MEXICAN MESSIAH

M E X I C A N

Messiah

Andrés Manuel López Obrador

⩗⩗⩗⩗⩗

GEORGE W. GRAYSON

The Pennsylvania State University Press | University Park, Pennsylvania

Library of Congress Cataloging-in-Publication Data

Grayson, George W., 1938–
    Mexican messiah : Andrés Manuel López Obrador / George W. Grayson.
       p.   cm.
Includes bibliographical references and index.
ISBN 978-0-271-03262-7 (cloth : alk. paper)
1. López Obrador, Andrés Manuel.
2. Mexico—Politics and government—2000– .
3. Mexico—Politics and government—1988–2000.
4. Distrito Federal (Mexico)—Politics and government—21st century.
5. Partido de la Revolución Democrática (Mexico).
6. Presidential candidates—Mexico—Biography.
7. Politicians—Mexico—Biography.
I. Title.

F1236.9.L66G73 2007
972.08'4—dc22
2007011754

The Pennsylvania State University Press is a member of the Association
of American University Presses.

It is the policy of The Pennsylvania State University Press to use acid-free
paper. This book is printed on Natures Natural, containing 50% post-
consumer waste, and meets the minimum requirements of American
National Standard for Information Sciences—Permanence of Paper for
Printed Library Material, ANSI Z39.48–1992.

CONTENTS

TABLES

ACKNOWLEDGMENTS

I wish to express my appreciation to the scores of people who assisted me in preparing this book. I owe an enormous debt to the *tabasqueños* who collectively took hundreds of hours to teach me about a state that bears the sobriquet of "Mexico's Eden." Among those who were especially generous with their time were Laura Beauregard de los Santos, Gonzalo Beltrán Calzada, Ernesto Benítez López, Darvín González Ballina, Ariel B. Córdoba Wilson, Isidra Correa López, María del Carmen Muriel de la Torre, Amador Izundegui Rullán, Bartolo Jiménez Méndez, Rodolfo Lara Lagunas, Candalaria Lázaro Lázaro, José Ramiro López Obrador, Elena Medina Beltrán, Armando Padilla Herrera, Francisco Peralta Burelo, Hermilo Pérez López, Pedro Reséndez Medina, and Fernandez Valenzuela Pernas.

Rafael López Cruz, a man whose knowledge of history is surpassed only by his devotion to social ideals, went through relevant parts of the book with a view to noting errors of fact and interpretation. His tireless efforts have earned my eternal admiration.

Although some members of López Obrador's entourage may not agree with my conclusions, I could not have progressed in my research without their assistance. These men and women include Martí Batres Guadarrama, Manuel Camacho Solís, Ramón Bolivar Zapata, Julieta Campos, Leonel Cota Montaña, Socorro Díaz Palacios, Horacio Duarte Olivares, Alejandro Encinas Rodríguez, Enrique González Pedrero, Laura Itzel Castillo, Pedro Jiménez León, Ignacio Marván Laborde, Aarón Mastache Mondragón, Ricard Monreal Ávila, Porfirio Muñoz Ledo, César Raúl Ojeda Zubieta, José Agustín Ortiz Pinchetti, José Maria Pérez Gay, Luz Rosales Esteva, Pedro Alberto Salazar, Cuauhtémoc Sandoval Ramírez, Enrique Semo Calev, Maricarmen Soria Narváez, Raquel Sosa Elízaga, and César Yañez Centeno Cabrera.

I was also privileged to speak with such cognoscenti of Mexican politics as Samuel Aguilar Solís, Ramón Aguirre Velázquez, Alberto M. Aguirre, Ricardo Alemán, Fred Álvarez Palafox, Sigrid Artz, José Eduardo Beltrán Hernández, Federico Berrueto Pruneda, John M. Bruton, Ángel Buendía Tirado, Roberto Campa Cifrián, Cuauhtémoc Cárdenas, José Carreño Carlón, Omar Castro Castillo, Emilio Chuayffet Chemor, Jeffrey Davidow, María de los Ángeles

Moreno, María Emilia Farías, Lourdes Galaz, Manuel Gómez Aguilera, Manuel Gurría Ordóñez, Francisco Labastida Ochoa, Adrián Lajous Vargas, Roberta Lajous Vargas, Antonio Lozano Gracia, José Luis Luege Tamargo, Juan S. Millán Lizárraga, Esteban Moctezuma Barragán, Fausto Mucio, Antonio Ocaranza Fernández, Ignacio Ovalle Fernández, José Francisco Paoli Bolio, Ricardo Pascoe Pierce, Isidro Pastor Medina, Luis Priego Ortiz, Graco Ramírez Garrido Abreu, Jésus Rangel M, Jesús Reyes Heroles, Francisco Rojas Gutiérrez, Liebano Saénz Ortiz, Carlos Salomón Cámara, Jesús Silva Herzog, and Leo Zuckerman Behar.

I especially appreciate the willingness of former Tabasco governor Leandro Rovirosa Wade and his charming wife, Doña Celia Sastre de Neme, to invite me into their home for stimulating conversation on two evenings. Guillermo Flores Velasco, Juan Gabriel Valencia Benavides, Carlos Heredía Zubieta, and Arturo Nuñez Jiménez—men who have forgotten much more about Mexican politics than I can ever hope to learn—agreed to share their wisdom with me on three or more occasions.

My biggest debt of gratitude goes to Professor Oscar Aguilar Ascencio, who helped map out the contours of a "messianic politician," with particular reference to López Obrador. I only wish Oscar's incredibly busy schedule had not prevented him from co-authoring the book and thus making an even greater contribution to this analysis.

I would be remiss without mentioning Professors Raj Nadella and Julie Galambush, colleagues at the College of William & Mary who gave excellent advice.

As I was telling Queen Elizabeth recently, "I hate name-droppers." However, I do want to thank President Felipe Calderón Hinojosa for sharing his views on the "Tlatelolco complex" that has afflicted several of his predecessors and limited the Mexican government's ability to crack down on wrongdoers.

The College of William & Mary's distinguished Class of 1938 and the Faculty Research Committee provided funds to assist my study. Bettina J. Manzo, research librarian at the College's Earl Gregg Swem Library, continually tracked down information that I thought could not be found, while the Interlibrary Loan Office ransacked libraries throughout the nation for books that I could not locate in either Mexico or the United States. William & Mary students Emily Unverzagt and Joseph H. Jenkins proved invaluable in conducting research, assisting with translations, and editing copy.

It goes without saying that this book would never have seen the light of day without the commitment and faith of Sanford Thatcher, director of the Pennsylvania State University Press, and the hard work of Cherene Holland, the managing editor at the Press, and editorial assistant Kristin C. Peterson. The editing of Suzanne Wolk, a professional with a remarkable rapport with the English language, was simply outstanding.

This book is dedicated to my wife, Bryan Holt Grayson, whose love and encouragement inspired my writing and made my breaks from the word processor an unalloyed joy.

With so many helping hands, any errors that have crept into these pages are my responsibility alone.

SELECTED ACRONYMS

ACNR—National Revolutionary Civic Association (Associación Cívica Nacional Revolucionaria)

ALDF—Legislative Assembly of the Federal District (Asamblea Legislativa del Distrito Federal)

AMLO—Andrés Manuel López Obrador

APPO—Oaxacan People's Popular Assembly (Asamblea Popular de los Pueblos de Oaxaca)

ARDF—Representative Assembly of the Federal District (Asamblea de Representantes del Distrito Federal)

CD—Democratic Current (Corriente Democrática)

Cedestab—Center of Studies on Tabascan Development (Centro de Estudios del Desarrollo Democrático, Económico y Social de Tabasco)

CEN—National Executive Committee (Comité Ejecutivo Nacional)

CESPES—PRI's Center for Economic, Political, and Social Studies (Centro de Estudios Sociales, Políticos y Económicos)

CEU—UNAM Student Council (Consejo Estudiantil Universitario)

CGH—General Strike Committee (Consejo General de Huelga)

CID—Current of the Democratic Left (Corriente de la Izquierda Democrática)

CNBV—National Banking and Securities Commission (Comisión Nacional Bancaria y de Valores)

CNC—National Campesino Confederation (Confederación Nacional Campesina)

CND—National Democratic Convention (Convención Nacional Democrática)

CNDH—National Human Rights Commission (Comisión Nacional de los Derechos Humanos)

CNOC—National Worker Peasant Council (Coordinadora Nacional de Organizaciones Campesinas)

CNOP—National Confederation of Popular Organizations (Confederación Nacional de Organizaciones Populares)

CNTE—National Coordination of Educational Workers (Coordinadora de Trabajadores de Educación)

COCEI—Worker, Student, Farmer, and Isthmus Coalition (Coalición Obrera Campesina Estudiantil del Istmo)

Cofipe—Federal Code for Electoral Institutions and Procedures (Código Federal de Instituciones y Procedimientos Electorales)

Conasupo—National Company of Subsistence Food for the People (Compañía Nacional de Subsistencias Populares)

Coplamar—General Coordination of the National Plan for Marginal Groups and Depressed Zones (Coordinación General del Plan Nacional de Zonas Deprimidas y Grupos Marginales)

CROC—Revolutionary Confederation of Workers and Peasants (Confederación Revolucionaria de Obreros y Campesinos)

CT—Congress of Labor (Congreso del Trabajo)

CTM—Confederation of Mexican Workers (Confederación de Trabajadores de Mexico)

CUD—Unified Coordination of Victims (Unified Coordinadora de Damificados)

D.F.—Federal District (Distrito Federal)

DGCS—General Directorate of Social Communication (Dirección General de Comunicación Social)

DIF—National System for Integral Family Development (Sistema Nacional para el Desarrollo Integral de la Familia)

EZLN—Zapatista Army of National Liberation (Ejército Zapatista de Liberación Nacional)

FDN—National Democratic Front (Frente Democrática Nacional)

FNDSE—National Front in Defense of Energy Sovereignty (Frente Nacional en Defensa de la Soberanía Energética)

Fobaproa—Banking Fund for the Protection of Savings (Fondo Bancario de Protección al Ahorro)

FPFV—Francisco Villa Popular Front (Frente Popular Francisco Villa)

GDF—Government of the Federal District (Gobierno del Distrito Federal)

ICAP—PRI's Institute for Political Training (Instituto de Capacitación Política)

IDN—National Democratic Left (Izquierda Democrática Nacional)

IEDF—Electoral Institute of the Federal District (Instituto Electoral de D.F.)

IEPES—PRI's Institute for Economic, Political, and Social Studies (Instituto para Estudios Políticos, Económicos y Sociales)

IFE—Federal Electoral Institute (Instituto Federal Electoral)

IMF—International Monetary Fund

IMSS—Mexican Social Security Institute (Instituto Mexicano del Seguridad Social)

INCO—National Consumer Institute (Instituto Nacional del Consumidor)

INI—National Indigenous Institute (Instituto Nacional Indigenista)

INVI—D.F. Housing Institute (Instituto de Vivienda del Distrito Federal)

IPAB—Institute for the Protection of Bank Savings (Instituto para la Protección al Ahorro Bancario)

ISI—Import-Substitution Industrialization

ISSSTE—Institute of Social Security and Services for State Workers (Instituto de Seguridad y Servicios Sociales de los Trabajadores del Estado)

IVA—Value-added tax (Impuesto al valor agregado)

MAS—Movement Toward Socialism (Movimiento al Socialismo)

MLN—National Liberation Movement (Movimiento de Liberación Nacional)

NAFTA—North American Free Trade Agreement

OET—Organization of Tabascan Students (Organización de Estudiantes Tabasquños)

PAN—National Action Party (Partido Acción Nacional)

PANAL—New Alliance (Partido Nueva Alianza)

PARM—Authentic Party of the Mexican Revolution (Partido Auténtico de la Revolución Mexicana)

PAS—Social Alliance Party (Partido Alianza Social)

PASC—Peasant and Social Democratic Alternative Party (Partido Alternativa Socialdemócrata y Campesina)

PCD—Center Democratic Party (Partido de Centro Democrático)

PCM—Mexican Communist Party (Partido Comunista Mexicano)

PDM—Mexican Democratic Party (Partido Demócrata Mexicano)

Pemex—Mexico's state oil monopoly (Petróleos Mexicanos)

PFCRN—Party of the Cardinista Front for National Reconstruction (Partido del Frente Cardenista de Reconstrucción Nacional)

PGR—Attorney General's Office of the Republic (Procuraduría General de la República)

PJF—Federal Judicial Police (Policía Judicial Federal)

PMS—Mexican Socialist Party (Partido Mexicano Socialista)

PMT—Mexican Workers' Party (Partido Mexicano de los Trabajadores)

PPS—Popular Socialist Party of Mexico (Partido Popular Socialista de México)

PRD—Democratic Revolutionary Party (Partido de la Revolución Democrática)

PRI—Institutional Revolutionary Party (Partido Revolucionario Institucional)

Prodecot—Program for the Development of Tabasco's Coastal Zone (Programa de Desarrollo de la Zona Costera de Tabasco)

Pronasol—National Solidarity Program (Programa Nacional de Solidaridad)

PRT—Workers' Revolutionary Party (Partido Revolucionario de los Trabajadores)

PSD—Social Democratic Party (Partido Social Demócrata)

PSN—Nationalist Society Party (Partido de la Sociedad Nacionalista)

PST—Socialist Workers' Party (Partido Socialista de los Trabajadores)

PSUM—Unified Socialist Party of Mexico (Partido Socialista Unificado de México)

PT—Workers Party (Partido del Trabajo)

PVEM—Green Ecological Party of Mexico (Partido Verde Ecologista de México)

SCJN—National Supreme Court of Justice (Suprema Corte de Justicia Nacional)

Sedue—Secretary of Ecology and Urban Development (Secretaría de Desarrollo Urbano y Ecología)

SHCP—Treasury Ministry (Secretaría de Hacienda y Credito Público)

SLP—San Luis Potosí

SME—Mexican Electricians Union (Sindicato Mexicano de Electricistas)

SNTE—National Union of Educational Workers (Sindicato Nacional de Trabajadores de Education)

SPP—Ministry of Budget and Planning (Secretaría del Presupuesto y la Planificación)

STPRM—Oil Workers' Union of the Mexican Republic (Sindicato de Trbajadores Petroleros de la República Mexicana)

STUNAM—UNAM Workers' Union (Sindicato de Trabajadores de la Universidad Nacional Autónoma de México)

SUTGDF—Single Union of D.F. Government Workers (Sindicato Único de Trabajadores del Gobierno del D.F.)

TEE—Tabasco State Electoral Tribunal (Tribunal Electoral Estatal)

TEPJF—Electoral Tribunal of the Federal Judiciary (Tribunal Electoral del Poder Judicial de la Federación)

UACM—Autonomous University of Mexico City (Universidad Autónoma de la Ciudad de México)

UJAT—Autonomous Juárez University of Tabasco (Universidad Juárez Autónoma de Tabasco)

UNAM—Autonomous National University of Mexico (Universidad Nacional Autónoma de México)

INTRODUCTION

Andrés Manuel López Obrador entered the final stretch of the presidential race as the leading candidate to succeed Vicente Fox Quesada. On the eve of the July 2, 2006, contest, he claimed to have a ten-point lead in a poll that he would not make public. After a partial recount of the nearly 42 million ballots cast in the election, the Federal Electoral Tribunal (TEPJF) found that the former mayor of Mexico City had lost by an eyelash to Felipe Calderón Hinojosa, the nominee of Fox's National Action Party (PAN). López Obrador blasted the outcome as "fraudulent" and moved to establish a government parallel to Calderón's.

Nonetheless, *el Pejelagarto* (or *el Peje*), as the erstwhile mayor is called,[1] ran an extremely competitive race, despite jarring blows that would have knocked most politicians out of contention and possibly landed them in prison. In early 2004, for example, agents filmed his finance secretary, Gustavo Ponce Meléndez, dropping big bucks at a blackjack table in a posh Las Vegas casino. No sooner had this exposé erupted than the nation's most popular morning TV show, hosted by Víctor Trujillo—a comedian-turned-television journalist armed with the mordant humor of *Saturday Night Live* or *The Daily Show with Jon Stewart*—detonated another bomb. Trujillo aired videos of René Bejarano Martínez, the mayor's top operative, greedily cramming thousands of dollars into his suitcase and pockets. This money was handed over by a shadowy Argentine entrepreneur with close ties to big shots in López Obrador's Democratic Revolutionary Party (PRD).

Two months later, the *videoescándalos* gave way to a concerted drive by Fox to strip López Obrador of his immunity as an elected official so that he could stand trial for having flouted a judge's order. After months of legal haggling, deputies in the once-dominant Institutional Revolutionary Party (PRI) joined their counterparts in the PAN. Thanks to this alliance, the Chamber of Deputies approved the *desafuero*—the formal term for divesting the mayor of his legal shield. The outcry at home and abroad against this egregious maneuver forced the chief executive to capitulate and recognize López Obrador's right to seek the nation's top office.

Although he had failed to resolve the capital's crime, pollution, traffic, water, and trash problems, Mexico City's former chief remained a formidable presidential contender as the nominee of the "For the Good of All" (*Por el Bien de Todos*) coalition, spearheaded by his leftist-nationalist PRD.

How did López Obrador vault such imposing hurdles to become one of his country's most popular politicians? Commentators have compared him to such Latin American populists as Venezuela's Hugo Chávez and Bolivia's Evo Morales. Indeed, he shares several of their characteristics: he proclaims tidings of change and hope, excoriates the status quo, assails the hegemonic political class, relies on the mass media to disseminate his positions, and decries neoliberal economic policies.

While elements of populism apply to López Obrador, he is in fact a political "messiah," a term that derives from the Hebrew word for "anointed one." Unlike a Chávez, for example, he is not just one more option for the masses. Rather, he is a "savior" prepared to rescue the humble from deceitful politicians and their neoliberal schemes that benefit the affluent. While others claim to "represent" the downtrodden, el Peje "incarnates" their struggle.

Central to the concept of a messianic politician is his conviction that he embodies the project of redemption, that he represents a viable mission—based on his moral principles and values—to uplift the "have-nots." The righteousness of his cause immunizes him from scrutiny and attacks. To question or assail him is to offend the interests of the disadvantaged whom he represents. López Obrador presents an alternative to the neoliberal creed, whose adherents constitute an "evil" so great that he refuses to utter the name of its principal protagonist, President Carlos Salinas de Gortari (1988–94), whom he derides as "the Unmentionable One" (*el Innombrable*).

Political messiahs explain economic, social, and political "reality" in a way that is credible to the masses. Their success also springs from convincing the faithful that they embrace the interests of the people and possess the strength and fortitude to transform their lives. As mayor, López Obrador continued to exhibit the honesty and austerity that he had demonstrated during a quarter-century of social activism. Upon reaching City Hall, he did not turn his back on the poor but created programs to assist them.

A messiah manifests his powers by performing miracles (Jesus) and in heroic achievements in the face of adversity (López Obrador). The pursuit of social justice—his most outstanding quality—arms him with moral force. The savior has two dimensions: he is both a national and political liberator and the spiritual and religious shepherd of his flock; he is at once a king and a redeemer, a political and spiritual hero. He enhances his credibility by thwarting his enemies' efforts to expel him from the political scene.

Detractors underestimate such a politician because they fail to appreciate his skill in "connecting" with the people by dint of the potency of his message of liberation. He draws strength from his conviction that he is not alone but instead basks in the support of the multitudes. He conveys to those struggling to survive the prospect of a better life that is unattainable in the iniquitous and cruel world of the marketplace. He holds out "another realm" infused with justice, equality, and well-being for its inhabitants. The messianic leader relies heavily on the mass media to project his "word," even as the "neoliberal empire" seeks to block his access to the throne of power. Through speeches, marches, and demonstrations, he warns the elite of the "dangers to democracy" and "stability" if it impedes his crusade of hope.

The term "messianic" is used in a descriptive, not a pejorative, manner. It refers to a person whose political vision and trajectory combine leftist, populist, nationalist, and corporatist elements in a way that separates him from other politicians. El Pejelagarto is a secular messiah who enunciates a doctrine of salvation by returning to the values of the 1917 Constitution—fairness for workers, Indians' rights, fervent nationalism, and anti-imperialism.

Whether by chance or by design, he employs strategies that are surprisingly similar to those used by Jesus of Nazareth two thousand years ago, when the Romans occupied Palestine. López Obrador makes no pretense of being divine. Yet he has called himself "the little ray of hope" (*el rayito de la esperanza*) for the dispossessed—a key to his extraordinary success. Once he and his faithful followers had recaptured his nation's Jerusalem (Mexico City), he immediately fixed his sights on the latter-day Rome (the presidency)—from which recent leaders had propounded despised neoliberal precepts.

Although he was born near the town of Bethlehem in the state of Tabasco, the political messiah's mother was not a virgin; nor were wise men bearing gold, frankincense, and myrrh guided to his birthplace by a luminous star in the East. Moreover, unlike Christ, about whom we know little before he reached age thirty, we have copious information about el Pejelagarto's life.

López Obrador shares several traits with the founder of Christianity. First, as Jesus claimed the role of spiritual liberator, the former mayor offers himself as a political redeemer. He is determined to deliver the people from the heinous liberalization that has yielded "monstrous social inequality," as well as dependence on the United States, the International Monetary Fund (IMF), and other exponents of the "magic of the marketplace."

Second, like Christ, he lives frugally. A widower during most of his term as mayor, he resided with his three sons and a housekeeper in a small home in an unpretentious neighborhood; he dressed simply, rode in a battered Japanese car, worked sixteen to eighteen hours a day, cut his salary, and promised to do the same if elected president. He also expected members of his entourage to forego creature comforts for the greater good. As was the case with Christ, self-sacrifice included placing a higher priority on one's mission than on one's family, and López Obrador demanded this of his employees as well as of himself. During his campaign for the presidency, he often assigned greater importance to his crusade than to his wife, children, parents, and siblings.

Third, at times López Obrador has emulated Jesus' habit of speaking in parables and coining memorable phrases. When he ran for mayor in 2000, el Peje adopted as his campaign slogan a modern rendering of Jesus' saying, "Blessed are you who are poor, for yours is the Kingdom of Heaven" (Luke 6:20): "For the Good of All, Above All the Poor" (*Por el Bien de Todos, Primero los Pobres*), which he abbreviated for his presidential campaign.[2] This emphasized his belief that the poor are the most deserving in society. On another occasion, he expressed his hostility to the elite's wrongdoing by asserting, "the people are sick and tired of so many petty political deals."[3]

Fourth, López Obrador is influenced by political icons in much the same way that the Old Testament prophets motivated Jesus. These visionaries include Father José María Morelos y Pavón (1765–1815), a champion of Mexican independence who strove to uplift impoverished Indians; President Benito Juárez (1806–72), an advocate of separating church and state who believed that public servants should live modestly; Francisco I. Madero (1873–1913), an idealistic advocate of "effective suffrage and no re-election" who sparked the overthrow of the encrusted dictatorship of Porfirio Díaz; and Lázaro Cárdenas, a muscular nationalist who organized peasants and workers, even as he accomplished sweeping land reform and nationalized the foreign-controlled petroleum sector. Of these four prophetic figures, el Peje exhibits a special affinity for Juárez and Cárdenas. He told a journalist just before he became mayor, "There are two presidents in Mexican history who continue to lead by their examples, two enduring presences: Juárez and Lázaro Cárdenas."[4]

Historian Enrique Krauze, who calls López Obrador a "tropical messiah," argues that Tabasco's fanatically anticlerical governor, Tómas Garrido Canabal, inspired his "puritanical, dogmatic, authoritarian inclination to hate and . . . redeemer-like" qualities.[5]

Meanwhile, López Obrador has treated PRD founder Cuauhtémoc Cárdenas, son of the late president, as an inept prophet because he failed as the D.F.'s mayor to achieve social justice for the masses. In fact, Cárdenas, who contemplated seeking the presidency a fourth time in 2006, rejected a hallmark of López Obrador's government—providing monthly stipends to senior citizens—and refused to support el Peje in 2006. Cárdenas even expressed concern that, if elected, López Obrador might seek to extend his tenure more than six years. "A messianic agenda resists limits and needs time: a sexenio is too brief a period," writes Krauze.[6]

Fifth, López Obrador has confronted the beneficiaries of the neoliberal model that Mexican presidents have trumpeted since the mid-1980s in a manner that parallels Christ's challenge to the Jewish establishment and their Roman protectors. He employs the idiom of class warfare by focusing his ire on the self-serving, corrupt "political elite" who have abandoned the revolutionary principles inspired by Morelos, Juárez, Madero, and Cárdenas. It is these grandees, who profited from the 1998 Fobaproa bank bailout, whom López Obrador attacks with the self-righteousness of Christ expelling the moneychangers from the temple.

He demonizes Salinas, who promoted the nation's market-oriented élan and helped forge the North American Free Trade Agreement (NAFTA). For López Obrador, the devil's sons are Roberto Madrazo Pintado, the wealthy former governor of Tabasco, who ran third in the presidential contest, and Calderón, the winner. El Peje alleged that either Madrazo or Calderón would reprise Salinas's ruthless policies if elected chief executive.

Sixth, as a "savior," López Obrador stands above the law just as Christ stood guiltless before Pontius Pilate. He is the conveyor of a message, and his persona cannot be separated from the actions of his government. As a result, he rejected transparency in his administration. If his goals were noble and his intentions pure, why should the press or other outsiders delve into his expenditures on, say, multimillion-dollar public works? Some of his collaborators may have committed "errors," but their actions did not impugn the integrity of the man who named them to key posts. El Peje has even claimed that his honesty makes him "politically indestructible."

Christ invariably took the offensive against his detractors, rebuking entrenched religious leaders as serpents: "Ye serpents, ye generation of vipers, how can ye escape the damnation of hell?" (Matt. 23:33). For his part, López Obrador, emphasizing the virtue of his mission, accused his own Pharisees of engaging in a "conspiracy." When Fox tried to prevent him from seeking the presidency,

López Obrador played the martyr's role, stating, "I do not lust after elective office. I am not obsessed about being president. I struggle for ideas, for an agenda."[7] He also averred, "I am convoking a movement of analysis, of reflection, of conscience. I might even speak of a spiritual movement. . . . Many people who see me, humble people, tell me that they are praying [for my success]."[8]

Seventh, a messianic politician has a monopoly on truth. Thus his positions are not debated but disseminated, because they hold promise for the political salvation of the destitute. In the same manner that Jesus challenged the emphasis that Jewish clerics placed on form over substance in interpreting the Torah, López Obrador has construed statutes to conform to his goals. He defines law as the "will of the people," as he construes it. Like Christ, he pays lip service to orthodoxies while continually reinterpreting the law. As mayor, he frequently gave short shrift to bills passed by the city council, known as the Legislative Assembly of the Federal District (ALDF). He treated legislators as latter-day Pharisees, Sadducees, and Scribes with whom Christ clashed as he invested the scriptures with "truer" meaning.

López Obrador borrows Jesus' strategy of calling simultaneously for conformity and change. Religious, civil, and customary laws were synonymous in Roman-occupied Palestine. Thus Christ was focusing on the central aspect of every life when he said, "Think not that I am come to destroy the law, or the prophets: I am not come to destroy but to fulfill. . . . Whosoever therefore shall break one of these least commandments, and shall teach men so, he shall be called the least in the kingdom of heaven: but whosoever shall do and teach them, the same shall be called great in the kingdom of heaven" (Matt. 5:17, 19).[9] For instance, el Peje gave assurances that he would pursue responsible macroeconomic policies and uphold NAFTA while simultaneously upbraiding the architects of Mexico's economic opening.

Eighth, unlike most populists, the messianic politician has long worked shoulder to shoulder with the poor and remains in constant contact with them. Even though he won election as Mexico City's mayor, López Obrador, like Christ, has spent most of his life among peasants. He preaches egalitarianism and forgives prostitutes and other sinners, using this relationship with the dispossessed to energize both himself and his followers. He denies that he is a populist but says he is as "one with the people," for governments are only legitimate if wedded to the masses.

Ninth, while unable to perform miracles like those attributed to Christ, the Tabascan magically revitalized his PRD, renovated the Historic Center, and provided monthly payments to the needy—his rendition of distributing "loaves and fishes." In calling Mexico City the "the City of Hope" (*la Ciudad de la Esperanza*), the mayor recognized the human need for symbols of transcendence and framed his works in a spiritual context in a country of quiet believers.[10]

His revitalization of the capital's crumbling historic zone—which had been invaded by tawdry bars, pimps, whores, drug dealers, and gangs—is a modern-day wonder that inspires optimism.

Tenth, like other messiahs, López Obrador relies on his own judgment and seldom follows the counsel of others. As his father-in-law said, "He doesn't hear and he doesn't listen."[11] Yet he is surrounded by a small group of confidants, his "apostles," who include at least one Judas-like betrayer. As was Christ's practice, López Obrador seldom compliments his subordinates but exhorts them to accomplish even more.

Eleventh, he has also taken a page from Jesus by welcoming into his entourage devoted females. These modern Mary Magdalenes have held prominent positions in his cabinet, worked faithfully and tireless to advance his mission, and helped his campaign in other ways.

Finally, even though an outsider—he broke with the PRI in 1988—López Obrador has risen to power within Mexico's electoral system. His ascent to the mayorship represented his "political beatification," just as reaching the National Palace would have constituted his "political canonization." Oscar Aguilar Ascencio has offered another analogy: "His capturing City Hall was tantamount to Christ's conquering Jerusalem; now the messianic López Obrador wants to seize Rome, the epicenter of the 'evil empire.'"[12]

Although he rejects the appellation "messiah," López Obrador has defined himself as a "mystic." Writer Carlos Marín has observed that "much of his rhetoric leads to the interpretation that he has found a kind of new political church—that of Saint Andrés Manuel." The mayor responded: "Messianic? No. There have been such interpretations, but what I have said [is that] when one has principles, when one has ideals, he is less vulnerable and can confront whatever adversary. It annoys my adversaries that I act in this manner. But I am a *juarista,* and Juárez said that you acquire authority from upright behavior.[13]

Fox, however, referred to el Peje's qualities when he warned about extravagant campaign promises: Messiahs are already embarked upon campaigns, offering the people "everything imaginable" (*el oro y el moro*) and confusing them by pretending to have "simple solutions" to complex problems.[14]

THE DEMONSTRATIONS OF AUGUST 29, 2004, AND APRIL 24, 2005

López Obrador's messianic traits were abundantly clear on August 29, 2004, when hundreds of thousands of his followers cascaded into the streets of the ancient Aztec capital to support their leader as he confronted the *desafuero* threat. If ousted from city hall, López Obrador would have faced charges of official misconduct, which the Procuraduría General de República (PGR) had leveled against him. The dispute swirled around the allegation that city officials had ignored an injunction against constructing a service road to a new hospital on private property in the city's Santa Fe area. The matter appeared trivial, yet failure to resolve it by January 2006 would have prevented López Obrador from seeking the presidency, as the Constitution prohibits anyone with legal matters pending against him from becoming a candidate.

This march "for Democracy and Legality" (*por la Legalidad y la Democracia*)—the largest ever staged by Mexico's Left—included many senior citizens, some hobbling on canes and walkers. They turned out to display their appreciation for the monthly allowance from the Government of the Federal District (GDF) of 680 pesos, later raised to 720 pesos. A group of elderly women held up a sign that read, "May God Watch over the Little Ray of Hope! (*¡Qué Dios te Cuide, Rayito de Esperanza!*). Meanwhile, a placard in the central plaza proclaimed, "Musical groups of the blind in the Historic Center are certain that you will be the next president."[15] The blind, like other disabled residents, also receive the monthly stipend of 720 pesos. Other beneficiaries of government programs include single mothers, scholarship recipients who come from poor neighborhoods, young people from newly established preparatory schools, and students at the Autonomous University of Mexico City (UACM), which López Obrador founded.

These demonstrators rubbed elbows with families that had obtained credits with which to purchase houses and with taxi drivers who had obtained loans with which to buy their own vehicles. Leaders of labor organizations signaled their presence with gaudy pennants. Members of the Mexican Electricians Union (SME) unfurled banners that praised the mayor's opposition to the nationalization of Mexico's electricity industry. Their counterparts in the UNAM Workers' Union (STUNAM) chanted slogans against neoliberalism and on behalf of el Peje.

Neighborhood organizations employed signs, slogans, and songs to express their solidarity with the mayor. These groups included the residents of the Venustiano Carranza neighborhood, whose members shouted, "the voice of the people is the voice of God!" Not only had López Obrador brought leaders of such organizations into his administration, he had also rewarded their loyalty by giving their members preferential access to housing credits, store sites, and areas of sidewalks where they could sell everything from jewelry to videos.

Big shots in his Democratic Revolutionary Party were ubiquitous. The PRD's yellow-and-black banners and balloons gave the demonstration the appearance of a field of black-eyed Susans. Especially prominent was Deputy Manuel Camacho Solís, an important convert from the PRI and a key strategist for the mayor. While there were no palm leaves, López Obrador occasionally broke his stride to accept flowers, salute well-wishers, or receive embraces from admirers who treated him more as a savior than as a popular run-of-the-mill politician.

Although a smile danced across his face, the mayor seemed to have retreated into his own thoughts, possibly about his plans for nation's lumpenproletariat. When he arrived three hours late in the Zócalo central square, the crowd opened a path for him. The spontaneous action was reminiscent of the Bible's account of God's parting the Red Sea so that Moses and the Israelites could flee their Egyptian foes.[16] A banner proclaimed, "The Voice of AMLO is the Voice of God!"

In his lengthy message, López Obrador elaborated on the theme of his inaugural address. He enunciated a twenty-point program that would constitute a "new social pact" in contrast to the neoliberal approach of President Fox. *Un proyecto alternativo de nación*—his blueprint for change—included reactivating the economy, creating jobs, and improving the lot of Indians, senior citizens, the disabled, poor students, single mothers, and others in need. Upon declaring his presidential candidacy, he expanded his platform from twenty to fifty planks.

He called for honesty and austerity in a government that would guarantee free public education at all levels, respect individual freedoms, and advance social rights. He averred that the best foreign policy is an effective domestic policy and that Mexico must conduct its relations with the United States on the basis of "respect and collaboration."[17]

Several months passed before he made it official, but the August 2004 march signaled López Obrador's announcement of his presidential candidacy in a race that promised to be one of the hardest fought in Mexican history. For the first time, traditional contenders would be running against a political messiah.

On April 24, 2005, more than a million loyalists took part in a "March of Silence" to protest the *desafuero* once again. Many of the same groups participated in this event, using the same slogans. This time, however, there seemed to be one change in the environment. The demonstrators not only manifested allegiance to López Obrador; they put the government on notice that they did not want it to destroy their dream of reaching the Promised Land.

FACTORS THAT GIVE RISE TO MESSIANIC POLITICIANS

Analysts have identified a number of factors that explain the appearance of messiahs. These include (1) weak, unrepresentative political institutions, (2) a lack of confidence in traditional politicians, (3) the yearning for a message of hope, (4) the presence of an individual who offers himself as a leader of the masses unrestrained by institutional fetters, (5) adeptness at capturing media attention, and (6) vague proposals complemented by symbolic acts that respond to the needs of the masses.[18]

These factors were present at the time of Jesus, when religious and political ferment roiled Palestine. The Hellenistic influence that had come to dominate the eastern Mediterranean had acutely affected Jewish society, and foreign myths, cults, and philosophies had made notable inroads. The Romans controlled Palestine, and the Jews were a repressed people whose quest for independence would erupt in the war of A.D. 66–73.[19] According to scholar Burton Mack, one important phenomenon of the Greco-Roman age was the appearance of the religious and philosophical entrepreneur, sometimes called the divine man, sometimes the sophist or sage. "The entrepreneur stepped into the void left vacant by the demise of traditional priestly functions at the ancient temple sites and addressed the confusion, concern, and curiosity of people confronted with a complex world that was felt to be at the mercy of the fates."[20]

The power structure in Palestine was riven. "The geographical division after the death of Herod had left conflict and resentment, the wealthy class and the priests had their differences, the priestly hierarchy was in internal conflict, and the Romans were sufficiently hated to spark a cleavage between the governor and the populace. The establishment could not offer a united front against a bid for power."[21]

Rather than dominance by Roman Legions, Mexico fell under the seventy-one-year rule of the PRI. In fact, López Obrador tends to praise the "revolutionary party"—to which he belonged until age thirty—before technocrats like Salinas hijacked the party in the 1980s. These infidels, he claimed, had forsaken the PRI's traditional goals. El Peje regarded the usurpers as latter-day Romans whose rule was illegitimate and who should be driven out of Jerusalem and defeated in their own citadel. Although Fox belonged to the center-right National Action Party, López Obrador scorned him for embracing the neoliberalism of Salinas and his successor, Ernesto Zedillo Ponce de León (1994–2000). He mocked the PRI and the PAN—he labeled them "PRIAN"—as ideological twins.

López Obrador acquired his distaste for neoliberalism in Tabasco. In the mid- to late 1970s, a petroleum boom uprooted tens of thousands of small farmers and fishermen who sought employment with Petróleos Mexicanos (Pemex), the national oil monopoly. The production of black gold—sometimes reviled as the "devil's excrement"—also contaminated the state's land, water, and air. Governors Leandro Rovirosa Wade (1976–82) and Enrique González Pedrero (1983–88) succeeded in securing federal government funds to compensate for the pollution and disruptions that afflicted the state. During their terms, Tabasco went from near the bottom to near the top of the nation's thirty-one states in per capita tax monies disbursed to its government.

In contrast to the achievements of his predecessors, Governor Salvador Neme Castillo (1988–92) ran a hugely corrupt regime, lacked strong allies in Mexico City, and was forced by Salinas to acquiesce in a sharp reduction in federal monies flowing into the state. To make matters worse, at the time of this cutback Pemex began to shift its operations to neighboring Campeche, where it took advantage of the enormous reservoirs of oil located off the state's coast without provoking the social unrest that occurred in Tabasco. Although the petroleum boom had allowed the construction of roads, bridges, ports, and airports, little had been done to diversify the Tabascan economy, which still relied heavily on the production of livestock and tropical fruits and vegetables.

The state was grossly unprepared for the tumbling of tariff barriers in the 1980s, which brought competition from less expensive items from north of the Río Grande. The resulting economic downturn accentuated the social, economic, and political dislocations sparked by the oil bonanza. As Neme, whom Salinas removed in 1992, fought for his political survival, Tabasco's poor and dispossessed looked for someone to champion their cause. López Obrador furnished this leadership. He not only excoriated Neme's and the PRI's corruption but also mobilized squads of small farmers, fishermen, and Indians to block access to oil wells in order to wrench additional monies from Pemex.

During its protracted hegemony, the PRI resembled both a religious and a political hierarchy that articulated the protean ideology of revolutionary nationalism. Yet by the early twenty-first century, the elites were at each other's throats. In his quest to succeed Fox, PRI president Madrazo (2002–5) helped scuttle the president's energy, judicial, labor, and tax reforms. As a result, when Pemex revenues are excluded, the Mexican government collects taxes equal to only 10.4 percent of Gross Domestic Product—a figure on par with Haiti. This means there are insufficient funds to augment spending on education, healthcare, housing, employment training, and other crucial items. PRI- and PRD-led opposition to inviting private capital into the energy sector also limits the output of oil, earnings from which generate 36 percent of government resources.

Fox's ineptitude weakened the presidency and his party's candidate, Calderón, reached the presidency in large measure because of López Obrador's mistakes during the campaign. Meanwhile, Madrazo failed to unify a PRI that was profoundly divided over his selection as its nominee.

The presidential contest took place as globalization continued to erode the PRI-spawned corporatist system, which brought social controls and stability to Mexico for more than half a century. At the same time, many of the economic reforms of the 1980s and 1990s have been implemented haphazardly, resulting in enduring monopolies and oligopolies in both the private and public sectors. These impediments to growth mean that nearly half the population lives in misery, while new technology displaces workers and exporters suffer mounting competition from China, India, and other Asian dynamos. Mexicans also face street violence, corrupt police forces, sticky-fingered bureaucrats, and an unscrupulous judiciary, with the exception of several high federal courts. Just as the Tabasco upheaval in the 1980s gave impetus to López Obrador's rise at the state level, current national conditions—ubiquitous poverty, high unemployment, debilitated labor unions, weakened peasant leagues, hostility toward the economic liberalism promoted by the United States, and disdain for Congress, politicians, and political parties—enhanced the attractiveness of López Obrador in 2006. Like Christ, he promised salvation from oppressive government programs.

Although he failed to win the presidency, the activities of López Obrador could profoundly affect Mexico's relations with its northern neighbor. The lack of security along the two-thousand-mile border has led the U.S. State Department to issue six "alerts" to American citizens in recent years and, on July 29, 2005, to close its consulate in violence-plagued Nuevo Laredo, where rival narco-traffickers engaged in a pitched battle. Drug cartels have grown in power and wealth to the degree that they operate as parallel governments in various localities. As a result, thousands of migrants cross into the United States illegally each day, and the nation's porous, crime-ridden southern flank has become an open door for lawbreakers seeking to use Mexico as an avenue to the United States.

OVERVIEW OF THE BOOK

Professor Oscar Aguilar Ascencio, a brilliant student of Mexican politics and a superb human being, not only laid out the theoretical design of this Introduction, but his invaluable ideas suffuse virtually every page of this volume. Chapter 1 examines the conditions in López Obrador's home state of Tabasco and the influence of his family, teachers, and prophets as he grew to maturity. Chapter 2 focuses on López Obrador's zealous commitment to social causes as revealed in his asceticism and extensive work with the Chontal Indians and the PRI. Chapter 3 concentrates on López Obrador's antagonism toward the evils of neoliberalism and its devilish advocate, Carlos Salinas. Also included is an overview of the PRI's hegemony.

Chapter 4 describes the corrupt political system against which López Obrador fought as the crusading gubernatorial candidate for the National Democratic Front in 1988. Chapter 5 analyzes how López Obrador took advantage of his presidency of the state PRD to launch an "exodus for democracy" against voting fraud in 1991, to create a party in Tabasco that emulated the practices of the traditional PRI, and to launch his gubernatorial bid against Roberto Madrazo.

Chapter 6 examines López Obrador's "miraculous" achievements in advancing the PRD's fortunes as its national president. It also discusses his animus toward the Fobaproa banking reform. Chapter 7 presents an overview of the political culture of Mexico City that fostered López Obrador's emergence as a political messiah.

Chapter 8 reviews his successful campaign for the second-most important post in the nation on the platform of "Por el Bien de Todos, Primero los Pobres." Chapter 9 illuminates how López Obrador employed crack-of-dawn news conferences—the *mañaneras*—both to gain legitimacy for his regime and to spread his gospel. Chapter 10 explores the programs that the *jefe de gobierno* launched as the savior of the capital's dispossessed, as well as the constituencies that he molded in the process. Chapter 11 discusses the mayor's various public works projects and the compromises he made with key power brokers to burnish his credentials for national office.

Chapter 12 identifies el Peje's closest male and female followers and sets forth the functions they perform, and describes the Judas who allegedly betrayed him. Chapter 13 recounts López Obrador's belief that law is the "people's will" as he interprets it, as well as his selective support for lawmakers, the courts, electoral institutes, and the concept of transparency. Chapter 14 looks at López Obrador's clashes with Vicente Fox, who, through the *desafuero* process, sought to prevent his running for president. Chapter 15 evaluates his fifty-point presidential platform, which, if enacted, would create his version of the Promise Land. Chapter 16 sets forth his strategy for expanding the ranks of his disciples so that he could succeed Fox, whom he hoped would be the last neoliberal president, and explains the mayor's efforts to allay fears abroad about his "leftist," "populist," and messianic orientation.

Chapter 17 assesses whether López Obrador's parallel government, which sprang to life at the "Democratic National Convention" of September 16, 2006, can thwart Calderón's reformist agenda and pave the way for the political messiah's election in 2012. Will "the little ray of hope" block proposed reforms, in a move that would exacerbate economic conditions and thus spur turmoil and bilateral tensions? Chapter 18, the concluding chapter of this book, addresses this pivotal question.

A CHILD IS BORN
IN TABASCO

Soon after his birth on November 13, 1953, the family of Mexico's political messiah moved to remote, fly-specked Villa de Tepetitán, which snuggles against the Tepetitán River, once the escape route for pirates who, legend has it, buried treasure in the town. Andrés Manuel's name was derived from those of his parents, Andrés and Manuela, who feared they might not be able to have more children. The name of the town, which lies in the municipality of Macuspana in the southeastern part of the state of Tabasco,[1] sprang from the Mayan words *tepetl* (mountain) and *titlan* (between). Now, as fifty years ago, the economy depends on cattle raising, fishing, and farming. Sombrero-wearing horsemen, load-bearing tricycles, and battered trucks vie with cars, beat-up buses, and scrawny dogs on the road that runs to the village. As a university student, Andrés Manuel read *Macando*, a Gabriel García Márquez novel. He immediately told a boyhood friend, Ernesto Benítez López, that "this book describes Tepetitán when we were growing up."[2]

His maternal grandparents, José Obrador Revuelta and Úrsula Gertrudis González Gúzman, migrated from northern Spain, where they had lived in Villa de Ampuero, near Santander on the Bay of Biscay.[3] López Obrador's mother, Manuela "Doña Manuelita" Obrador González, was born in Frontera, Tabasco, on December 24, 1922.[4] She was one of six children, including sisters Pilar Lucía and Gloria Juana and brothers José Féliz and Esteban Ramón.

José Obrador, a successful merchant, initially opposed his daughter's marrying Andrés López Ramón. She was the only child still living at home, and her suitor was eleven years her senior. Moreover, his parents, Lorenzo López Sandoval and Candelaria Ramón Carrillo, were as poor as church mice. López Sandoval, whose wife died giving birth to Andrés López Ramón, was said to live behind a plow in Cosamaloapan, Veracruz, where they scratched out a living.

When the bride's father finally consented, Manuela and Andrés López Ramón were married in the church of the Virgin of the Assumption in Tepetitán on October 30, 1952. Of the marriage, Doña Manuelita Obrador de López later said, "It was the best thing that could have happened to me. I found a man who was affectionate, a homebody, and attentive to the children. What more could I ask of God?"[5]

After his employer, a Pemex contractor, transferred López Ramón from Agua Dulce, Veracruz, the newlyweds finally settled in Tepetitán, but he worked outside the town. In Tepetitán, Doña Manuelita's father, José Obrador Revuelta, and his wife, Ursula, operated La Revoltosa, a store that sold general merchandise, freshly baked bread, and patent medicines. While Obrador Revuelta was neither a pharmacist nor a physician, he dispensed medical advice, gave injections, and prepared remedies. If the first nostrum did not work, he urged his customer to come back for another concoction. Although teased for being "Gauchupines" or Spaniards, José Obrador and his wife, who had a smile for everyone, were beloved by the townspeople. "My maternal grandfather was a person with a big heart," remembers one of his grandsons. "Whenever he was needed to give an injection or take care of someone, he went and did not ever charge for his services."[6]

Doña Manuelita enticed her husband to open another store. "Listen, old man. . . . Why not quit your job at Pemex so we can work together? Possibly we will earn less, but in the final analysis money doesn't interest us . . . as much as you and I being happy. Let's be reunited, let's be together . . . !"[7]

Her husband, a stocky, gregarious man, agreed, and he worked with his wife in the several family businesses they established.[8] He also enjoyed sitting in his favorite chair and drinking Carta Blanca beer. The "Gambler" (*Tajúr*), as friends called him, delighted in playing cards, shooting pool, and throwing dice—often for more money than he could afford to lose. It was the strong-willed Doña Manuelita who took the lead in running the business and raising their seven children.

She distinguished herself as a shrewd businesswoman through the operation of their small enterprise on Calle Hidalgo, one of the town's three streets. Miscelánea Manuelita, as they named the store, was located on the banks of the Tepetitán River, where iguanas scurried among the almond, tamarind, and guayacán trees.

They sold a little of everything—produce, butter, cloth, medicines, hardware, cigarettes, soft drinks, and so on. She skinned fish, including the *pejelagarto*.

Though the muddy roads were impassable most of the year, the river linked the town to the rest of the state. Doña Manuelita would arise at 4:00 A.M. to make purchases—with the aid of her brother José Félix, one of her sons, or a helper—from villagers who came by *cayucos* to sell her rice, corn, beans, bananas, chickens, and other items.[9] She also bought finished goods and sold merchandise to the owners of ships—the *Puxcatán,* the *Armandito,* the *Ana Luisa,* and *El Carmen*—that arrived from Campeche and other venues. In addition to foodstuffs bought from villagers, she purchased coffee, rice, and grain in bulk. When the distributors tried to cheat her by manipulating the scales, Doña Manuelita—a short, stout, unpretentious woman—would hoist a sack of rice off the scales and order the *coyotes* to recalibrate the device for accuracy.

Her friendliness and her readiness to extend credit to customers and acquaintances earned her a place as "the most beloved person in the village," according to a neighbor and close family friend.[10] Indicative of this esteem, she and her husband were godparents to a large number of children from the area. "They acted as if they were at the same level as everyone else, as if they were humble," Nelly León, seventy, a teacher at the elementary school, told a reporter.[11]

A strong believer, Doña Manuelita looked forward to August 15, when *tepetitecos* paid homage to the Virgin of the Assumption, whom López Obrador's mother believed shared many qualities of the Virgin of Santander in Spain. Doña Manuelita's last pregnancy had produced twins (Candelaria Beatriz and Martín Jesús), and the delivery was extremely difficult. She promised the lord that if she lived, she would donate a statue of the Virgin of Carmen to the nearby village of Límbano Blandín, which lacked a patron saint. She survived and made good on her word. The Virgin holding the Christ child still stands to the left of the priest when he says Mass in Límbano Blandín's simple, picturesque church.[12]

At the same time, Doña Manuelita exhibited a social vision, expressed sympathy for the indigenous population, and inculcated the value of the Golden Rule in her children. The success of their businesses meant that the family, though by no means rich, had more money than most of their neighbors. She and her husband encouraged the youngsters to share toys with playmates and to lend a hand to others.[13] When his mother scolded Andrés Manuel for coming home from school without his pencil, he answered that he had broken it in half and shared the pieces with poor classmates. "Ever since he was a child, he wanted to give to others," said Emiliano Gómez, a rancher and family friend.[14] Later, when operating a restaurant in Palenque, Doña Manuelita provided free food to striking workers in the tree-cutting industry.

Their children remember Doña Manuelita and Andrés López as caring, loving parents who would sometimes have to discipline their children. When young Andrés Manuel fell into bouts of ill temper, his father cured the "disease" by giving his son a quick spanking. The boy "said 'ouch!' and the illness went away."[15]

There was little entertainment for children in Tepetitán, whose population numbered fewer than a thousand inhabitants. As a result, Doña Manuelita organized social activities that included competitions for young men such as climbing twenty-meter greased polls, chasing greased pigs, and attempting on horseback to spear pieces of paper hanging from tree branches. If the intrepid rider succeeded, the young woman whose number corresponded to that on the target would hang a garland around his neck. In the evening, dances attracted young people from across the region. Many of the rough-hewn boys, who worked on nearby ranches, donned their finest shirts and rode into town on the best steed available. Doña Manuelita insisted that they leave their guns at her store. After the dance they would drink in cantinas before falling asleep. The next morning they collected their pistols and galloped out of town, shooting wildly into the air.

On Saturdays, young Andrés Manuel and his brothers paid fifty centavos to attend movies at the Cine Municipal. His favorite character was The Saint (*El Santo*), a wrestler played by Rodolfo Guzmán Huerta, who defended the poor against zombies, female vampires, witches, the offspring of Frankenstein, and the forces of darkness. Many of the fifty-four *El Santo* films portrayed wrestlers as law-abiding citizens who fought the evil and corrupt *rudos* in a society devoid of order and justice.[16] El Peje devoured comic books featuring *El Santo*. In addition, he shot marbles on the town's dirt streets, swam and fished in the river, and played cowboys and Indians.[17]

As a child, Andrés Manuel developed a passion for baseball and, like many youngsters, aspired to become a professional player. His fondness for the sport persists, and as mayor he often garnished his speeches with baseball metaphors, describing the percentage of questions answered at news conferences as his "batting average," for example. There was no TV in Tepetitán in the 1950s, and electricity was available only a few hours a day. Still, he listened to Major League games on the battery-powered radio of Don Pepe, who shared his love of the sport and umpired local games. The town's baseball field bears the name of el Peje's grandfather.

The boy's beloved team was the New York Yankees, but his favorite player was Dodgers pitcher Sandy Koufax. Another outstanding big leaguer whom he admired was Roberto Clemente, a Puerto Rican who starred in right field for the Pittsburgh Pirates. Clemente was inducted posthumously into baseball's Hall of Fame after his death in a plane crash.

Andrés Manuel also enjoyed playing baseball. He took the game seriously. On one occasion he streaked after a long fly, snagged the ball, and held on to it even after colliding with a barbed-wife fence.[18] His brother José Ramiro recalled that Andrés Manuel was a power hitter who played both third base and the outfield.[19] Other baseball enthusiasts said that he manipulated the bat with such skill that he could hit singles to any part of the field—a talent he demonstrated later in responding to the queries of reporters. López Obrador held catchers in the highest regard: they called the pitch, moved defensive players around the field, and enjoyed a strategic overview of the contest. Nevertheless, he left this position to his younger brother, José Ramón, known as "the sheep" (*el Borrego*) because of his size and strength. *El Borrego* had a fierce temper and would charge the mound with his bat if the pitcher struck him out. On other occasions he would simply take the baseball home, ending the contest. As a rule, the youngsters made their own baseballs by wrapping rags in the wet sap of rubber trees.[20]

Enemies accused López Obrador of seriously injuring a teammate during a game in 1961. According to PRI deputy Carlos Manuel Rovirosa Ramírez, eight-year-old Andrés Manuel lost a fight with a fellow player, José Angel León Hernández. The youngster became so enraged that he reportedly hurled a baseball at León Hernández's head. The impact of the ball allegedly caused the victim to bleed profusely, develop epilepsy, and remain in a near vegetative state until his premature death in 1995. There is no official record of this incident, and I could find no one in Tepetitán to verify it. A newspaper article about the affair appeared in the anti–López Obrador *Tabasco el Día* on October 5, 1995. Writer Rafael Soberanez León claimed to have interviewed the injured boy's parents, who are now deceased. One version of the story suggests that surviving family members refuse to talk about the matter.[21] López Obrador's elementary school teacher denies this account and says that he avoided schoolyard scuffles.[22] Moreover, a close family friend who knew León Hernández characterized the incident as "a lie, which the PRI had concocted to disparage López Obrador."[23] When I spoke with Rovirosa Ramírez at a beer party and cockfight at his Rancho Chubasco outside of Tepetitán, he was vague about the incident and cut short the conversation.[24]

Still, violence was no stranger to Tepetitán. On August 15, in the early 1960s, the day of the Virgen de la Asunción and the town fair, Captain Próspero González and a dozen mounted state police arrested Esteban Reyes for allegedly stealing a horse. Even though Reyes, twenty-four, had an impeccable reputation, the drunken officers bound his hands and feet, took him to a nearby ranch, made him dance by firing shots near his feet, and ultimately killed him. The outraged men of Tepetitán captured and executed Captain González. One observer said he was sliced into small pieces (*picadillo*);[25] another claimed that he was shot, along with several of his men.[26] No legal repercussions ensued because authorities were told that "the town" had carried out the execution. After this experience with traditional justice, the police steered clear of Tepetitán.

Andrés Manuel completed his first years of education at the local Marcos Becerra Primary School, where he was always the first student to finish his work. There were no advanced schools in Tepetitán, and Doña Manuelita arranged for him to continue his studies at the Rómulo Hernández García Secondary School in Macuspana. An obedient youngster, he stayed with a middle-class family headed by José Hernández Hernández and María del Carmita Domínguez. Hernández was a well-to-do merchant who shared Doña Manuelita's devotion to Catholicism. Andrés Manuel returned home on weekends by bus. The boy even served as an aco-lyte for a Father Carlos at the San Isidro Labrador Church in Mac-uspana and—despite claims to the contrary—remains a Catholic, according to his sister, Candelaria Beatriz. "He doesn't talk about his religion, perhaps to avoid problems with other faiths," she added.[27]

The family's fortunes worsened, though, when Andrés Manu-el's father defied the advice of Doña Manuelita and purchased a business that made giant cheeses weighing twenty-five to thirty kilograms. Unable to compete against larger producers, he lost money hand over fist and wound up deeply in debt. To improve their economic lot, Doña Manuelita insisted that the family move to Villahermosa, the state capital. Although her husband yearned to return to his native Veracruz, he acquiesced in her decision. "Yes, Mamacita," he agreed. In Villahermosa they bought a house from Diego Rosique Palavicini, a friend and affluent cattle raiser who owned a chain of stores in addition to a ranch near Tepetitán. Doña Manuelita and Andrés sold cloth and clothing at Novedades Andrés and shoes at La Gota, small stores at the corner of Primav-era Street and Progreso, next to the Pino Suárez market.

TRAGEDY STRIKES

Tragedy struck the family in 1969. At 4:00 P.M. on July 8, Andrés Manuel and his younger brother, José Ramón, were minding the fabric store while their parents were out. According to a contempo-rary newspaper account, José Ramón decided to scare an acquain-tance who worked in a nearby store. He took from the cash drawer a Super Colt .38-caliber pistol, which their father had accepted as payment for an eight-hundred-peso debt. Andrés Manuel noticed that his brother, who also had a white toy pistol, had put a bullet in the Colt and was handling the weapon carelessly. "Stop playing with the pistol," he commanded. José Ramón answered, "Don't be afraid. You are a scaredy cat. Everything frightens you." Andrés Manuel remembers turning his back, only to hear the weapon discharge. José Ramón died immediately when a bullet pierced the right side of his head. Passersby reportedly told Licenciado Arnulfo Sánchez Méndez, who investigated the incident, that the dead boy's brother was playing with the weapon.[28] By another account, both boys were tugging at the trigger.[29] In yet a third version, the fourteen-year-old José Ramón was twirling the pistol like a gunslinger when it fell to the floor and went off, sending a bullet through the boy's temple.[30] The State Judicial Police reportedly seized the fifteen-year-old Andrés Manuel, struck him on the face, neck, and back, and held him in custody until midnight before determining that they had no proof of homicide.[31]

The politically powerful Rosique intervened with Governor Manuel R. Mora Martínez to shield the family from legal action.[32] Since the administration of González Pedrero, the police report of the shooting has been missing from the official records of Villahermosa. José Ramón was interred in the Panteon General of Villahermosa, where his parents were later buried. Political adversaries continually dredge up this accident to impugn López Obrador's character, and José Ramón's death "remains a shadow over his life."[33] Critics even castigate López Obrador as "Cain," after the first-born son of Adam and Eve, who killed his brother, Abel.

The 1969 event inevitably invites comparisons with another incident. In December 1951 future president Carlos Salinas, then three years old, allegedly shot and killed a family maid. Carlos and his brother Raúl, age five, along with an eight-year-old friend, were playing war games with a loaded .22-caliber rifle that their father had left in a closet. They condemned their twelve-year-old maid to death, instructed her to kneel, and one of them shot her. When asked what had happened, Carlos said, "I killed her with one shot. I'm a hero." No one was ever charged with a crime, as the authorities ruled the incident an accident.[34]

The distraught Andrés Manuel engaged in no such braggadocio. Yet his father never forgave him for the death of Jose Ramón, who was the apple of his eye. In light of this hostility, Andrés Manuel began to support himself by selling shoes and clothing provided by his mother in various neighborhoods of Villahermosa. He frequently spent the night in the homes of friends to avoid his father's ire. Soon he began traveling to Chetumal, near the Mexico-Belize border, through which black market items entered the country, to broaden his array of merchandise. At school he became known as "El Americano" because he wore foreign-made shirts.[35]

THE FAMILY ODYSSEY CONTINUES

López Obrador's grieving parents attempted to mute the horror of José Ramón's death by relocating to Agua Dulce, Veracruz, where Doña Manuelita's sister, Gloria Juana Obrador González, lived. They supported themselves by opening yet another store, which they called Amor y Paz. By this time Andrés Manuel had dropped out of sight. For more than a year his parents knew nothing of his whereabouts until a journalist reported that he was studying at UNAM in Mexico City.[36]

In 1972 the family's pilgrimage continued. In pursuit of a less humid climate that would help Doña Manuelita's health, they wound up in Palenque, a small town in Chiapas near the Tabasco frontier and site of world-renowned Mayan ruins. In the Pakaná section of Palenque, Doña Manuelita and her husband purchased El Palomar restaurant and a small hotel, the Ki-Chan—"friend" in Mayan—which they enlarged to twenty-three rooms. They also acquired two ranches, one near the hotel, another sixteen miles from town. They lived in Palenque until both died in 2000.

Doña Manuelita served as role model, inspiration, and motivator for her seven children: Andrés Manuel, José Ramón, José Ramiro ("Pepín"), Pedro Arturo, Pío Lorenzo, and the twins, Martín Jesús and Candelaria Beatriz ("Candy"). Table 1 lists the dates and places of the children's birth, as well as their current occupations.

As the eldest child, Andrés Manuel was the favorite of Doña Manuelita, and she encouraged him to work hard at school and prepare for a university education. She also urged his siblings to study like Andrés Manuel so they could improve their lives.

José Ramiro spent four semesters taking economics courses at UNAM before returning to Tabasco, where he worked in the Casa de Cultura in Villahermosa, opened a laundry, and helped with a family business.[37] Although he joined Andrés Manuel in founding the

TABLE 1. *Birth Date, Place of Birth, Occupation of the López Obrador Children*

NAME	DATE OF BIRTH	PLACE OF BIRTH	OCCUPATION
Andrés Manuel	November 13, 1953	Macuspana	Mayor of D.F. (2000–mid-2005)
José Ramón ("Moncho"/ "Borrego")	December 20, 1954	Macuspana	Died in a shooting accident on July 8, 1969
José Ramiro ("Pepín")	March 19, 1956	Macuspana	Mayor of Macuspana (2003–6)
Pedro Arturo	October 21, 1957	Tepetitán	Federal government's representative to Diconsa in Tlaxcala
Pío Lorenzo	May 21, 1959	Tepetitán	Human rights worker in Tuxtla Gutiérrez, Chiapas; and political organizer for Andrés Manuel's presidential campaign
Candelaria Beatriz ("Candi")	November 14, 1964	Villahermosa	Homemaker in Tuxtla Gutiérrez, Chiapas
Martín Jesús	November 14, 1964	Villahermosa	Businessman in Veracruz with activities in Baja California Sur; estranged from Andrés Manuel and most of the family

PRD in Tabasco, Andrés Manuel opposed José Ramiro's running for mayor of Macuspana in 2003. The only other child to earn a degree was Pedro Arturo, who studied civil engineering at the University of Veracruz. He later served as director of public works in Tabasco's Emiliano Zapata municipality (1985–88), became a carpenter, and in 2002 was named delegate in Tlaxcala for Diconsa—the federal government's food distribution program. He is married to Carmen Herrerías Alamina, whose brother was the private secretary to Octavio Romero Oropeza, official mayor or chief administrative officer of the D.F. under López Obrador.[38]

Pío Lorenzo, who participated in the agrarian leagues in Tabasco, studied sociology at UNAM, supporting himself by serving in Tabasco's representational office in the D.F., correcting galleys for *La República* and editing speeches for PRI politician Alfredo del Mazo González. He also worked in the Chiapas state government before helping to organize a citizens' network to assist his brother's presidential campaign.

Martín Jesús earned the label of the black sheep and playboy of the family for using Andrés Manuel's name to promote business ventures in Veracruz and Baja California Sur. His twin, Candelaria Beatriz, is a homemaker in Tuxtla Gutiérrez, Chiapas.

In the 1970s Doña Manuelita dropped a tray while serving diners at El Palomar. X-rays revealed that she not only had a fractured shoulder but also a cancerous growth.[39] In response to a physician who warned that her days were numbered, she replied that she would outlive him. According to a cousin, she also said, "I cannot die; I have a flock of children to raise."[40]

Doña Manuelita took various remedies, such as *cancerillo*, a widely available herb believed to have curative powers. In addition, she went to Mexico City for forty days of cobalt treatment. Although this therapy destroyed her cancer, it left her with severe allergies—to the point that she required an oxygen device to help her breathe. She also suffered from acute phlebitis. She encouraged Andrés Manuel's activism and she and her husband assisted him with small amounts of money.

Until their deaths, his parents worried intensely about López Obrador's future. Doña Manuelita remained committed to his ideals but said that his activities caused her "moral suffering." In contrast, Andrés López Ramón thought little of his son's pursuit of peaceful change. "Peace flags are worthless. Those who enjoy power and harm the people will not respond to peaceful means. For this reason, the people must find the right moment to take up arms and thus change things," he insisted.[41]

Doña Manuelita died of a heart attack in Veracruz on May 6, 2000, just two months before her son won the mayorship; her husband passed away on December 7, 2000, at the age of eighty-eight. The last thing Doña Manuelita told two of her closest friends was "to take care of my son Andrés; they will try to kill him."[42] Despite the urging of his brothers, Andrés Manuel seldom visited his parents when they were hospitalized in Mexico City. Rather than impose on the PRD's candidate for mayor, family members often asked other federal officials from Tabasco to help obtain passes so that they could see their father and mother in the hospital outside normal visiting hours.[43] One of López Obrador's collaborators explained that, because of his political activities, "he seldom finds time even to go to the bathroom."[44] For years Andrés Manuel and his brothers and sister gathered in Palenque on December 24 to honor the birthday of their mother. They also conducted family business with Andrés Manuel, the eldest sibling, serving as paterfamilias.

THE INFLUENCE OF MAESTRO RODOLFO LARA LAGUNAS

From 1965 to 1968 López Obrador attended Federal Secondary School no. 1 in Villahermosa. He cited one of his teachers at this school, Maestro Rodolfo Lara Lagunas, as a powerful force in raising his social awareness.[45]

Born in 1942 to an impoverished shoemaker's family, Lara Lagunas and his eight brothers and sisters grew up in the Carolina section of Cuernavaca, which was so dangerous that police seldom ventured into the poor neighborhood. He managed to land a job in a rural school, more than an hour's walk from his home, while he worked on his undergraduate degree at night. He later earned a degree in educación cívica from the Escuela Normal Superior de México. In 1964 Lara Lagunas came to Villahermosa to teach civics; two years after his arrival, he entered the law school at the Autonomous Juárez University of Tabasco (UJAT).

Introduction to Benito Juárez

Lara Lagunas venerated Benito Juárez, the Liberal president of the mid-nineteenth century who championed the cause of the downtrodden against a markedly unjust political system. Finding that students knew so little about his idol, Lara Lagunas wrote a textbook entitled *Juárez: De la choza al Palacio Nacional; historias y testimonios* (2004), which emphasized the overwhelming obstacles faced by Juárez: he was orphaned at age three, suffered physical abuse at the hands of an uncle, grew up speaking only his native Zapotec, and experienced ugly discrimination by teachers. He persevered and gained admission to a seminary, which he left to study law in the newly established Instituto de Ciencias y Artes. As a young attorney, he found the ecclesiastical and lay courts extremely biased against the impoverished Indians whom he defended. He was even imprisoned on trumped-up charges. Rather than cow Juárez, these experiences strengthened his resolve to "destroy the wrongful power of the privileged classes."[46] He chose a political route to achieve this goal, winning local elections before serving as a federal deputy and then as governor of Oaxaca in 1847.

The Oaxacan joined the Liberal movement, which backed a constitutional government, the elimination of *fueros* for military personnel and the clergy, and the redistribution of the church's extensive landholdings to the peasants who toiled on them. After being exiled by Antonio López de Santa Anna, Juárez returned to Mexico in 1855 and, as justice minister, crafted the "Juárez Law," which diminished the power of the army and the church. Juárez served as provisional president for the Liberals in the War of Reforma (1858–60) against the Conservatives. When the Liberals triumphed, he won election as president in 1861.

Upon taking office, Juárez found the government's finances in disarray and stopped payment on loans from European countries. France's Napoleon III used this maneuver to justify an invasion and named a Hapsburg prince, Maximilian, emperor of Mexico. After its Civil War, the United States forced the French to withdraw. Maximilian was executed, and Juárez again became president in 1867. He was reelected in 1876. He is revered (or reviled) for separating church and state, promoting religious toleration, and accomplishing land reform.

Lara Lagunas also emphasized Juárez's egalitarianism and unpretentiousness. He believed that members of his government should lead dignified lives, but should neither abuse their power nor enrich themselves at the public's expense. Juárez's rule was no paragon of democracy, however. In 1858 he assumed the presidency as a result of a coup d'état. Moreover, he created a political machine to maintain his grip on power. Nonetheless, Mexico was the scene of Hobbesian politics in which most, if not all, players employed undemocratic tactics.

For Lara Lagunas, the antithesis to Juárez was Porfirio Díaz, a hero of the war against the French, who dominated the presidency from 1876 to 1911. The general-turned-politician ruled with an iron fist, dispatching his Guardias Rurales to intimidate, torture, and kill his enemies. Although he sought the presidency with the slogan "effective suffrage, no re-election," Díaz believed in "little politics and much administration." In 1880 Díaz selected as his successor Manuel González, telling him that he was leaving politics. González immediately yanked open the drawer of his desk and began feverishly searching for something. "What are you looking for?" Díaz asked. "Some *pendejo* who will believe that you are really going to exit the political arena," he replied. After four years, Díaz returned to the presidency, where he stayed until he was ousted by the Revolution. Díaz and his advisers, known as "scientists" (*científicos*), rolled out the red carpet for foreign corporations, repressed nascent trade unions, and concentrated land in the hands of a few.

Lara Lagunas's teaching may have imbued López Obrador with the cyclical view of history that periods of enlightenment are invariably followed by periods of darkness.[47] This concept appeared in López Obrador's book *Del esplendor a la sombra: La república restaurada*, which was published in 1986.

In addition to regaling his students with lectures on Juárez, Lara Lagunas taught them about Mahatma Gandhi's civil disobedience, Fidel Castro's revolution against the Batista dictatorship in Cuba, and U.S. aggression in Vietnam. Lara, who emphasized that "you can never know the impact that you have on students," found el Peje "a quiet and attentive boy," a good student but not outstanding. "He was timid and the girls liked him, but he did not show much interest in them. I never imagined that he would grow up to be a leader," he noted.[48]

The impact of the teacher proved profound. In later years López Obrador praised the accomplishments of Juárez, especially as an advocate for the "have-nots." At UJAT Lara Lagunas became a leader in the student movement, which demanded the removal of the repressive Governor Mora. In late May 1968 the young teacher participated in a hunger strike and was later jailed, as student protests spread like wildfire across Mexico.[49] While Lara Lagunas was behind bars, López Obrador and classmates brought him food and reading material.

OVERVIEW OF TABASCO'S HISTORY

López Obrador also learned that as the twentieth century unfolded, the nation's industrialization took place in the Mexico City-Guadalajara-Monterrey triangle. Later, twin assembly plants sprang up along the U.S.-Mexican border. Since the 1930s the federal government had spent vastly more in the north than in southern states like Chiapas, Oaxaca, Guerrero, Campeche, and Tabasco. Until the end of World War II, travel from Villahermosa to the D.F. meant going by boat to Veracruz and then overland to the capital. Banana and cocoa growers sent shipments to New Orleans, Louisiana, or Brownsville, Texas, not to Mexican ports. Attention turned to Tabasco only when Pemex found giant oil deposits in the 1970s.

A number of strong, capricious leaders filled the vacuum left by weak institutions within the state. According to López Obrador, three men compete for the title of Tabasco's best governor in the twentieth century.[50] These are Francisco J. Mújica, Tomás Garrido Canabal, and Carlos A. Madrazo Becerra. Like all governors of the state until the election of Manuel Andrade Díaz in 2001 and Andrés Granier Melo in 2006, these men made their political careers outside Tabasco.

Francisco J. Mújica

General Mújica, a staunch nationalist, ran the state from 1915 to 1916. Not only was he a fervent Jacobin and important architect of the 1917 Constitution, he also exhibited the nationalism that infused the 1910–16 Revolution. For example, he expelled a North American company from property that it had taken from peasants in the municipality of Jonuta. When Venustiano Carranza, the head of the constitutional army, ordered the property returned, Mújica reminded his chief of the land distribution goals of the Revolution, thus persuading Carranza to change his mind. As a result, the governor created the first *ejido*, La Isla del Chinal, during the Revolution. Mújica later made a name for himself in Michoacán politics.

Tomás Garrido Canabal

Thanks to support from General Alvaro Obregón, Garrido Canabal held sway for much of the period between 1919 and 1935 and gave the first major impetus to Tabasco's development. He earned national attention with his brutal anticlericalism in a state that the Roman Catholic Church had ignored during the colonial period. His so-called "defanatization" (*desfanatizadora*) initiative limited the number of churches to one for every six thousand inhabitants and required that priests must be Mexican born, with at least five years of residence in Tabasco. These clergymen had to be more than forty years of age, married, graduates of state primary and secondary schools, and of good character.

He authorized the "Red Shirts" to spearhead a *Kulturkampf* against Catholicism. The Garrido government outlawed writings that made reference to God and prohibited the placing of crosses at burial sites. In addition, religious festivals were transformed into secular events, and Tabascan towns bearing the "sectarian and fanatic nomenclature" of saints or other religious figures were rechristened with the names of artists, intellectuals, teachers, and local heroes. The zealous governor even endorsed the use of force to "destroy the roots of the religious virus,"[51] and converted churches into "rational schools" characterized by military discipline and "scientific" education, where students learned the virtues of reason, agricultural technology, and physical exercise.[52]

According to López Obrador, the governor "was a visionary with great sensitivity who knew how to combine politics and economics harmoniously."[53] His ability to achieve growth by sharply expanding the exportation of bananas gave him the freedom of action required to harass the church.

Garrido earmarked half the state's budget for education, fought alcoholism, granted the vote to women, and sprinkled his speeches with socialist terms. Yet he organized society in a corporatist, authoritarian fashion, creating leagues of peasants, workers, women, and cattle ranchers. At various times he allowed "seat warmers" to occupy the governorship, giving rise to the saying, "more than a man, Garrido is a flag, a doctrine, and an example."[54]

Garrido knew how to ingratiate himself with national politicians. When presidential aspirant Obregón visited the state in 1928, the governor assembled five thousand peasants, dressed in white, on the bank of the Grijalva River where it emptied into the Gulf of Mexico. The visitor responded to the welcome by declaring Tabasco the bulwark of the Revolution, and President Cárdenas later praised the state as the "laboratory of the revolution" and said it would be good to "tabasqueñizar a México." Garrido, a loyalist of former president Calles, embarrassed Cárdenas by continuing his anticlerical diatribes as a cabinet member and unleashing his Red Shirts in Mexico City. He ultimately went into voluntary exile in Costa Rica.[55]

Carlos A. Madrazo Becerra

Madrazo Becerra, the next governor to concentrate on development, began his career as a disciple of Garrido. The son of a rural teacher and a low-level state employee, Madrazo received a university scholarship from the governor, joined the revolutionary party, organized the Red Shirts, and spoke out in favor of teaching socialist tenets in the schools. Although deeply authoritarian and devoted to one-party rule, he believed that the revolutionary party should become more responsive to its members.

He found himself engulfed in a scandal when serving as a federal deputy. His enemies accused him of profiting from the sale of jobs in the *bracero* guest-worker program with the United States. He was later exonerated, and it turned out that his real crime had been to support Mexico City mayor Javier Rojo Gómez for the party's presidential nomination in 1945 when the PRI's mandarins had lined up behind Veracruz governor Miguel Alemán Valdés.

Madrazo governed with an iron hand. When Cuauhtémoc Cárdenas visited the state with *tabasqueño* Santiago Wilson to promote the ex-president's progressive, anti-imperialist National Liberation Movement (MLN), Madrazo informed them in no uncertain words: "Tell the general [Cárdenas] that he runs Michoacán, but I run Tabasco." To Wilson, he added, "I don't want to see you in Tabasco again . . . because if you don't leave I will crush you like a fly," striking his right leg for emphasis.[56] Elections expert Citlallín de Díos Calles remembers that when her father, Jesús Ezequiel de Díos, a Tabascan writer, criticized Madrazo, he warned him to remain in the D.F. or "I will kill you."[57]

On December 7, 1964, three weeks after leaving the governorship, President Gustavo Díaz Ordaz named Madrazo head of the national PRI. Madrazo believed that, in addition to nominating candidates, the PRI should have a social agenda—focusing on agricultural production, credit availability, salary levels, education, and the strengthening of municipal administrations, among other important issues. "The party is not the government, nor must it be subservient to the government, but at the vanguard of ideas, combining hopes, finding means [to fulfill those hopes], and charting directions," he insisted.[58] To circumvent governors and other opponents of change, Madrazo organized regional and municipal committees.

The revitalized PRI went beyond meetings and engaged in economic development projects. Governors regarded such activism as blatant trespassing on their terrain. Madrazo also opposed a move by PRI greybeards to allow the re-election of legislators. He believed that the people could work through political parties to advance their interests. Thus re-election would only insulate lawmakers from popular sentiment and in the process weaken the PRI and other parties. In addition, multiple terms would impede the emergence of new leaders. Madrazo's persistence persuaded the PRI's three sectors to oppose the legislation, which ultimately failed.

A Child Is Born in Tabasco

Madrazo also insisted that PRI members select candidates via secret ballot. Intramural democracy, he reasoned, would fortify the public's respect for the ruling party, which had been under attack by Cárdenas's MLN for catering to affluent businessmen. Madrazo advocated selecting new party leaders nationwide, choosing candidates through primaries, and implementing individual affiliation rather than membership by sector. With the president's consent, he managed to hold an internal election to select the gubernatorial candidate in Baja California.

At this point, he suffered a barrage of attacks in the media. The coup de grâce took the form of a cartoon on the cover of the popular magazine ¡Siempre! that could not have been published without the government's permission. It depicted Madrazo as a little boy in short pants. While he sat on the ground destroying a doll that represented the PRI, President Díaz Ordaz observed his behavior from behind a wall. A few days later, Madrazo resigned as PRI president.

The so-called "Cyclone from the Southeast" exchanged letters with his followers, made speeches in seventeen states, and advocated the formation of a "national front" of "progressive men" on the grounds that the PRI no longer boasted "the support of the immense majority" of Mexicans.[59] He even launched a new organization—Patria Nueva—for which José Francisco Paoli Bolio drafted the preliminary documents. Madrazo was especially popular with young Mexicans,[60] and suffered a profound emotional crisis after the October 2, 1968 "Tlatelolco Massacre." His opponents accused him of being an *oculto* leader of the student movement and a provocateur of the violence that erupted. On June 9, 1969, he, his wife, and tennis star Rafael "El Pelón" Osuna, who happened to be aboard, died, along with seventy-six other passengers, when their plane crashed near the Pico del Fraile mountain in Nuevo León. To this day, many observers believe that Madrazo's enemies in Los Pinos and the PRI were responsible for his death.[61]

LÓPEZ OBRADOR STUDIES POLITICS AT UNAM

Unbeknownst to his family, López Obrador continued his study of politics and history in Mexico City. He followed his mother's advice and gained admission to UNAM, where he majored in political science and public administration from 1973 to 1976. Famous for its leftist orientation, UNAM was a hotbed of radicalism. Students and professors remained outraged at the Tlatelolco blood-letting, in which federal troops killed hundreds of unarmed students and other middle-class protesters in Mexico City.

Bartolo Jiménez Méndez, a close friend, recalled that the long-haired López Obrador admired former governor Madrazo, Juárez, Gandhi, and Castro. He was obsessed by dialectical materialism and read Louis Althusser, Friedrich Nietzsche, and Karl Marx. "He assimilated little; as a result, he studied a great deal," stated Jiménez Méndez. López Obrador also sat in on lectures by Dr. Enrique González Pedrero, the director of the Facultad de Ciencias Políticas y Sociales, who thundered against the exploitation and poverty of Mexico's peasants and workers.

El Peje dropped out of UNAM several times because he was a "lazy" student and suffered bouts of depression arising from his brother's death.[62] He failed economics, mathematics, and statistics, struggled in courses on political parties, social psychology, and political philosophy, compiled only a 7.6 grade point average on a 10-point scale, and did not complete his degree until 1987.[63] He was involved in the Organization of Tabascan Students (OET)[64] and lived in a Tabascan student center known as Cedet, A.C. While OET was essentially a social organization, he was also active in the politically focused Center of Studies on Tabascan Development (Cedestab). This group enjoyed the support of future governor Leandro Rovirosa Wade, then secretary of water resources under President Luis Echeverría Álvarez (1970–76).

López Obrador, Víctor Manuel López Cruz, Jorge Miguel Luna Cabrera, and other Cedestab members relished discussing politics in the home of acclaimed poet and fellow *tabasqueño* Carlos Pellicer Cámara, a champion of indigenous communities. Pellicer created the famous La Venta Park in Villahermosa, a regional anthropology center that bears his name and houses collections of Indian artifacts, and other museums. Like the Indians, Pellicer wore *huaraches* and pants and shirts made of *manta* when in Tabasco, and he referred to himself as the "Apostle of the Chontales," an indication of his solidarity with Nacajuca residents.

Pellicer's *Canto a Juárez* is considered one of the greatest works of Mexican poetry. López Obrador idolized Pellicer. Of the indigenous population, Pellicer wrote, "Not with all the honey in the world could you sweeten the bitterness of the Chontal."[65] Pellicer befriended López Obrador, who sometimes accompanied him on speaking trips.[66] On one occasion, el Peje invited Pellicer and fellow students to visit Palenque. While there, the young men were swimming in the Baña de la Reina when a strong current pulled López Obrador under the water. "After the experience," according to a biographer, "he told his friends that in this moment the only thing that passed though his mind was that he could not die because he had a mission in life."[67]

Pellicer did more than make speeches; he sold his José María Velasco paintings for 7 million pesos to finance a broom factory, a workshop that produced drums, and the production of tomatoes, beans, corn, and yucca.

Although considered a "serious student" by at least one colleague,[68] López Obrador was called a "water snake" by fellow students because he was "continually moving, appearing, and disappearing."[69] Despite mediocre grades, the young Tabascan developed an intense interest in community development, the subject of his UNAM thesis.[70] On one occasion, he was doing research on how the increased production of the *pejelagarto* fish might improve the lives of local Indians. When Jiménez Méndez and another student teased him about the project, López Obrador became angry and challenged them to a fistfight.[71]

López Obrador did not attend his graduation ceremony at UNAM. "He came to tell me that he had passed his courses, but that the [graduation] party was to be in an extremely luxurious hotel and cost a great deal. He did not have money for this," said his mother. "This is like my *Negrito*," she said, using her affectionate nickname for her dark-skinned son. "He did not like expensive things."[72] The fact that he did not complete his degree for another fourteen years may have contributed to his absence.

Doña Manuelita, Maestro Lara Lagunas, and Carlos Pellicer played crucial roles in forging López Obrador's outlook. His mother taught him the value of hard work, as well as the importance of Christian compassion. In Tepetitán he witnessed poverty, gained a strong sense of community where isolation and violence were frequent companions, and learned how humble people employed traditional means to redress wrongdoing. His brother's death and the subsequent estrangement from his father undoubtedly affected him, but only he knows how deeply. Lara Lagunas immersed him in the ideals of Juárez, whose republican austerity became the watchword of the emerging political messiah, who was also attracted to the crusading zeal of Garrido. His teacher also lauded the accomplishments of Cárdenas, whom López Obrador came to admire as Mexico's greatest modern president. Pellicer opened the young man's eyes to the "other Tabasco," where Indians eked out an existence amid squalid conditions and blatant discrimination. The "providential man," as Krauze has called him, began to pursue his "mission" in his home state. In keeping with a zealous determination to uplift the dispossessed, he sought to reform a PRI that had abandoned the beneficiaries of the Mexican Revolution.

BLESSED ARE THE POOR

As a result of the oil boom of the late 1970s, López Obrador returned from UNAM to a state even more socially, economically, and politically convulsed than it had been before.[1] Mexico's energy fortunes soared in 1972, when Pemex discovered the prolific Reforma fields below the thick tropical vegetation that blankets the state. Many farmers and fishermen abandoned their traditional pursuits to work for Pemex, whose crews spurred the flight from land- and water-related work by destroying large tracts of fertile terrain and contaminating productive rivers and estuaries. "This has turned the hydrological system upside down," said a respected biologist.[2] Detractors of the oil firm often neglected to mention that the cutting of forests and jungle by cattle raisers had played havoc with the state's environment well before drilling surged in the 1970s.

TABASCO'S REGIONS

The state of Tabasco comprises four zones—the most prosperous, embracing Villahermosa and surrounding areas, is the center of Pemex operations. Once a steamy, gregarious provincial capital, Villahermosa was transformed into an expensive peso-chasing boomtown. Black gold detonated an explosion in the city's population, which grew from 33,000 inhabitants in 1950 to 99,000 in 1970 and 250,000 in 1980. Twenty-five years later, the number of inhabitants had soared to 543,548. Private and commercial flights into the local airport increased sharply, helicopters ferried workers and equipment to oil facilities, traffic on the capital's narrow streets and roads multiplied, and hotels and restaurants sprang to life to accommodate Pemex employees and suppliers. Businesses opened to meet the needs of the rapidly growing population, and fans arrived at the Centenario baseball stadium to watch their beloved Olmecas play, only to find that oil workers had purchased the best seats. On the seamier side, even the prices charged by prostitutes, who came from far and wide, rose sharply. Though prosperous ranches produced bananas, cocoa, and livestock, thousands of poor people lived in fetid shacks that clung like swallows' nests to the banks of the Grijalva, which, until a few years earlier, had been alive with the splash of expatriated Mississippi steamboats.

The oil boom also affected the Región de la Sierra, which encompasses the municipalities of Teapa, Tacotalpa, Jalapa, and Macuspana. Pemex had begun drilling in the 1950s in Macuspana, where Ciudad Pemex was located. So remote was this huge gas-processing and distribution complex that it became the monopoly's "Siberia" for employees out of favor with management.[3] As in the Villahermosa area, Pemex's construction of roads, bridges, and ports promoted commerce and created jobs. Teapa continued to produce bananas and Jalapa remained a cattle-raising area, yet thousands of men from these municipalities sought the high-paying jobs at Pemex.

Meanwhile, the petroleum bonanza hardly touched hundreds of thousands of *tabasqueños* in the isolated and impoverished Región de los Ríos, also known as the Usuamacinta region. Here the municipalities of Balancán, Centla, Emiliano Zapata, Tenosique, and Jonuta accounted for 40 percent of the state's territory but only 15 percent of its population. Major tributaries of the Usumacinta, the largest river in Mesoamerica, separated the region from the rest of the state and forced reliance on radio broadcasts and makeshift launches known as *pangas* for communication with neighboring municipalities. Only its largest towns had potable water, electricity, and plumbing. The widespread business of cattle ranching generated few jobs, and the lack of paved roads, machinery, credit, and technical assistance, combined with the constant danger of flooding, made subsistence farming a risky business. As a result, the output of corn, beans, and rice declined steadily alongside the harvesting of valuable trees like mahogany, cedar, and guanacaste—once a source of employment and income.

Pockets of poverty coexisted with areas of development in the Región de la Chontalpa. The more advanced municipalities in this zone include Cárdenas, Huimanguillo, Paraíso, and the oil- and cocoa-producing Comalcalco. Still, this area also embraced the extremely poor municipalities of Jalpa de Méndez, Cunduacán, and Nacajuca. Nacajuca is home to the Chontal Indians with whom López Obrador worked as state coordinator of the National Indigenous Institute (INI).

In the mid-1970s, López Obrador began assisting the indigenous population. He understood the PRI's shortcomings, but he joined the party in hopes of accomplishing change "from within."[4] He also realized that the PRI was the only party that could win. In 1976 PRI president Porfirio Muñoz Ledo recruited Carlos Pellicer as a senatorial candidate in Tabasco. Striving to inject new blood into the party's ranks and improve its image, Muñoz Ledo persuaded presidential nominee José López Portillo to endorse more notables, females, and young people for congressional seats. The PRI hierarchy deplored this innovation, but many leaders had offended the party's presidential contender by backing government secretary Mario Moya Palencia in the run-up to the nomination.

Secretary of water resources Rovirosa Wade, who was destined to become the PRI's candidate for the statehouse, enthusiastically endorsed Pellicer. His candidacy helped diminish the growing power of David Gustavo Gutiérrez Ruiz, the ruthlessly ambitious and extremely wealthy head of the state party's Popular Sector (discussed in the next chapter), former interim governor of Quintana Roo (1971–74), and an undisguised aspirant for the governorship.[5]

Once convinced that he should run for office, Pellicer threw himself into the campaign. Despite his remarkable art collection, the nonmaterialistic poet lacked the finances to wage a vigorous statewide race. Thus he welcomed the young people who flocked to his side, especially skilled organizers like López Obrador, whom he treated like a son. In fact, el Peje may have persuaded Pellicer to use campaign funds from the PRI to purchase sewing machines for poor communities.[6] Among the other young idealists who came from Mexico City to lend a hand were Jorge Miguel Luna Cabrera and José Isabel Jiménez Félix.

After winning the Senate seat, Pellicer campaigned for Rovirosa Wade. The poet told the candidate that he had just a single recommendation for his administration: "I want to tell you with all my 'force' that there is only one person who enjoys all the Indians' confidence. He is López Obrador. You must, however, insist that he finish his degree at UNAM."[7] When Rovirosa Wade won, Pellicer asked whether he had "thought any more about López Obrador."[8] "The Senator of the Chontales," whose work indelibly marked López Obrador, died a few months after taking office.

With all of the folderol associated with his January 1, 1977, inauguration, the new governor had forgotten about Pellicer's request until other young activists, Humberto Mayans Canabal and Pascual Bellizia Rosique, reminded him of his commitment. Though Rovirosa Wade had already named his cabinet, he agreed to meet with Pellicer's protégé, who was waiting in an anteroom. Before laying eyes on López Obrador,[9] the governor used his "red telephone," which connected all government officials, to contact

Ignacio Ovalle Fernández, head of the INI. He asked Ovalle to appoint López Obrador as the institute's Tabasco coordinator. Ovalle agreed to talk with the young man but emphasized that all state directors had to take courses that would sensitize them to the Indians' culture and abject poverty.[10] Only after arranging the appointment did Rovirosa Wade meet el Peje, who impressed him as a person possessed of "a great spirit of service."[11]

INI AND COPLAMAR

When Ovalle interviewed López Obrador, he found that the twenty-four-year-old's "head was full of ideas, that he showed incredible imagination, and that he proposed sensible projects."[12] In view of the young man's knowledge and sensitivity, Ovalle excused him from undergoing the obligatory training. Ovalle recalled his belief that he was in the presence of a person with "a grand soul" who had a strong "interior force." Nevertheless, López Obrador insisted on taking the classes, lest it appear that he was receiving preferential treatment. "I have to follow my own rules," he said.[13]

By virtue of becoming the head of Tabasco's INI, López Obrador also assumed the state directorship of the General Coordination of the National Plan for Marginal Groups and Depressed Zones (Coplamar). The purpose of this program was to use oil revenue to improve the plight of the poor. However, Ovalle, the architect of the program, had a staff of only a few people and a meager budget. After two years he explained to the chief executive that without more funds his government would fail the indigenous population and other disadvantaged groups.

Ovalle obtained additional resources, which he stretched by allying with other state agencies that had offices and personnel in most of the country. These included INI, the Mexican Social Security Institute (IMSS), the Ministry of Public Education (SEP), and the National Company of Subsistence Food for the People (Conasupo). Such joint ventures meant that there was no need to create a sprawling bureaucracy. Coplamar was the "embryo" for Salinas's National Solidarity Program (Pronasol), Fox's Contigo Program of Attention to 250 Micro Regions, and Fox's Opportunities initiative to promote education, healthcare, and nutrition among the poorest of the poor and similar Calderón-backed initiatives.[14]

According to López Obrador's secretary, Ernesto Benítez López, the linkage between Coplamar and Conasupo infuriated Gustavo Rosario Torres, who was accustomed to running the giant food distribution agency's operations in Tabasco. Benítez López remembers that López Obrador was invited to a party at a Coplamar-Conasupo warehouse in Boca de Cerro, near the Guatemalan border. The building where the fiesta was held overflowed with gorgeous women, upbeat dance music, and the aroma of whiskey. Fearing that his enemies were trying to entrap him in a compromising situation, the puritanical López Obrador immediately told the driver, "Let's get out of here."[15]

Contrary to the claims made by Rovirosa's predecessor, Mario Trujillo García (1971–76), that there were no Indians in Tabasco, tens of thousands of Chontales, Chols, Tzeltals, and other Maya descendants eked out a living in the state. In most cases they suffered from malnourishment, primitive housing, and a lack of education. Trujillo treated them like bastards whom he wanted to crop out of a happy family portrait, while other elites denigrated them as "water dogs" because of the swampy areas in which they lived.

As chief of INI and Coplamar, López Obrador repainted this picture. He built a thirty-member team that included Baldemar Hernández Márquez, subdirector of organization; Rafael Coronel Carrillo, coordinator of housing programs; and Omar Castro Castillo, financial administrator.[16] He also established an informal group of Chontal advisors, composed of individuals well acquainted with their neighborhoods, and cultivated older men so as to gain legitimacy for his endeavors.[17]

López Obrador visited the government offices in Villahermosa on a regular basis. "Why do you insist on going every day?" asked his co-worker Omar Castro. El Pejelagarto's response revealed his astuteness: "I drop in to report on our programs so that 'the Turk'"—*el Turco*, the hard-boiled government secretary Salvador Neme Castillo—"doesn't send his police out here to investigate our activities."[18]

Ovalle rated López Obrador's performance at INI as "excellent." While forty-nine of the fifty state coordinators lived in towns near an indigenous community, López Obrador refused to do so. One of his first acts was to move the INI's modest headquarters from Villahermosa to Nacajuca, where he built a small office that also served as storage shed and workshop. The director's house consisted of a simple kitchen, two bedrooms, a living room, and a small bathroom.[19] Ovalle recalls visiting Nacajuca at the invitation of Governor Rovirosa. They found López Obrador, who by now had married and begun a family, living in a one-room hut known as a *choza*. His young wife was cooking on a crude stove perched on the earthen floor, while their youngest child slept on a folding cot. When the visitors left, a group of Chontales shouted, "López Obrador for governor!"[20]

The INI coordinator obtained land for the community, helped them gain legal title to the property on which they lived, assisted in paving the dirt roads that snaked through the indigenous zone, created a transportation cooperative, ordered the building of the so-called *casas Sandinistas* with Cuban technical assistance, established schools, promoted literacy programs for adults, and awarded scholarships to youngsters so they could continue their education. Under el Peje's supervision, the INI also launched a ceramics factory, vaccinated thousands of children, and brought electricity to many areas that had previously depended on gas lanterns and candles.

In addition, he granted credit based on one's word (*a la palabra*). A co-worker remembers accompanying López Obrador with a satchel of cash, forking over pesos as agreements were reached.[21] This practice of making loans based on a verbal commitment to repay the money conveyed his trust of the recipients and morphed into another INI program in which cows were made available *a la palabra* with the understanding that a cow's first female calf would be returned to the institute to be lent to another family.[22] In addition, López Obrador oversaw the preparation of a dictionary in Chontal, recorded traditional Indian music, and founded Radio Chontal, which broadcast in the Indians' language.

XENA, the 500-watt "Voice of the Chontales," began operating in 1981. It featured native music and culture and news about housing, roads, potable water, electrification, and other INI initiatives. In addition, broadcasts disseminated information about births, deaths, marriages, and social events in the Indian communities, innovations in medicine, and the risks of alcoholism. Some messages were transmitted through regular programs like *Por el Camino de la Salud,* literally the "Road to Good Health." Candelaria Lázaro Lázaro and other producers also embedded lessons in soap operas that included the character *Chucho el Roto* (Chucho the Broken One), whose poverty and philandering sprang from his incessant drinking.[23] The state government subsequently shuttered Radio Chontal, alleging that it had become a conduit for anti-PRI propaganda. Sixteen years later, local indigenous leaders petitioned Xóchitl Gálvez, Fox's national coordinator for indigenous communities, to recommence broadcasts.[24]

The Indians became devoted to the outgoing, spontaneous López Obrador. While enthusiastic about this work, he exhibited a sense of sacrifice and privation much like Franciscan monks and primitive Christians. If nightfall found him in a remote village, he would sleep on a mat or hammock just as the local residents did. Then he would get up early and labor side by side with them all day. "We liked the fact that he was not a man who stayed in his office," a Chontal leader said.[25] They referred to him as *lesho,* which in Mayan connotes affection bordering on adoration.

Mutual respect characterized the relationship between Rovirosa Wade and López Obrador. The governor told Reséndez Medina, his chief administrative officer, to give the INI coordinator whatever he needed for social projects.[26] El Peje disdained sycophantic groveling, or *lambisconería,* and seldom praised the governor for INI's accomplishments. Instead, he extolled the people and their success in the face of insurmountable obstacles. López Obrador's uncanny ability to identify with the dispossessed held him in good stead as he ascended the political ladder.

Rovirosa Wade also taught López Obrador a lesson in wringing money out of Mexico City. Although an affluent entrepreneur, the governor was committed to social objectives. To obtain more resources, he ordered his private secretary, the politically shrewd Angel Buendía Tirado, to organize the closure of roads to oil wells. López Obrador and Víctor Manuel López Cruz participated in this initiative, which convinced Pemex officials to send more funds to the state for security.[27]

López Obrador befriended Graco Ramírez Garrido Abreu, a young activist in the Socialist Workers' Party (PST), who assembled Cuban-made prefabricated houses. López Obrador liked Ramírez Garrido's work and contacted Ovalle about expanding the program to Nacajuca. The INI director explained that, while it might be a worthwhile project, there were no resources available; but the dynamic Tabascan insisted he was not asking for money, only "authorization" to proceed.[28] With Ovalle's approval, López Obrador obtained materials and technical assistance from the Havana government to construct dwellings for the Chontales.[29]

CAMELLONES CHONTALES

López Obrador devoted even more time and energy to advancing agricultural projects in indigenous communities. He paid particular attention to increasing output by employing techniques once used by the Mayas. Until the 1970s, the government had endeavored to drain, dry, and divide swamp land in order to grow crops and trees—though flooding invariably frustrated these ventures.

Rather than dredging and attempting to dry out low-lying areas, INI used human labor and machinery to build up rectangular, waffle-like platforms of fertile soil that were high enough to evade normal flooding. Local residents could then cultivate the area without relying on technical assistance. They planted corn, beans, yucca, and other crops for family consumption. Fish spawned in the water around the earthen platforms. A family of five could live well on the output from a two-thousand-square-meter parcel. López Obrador became a forceful advocate for this program, and the cultivated plots became known as *camellones chontales*.[30]

Mother María del Carmen Muriel de la Torre, a member of the Congregation of the Helpers of Purgatory (*Auxiliadoras del Purgatorio*), had been working with the Indians in Nacajuca since 1971. A member of a distinguished Mexico City family, her desire to help the downtrodden led her to join a religious order. After ministering to the poor in a half-dozen countries, she happened to stop in Nacajuca. She found the Chontales "so poor, so sick, so badly clothed, so ill-housed, and so afflicted by discrimination" that she simply could not leave. Females in the swampy municipality were often victimized by local uses and customs. One of these was a practice known as *sarna,* whereby women in an advanced stage of pregnancy were bound by their wrists to beams in their dwellings. Then local healers, or *curanderas,* built fires, laced with Chili and other herbs, under their feet, supposedly to ease the birthing process and ensure the good health of the baby.

Madre Muriel introduced modern methods of childbirth. In addition, she recruited teachers, set up clinics, provided cooking classes, founded a high school and cultural institute, created a computer center and ceramics factory, and established a retirement home. The religious sister and López Obrador developed an uneasy relationship—in part because he "did not like to share credit for projects."[31] In truth, she initiated the *camellones chontales* on the basis of plans sent from Holland,[32] but the INI director never recognized her role in this endeavor. Nacajuca was only big enough for one messiah and it should be he, not Madre Muriel, whom he supplanted as the leader of the community. In 2001 the Fox administration selected her as "Volunteer of the Year."[33] "Still," she recalled, "López Obrador never gave me credit. God help us if he reaches the presidency."[34]

Rovirosa Wade agreed that Madre Muriel had launched the *camellones* project but insisted that López Obrador had introduced key designs to mitigate flooding and improve the circulation of water. In the final analysis, the ex-governor concluded that the program did more to bolster the dignity of the Chontales than to accelerate economic growth.[35]

Ovalle received visits from Doña Manuelita while her son was involved with INI. When she first asked for a meeting, Ovalle assumed that she would seek a salary increase or other benefits for Andrés Manuel. Instead, she thanked Ovalle profusely for taking such an interest in her son and supporting his work, always adding that "he likes you very much."[36]

MARRIAGE TO ROCÍO BELTRÁN MEDINA

Soon after his return to Tabasco, López Obrador taught education classes at the Autonomous Juárez University of Tabasco. There he fell in love with one of his students, Rocío Beltrán Medina, who came from a lower-middle-class family in Teapa. Before attending law school in his forties, her father, Gonzalo Beltrán Calzada, had owned a small, rustic ranch in Teapa, where Rocío and her mother cooked on a crude stove and the family cut its own firewood. "It was also easier to have food than money," observed Rocío's half-brother, Luis.[37] Her father operated a small country store before becoming a lawyer and public defender. According to her father, Rocío and Andrés Manuel dated clandestinely, sometimes meeting in Villahermosa, other times in Teapa. She noted during their courtship, "Andrés Manuel is so passionate about his work that he set about it as if it were a mission. . . . Rather than go to the movies or park with me, I often accompanied him to meetings or assemblies to take advantage of the little time we had together."[38] Rocío's father learned of their intention to marry only when Rocío presented him with an invitation to the wedding.[39] The murder of López Obrador's close friend, Nabor Cornelio Álvarez, a lawyer and human rights leader, gave focus to his life and convinced him that it was time to marry. He was twenty-six years old; she was twenty-three. The ceremony took place on March 30, 1980, in the home of Rocío's father in Teapa, a house so small that one of Rocío's cousins observed that his car was longer than the structure was wide.[40] The simplicity of the nuptials did not prevent the attendance of future governor Neme. Also present were Governor Rovirosa Wade and his wife, Celia Sastre de Neme, who served as witnesses to the marriage. The bride's mother said the newlyweds were too busy for a real honeymoon, but they did make a brief trip to Cuba.[41]

Rocío took care of the home, managed their small budget, and cooked excellent meals, while Andrés Manuel threw himself into politics. A devout Catholic, she would make the sign of the cross on her husband's face every morning before he left the house. When they lived in Nacajuca, she worked for the Ministry of Public Education in Villahermosa. She shared her husband's social goals and, upon returning home each day, would make a beeline for the Indian children from distant areas whom INI fed, clothed, and housed in a dormitory so that they could attend school.[42] She sometimes sat in on political meetings in their home, but rarely spoke out—except to comment shrewdly on someone's character. "I don't like that man," she would say privately to her husband, and her impression often proved correct.[43] She was "López Obrador's general," insisted Armando Padilla Herrera, a fellow Tabascan.[44] She later took exception to López Obrador's passing over longtime allies when awarding legislative nominations to former members of the PRI.[45]

A beautiful woman, her large brown eyes conveyed the hardships she experienced: a husband whose first commitment was politics, three boys to raise, bouts of illness, and a modest income. Indeed, López Obrador frequently asked his long-suffering wife to give him a portion of her meager funds so that he could help a beleaguered PRD committee pay its bills. Rocío sometimes had to borrow money from her parents and other family members to make ends meet,[46] and on several occasions López Obrador even mortgaged their home to obtain cash for the party.[47]

When Andrés Manuel and Rocío acquired a house in Villahermosa, Don Gonzalo paid them a monthly allowance because her mother, whom he had divorced, lived with them.[48] In the mid-1990s a friend inquired about the family's finances. Rocío replied, "Carlos, I am extremely content. For the first time we have opened a savings account." Within two months Andrés Manuel had withdrawn the money to lend to a Tabascan who had asked for a loan to start a business.[49]

Nevertheless, Rocío shared her husband's belief in unpretentiousness. In lieu of fancy toys they tied an inflated plastic bag to the side of their children's playpen, amusing the young boys with the sound the bag made when they hit it.[50] In Villahermosa, law enforcement agents regularly staked out their modest home at 123 Jupiter Street in the Galáxias neighborhood; at times, helicopters hovered overhead as police tried to keep track of López Obrador's whereabouts. When el Peje openly challenged the PRI, former friends would cross the street to avoid speaking with Rocío and her boys, even as "death to the traitor" and other graffiti appeared on nearby walls. A young friend of the couple emphasized Rocío's "moral power," her attentiveness and gentleness, and the "refuge" that her home provided for el Peje. "Theirs was 'the purest of loves,'" she added.[51]

After Rocío's death in 2002, López Obrador wrote: "To marry Rocío was the most important decision of my life; not only was there love but companionship. She protected and advised me until the end. I could have done nothing truly important without her support. She gave me courage in difficult moments and shared with me the humanism and faith in the reforms for which we struggled."[52]

Such words of endearment aside, López Obrador's messianic drive often blinded him to his wife's medical needs. When her fingers began to swell, she received cortisone for what appeared to be arthritis. A friend, a former medical student, administered the drug with a syringe but urged Rocío to consult an expert. Despite repeated advice from family friends, López Obrador never seemed to find time to take her to a specialist for the treatment she required.[53] He always promised that they would go during their vacation. "He will never do it," Rocío's mother told an acquaintance.[54] Rocío also took pride in having used public health facilities rather than relying on private healthcare providers.

LÓPEZ OBRADOR AND GONZÁLEZ PEDRERO

López Obrador's organizational prowess attracted the attention of Enrique González Pedrero, who invited him to play a key role in the 1982 gubernatorial campaign. A renowned intellectual and outspoken leftist, González Pedrero had distinguished himself at UNAM. The candidate had begun his political career in university politics before President Echeverría urged him to run for the Senate from Tabasco. After completing his term, he returned to UNAM and began the first of his three-volume study on Santa Anna during the sexenio of López Portillo, for whom he had no affinity.

González Pedrero reentered politics in 1979, when, following the recommendation of education secretary Fernando Solana Morales, the president placed him in charge of the National Commission on Free Textbooks. This prevented his accepting the post of chief administrative officer at the Government Ministry, which he was offered several weeks later. The interest in González Pedrero prompted López Portillo to ask, "Why does everyone want this man?"[55]

González Pedrero worked on the 1982 presidential campaign of Miguel de la Madrid Hurtado (1982–88). Like all "people from the provinces, I wanted to return to my *patria chica*," the Tabascan admitted. Upon his election in July, de la Madrid flashed him the green light to run for governor of Tabasco.[56] His long absence and relative anonymity in the state hardly bothered Tabascans, who "were used to going out to the airport to learn who our next governor would be," as a political activist ironically put it.[57] González Pedrero had only a small group of supporters. Among them was the so-called Conasupo Group, whose leader, Gustavo Rosario Torres, served as state delegate of the national food distribution company. Other members of this faction were Josue Xicoténcatle Sánchez, Pedro Jiménez León, Fredy Chablé Torrano, and Rodolfo Jiménez Damasco. The last three young men had studied at the PRI's Institute for Political Training (ICAP), which González Pedrero had headed. The PRI candidate also brought with him several young men from outside the state to work in his campaign. These "out-of-staters" (*extraestatales*)—a play on the titles of films about extraterrestrial creatures then in vogue—included Adán Pérez Utrera, Roberto Salcedo Aquino, Wilfrido Robledo Madrid, and José Antonio Álvarez Lima.

Several months before the vote, López Obrador turned over the day-to-day operations of INI to his subordinates so he could devote himself full time to González Pedrero's election. Other *tabasqueños* who worked on the campaign would become prominent politicians, including José Eduardo "Chelalo" Beltrán, Juan José Rodríguez Prats, Nicolás Haddad López, César Raúl Ojeda Zubieta, and Padilla Herrera. Mayans Canabal, a good friend of Beltrán's, also joined the group. The young Tabascan activists frequently found themselves at odds with the Conasupo Group.

González Pedrero and Julieta Campos de la Torre, his Cuban-born wife and an illustrious intellectual in her own right, befriended López Obrador. In fact, one confidant of López Obrador avers that Campos had a greater influence on the young leader than her husband did, because "she felt the needs of the indigenous people in her heart."[58]

As González Pedrero's campaign slogan was "Let Tabasco Speak!" López Obrador was put in charge of organizing meetings to hear the concerns of residents. He also headed the PRI's Center for Economic, Political, and Social Studies (Cespes), which helped devise the governor's program. Following the *priísta*'s landslide, González Pedrero invited López Obrador and Víctor M. Barceló to participate in the Committee on the Planning and Development of Tabasco State (Copladet). This program provided the mechanism for preparing state and municipal development plans based on ideas received during the previous months.[59]

LÓPEZ OBRADOR AS PRI PRESIDENT

González Pedrero placed López Obrador at the head of the party because "he communicated so well with the people."[60] During the campaign, López Obrador had accompanied González Pedrero throughout the state and helped him learn about the municipalities, their people, and their problems. In making this appointment, the governor was following the advice of former government secretary Jesús Reyes Heroles: "If you want to know a man, give him power."[61]

On January 28, 1983, López Obrador was formally elected PRI president. In his acceptance speech, he echoed the "moral renovation" theme that de la Madrid had articulated during his presidential race. He also called for the renovation of PRI sectional committees, the recruitment of young people and women, and popular consultations on key issues. While declaiming the contributions of "old militants," he stressed the need to engage in self-criticism, respect adversaries, fight against "new bosses" in economic and political power, and promote "democracy and social justice." Early in his tenure, López Obrador made it clear that he would not tolerate interference in his leadership of the party when he rejected a request from Government Secretary Beltrán to remove two appointees, Milton Lastra Valencia and Joel Cárdenas Arronis.[62]

The youthful idealist viewed the party as a "pact of revolutionaries"—that is, as a "party that had the duty to always act in behalf of the poorest classes of society." As the majority party, López Obrador said, "the PRI must stand at the vanguard of political reform and constitute the principal agent of modernization in the whole political system."[63] As party head, López Obrador attempted to restructure the PRI along the lines proposed by Carlos Madrazo in the mid-1960s. In addition, he sought to put into practice the belief of his boss that the party should link society and government. The new party chief even commissioned Alberto Zentella Rodríguez to write a party anthem that stressed the role of the PRI as a "vanguard party":

> Advance, advance with the PRI
> Companions, advance
> Liberty, unity
> Democracy and social justice
>
> We are militants of the Party
> Drops of water that form an ocean
> We are progressive leaders
> Democrats and revolutionaries

Zealous protectors of the Party
We will not permit the undermining of our Country
Outsiders, misfits, and traitors
In moments of crisis, or in good times

Advance, advance with the PRI
Companions, advance
Liberty, unity
Democracy and social justice

One day we will overthrow tyranny
With no re-election and suffrage
This great day we will construct
A country that is just, free, and sovereign

National unity is foremost
In revolutionary columns
For this women and men
Forge a vanguard party

Advance, advance with the PRI
Companions, advance
Liberty, unity
Democracy and social justice

López Obrador wasted no time in asserting his authority. In early 1983 he removed Oscar Priego Gallegos, who was associated with old guard governors Trujillo and Rovirosa Wade, as head of the PRI's popular sector, CNOP. He replaced him with Chablé Torrano, a González Pedrero loyalist. As a sop to the veterans, he allowed Deputy Oscar Llergo Heredia, a Rovirosa ally, to remain at the helm of the state National Campesino Confederation (CNC).[64] Meanwhile, the PRI's labor sector in the state suffered divisions because Andrés Sánchez Solís, local secretary-general of the Confederation of Mexican Workers, was at odds with his union's national leadership.

MINIMAL MUNICIPAL PROGRAMS: "CONTRACT WITH TABASCO"

In public assemblies, candidate González Pedrero had insisted that mayoral candidates agree to "minimal municipal programs," to which they would adhere when elected. These plans varied throughout the state and embraced proposals made in public meetings during the campaign. González Pedrero served as the "witness of honor" as the aspirants solemnly signed these pledges, which resembled the "Contract with America" that Representative Newt Gingrich asked Republican candidates to sign in the 1994 U.S. congressional elections. After the mayors took office, the brash young party president strove to ensure that the mayors kept their pre-election commitments and did not divert public monies to their personal bank accounts.

At the new governor's urging, de la Madrid sought to compensate Tabasco's oil-rich area for the inflation, contamination, and employment dislocations arising from the petroleum boom through the creation of the Program for the Development of Tabasco's Coastal Zone (Prodecot). González Pedrero asked López Obrador to lead Prodecot, but the young activist turned down the offer. The program sought to organize communities where antipollution protesters, known as the Ribereño Pact, exercised substantial influence. The goal was to promote coherent development with resources from Pemex, whose exploration and production had contaminated the region, so that fishermen and peasants could undertake productive activities that would improve their condition.[65]

López Obrador wanted to reverse the *cacique*-dominated structure of the PRI by placing rank-and-file members on the top and the elite on the bottom. Through the democratic selection of leaders, he sought to weaken, if not break, the grip of local strongmen. He emphasized that such grassroots participation was crucial to "broaden and reinforce the links between the PRI and the people."[66] It would also put pressure on mayors to fulfill their campaign promises.

López Obrador found that "PRI militants responded enthusiastically and responsibly to this democratizing process." He conceived of the local PRI as an essentially political apparatus during electoral campaigns but as a social movement in other times. Through "democratic assemblies," he and his colleagues instructed six thousand local leaders in such subjects as social development, community planning, efficient local administration, and the evaluation of governmental actions.[67]

The party and government were indistinguishable and, thanks to a generous social development budget, López Obrador had dozens of people working in his various endeavors. Among his closest collaborators were architect Ramón Bolívar Zapata, Luz Rosales Esteva, CNC leader Darvín González Ballina, and Professor Luis Barjau Hernández.

CROSSING SWORDS WITH THE MAYORS

This party-centered activism raised hackles among state and local officials. "Mayors considered the PRI an appendix of their municipalities and were afraid of the representativeness, force, and dynamism of local party committees."[68] Once elected, they were used to behaving as lords over their fiefdoms with little supervision, few restraints, and no obligation to fulfill campaign promises. "Most municipal presidents were invariably trying to enrich themselves," said former governor Rovirosa.[69] Another prominent Tabascan described local presidencies as "factories for the nouveaux riches."[70]

They acted like "Chavo Broca," a Tabascan *cacique* who, according to legend, visited a small town when running for office. "I will be the people's candidate!" he roared, to the delight of the assembled villagers. "I will get you public works!" he intoned to growing applause. "I will start by getting you a bridge!" he promised his snaggle-toothed, shoeless audience. At this point, someone shouted, "But Don Chavo, we don't have a river here." "Then I will get you a river!" he exclaimed to a crescendo of cheers.[71]

Before launching major reforms, González Pedrero needed time to reacquaint himself with the state and consolidate his power over various political factions. The cerebral governor took office in January 1983, and before he could organize his administration, López Obrador began to launch sweeping changes and alienate local powerbrokers.

González Pedrero also directed Francisco Peralta Burelo, his press chief, to help the governor shed his image as a "communist" so that he could develop a better rapport with the state's movers and shakers.[72] In addition to heading a left-wing faculty at UNAM, González Pedrero had participated with Carlos Fuentes and other intellectuals in founding *El Espectador,* the first antigovernment magazine to urge the creation of a new, less dogmatic, more sophisticated Left. González Pedrero next wrote for *Política* (1961–67). Although the future governor and his wife had long since become disenchanted with Castro, *Política* praised the Cuban government, backed the Sandinista revolution in Nicaragua, and harshly criticized U.S. foreign policy.[73]

A majority of the mayors raised a ruckus over López Obrador's behavior. The ringleader was Rosario Torres, who by virtue of heading Villahermosa boasted more power than his colleagues. Others who joined with him were Dr. Eugenio Amat de la Fuente (Cárdenas), Jesús Dagdug Jaidar (Comalcalco), and Abenamar de la Fuente Lazo (Huimanguillo). The party president also crossed swords with municipal presidents whom he had recommended for their posts, among them Joaquín Cabrera Pujol (Emiliano Zapata), Baldemar Hernández Márquez (Jalpa de Méndez), and Carmen Jiménez de la Cruz (Nacajuca).[74] Even López Obrador's modest request that mayors spend 10 percent of their budgets on social needs drew sharp criticism from the officials, who considered their spending and hiring practices sacrosanct.

Following the uproar, the governor convened a session that included López Obrador and the seventeen municipal presidents. After hearing the mayors' complaints, González Pedrero concluded that their differences with the party president were "definitive and irreconcilable."[75] He told the PRI leader, "Tabasco is not Cuba."[76] Nevertheless, the governor made it clear that he wanted López Obrador to remain on his team and appointed him the state's chief administrative officer, who, among other things, was in charge of contracts for goods and services. In this post, González Pedrero believed that el Peje could learn how the structures of the state functioned.

Government Secretary Beltrán told the ex-PRI leader, in effect, "You will no longer have to ask for money. Here you will have everything."[77] This was a reference to the cutback in funds that the party had suffered earlier in the summer, as the state attempted to rein in the overzealous López Obrador. During this period, party workers were either not paid or paid only partially.[78]

The impetuous young man received the assignment on August 15 and resigned at 10:00 P.M. the same day. He briefly visited the office of the *oficial mayor* but said, "this is not the place for me." He found incumbent Peralta Burelo and his co-workers too *fifi*—that is, immaculately dressed in silk shirts and stylish slacks, with fancy watches adorning their wrists.[79] But only after he had accepted the job did he phone Rocío to tell her of his move. Her response was strident: "Why are you taking a post that you will not hold!"[80]

The night following the appointment, González Pedrero received a phone call from Jorge Calles Broca, director of the newspaper *Presente*. Calles said he had received a notice that López Obrador had resigned as *oficial mayor* and party president. Should the newspaper publish this item? Although this was the first the governor had heard of the resignation, he told Calles, "By all means publish it."[81]

Below is the text of el Peje's resignation letter:[82]

C. Lic. Enrique González Pedrero
Governor of the State of Tabasco
August 16, 1983

Señor Governor,

My work has always been to serve the interest of the majority of my people. Today, you offered me the opportunity to occupy the honored post of Chief Administrative Officer of the Government, which I sincerely feel is at odds with my fundamental goal.

Consequently, I thank you for the good will and support that you have always given me, but I hope you will understand the irrevocable character of the resignation that I am presenting.

Sincerely,

Lic. Andrés Manuel López Obrador

Graco Ramírez had warned López Obrador that he would be fired because his concept of a socially committed party clashed with the objectives of the special interests of the party, including cattle-men, fruit and vegetable producers, and the Oil Workers' Union of the Mexican Republic (STPRM).[83] Nonetheless, González Pedrero doubted that the ex-PRI president had planned to accept the chief administrative officer's post only to reject it in a sensational man-ner. More likely, the offer of the position caught him by surprise and, after mulling over alternatives during the day, he decided to refuse it.[84] Before López Obrador renounced the position, however, outgoing official mayor Peralta Burelo shifted control of the state printing office from the office of the chief administrative officer to the State Education Ministry, lest López Obrador and his political allies use the equipment to print political material.[85]

In solidarity with their leader, many party officers and López Obrador sympathizers within Prodecot stepped down.[86] The pro-testers explained their action in a large advertisement published in *Nuevo Rumbo*, a local newspaper.

Rodolfo Jiménez Damasco assumed the reins of the state PRI, which had only one staff member once López Obrador had departed. Nonetheless, the new president announced that "the party will be the vanguard of the revolutionary work that Governor Enrique González Pedrero is undertaking in Tabasco." "It is not for us to question him," Jiménez Damasco added, "but to support him in conformity with our statutes and declaration of principles."[87]

Rather than exhibit animus toward González Pedrero, López Obrador expressed a sense of betrayal by a mentor who had shared his social and political values and objectives, only to curry favor with big businessmen, cattle ranchers, and other interest groups. Despite an especially difficult first year in office, González Pedrero became one of the state's most effective leaders.

In the 1990s the two men reconciled. In 1997 González Pedrero received a call from a PRD leader in Tabasco explaining that the party had unanimously nominated him for federal deputy. The ex-governor thanked the caller for the "display of confidence" but insisted that he was "too old to run for the Chamber of Depu-ties." As national PRD president, López Obrador phoned González Pedrero and said, "Maestro, I need to talk with you." When González Pedrero reiterated that he would not run for deputy, López Obra-dor asked if he would consider becoming a Senate candidate. El Peje promised that he would have "autonomy" and "could vote in accord with his conscience." González Pedrero made speeches before university audiences to garner support even as a PRD out-sider and unopposed candidate. He won the seat and served from 1997 to 2000.[88] As mayor of Mexico City, the Tabascan appointed Julieta Campos secretary of tourism. In October 2005 he named six "counselors" who represented the "best" that Mexico had to offer. Among this select group, González Pedrero was given responsibil-ity for advising the candidate on domestic policy.

Inspired by Carlos Pellicer, López Obrador worked zealously at INI and Coplamar to improve the material and moral standards of indigenous communities. This mission took precedence over other aspects of his personal life, including his family. The increasingly messianic young man deeply believed that the PRI offered the best vehicle for elevating Tabasco's downtrodden and resurrecting the indigenous culture that he so respected. But the refusal of the state's mayors to fulfill promised reforms opened his eyes even wider to the authoritarian character of local governance. His conflict with the PRI establishment and the governor's refusal to press for immediate changes infuriated López Obrador, who adamantly believed in the righteousness of his cause and wanted to accomplish root-and-branch reforms at once. His ouster as state president soured the champion of the dispossessed on the revolutionary party, which he was destined to leave. In working for Rovirosa Wade, though, he had learned how to mobilize the masses to put pressure on the federal government—a skill that he used repeatedly as a PRD leader and as a presidential candidate.

THE DEVIL AND
HIS IDEAS

LÓPEZ OBRADOR RETURNS TO MEXICO CITY

González Pedrero's action shattered López Obrador's dream of democratizing the state PRI. Disillusioned by this treatment, the young man left Villahermosa in an old Volkswagen Beetle with only a few pesos in his pocket. He first visited his parents in Palenque, where he relaxed by fishing, swimming, and reading. When journalists continued to pester him, he drove to his aunt's home in Agua Dulce. After a few days there, he headed for the D.F.

Fortunately, he had a friend in Pedro Reséndez Medina, who thought highly of his cousin, Rocío. López Obrador contacted Reséndez, who was vacationing in Acapulco, to ask for help. He explained that he was leaving Tabasco and would need a place to live until he found permanent housing. Reséndez gave López Obrador keys to his apartment in the middle-class Yacatas neighborhood of Colonia Narvarte.[1] While many PRI politicians kept their distance from el Peje lest they run afoul of Tabasco's powerful governor, Reséndez had no such qualms. He had served as chief administrative officer in Trujillo's and Rovirosa Wade's regimes, had a nest egg, and had not been invited to join González Pedrero's administration. Thus he did not hesitate to lend a hand to his beloved cousin and her husband. The López Obradors lived in Reséndez's apartment for approximately one year. Rocío asked her cousin for two things: the name of a reliable notary and a loan. He supplied both. After six months, she returned the full amount that she owed, even asking how much interest was due.[2]

With the help of Jorge Abdo Francís and others who also had broken with Gónzalez Pedrero, López Obrador found various jobs. He gave lectures on economic development and the political problems of Mexico and delivered uncompensated talks on the future of the PRI at the party's Institute for Political Training (ICAP), headed by fellow Tabascan Arturo Núñez Jiménez. In addition, he did freelance political consulting. He also maintained ties to his home state by writing for the *Revista de la Universidad,* published by UJAT. One of his articles focused on the anniversary of the Mexican Revolution; another concentrated on the oil industry.[3] Rocío remembered the financial hardship. "At this time my husband was without work . . . we did not have even a centavo."[4]

In an effort to find permanent employment, López Obrador reached out to Ovalle, who was about to leave Mexico to become ambassador to Argentina. The former INI director immediately contacted his good friend and social activist Clara Jusidman de Bialostozky, whom de la Madrid had recently placed at the head of the National Consumer Institute (INCO). Ovalle asked for an appointment with a view to landing a job for his young friend from Tabasco. The Salinas administration was considering transferring INCO's functions to the federal attorney general for consumers. To preserve the agency and its programs, Jusidman was seeking to replace a number of employees with more dynamic personnel, and she was looking for a new director of promotion who would be "sensitive to social problems and a hard worker." Ovalle suggested López Obrador for the job, and Jusidman hired him.[5]

Jusidman, a highly respected champion of progressive causes who later served as secretary of social development under Mayor Cuauhtémoc Cárdenas (1997–99) and Interim Mayor Rosario Robles Berlanga (1999–2000), recalled that López Obrador made an "excellent impression" during their initial meeting. She was struck by his "empathy for the downtrodden, his democratic leadership in Tabasco, and his ability to connect with people."[6] Later, she concluded that he followed a "higher mandate."[7]

As director of promotion, one of INCO's four divisions, López Obrador supervised approximately forty people who worked in the city's sixteen boroughs and developed materials for the institute's thirty-one state offices. His staff organized classes and developed workshops on consumer education and home economics for lower-middle-class residents and trade union members in Mexico City. Still aspiring to bring the PRI closer to its base, López Obrador met with PRI leaders in the hope that they would endorse an ambitious program of grassroots consumer education, but they turned him down.[8] Jusidman instructed López Obrador in management skills. In accord with his freewheeling style, he had embarked on a dozen or more programs in Nacajuca. She insisted that he define his goals clearly, set priorities, and limit himself to three or four initiatives.

INCO was heavily involved in relief efforts after earthquakes in the D.F. in 1985. The institute had good ties with the business community, whose products it evaluated, as well as with average citizens, who were accustomed to contacting INCO, which used a catchy jingle to broadcast its telephone number. These relationships enabled the organization to function as an intermediary between firms that were prepared to lend or donate items (rubble-clearing machinery, wood, and water, for example) and citizens who required such items (tenants who were searching for friends and loved ones in collapsed structures).[9] López Obrador was personally involved in an institute brigade that removed debris from the building in which the organization's technical director, Alejandro Delgado, perished.[10]

El Peje spent most of his time designing strategies and advancing his personal political project. In addition to Ramón Bolivar, an architect and friend from Tabasco, he developed a close rapport with Rodolfo F. Peña, his subdirector and the person responsible for the educational materials in the area of promotion. A well-respected journalist, Peña also contributed to the small, leftist newspaper *Unomásuno*. As a strong defender of workers' rights, he and López Obrador talked at length about the country's future and its growing inequities. Peña, who later wrote for *La Jornada*, "was a very important person for Andrés Manuel," noted Jusidman.[11]

López Obrador also worked with Flavio Ruiz, whose father was an officer in the Congress of Workers (CT)—an umbrella organization for PRI-affiliated unions. In addition, he became acquainted with Gustavo Ponce, a well-prepared economist, who served as subdirector under Alejandro Delgado. As finance secretary in Mayor López Obrador's cabinet in 2004, he embarrassed his boss by playing blackjack in Las Vegas.[12]

At INCO, the Tabascan received a regular paycheck that allowed him to put a roof over his family's head. Thanks to recommendations by Ovalle, Núñez, and others, the housing fund of the Institute of Social Security and Services for State Workers (ISSSTE), a social agency for public employees, helped Andrés Manuel and his wife purchase a sixty-square-meter apartment in Copilco, near where his sons live today. Rafael Marín Mollinedo and Gonzalo Beltrán later helped the family move into a larger home.[13]

ANIMUS TOWARD NEOLIBERALISM

In addition to his involvement at INCO, López Obrador broadened his contacts among politicians and his knowledge of political affairs. Núñez introduced him to PRI president Adolfo Lugo Verduzco, whom López Obrador admired because of his efforts to democratize the party. After this meeting, Lugo told Núñez that el

Peje was "a good man. How unfortunate that González Pedrero did not contact me so I could have found a job for him in the national party."[14] Of course, Lugo was dissembling, because he surely did not want to offend González Pedrero—who appeared to be on the fast track to becoming either secretary of government or public education. Rumors abounded that he might even succeed Salinas as president in 1994.

López Obrador also talked with individuals who belonged to other parties, including Heberto Castillo Martínez, who, as the candidate of the Mexican Socialist Party (PMS), bowed out of the 1988 presidential contest in favor of Cuauhtémoc Cárdenas.

While at INCO, López Obrador spent a great deal of time reading, thinking, and writing about the history of Tabasco. He took advantage of his 3:00 to 5:00 P.M. lunch period to work on books and articles with his brother Pío Lorenzo, often returning to his writing after his workday ended at 8:00 P.M. In 1984, under the auspices of UJAT, he published *Los primeros pasos: Tabasco, 1810–1867*, an expansion of his UNAM thesis. He benefited from the assistance of Carlos Ruiz Abreu, a historian well versed in the nation's archives. For months Ruiz Abreu helped him amass materials for *Del splendor a la sombra: La República restaurada, 1867–76*, which was published in 1986.

López Obrador impressed Ruiz Abreu, who had no great love for politicians, as "an integral human being who appreciated and respected the work of bureaucrats." The historian remembered the Tabascan's commitment to social service and his fondness for the moralism attributed to political reformer Reyes Heroles: "Politics is so clean that not even the dirtiest of politicians can soil it."[15] López Obrador's puritanical streak came into play when Abreu, who had just completed his UNAM thesis, asked him if he could make ten copies of the 220-page manuscript on the INCO copier. Even though Abreu had helped the Tabascan with his research free of charge, el Peje neither acceded to this request nor offered to pay for the reproductions.[16]

EL PEJE DISCOVERS THE DEVIL

In the course of conversing, reading, and writing, López Obrador pondered the betrayal of the Mexican Revolution by neoliberal technocrats who advocated throwing open the economy to trade, investment, and influence from the United States and other countries. He despaired over de la Madrid's commitment to the belt-tightening policies demanded by the IMF and foreign banks as a condition to granting the country new loans. He characterized this policy as "fatal" for the majority of Mexicans. In his view, the inflation-fighting austerity deprived the economy of incentives and meant that average citizens worked to cover the service on the nation's external debt. "International bankers and a small group of financial speculators tied to government officials were the only beneficiaries of Miguel de la Madrid's economic policies. The government converted the country into a huge casino where financial speculators harvested wealth," he averred.[17] Indeed, López Obrador became so fixated on the debt issue that he urged Ovalle to convince de la Madrid to hold a plebiscite on whether Mexico should pay its foreign obligations. Ovalle did not comply.[18]

Still, el Peje was not ready to give up on the PRI. Before the 1985 local elections in Tabasco, he asked Omar Castro Castillo, a good friend and his replacement as INI state director, to pick him up at the Villahermosa airport and take him to meet with González Pedrero about entering the primary for mayor of Macuspana. Once in the car, he whipped out a sheet of paper on which he had carefully mapped a development scheme for the municipality, including the names of individuals who might occupy important government positions. While impressed by the detail of the projects and personnel, Castro remarked, "What you have here will take at least six years to accomplish." "That's true," López Obrador replied, "but if we work hard, we can achieve in three years what others would take six years to complete."[19] Although he does not remember the incident, the governor reportedly rejected this request. El Peje commiserated with Castro at El Tumbapato restaurant before returning to the capital that evening.[20]

EVOLUTION OF REVOLUTIONARY PARTY

The actions of party leaders in the 1980s clashed with the tenets that López Obrador believed the party should uphold. Many of these principles appeared in the socially progressive 1917 Constitution, adopted after the bloody 1910–16 Revolution. This fundamental law endowed the state with control over the nation's mineral and hydrocarbon wealth, enumerated the rights of working people, including the organization of unions, and ensured that the *ejidos* on which small farmers lived could not be divided, sold, or mortgaged.

Influence of Lázaro Cárdenas
One of López Obrador's foremost heroes was President Cárdenas, who invested meaning in the concept of "revolutionary nationalism" that impregnated the Constitution. He distributed land to peasants, encouraged the unionization of workers, and boldly challenged international corporations. In 1929 President Plutarco Elías Calles had created the first iteration of the revolutionary party after the assassination of President-elect Obregón amid the Cristero Rebellion—a conflict between the Jacobin government and militant Catholics who were subjected to the Constitution's

harsh anticlerical provisions. Determined to avoid a breakdown of order, Calles assembled a group of generals, local bosses, agrarian chiefs, and leaders of small parties in Querétaro. They founded the National Revolutionary Party as a loose confederation of power brokers, with the president serving as *primus inter pares*. In 1934 Calles used the "big finger," or *dedazo,* to handpick Cárdenas in an effort to find not just another malleable successor but one who would appeal to progressives vexed by the growing conservatism of Calles's rule.

Cárdenas, a youthful and ambitious revolutionary general from Michoacán, had a mind of his own. During his presidential race, he barnstormed the country to attain national recognition, acquaint himself with the country's problems, and recruit loyal cadres. Once in office, Cárdenas scorned the royal trappings of his predecessors and proved his sensitivity to the plight of ordinary citizens by moving his official residence from Chapultepec Castle, the luxurious quarters of the nineteenth-century emperor Maximilian, to the less ornate former hacienda known as Los Pinos.

As president, Cárdenas broke completely with Calles and reshaped the federal "revolutionary party" into an authoritarian corporatist organization, which he renamed the Party of the Mexican Revolution. In this restructuring, Cárdenas imported aspects of Benito Mussolini's "corporatist state," which accentuated political participation through citizens' occupations or businesses, a concept that found wide expression in Latin America.

Cárdenas emphasized group-focused participation for segments of Mexico's society whose support he deemed crucial for the centralized exercise of power. He built into the hegemonic party's machinery access for three major constituencies, each of which exerted top-down influence through a mass membership organization with smaller constituent parts: the Confederation of Mexican Workers (CTM), the National Campesino Confederation (CNC), and the short-lived military sector. Although Cárdenas was chiefly interested in workers and peasants, he reluctantly agreed to establish a "popular" sector that his successor formed as National Confederation of Popular Organizations (CNOP). Cárdenas extended the corporatist framework to the business community, which statutes barred from affiliating with the party. Rather than offer them a sector, he mandated that firms, banks, and commercial enterprises join such "peak" bodies as the National Confederation of Chambers of Commerce and the Confederation of Industrial Chambers. The former linked state and local chambers of commerce to the national organization; the latter embraced small-scale manufacturers.

By the time he left office in 1940, Cárdenas had adroitly pulled together most of the major components of society under the party's tri-colored tent, while expanding state control over the national economy. He also immunized the autocratic system from serious challenges by providing lucrative opportunities and political protection for the relatively small number of union and *campesino* leaders. Access to money, land, jobs, business ventures, and influence ensured that their loyalties lay not with their constituents but with the president and the official party to which they owed their valued posts. Many of these leaders accumulated vast fortunes, giving birth to the adage "Show me a politician who is poor, and I will show you a poor politician."[21]

Mexico's "Economic Miracle"

The corporatist system's top-down control enabled Mexican presidents to adopt a new economic policy, import-substitution industrialization (ISI), that spurred an "economic miracle" for nearly three decades after World War II. The success sprang from political stability, the application of protectionist measures that fostered the replacement of imports with homegrown products and services, the provision of cheap, abundant energy, and the establishment of twin plants. The last program—the so-called *maquiladora* initiative—provided that Mexicans would do the labor-intensive work on radios, television sets, and other items, which would then be exported to the United States at a low tariff for final assembly.

Certain shortcomings disfigured the economic boom. The high price and indifferent quality of Mexican goods made them uncompetitive internationally, forcing the country to rely on oil, minerals, tourism, and *maquiladoras* to earn foreign exchange. Much of the new industry was heavily mechanized and did not generate enough jobs for the nation's rapidly growing population. The ranks of the dispossessed expanded, while the affluent added to their princely assets: 40 percent of the nation's wealth lay in the hands of 5 percent of the population. Most peasants worked on small, inefficient plots, and Mexico became a net food importer in the 1970s.

The revolutionary party, which evolved into the PRI in 1946, increasingly resorted to patronage, electoral fraud, and outright suppression to maintain its hegemony. Furthermore, the absence of a professional civil service meant that functionaries had no job security when a new president took office. Insiders referred to the last year of the sexenio as the "Year of Hidalgo" (*Año de Hidalgo*)—after the austere priest whose stern, pinched face once graced the peso coin—when public officials stole egregiously to provide for an uncertain future.

The political structure resembled a triangle with a monarchial chief executive at the apex, flanked on one side by a disciplined revolutionary party and on the other by a distended, inefficient, and corrupt bureaucracy. In addition to the *dedazo,* the president's power was buttressed by his access to enormous amounts of money and his ability to name and remove governors and other officials like handmaidens. While authoritarian, the PRI's Mexico was not a strong state, as evidenced by the high level of tax evasion that it suffered.

Rules of the Corporatist Game

The chief executive and other actors subscribed to a set of formal and informal rules of the game. There was a prohibition on re-election to the presidency; the bureaucracy established a viselike grip on both the party and the military; the armed forces obeyed orders issued by civilian leaders rather than deliberating over their own course. In addition, the regime's leaders continually evoked the protean legacy of the Revolution to enhance their own legitimacy and discredit opposition forces on the Left and Right; the party-state amalgam forged an implicit alliance with private capital; unsuccessful aspirants promptly and publicly threw their support behind the PRI nominee, for which they received remunerative posts as attractive consolation prizes; and the party's three sectors operated on a "one for all, all for one" basis in backing each other's candidates for elective positions at all levels; and, excluding debilitating illness, high officials retained their posts unless removed by the president. Finally, the mass media abstained from openly criticizing the regime, especially the decisions and actions of the chief executive.[22]

Challenge to the Corporatist System

On October 2, 1968, the top political operative of President Díaz Ordaz (1964–70) ordered troops to fire on a large crowd of unarmed students, housewives, and office workers, killing hundreds of anti-government protesters. Some demonstrators had taken to the streets to decry the PRI's antidemocratic rule, while others condemned the lack of economic opportunities. The "Tlatelolco Massacre" signaled the beginning of the end of the ISI venture that had enriched a favored few at the expense of the nation's 48 million people. El Peje's professors had experienced the 1968 crackdown and emphasized to their students the venality of a regime that could inflict such horror on its own people.

Thanks to the discovery of Mideast-sized oil reservoirs in Tabasco and Chiapas, the corporatist regime achieved another spurt of growth in the late 1970s and early 1980s. Yet various considerations—a sharp downturn in petroleum prices, the regime's ineffectual response to the September 1985 earthquakes that struck the D.F., and soaring prices amid joblessness—spurred opposition to a system that could not create opportunities for the urban poor, peasants, elements of the business community, and a substantial segment of the middle class.

The mid-1980s also marked the period when, in López Obrador's view, de la Madrid and Carlos Salinas sacrificed the social goals of the 1917 Constitution by propelling the country into the international arena, notably by Mexico's 1986 entry into the General Agreement on Tariffs and Trade (now the World Trade Organization). De la Madrid's naming of Salinas as his successor ensured "six more years of the market-oriented policies."[23]

Fault Line in the PRI

In the 1980s, his friends recall, López Obrador increasingly regarded the PRI as "worn out," a disenchantment that coincided with a widening fault line within the party. The ascendancy of Salinas and fellow "technocrats" alienated ex-Michoacán governor Cuauhtémoc Cárdenas, former cabinet secretary and party president Porfirio Muñoz Ledo, and other stalwarts who formed the Democratic Current (CD) in 1986. Although these activists rhetorically advocated intraparty "democracy," their real goal was to thwart the growing influence of the technocrats. Cárdenas and his allies bemoaned the diminished subsidies at home and the tumbling of trade barriers that fostered Mexico's linkage to the global economy. They also despaired over curbs on wages, reductions in government investment, diminished social spending, privatization of key industries, and deregulation of foreign investment. For his part, Cárdenas, the son of the late president, fervently believed in protectionism, a sprawling welfare state, muscular restrictions on private investment, and national ownership of key sectors that would safeguard the ideals of the Constitution. Ten *priístas* signed "Working Document Number One," which encapsulated the CD's goals and mirrored López Obrador's concerns about the country's direction.[24] A factor in the tension was the refusal of de la Madrid to accede to the request of the redoubtable "Doña Amalia" Solórzano—the widow of General Cárdenas—to name Cuauhtémoc Cárdenas director-general of Pemex.[25]

In pursuit of their objectives, CD activists openly campaigned for Cárdenas's selection as the PRI standard-bearer—an action that violated the unwritten rule that the incumbent president handpicked his successor. Party president Jorge de la Vega Domínguez's excoriation of the rebels, combined with Salinas's candidacy, dashed CD leaders' hopes for either internal reform or changing the party's neoliberal doctrine.

Formation of the National Democratic Front

Cárdenas accepted the nomination of the small Authentic Party of the Mexican Revolution (PARM), which was composed of old-line *priístas* whose party had orbited the PRI as a subsidized satellite. But when the PRI allowed the PARM to lose its registry in 1982, its erstwhile ally cast its lot with Cárdenas. The more ideological Popular Socialist Party (PPS) followed suit. It castigated Salinas as part of the "reactionary," "counterrevolutionary" clique that kowtowed to the "retrograde bourgeoisie."[26] As a reprisal for Cárdenas's "violation" of statutes by accepting these nominations, the PRI expelled him and his allies, who became the nucleus of the National Democratic Front (FDN). The "Front," which crystallized formally on January 12, 1988, embraced four parties with legal registration—the PMS, the PPS, the PARM, and the Party of the Cardinista Front for National Reconstruction (PFCRN)—several quite small parties that lacked official recognition,[27] and a handful of popular and civic movements.[28]

In 1987 Graco Ramírez and various *tabasqueños* had invited López Obrador to join the FDN's ranks. Cárdenas also encouraged him to affiliate. Like these men, López Obrador had concluded that the so-called revolutionary party had abandoned the objectives of the Constitution and had no interest in defending the people against the rapacious forces of capitalism. Before reaching his decision, he discussed the matter with his wife, his brothers Pío Lorenzo and José Ramiro, his parents, Abdo Francís, Bolivar, Rosales, Omar Castro, Peña, and other confidants. Ultimately, he declined to join the FDN because he believed it had no future.

Having left the mother ship, Cárdenas and the other PRI apostates were eager to recruit new talent for their political explorations, and they continued to court the self-righteous López Obrador. In him they found a zealous soul mate who applauded Father Hidalgo's devotion to the downtrodden, Juárez's austere republicanism, Madero's reformist goals, and the social changes wrought by the strong-willed Lázaro Cárdenas. El Pejelagarto believed that the technocrats had broken faith with the PRI's commitment to revolutionary nationalism. He would come to regard Salinas as the satanic embodiment of neoliberalism, which had to be exorcized to liberate the great majority of Mexicans.

LÓPEZ OBRADOR TAKES ON
THE ROMANS: THE 1988
GUBERNATORIAL CAMPAIGN

Cárdenas lost the July 6, 1988, election after flagrant manipulation
of the vote tally by the Government Ministry. Two weeks later he
rallied three hundred thousand people in the Zócalo to protest the
"electoral fraud"; yet unlike López Obrador eighteen years later, he
declined to foment national unrest in what he knew would be a
fruitless attempt to change the outcome. Muñoz Ledo, a firebrand
in López Obrador's entourage nearly twenty years later, favored a
militant challenge to the validation of Salinas's victory. He hoped to
force the PRI to install an interim president and negotiate a political opening. The more cautious Cárdenas, however, insisted that
the FDN lacked the structure, cohesion, and communications to
spearhead a successful nationwide protest. "In the FDN, old political enemies suddenly found themselves working on the same side.
They resisted cooperation with people they did not trust. Enemies
accused each other of infiltrating the FDN to work for the PRI, sab-
otaging FDN events, and passing information to its foes."[1] One of
its leaders called it "a semi-anarchic movement."[2] The front did not
even have the means to contact its rank-and-file supporters so that
they could turn off their house lights for twenty minutes at the
same time to symbolize their opposition to the electoral fraud.[3]

When some hotheads said, "Let's take up arms!" Cárdenas
responded, "Where will the arms come from?" He knew that rev-
olutions took years to plan and that in a confrontation with the
regime, the army would prevail over the FDN.[4] Following the violent path would also damage, if not end, his political career. As
he argued in mid-September, the PRI "would like us to call for a

confrontation . . . so they could respond with a bloodbath and a devastating wave of repression."[5]

While PAN deputies voted against ratifying Salinas's election, they refused to agree that Cárdenas had won because of their animus toward the Left. A newly elected *panista* deputy from Guanajuato, Vicente Fox, scorned the affirmation of Salinas's triumph by speaking from the podium with ballots affixed to the side of his head, in a parody of the new chief executive's protruding, sheeplike ears. While the gesture elicited laughs, Cárdenas was on the lookout for a serious means to take advantage of the momentum that the FDN had built.

LÓPEZ OBRADOR AND THE FRENTE DEMOCRÁTICA NACIONAL

The next elections were the October 2 local contests in Veracruz, where the strong leadership of Governor Fernando Gutiérrez Barrios guaranteed PRI hegemony. A better opportunity presented itself in the November balloting for the statehouse in Tabasco, where there were signs of growing opposition to the PRI.[6] Cárdenas asked Ramírez Garrido to help him find a candidate for that contest. The unofficial recruiter first approached Peralta Burelo, the forty-nine-year-old former communications director for González Pedrero and ex-PRI mayor of Comalcalco,[7] who enjoyed a reputation for independence, courage, and honesty. When he turned down the offer, Ramírez Garrido again sounded out López Obrador.[8]

On July 13 López Obrador met with Cárdenas at La Cochera del Bentley in the Barranca del Muerto section of the D.F. At this meeting Ramírez Garrido told the FDN leader that the Tabascan would not only make an attractive gubernatorial standard-bearer but had the potential to be "a great leader in the southeast of the nation." Eager to amplify the influence of his movement, Cárdenas encouraged López Obrador to run, and the young man asked for a week to think over the request.[9]

At first Rocío was opposed to the move, asking how the family would eat if he did not have a job. Doña Manuelita remembered telling her daughter-in-law that "we are ignorant and we must do all in our power so that he, as a professional, moves ahead. She embraced me and went to tell him that she agreed with his candidacy."[10]

The PRI's heir apparent was Salvador Neme Castillo, the Senate leader who had vied for the PRI nomination with several party notables.[11] His chief rival was Roberto Madrazo Pintado, son of the former governor.

López Obrador asked Rovirosa Wade to support his candidacy for governor; but the ex-state executive said that he had already committed himself to Neme and urged López Obrador to talk with the PRI nominee. "You, Andrés Manuel, are young. Why not participate in Neme's campaign to position yourself to seek the governorship in 1994?" he suggested.[12] At first el Peje demurred on the grounds that he had to find positions for eight or ten of his allies. Rovirosa Wade believed that the pragmatic Neme would agree to back López Obrador's loyalists for state legislative seats or municipal presidencies. After all, the two men had developed a working relationship when they served in Rovirosa Wade's entourage. Following his meeting with Neme, López Obrador thought that they had struck a deal: he would work on the campaign provided that the PRI nominee find positions for Julio César Pérez Oropeza, Benitez López, and other supporters.[13] When none of these men received nominations, el Peje again visited Rovirosa Wade—not to seek counsel but to inform him of his decision to run for the statehouse.[14]

Neme faced a dilemma, according to the former governor, from whom he also sought advice.[15] The PRI candidate had nothing personal against López Obrador, but when he resigned from the state party presidency in 1983 el Peje had excoriated González Pedrero, who was well connected in Mexico City. He boasted extremely close ties to de la Madrid and had an excellent rapport with his heir apparent, Salinas. In fact, Salinas invited him to head the Institute for Economic, Political, and Social Studies (IEPES)—the PRI's think tank—during his campaign, and it was González Pedrero who seemed destined for a major cabinet position. Should Neme accede to López Obrador's request, he foresaw a possible confrontation with one of the country's most powerful men.[16] Crossing swords with González Pedrero, he reasoned, could mean a cut in funds flowing to Tabasco. In addition, Neme came to power intent on enriching his cronies, while ensuring a comfortable retirement for himself and his friends. López Obrador was neither his confidant nor a man whom the governor-designate could manipulate. Why do him any favors?

"NEW CRUSADE"

López Obrador had asked to meet with his friend Ovalle, who was serving as ambassador to Cuba. "Two days went by and he didn't show up," Ovalle recalled. "Then Andrés Manuel phoned to say that he would not be coming to Havana because he had already reached a decision about the matter on which he was going to solicit advice."[17] Meanwhile, in late July, Benítez López received a call from his close friend López Obrador, who asked him to convene a meeting of his key political allies.[18] At this meeting el Peje told them that he planned to challenge Neme, who in his view represented politics as usual. "The new crusade that I am about to undertake won't be easy, but we must act for the sake of our children," he said, adding that he would "understand if you cannot not join me."[19]

López Obrador proclaimed his own gubernatorial aspirations in front of the PPS headquarters in Mexico City on July 29, 1988. Much to Neme's chagrin, Dr. Gonzalo González Calzada, nominee of the PMS and PARM, gave López Obrador his registration. Román Ramírez Contreras and Ángel Zamora Andrade, candidates of the PPS and the Party of the Cardinista Front for National Reconstruction (PFCRN), respectively, also stepped aside.

One of the few elected officials who cast his lot with el Pejel-agarto was PRI deputy-elect Darvín González Ballina, who resigned his post as secretary-general of the state's National Campesino Confederation.[20] In a "manifesto," González Ballina deplored the PRI's agrarian operators for their "corruption," "lies," "demagogy," and indifference to the plight of peasants. Efforts were under way to convert the organization's leaders into "servile instruments to propitiate" their constituents, he asserted.[21] González Ballina was also upset that Neme had awarded candidacies for municipal president to only two CNC stalwarts, though the League of Agrarian Communities and local peasant unions made up the largest PRI sector in the state. In reaction to this move, national CNC head Héctor Hugo Olivares Ventura immediately flew to Villahermosa to castigate González Ballina as a "cynic," "political adventurer," "chaquetero," and "traitor."[22] "It was an extremely nasty meeting, replete with vulgar name calling," observed one of the Tabascan's confidants who was present.[23] Another defector from the PRI was local deputy Nicolás Heredia Damián, who agreed to take part in López Obrador's new crusade.

No sooner had López Obrador announced his candidacy than Salinas requested that Ovalle dissuade the renegade from running. The president-elect promised to give the Tabascan "a cabinet-level position in the area of social affairs" if he stepped down. As instructed, Ovalle met with the FDN standard-bearer in Palenque, where they talked at length, but, he says, "I in no way attempted to apply pressure on my friend." When López Obrador turned down the offer, Ovalle told him, "I see how enthusiastic you are about running. The worst thing I could do is try to dissuade you. I have delivered a message. I have completed my assignment. Continue with your campaign."[24]

NEME–LÓPEZ OBRADOR CONTEST

The ruling party's national leadership wanted no surprises in the November 9 face-off between Neme and López Obrador. Although the state was one of the PRI's most rotten boroughs, surveys indicated that the challenger posed a definite threat to the garrulous, self-absorbed nominee. So popular was the FDN that PRI polls would later show that López Obrador would have won the governorship if the contest had taken place two or three weeks after the controversial national election.[25] Even a respectable FDN showing would have lent credence to charges that the PRI had manipulated the results of the factious presidential showdown. In addition, it was feared that González Ballina's defection might spark a fissure in the CNC, whose leadership was infamously corrupt.

In effect, Cárdenas was continuing his presidential campaign through López Obrador's candidacy in Tabasco—a state where the PRI had never faced a serious threat. Although Salinas had reportedly received three out of every four votes cast in the state, there were complications for the ruling party. For instance, Joaquín "La Quina" Hernández Galicia, leader of the Oil Workers' Union of the Mexican Republic (STPRM), favored Cárdenas and had thousands of members in the state.[26] In the view of Manuel Camacho, Salinas's virtual alter ego, who had been designated party secretary-general, "it was a test whether the PRI could maintain its position or be supplanted by the FDN."[27] On August 7 Camacho flew to Villahermosa. He met with ex-governors Rovirosa Wade, Mario Trujillo, and González Pedrero, former and future aspirants for the statehouse and other party notables, businessmen, ranchers, and indigenous leaders.[28]

He also replaced González Ballina with Héctor Argüello López as head of the local CNC. At the end of the party conclave—the "Constitution of the Democratic Movement of Revolutionary Unity of Tabasco"—Camacho vowed that, "after hearing from the principal leaders, we know that Tabasco's *priístas* will continue being the PRI."[29] Despite these brave words, the PRI official found the local party divided, estranged from major business and labor groups, and oblivious to the challenge it faced.

Nine days later Camacho returned to Villahermosa, accompanied by the party's secretario de organización, Pedro Joaquín Coldwell. Their mission was not to rally the PRI's complacent old guard but to take control of what Camacho perceived as a rapidly deteriorating situation. José María Peralta López, the government secretary who had assumed the interim governorship when González Pedrero went to IEPES, had no idea how to organize a campaign.[30] González Pedrero had shaken up the old boys' network with his reforms. His use of primaries to select mayoral candidates in 1985 had sparked concerns among the party's old guard that he might employ the same method to choose the gubernatorial nominee in 1988. In fact, Beltrán, the favorite of González Pedrero, had considered challenging Neme. The revolutionary party was beset by confusion, disorder, and fragmentation. During his second visit, Camacho spurned platitudes about laying down the law to party stalwarts. He demanded that PRI leaders unite behind Neme, supplanted the incumbent government secretary with González Pedrero's ally, Mayans Canabal, replaced the PRI state president with the thirty-six-year-old senator-elect, Roberto Madrazo, and installed Fernando del Villar Moreno as the PRI's new delegate to the state and Neme's de facto campaign manager.

There was substantial sentiment in favor of substituting Madrazo for Neme, who seemed impervious to the consequences of the July 6 national election for his state.[31] But Neme had ingratiated himself with fellow senator Raúl Salinas Lozano, the father of the president-elect. Don Raúl frequently imbibed too much, and Neme took pains to ensure that he got home safely without embarrassment. Meanwhile, Doña Celia, the candidate's spouse, deftly practiced "the politics of the basket" (la política canastera). She ingratiated herself with Don Raúl and his wife, Doña Margarita, by bringing them baskets of fruit, chocolate, and other items from Tabasco. Don Raúl was not shy about suggesting candidates to his son. In addition to Neme, he recommended other fellow senators for governorships, including Víctor Manzanilla Schaffer (Yucatán), and Miguel Borge Martín (Quintana Roo).[32] Neme also enjoyed the backing of former governors Trujillo and Rovirosa Wade, wealthy Popular Sector chief David Gustavo Gutiérrez Ruiz, party activist Jesús Madrazo Martínez de Escobar, and Fausto Méndez, who was the grandmaster of Tabasco's Masonic Lodge.

Soon after Camacho had reconfigured Neme's campaign, he embarked on a trip to western Europe to counter the attacks that PRD president Muñoz Ledo was leveling at the PRI. Upon his return, Salinas suggested that perhaps the trip had been "too successful," a comment that hinted at the president's jealousy of Camacho and presaged the break between the two men five years later. Another bad omen for the PRI secretary-general's own political prospects appeared in Luis Donaldo Colosio's having supplanted him as the PRI's interlocutor with Tabasco's political elite.[33]

López Obrador's Campaign

Although possessed of only a small fraction of his adversaries' resources, López Obrador crisscrossed the Maryland-sized state. With his close friend Jesús "Chuy" Falcón behind the wheel and his secretary Alberto Pérez Mendoza at his side, he launched his campaign with an August trip to Nacajuca, home to a large Chontal community. He chose this site, he said, because "it is the most ancient and deeply rooted [population] of Tabasco. Besides, its thousands of people lack the most elementary social services, which demonstrates that they have always been forgotten by previous administrations."[34] He hoisted the FDN banner, and representatives of its constituent groups appeared at their candidate's kickoff rally in Nacajuca.

As he proceeded from village to village, López Obrador's old van succumbed to the state's rut-engraved roads, and he had to abandon the vehicle to ride with Laureano Naranjo—who had been trailing them in a Ford Fairmont. The well-to-do Nicolás Bellizia Aboaf came to the candidate's aid when he lent him a 1981 Volare K, which was baptized "El Mensajero de la Democracia," "El Paloma de Obrador," and "El Granma Tabasqueño."[35] The last nickname referred to Castro's small boat, which took him and eighty comrades from Mexico to battle the dictator Fulgencio Batista in 1956.

The candidate delivered his message through a loudspeaker mounted on the hood of his car. Although a few women would fling open the windows of their homes to see the cause of the commotion in the streets, he attracted few followers. "I told him," recalled his right-hand man, "Licenciado, it's better that we leave [for] no one likes us here . . . but, as always, he was obstinate and said that the people were reactionaries."[36]

Neme's forces often resorted to violence, and the worst aggression occurred in Mazateupa. There, masked thugs threatened López Obrador's entourage, but Chole Indians overwhelmed the attackers and threw them in jail. This episode accentuated concerns about Neme's candidacy in the PRI's national headquarters.[37]

The FDN nominee issued a twenty-five-point platform that emphasized social justice, secure land titles, efficient administration, increased educational opportunities, improved nutrition and healthcare, political reform, economic development, and conservation of the state's cultural heritage.[38] He relied on multiple visits from Cárdenas, Muñoz Ledo, and other well-known foes of the regime to help drum up support. Muñoz Ledo estimated that he made at least thirty visits to Tabasco on behalf of López Obrador during the 1988 and 1994 gubernatorial campaigns.[39]

The Election Outcome

Despite López Obrador's dawn-to-dusk campaigning, the official figures showed that Neme had trounced his adversary (77.9 percent to 21.2 percent, as presented in Table 2). PRI operatives had pulled out all the stops for the victory. Their spokesmen excoriated López Obrador as a "communist" and "traitor," spread rumors that he had killed his brother, warned Protestants that he would curb "religious freedom," tapped his phone, prevented the FDN from running coalition candidates at the local level, impeded the FDN's placing representatives in polling places, and accused the gubernatorial candidate of inciting Indians to violence. In addition, allies of the unscrupulous Neme, who had eliminated most of González Pedrero's reforms, manipulated the voting rolls, reportedly invested 40 million pesos of state funds in his campaign, actively discouraged López Obrador's followers from casting ballots, and convinced the establishment media to lambaste the FDN candidate.[40] The PRI allegedly "bought" FDN candidates, including Marcial Osorio, who left the race for the municipal presidency of Nacajuca in exchange for a house and 40 million pesos.[41]

The PRI also altered vote tallies. In one polling station in Comalcalco, Neme won 433 to 15; in another, he trounced López Obrador 181 to 1. Meanwhile, in Precinct 3 in Humanguillo and in Precinct 8 in Teapa, the FDN standard-bearer suffered *zapatos:* he was shut out, while the PRI candidates won 577 and 411 votes, respectively.[42]

TABLE 2. *1988 Presidential (July 6) and Gubernatorial (November 9) Results in Tabasco*

PRESIDENTIAL CANDIDATE	NUMBER OF VOTES RECEIVED	%	GUBERNATORIAL CANDIDATE	NUMBER OF VOTES RECEIVED	%
Carlos Salinas de Gortari (PRI)	199,860	74.23	Salvador Neme Castillo (PRI)	205,515	77.94
Cuauhtémoc Cárdenas (FDN)	53,275	19.79	Andrés Manuel López Obrador (FDN)	55,874	21.19
Manuel Clouthier (PAN)	14,329	5.32			
Minor Party Candidates Gumersindo Magaña (Mexican Democratic Party—PDM); Rosario Ibarra (Workers' Revolutionary Party—PRT)	1,715	0.64	Miguel Augusto Castillo Pérez (Mexican Democratic Party—PDM)	2,309	.88
Number of Registered Voters	634,687		Number of Registered Voters	679,110	
Valid Votes	269,179	42.41	Valid Votes	263,698	38.83
Nullified Votes	71	.03	Nullified Votes	22,644	3.33
Abstentions	365,437	57.58	Abstentions	392,768	57.84

SOURCE: López Obrador, *Tabasco, víctima del fraude electoral*, 109, 137; and Federal Electoral Institute, www.ife.org.mx.

In some areas, totals exceeded the number of registered voters. In addition to stuffed ballot boxes and the illegal voiding of ballots, sharp differences appeared between the FDN tally in the presidential race and in the gubernatorial contest.

All told, the FDN reported "irregularities" in sixty-seven of the state's 1,062 voting places. The FDN lodged sixteen written complaints with the State Electoral Commission, which was headed by Government Secretary Mayans Canabal. The commission determined that seventeen of the complaints were unjustified—rejecting one more complaint than was submitted.[43]

Some observers allege that López Obrador and Madrazo exaggerated the FDN threat, the former because he sought to play the valiant martyr struggling against oppressive forces, the latter because he wanted to accentuate his prowess as party leader. Sixteen years later, Camacho remained one of the few people convinced that without the national PRI's involvement, the party could have lost the contest.[44]

Maneuvers by Camacho Solís

After the election, the PRI sought to calm the roiled Tabascan waters. Camacho contacted FDN senator Roberto Robles Garnica, a Cárdenas confidant, to arrange a meeting with López Obrador. The losing candidate took the high road. He rejected the overture on the grounds that state electoral authorities had already received official complaints of the fraud perpetrated in the election. For him, the people's will was not "negotiable."[45]

PFCRN leader Rafael Aguilar Talamantes proved to be less high-minded. Muñoz Ledo nicknamed his small party the "railroad" because its initials were similar to those of Mexico's Ferrocarriles Nacionales de México, another agency owned lock, stock, and barrel by the government. Aguilar Talamantes had attracted attention by staging a hunger strike in the national Congress on November 17. He decried both the electoral fraud and the "aggression" visited on his party's militants and elected officials. While all of the opposition verbally backed Aguilar Talamantes's maneuver, only deputies from the PARM and the Democratic Current fasted during the twenty-four-hour protest.[46] Among their demands were the removal of Government Secretary Mayans Canabal and the mayor and police chief of Cárdenas. Camacho rewarded Aguilar Talamantes for recognizing the legitimacy of the results by firing the Cárdenas police chief, giving the PFCRN two state legislative seats, and providing his party with typewriters and furniture.[47] Aguilar Talamantes was true to his creed: "It's much better to make a detour than drive around in circles."[48] A facile writer, López Obrador chronicled the real and perceived abuses of the 1988 election in a book entitled *Tabasco, víctima del fraude electoral*.

PARTY BUILDING IN TABASCO

In contrast to Cárdenas's indifference to institutions, López Obrador commenced the construction in Tabasco of the newly founded PRD, which provided a vehicle for Cárdenas's followers to continue their political struggle against the PRI. Before López Obrador entered the fray, the Left simply did not count in the state. Central to el Peje's strategy was the fashioning of a parallel government. The PRI old guard conducted business in the governor's palace, the Quinta Grijalva, the Congress, the party's back room, business headquarters, private clubs, and other conventional sites. In contrast, López Obrador sought out people in the streets, municipal squares, and union halls, on communal farms, and in other venues. He attracted them with his relentless attacks on the pollution— both political and ecological—that enveloped Tabasco. He and fellow *perredista* professionals traveled throughout the state to help Indians and other poor people with their problems.

Pro-PRD lawyers helped low-income citizens apply for state and federal health, social, and educational programs for which they were eligible. In addition, the attorneys aided them in obtaining titles to the property on which they lived. Lic. Payambé López Falconi, a notary public, provided legal services. Architect Armando Padilla Herrera designed low-cost houses for squatters who had "invaded" vacant properties with the PRD's support. In Villahermosa (Medellín y Pigua neighborhoods), thirty-two lots were turned over to families in 1991; in Teapa (Vicente Guerrero Lerma),

104 two-hectare lots were allocated in 1993; and in Tepetitán, 154 lots were distributed in 1996.[49]

In the Cárdenas municipality, Dr. Carlos Alberto Wilson Gómez distributed books in the public schools; physicians Wilson, Guadalupe Mendoza Rodríguez, and José Manuel Lizárraga charged only a nominal fee to low-income patients; and veterinarian Miguel Cuitláhuac Vázquez cared for people's animals. In the process, the PRD spawned an independent *campesino* organization and a union of cocoa workers.[50] While the established media formed part of the PRI elite, the PRD distributed the muckraking *Corre la Voz,* edited by Pérez Mendoza, which exposed dishonesty in Neme's administration. In an attempt to find out the newspaper's sources, state and federal authorities stationed agents outside López Obrador's house in Colonia Galaxias, and two official vehicles followed him whenever he left home.[51]

The PRD even operated an informal utilities firm. The state power company pulled the plug on customers who refused to pay electric bills in protest of government policies. One mayor placed the evasion level at 60 percent.[52] Thus, most PRD local committees had technicians within their ranks who could reconnect the lines. Although some of its elements were different, the PRD's parallel government mirrored practices of the corporatist PRI. López Obrador's party provided goods and services that spawned client groups, who were expected to lend bodies to PRD demonstrations and vote for its candidates, in exchange for benefits received. Table 3 provides the names of the professionals and the services they provided.

In addition, López Obrador spearheaded a civil resistance movement against Pemex, highlighted by marches, sit-ins, and road blockages throughout the state. "He was telegenic, and his plainspoken eloquence, in the sibilant tongue of the gulf coast, appealed to the poorest people of his state."[53] The PRD focused on the contamination by the oil monopoly, which operated 1,110 installations covering 25 percent of Tabasco. One of the first protests involved pollution in Nacajuca, where abject poverty surrounded the Sen petroleum field, which had befouled local rivers and lagoons. Chontal demonstrations were met with brutal repression, prompting López Obrador and his followers to demand that Pemex indemnify the victims of contamination and introduce a social program in the most affected *ejidos.* During one demonstration, a policeman or strikebreaker smashed el Peje in the face. He appeared on the cover of *Proceso* magazine as the blood-drenched victim of repressive forces. When the STPRM elected a local president who sympathized with the Indians, the government threw him behind bars. The PRD spearheaded demonstrations that attained his freedom. They also obtained the release of nine political prisoners in San Carlos, Macuspana.[54] The party protested official torture to the National Human Rights Commission (CNDH). The issue

TABLE 3. *PRD's Parallel Structure in Tabasco*

FUNCTIONS ASSUMED BY PRD	ACTIVISTS	COMMENTS
Legal Advice	Rafael López Cruz Payambé López Falconi	Free service
Medical Assistance	Dr. Wilbert Narváez Narváez Dr. Guadalupe Mendoza Rodríguez Dr. Carlos Alberto Wilson G. Dr. José Manuel Lizárraga P. Dr. Adán Magaña Gómez	For instance, Dr. Wilson charged 5 pesos for an office visit
Ophthalmological Care	Dr. Guillermo Morelos García Jesús Falcón Becerra drove patients to their appointments.	Free service
Veterinary Care	Dr. Cuitláhuac Vázquez Hidalgo	Free service
Land Acquisition (Advice and leadership in squatting on vacant property)	Arq. Armando Padilla Herrera	
Housing	Arq. Armando Padilla Herrera	Free service
Utilities	Anonymous electricians	Free service
Communications	Alberto Mendoza Pérez José del C. Chablé Audelina Macario Rodríguez Armando Guzmán Zurita	*Corre la Voz* and, later, *La Verdad del Sureste*
Distribution of free textbooks	Dr. Carlos Alberto Wilson G. (Cárdenas)	
Social Assistance	Dorilián Díaz Pérez Nicolás Heredia Damián Prof. Minerva Ocampo Magaña Dr. Cuitláhuac Vázquez Hidalgo Prof. Manuel Cordero Martínez	Assisted the poor in signing up for social programs
Representation before federal and state electoral authorities	Arq. Armando Padilla Herrera Julieta Uribe Caldera Rafael López Cruz	Free service
Assistance with farming	Auldarico Hernández G. Javier López Cruz Miguel Gonzalo González Pascual Alor Pérez Benito Blé Taracena	Free service
Blocking Pemex installations to seek compensation for environmental damage	Darvín González Ballina Dorilián Díaz Pérez Dr. Wilbert Narváez Narváez Aurelio Cordero Aquino Nicolás Heredia Damián	Free service

SOURCE: Arq. Armando Padilla Herrera, electronic mail to author, January 21, 2006.

arose when, on September 4, 1989, the State Judicial Police sought evidence by handcuffing, blindfolding, beating, and submerging in water four Villahermosa residents. When one of the victims died, authorities attempted to bury him secretly, claiming that "pulmonary aspiration" had caused his death. While top officials escaped scot-free, lower officers were punished.[55]

The monopoly's officials offered several responses to these tactics. Francisco Rojas Gutiérrez, Pemex director-general from 1987 to 1994, was convinced that there was enough evidence to put López Obrador in prison. He cited the Tabascan activist's involvement in "beatings, threats, [and] abductions" that occurred in connection with blocking access to Pemex facilities. The ex-Pemex chief complained that he could not get Attorneys General Ignacio Morales Lechuga (1988–91), Miguel Montes García (1991–92), or Diego Valadés Ríos (1992–93) to press charges.[56]

These men seemed to empathize with the poor Tabascans, suffering from oil-induced pollution at the hands of the wealthy oil company. After all, the head of the monopoly in Tabasco managed a budget larger than that of the state government. In addition, there was an unwritten rule—since broken on numerous occasions—that attorneys general did not prosecute politicians for what were essentially political acts. Rojas Gutiérrez remembered receiving greater cooperation from Valadés's successor, Jorge Carpizo McGregor (1993–94), and his deputy Mario Ruiz Massieu."[57]

Local officials were also loath to crack down on poor farmers and fishermen whose livelihood was imperiled by the boom sweeping the state. Like Rovirosa Wade, Governors Neme, Gurría, and Madrazo used López Obrador to advance their own interests. State executives implored Pemex for additional funds to undermine López Obrador's appeal and insisted that without this assistance he would become stronger and cause even greater problems. Meanwhile, the executives relished the additional resources pouring into their state because of el Peje's activism.[58] These outlays meant they could spend less on social programs. Journalist Mario Ibarra christened this lucrative artifice to extract millions of dollars from Pemex the "Reclamation Industry."

Rather than lose hundreds of thousands of dollars a day in foregone revenue, the oil monopoly made payments to López Obrador, who in turn distributed funds to men and women who suffered from the ubiquitous contamination. Jailing the PRD leader this time, as his foes recommended, could have catalyzed even bigger and more violent demonstrations. In fact, violence mounted after Adrián Lajous Vargas, who became director-general of Pemex in 1994, halted the disbursement of cash to those with credible grievances, giving them in-kind compensation instead.[59]

Additional pesos flowed into the state after López Obrador filed a complaint against Pemex with the CNDH in early 1990. The commission ordered the monopoly to compensate the peasants for the losses they had incurred.

López Obrador viewed the provision of social services and the staging of sit-ins and blockages as crucial to building a grassroots party. In the mid-1990s his colleague and co-PRD founder Rafael López Cruz suggested that the party bring in an array of experts from UNAM, the Instituto Politécnico Nacional, the Chilpancingo

TABLE 4. *Key Municipal Leaders in Tabasco*

MUNICIPALITY	KEY LEADER(S)
Balancán	Darvín González Ballina
	Omar Jasso García
	Guadalupe Palomo
Benito Juárez	Alejandrino Álvarez Peralta
Cárdenas	Carlos Alberto Wilson Gómez
	Héctor Muñoz Ramírez
Centla	Carlos Chiñas
	Deputy Eber Sánchez Alejandro
	Jorge Lugo Romellón
Centro	Alberto Pérez Mendoza
	Julieta Uribe Caldera
Comucalco	Javier May Rodríguez
	José Manuel Copeland
Cunduacán	Benito Blé
	Gregorio Díaz Vázquez
Humanguillo	Miguel Gonzalí González
Jalapa	Wilberth Narváez Narváez
Jalpa de Méndez	Dolián Díaz Pérez
Jonuta	Adelino García Pérez
Macuspana	Minerva Pérez Pérez
Nacajuca	Adán Magaña Gómez
Paraíso	Minerva Ocampo Magaña
	Humberto Hernández
	René Brondo Bulnes
Tacotalpa	Wilberth Narváez Narváez
	Paulino Jiménez Ballestero
Tenosique	Enrique Martínez Martínez
	Hómero Margally
Emiliano Zapata	Norma Argaez Zurita
	Arturo López Obrador
	José Ángel Geronimo Jiménez

SOURCE: Bartolo Jiménez Méndez, interview by author, August 9, 2004; Armando Padilla Herrera, interview by author, January 14, 2005; and Alberto Jiménez Flores, interview by author, June 16, 2005.

agricultural and forestry research center, and other institutions to assess carefully the damage that Pemex had caused to the air, water, and soil. The economists and other experts could then rationally determine the amount of money required to eliminate the toxicity from rivers and lagoons, decontaminate the soil, and restore vegetation and wildlife. Such an approach would also involve a fair indemnity to individuals, families, and businesses harmed by Pemex operations. López Obrador derided this suggestion as "extremely legalistic" and reprised an old PRI saying that "politics kills law." Besides, he added, if we resolve all their problems, "how will we recruit people for marches and blockades?"[60] This response underlined the need for a messianic politician to mobilize his flock to achieve political goals. This approach helped build a solid PRD structure throughout the state. Table 4 lists the names of key leaders.

Allegations of fraud in the 1991 congressional and municipal elections prompted López Obrador to lead PRD militants in a protest movement. At first they considered occupying Villahermosa's Plaza de Armas, but Doña Manuelita advised her son that "nothing would be resolved" in Tabasco. Thus, on November 23, el Peje launched a march of five hundred people to the D.F. He modeled his demonstration on the "March for the Dignity of San Potosí," which anti-PRI candidate Dr. Salvador Nava Martínez had led to protest "massive fraud" in the 1991 gubernatorial race in San Luis Potosí. Nava never became governor, but Salinas ousted the man originally declared the winner.

López Obrador searched for a name to dramatize his demonstration. He considered "Caravan for Democracy" and "March Against Fraud" before adopting his wife's suggestion to call the six-week odyssey from Villahermosa to Mexico City the "Exodus for Democracy." His followers were presumably the "chosen people" who, to escape the repression of "Pharaoh" Neme, would reach the "promised land" of democracy once they arrived at the capital.[61] The dispute centered on the outcome of local elections in Cárdenas, Macuspana, and Nacajuca. Table 5 summarizes information about López Obrador's various protest marches.

López Obrador and his followers reached the capital on January 11, 1992, and immediately camped in the Zócalo. Their leaders met extensively with the secretary of the government, Gutiérrez Barrios, the undersecretary, Núñez, and Camacho, whom Salinas had named regent or appointed mayor of the D.F. Exacerbating pressure to conclude an agreement were plans for a major international event on January 16. On that date, El Salvador and its longtime guerrilla rivals were scheduled to sign a peace accord in Mexico City. Salinas did not want this ceremony, when the city would be full of diplomats and reporters from around the world, marred by Tabascan malcontents.

The negotiators finally agreed to award the municipality of Cárdenas to the PRD, while establishing PRI-majority interim councils until new elections could be held in Macuspana and Nacajuca.[62] In addition to providing the demonstrators with portable toilets and potable water, Mayor Camacho Solís reportedly gave López Obrador a generous sum to remove the demonstrators.[63] One Tabascan politician put the figure at 8 billion pesos.[64] The government also made dozens of buses available to transport the Tabascans home. Camacho stressed that he held conversations with López Obrador, Gutiérrez Barrios, Núñez, Pemex's director-general, and the labor secretary. "In view of the likelihood that López Obrador and the protesters stood a good chance of receiving compensation from the courts, we all agreed that it was better to provide them with funds

TABLE 5. *López Obrador's Crusades*

DATE	NAME OF MARCH	REASON FOR PROTEST	NUMBER OF PARTICIPANTS	OTHER GROUPS INVOLVED	OUTCOME
DEPARTED: November 23, 1991 ARRIVED: January 11, 1992	El Éxodo por la Democracia	Fraud in the 1991 elections in the Tabascan municipalities of Cárdenas, Nacajuca, and Mascupana	500	Enjoyed support from *La Jornada* journalists, from Dr. Salvador Nava, and from Cárdenas and other left-of-center politicians	Eager to rid Mexico City of protesters on the eve of the signing of a peace accord between the El Salvadoran guerrillas and its government, the Salinas administration agreed to give the PRD control of Cárdenas—with new elections scheduled for Macuspana and Nacajuca
DEPARTED: November 24, 1994 ARRIVED: November 29, 1994 RETURNED HOME: December 10, 1994	La Caravana por la Democracia	Fraud in the 1994 Tabasco gubernatorial election	2,000		
DEPARTED: April 23, 1995 ARRIVED: June 3, 1995	Éxodo por la Dignidad y la Soberanía Nacional	Fraud in the 1994 Tabasco gubernatorial election; goal of joining other parties in forging the Alianza Nacional Democrática	300 left Villahermosa; they numbered 2,500 by the time they reached Nezahualcóyotl on the outskirts of the D.F.	On May 14, joined in Veracruz by activists in various social and civic organizations; in puebla, met with Heberto Castillo and received communication from the EZLN	On June 9, 1995, received 45 boxes of materials showing extraordinary expenditures by Madrazo's gubernatorial campaign

SOURCE: Gerardo Albarrán de Alba, "El PRI 'pierde y tiende a desaparecer' López Obrador, por un nuevo proyecto de nación, con bipartismo PAN-PRD," *Proceso*, June 5, 1995. http://www.proceso.com.mx/.

with which to disband their demonstration and return home," he said.[65]

Some of López Obrador's demands could be satisfied only by Tabasco's government. Camacho sought the assistance of Interim Governor Manuel Gurría Ordoñez, who had just replaced Neme. For the first twenty minutes of their telephone conversation, Gurría was "impossible" to deal with, insisting that it was "better to have the demonstrators in the Zócalo than in Villahermosa." Finally Camacho told him in no uncertain terms of the president's interest in resolving the dispute, and Gurría quickly flew to Mexico City to help achieve this objective.[66]

When López Obrador's adherents returned to Villahermosa, word spread like wildfire that González Ballina, then the PRD state president, had a trove of pesos to distribute among those who had protested in the capital. To one observer, it appeared like a latter-day "California gold rush," as hundreds of people descended on Ballina's home, claiming to have taken part in el Éxodo.[67]

NEME'S OUSTER

The agitation associated with the march, combined with the governor's exclusion of his adversaries' allies from his cabinet, undermined Neme's standing. PRI state president Madrazo especially resented the governor's failure to find posts for his supporters, but Neme's motto was "Tabasco for the tabasqueños," which he translated as "Tabasco for my friends." In addition, his venal, maladroit management of state affairs and nepotism diminished his standing. Muñoz Ledo even coined the neologism Nemepotismo to mean "a form of tropical bossism in which a single family uses and abuses power in a disproportionate manner and organizes multimillion-aire business deals in elaborate public works to enrich themselves through a system of shady contracts."[68]

The oil bonanza helped to fill the state's coffers, and opportunities for payola abounded. One case involved the decision of the secretary of public works to purchase a barge-mounted dredge to clean the Laguna de las Ilusiones just outside Villahermosa. While a Florida firm offered to sell the equipment for $209,775, the chief administrative officer created a shell company, which bought the dredge from a U.S. firm and resold it to the local government for more than twice the original price.[69]

Neme also spied on his rivals. His government secretary and police chief kept an eye on politicians, especially when they attended parties. If they drank during the festivities, police would arrest them for drunk driving and throw them in jail. The next morning, Neme would agree to drop the charges in return for their support. Failure to cooperate would land them in a public scandal.[70]

Such antics gave rise to several anti-Neme groups, the most important of which was made up of Carlos Hank González and his allies. The egregiously powerful politician-turned-billionaire had served as mayor of Mexico City, governor of México State, and in several cabinet posts, and he sought to make Tabasco the keystone in a Gulf Coast arch that extended from the southeastern United States to Central America. He needed a few years to accomplish his project and was thus intent upon inserting Gurría into the governorship for three years, after which his protégé, Roberto Madrazo, could win a full six-year term. Gurría, who was a senator, had served as a surrogate big brother and political mentor to his cousin Roberto after his parents had died. Hank spread the word to the president and other key officials that "if Neme remains . . . in power, the PRD will continue to advance."[71] In light of the controversial 1988 election, Salinas was ready to take whatever steps necessary to thwart the party's rise.

The completion in 1994 of the striking fifteen-story Torre Empresarial, overlooking the Grijalva River in Villahermosa, represented a tangible icon of Hank González's southeast strategy. As part of his master plan, he also ordered the construction of a highway to link El Ceibo, in southern Tabasco, to the Petén region of Guatemala. This roadway became a white elephant. The economic crisis that erupted in December 1994 stymied Hank's grand scheme, which President Fox resurrected as the Plan Puebla-Panamá in mid-2001 and Calderón sought to revive in 2007. Although he was a friend of the Salinas family, Neme had also clashed with Salinas's handpicked national PRI president, Colosio, who was eager to give the party a facelift. In the selection of the local party leadership, the governor arrogantly imposed his slate over that favored by the national PRI.[72] This highhanded act precipitated a violent conflict between the contending factions. Thus Colosio sent PRI stalwart Jesús Salazar Toledo to annul the contest.[73]

Neme could have saved his skin had he followed the advice of government secretary Gutiérrez Barrios. "Don Fernando" sent a message through Chiapas governor Patrocinio González Blanco Garrido that Neme could remain in office provided he dismiss his government secretary, prosecutor, and chief justice. Neme told the messenger, "You run things in Chiapas, and I will run things here."[74] This intractability guaranteed his downfall. In early 1992 Salinas administered the coup de grâce. Meanwhile, the chief executive directed Rovirosa Wade, Arturo Nuñez, and González Pedrero to throw their full support to Gurría.[75]

The ouster of Neme rocked the PRI establishment in Tabasco, because even some of the governor's detractors abhorred Mexico City's interference in local affairs. The change at the state's helm made no difference to López Obrador, who continued to mount protests against the government even as he traveled from municipality to municipality.

Following the Neme debacle, the PRD's State Council adopted its own version of the "Ten Commandments" to ensure that militants and recently elected officials did not "fall into sinful ways." As read by Darvín González, these commandments were:

1. Place the interests of Tabasco above all others, including your personal ambitions.
2. Do not swear false allegiance to the Political Constitution of the United States of Mexico, the Free and Sovereign State of Tabasco, and comply with all laws and regulations that emanate from them.
3. Celebrate October 19 [election day] as the date on which the people placed their confidence in you to represent them.
4. Honor the Party of the Democratic Revolution as the forge of your political career.
5. Do not destroy the confidence that the people have invested in you.
6. Do not be a political prostitute.
7. Do not rob public funds.
8. Neither disparage nor abandon your allies with lies.
9. Do not lust after ill-gotten riches.
10. Do not covet positions of power that you do not deserve.

LÓPEZ OBRADOR'S PRAGMATISM

López Obrador combined the messianic impulses of these tenets with the pragmatism to advance his mission of redemption. For decades the most popular radio program in Tabasco had been *Telerreportaje,* whose original host, Jesús Antonio Sibilla Zurita, had turned the microphone over to his son, Jesús Sibilla Oropeza. Broadcast on XEVA from 6:00 A.M. to 10:00 A.M. every day, the program not only provided news and entertainment but served as a forum through which families could inform relatives of births, deaths, illnesses, and marriages in the Tabascan archipelago, where the population was scattered, phones were few, and roads and bridges were scarce. *Telerreportaje* even criticized the state government, and in 1994 López Obrador had written in Jesús Antonio Sibilla Oropeza's name for governor.

Three years later, el Peje invited the radio personality to become a PRD congressional nominee for a proportional-representation seat, which guaranteed his election. Although Jesús Antonio Sibilla Oropeza graciously turned down the opportunity, he recommended his cousin Octavio Romero Oropeza, who was promptly elected. When challenged by a PRD stalwart about recruiting a dyed-in-the-wool PRI member as a candidate, López

Obrador replied, in effect, "Ingratiating ourselves with the Jesús Sibilla clan will ensure us access to *Telerreportaje,* through which we can reach tens of thousands of people—many more than in our rallies." Rafael López Cruz, a PRD founder in the state, scorned Romero Oropeza as one of the most "ominous elements in the PRI," a man whose selection constituted the first crack in what had been the PRD's "happy family" in Tabasco. Not only did Romero Oropeza serve in the Chamber of Deputies, he also became a López Obrador confidant and the man who handled the politician's financial affairs. For López Cruz, it was "as if Luther had gained control of the Roman Catholic Church"[76]—aiming to restore it to its "original" state, before wayward leaders had allowed the church to drift into sin and corruption. Apostles like Romero Oropeza would help López Obrador build a party similar to the PRI before de la Madrid delivered it into the hands of neoliberal technocrats. In other words, he wanted to construct a party that embraced "revolutionary nationalism" and reflected "original" PRI values. Opportunistic or not, López Obrador's activities produced a fourfold increase in the PRD flock between 1988 and 1994. Like a good savior, he convinced his constituency that he embodied their dreams for a better life.

Upon turning over the reins of the party to González Ballina in May 1992, López Obrador went to work in Heberto Castillo's campaign for governor of Veracruz. This experience further soured him on the Salinas-run ruling party. "There I saw firsthand how the PRI imposed [Patricio] Chinos with 400,000 false ballots in remote districts where, according to official figures, 80 percent of eligible voters participated."[77]

As an opposition candidate, López Obrador ran into a buzz saw of vote theft, intimidation, and calumny by the official party. In the face of this onslaught, he became even more determined to vanquish his foes. Long gone was his hope of transforming Tabasco's PRI. Instead, he created a parallel party that engaged in PRI-style clientelism, thereby helping to attract converts. In blocking access to oil facilities and in launching *El Éxodo por la Democracia,* he honed his skill in obtaining resources from unsavory powerbrokers in Mexico City. He also evinced his contempt for laws enacted by an illegitimate power, and disseminated his Ten Commandments to discourage corruption within the PRD's ranks. He grew increasingly determined to enhance his political strength to save the poor. In selecting Romero Oropeza for a congressional seat, he demonstrated a readiness to make common cause with former enemies—now converts—to defeat the latter-day Romans who had occupied his land.

LÓPEZ OBRADOR
FIGHTS THE ROMANS
A SECOND TIME

López Obrador again vied for the Tabasco governorship in 1994. His campaign took place amid uncertainty and fear exacerbated by kidnappings, the EZLN revolt, and assassinations, including that of PRI presidential standard-bearer Colosio. After obtaining the *dedazo*—in this case a *dedillo*—to become the substitute candidate, Zedillo received a visit from Salinas, who asked if he had talked with López Obrador in light of the fluid situation in Tabasco. When Zedillo said he had not, Salinas suggested that Carlos Salomón Cámara, the nominee's communications secretary and a Tabascan, would be the ideal person to arrange a meeting. In mid-May, Zedillo and López Obrador dined in Salomón's home, where Zedillo invited the Tabascan to run for governor as the nominee of both the PRI and PRD. López Obrador agreed in principle but said he would have to talk it over with Cárdenas. Three days later Zedillo received word that Cárdenas had vetoed the joint candidacy, arguing that it was "a question of power or democracy."[1] When he later wrote about this episode, el Peje did not mention his readiness to accept Zedillo's offer. Instead, he pontificated that his main goal was not the governorship but "fair and free elections."[2] Moctezuma Barragán, Zedillo's chief political operator during the campaign, knew nothing of the overture, but he admitted that the president often played his cards close to his chest.[3] Unless Salinas was laying a trap for his successor, it remains a puzzle why he would have encouraged a deal between Zedillo and López Obrador to the detriment of Madrazo, his ally.

The tragic death of Madrazo's father's imbued the Tabascan with a certain messianic outlook. In 1991 he said, "I also have a double commitment: to be worthy of the political and ideological legacy of my father, the man whom I will always carry in my blood and heart . . . el Lic. Carlos A. Madrazo."[4]

Luis Priego Ortiz, who had worked closely with Carlos Madrazo, said that the son was the "antithesis" of his father.[5] He ignored his father's iconoclasm to follow the traditional artifices taught by mentors Manuel Gurría and Hank González. Even though he boasted overwhelming advantages in the gubernatorial contest, his supporters handed out gifts, rigged exit polls, and deployed public funds on behalf of their candidate. López Obrador reported that officials even disqualified the beauty queen of Nuevo Chablé in the Emiliano Zapata municipality because her family sympathized with the PRD.[6]

The local media operated as an extension of Madrazo's campaign, with the exception of radio station XEVT and the pro-PRD newspaper *La Verdad del Sureste,* which was edited by Pérez Mendoza. NGOs found that from September 12 to October 26, the coverage of the five local daily newspapers favored Madrazo (50 percent) over el Peje (25 percent) and PAN nominee Juan José Rodríguez Prats (15 percent).[7]

A week before the election, López Obrador, future government secretary Moctezuma Barragán, Federal Electoral Institute (IFE) councilor José Agustín Ortiz Pinchetti, and the PRD's Muñoz Ledo dined in the home of IFE councilor Santiago Creel Miranda. Representing Madrazo was Manuel Andrade Díaz, Tabasco's undersecretary of government. At this gathering, López Obrador pledged to overlook previous irregularities if the PRI agreed to play fair on Election Day.

Moctezuma agreed and sent one of his advisers to observe the November 20 contest.[8] He selected Juan Gabriel Valencia, a colleague with whom he had worked in the Ministry of Budget and Planning and who enjoyed a reputation for reliability and political astuteness, to act as his troubleshooter. A former security specialist at the Government Ministry, Valencia had gone to Chiapas at Zedillo's request to monitor events after the March 23 murder of Colosio. In the same capacity, he observed the November 14 fraud-ridden elections in Veracruz.[9] From Veracruz Valencia returned to Tabasco, where the gubernatorial race was scheduled for the following week. As early as September, he had begun—on behalf of Moctezuma—to make contacts. It was unusual for Moctezuma, the president-elect's chief political adviser, to involve himself in an election before his boss had even been inaugurated, but he and Zedillo were eager to clean up the Augean stable that their party had contaminated. To this end Valencia made clear to Alberto Rébora, coordinator of Governor Gurría's advisers, that those responsible for irregularities would be jailed when Zedillo took office. Madrazo was concerned that he might be removed in a deal with the opposition. At a September meeting at the Passy restaurant in the D.F., Valencia assured him that the way to prevent a deal was to make the election as transparent as possible.[10]

In the run-up to the election, Valencia was especially concerned about possible fraud in Macuspana, Jalpa, Nacajuca, and around Villahermosa. He thus asked the commander of the local military zone to have patrols ready to break up any demonstrations that might interfere with the contests.[11]

On November 13 Zedillo flew to Villahermosa for the closing event of the campaign. On the bus with Madrazo's entourage en route to the rally, he said that López Obrador had contacted him about entering into parleys. "I told him," Zedillo reportedly said, "that the decision will be made at the ballot box, not through negotiations." He then informed the prominent *tabasqueños* that "none of you is going to be governor." In other words, there would be no negotiated outcome á la Salinas. He urged the candidate to "win well, Roberto," adding, "my grandmother always said that one colored chicken was worth more than twenty plain ones."[12]

On Election Day, Valencia visited Madrazo's luxurious house. Around 1:30 P.M., he phoned López Obrador, who claimed that "the PRI was initiating a [vote-stealing] operation." Valencia asked for more information so that he could stop any chicanery. López Obrador, who was on his way to Macuspana, said that he could not meet with Valencia until 3:00 P.M.

In mid-afternoon Valencia visited López Obrador's home with Ovalle, then a federal deputy who was observing the contest. According to Valencia, the PRD candidate, who continued to allege that fraud was afoot, appeared "arrogant and fatalistic." Still, he provided no convincing facts. Soon after the men reached his residence, reporters from *La Jornada, El Financiero,* and other newspapers showed up. Their host, who obviously did not want to be seen chatting with *priístas,* urged Ovalle and Valencia to hide while he talked at length with the journalists outside his house.[13] In the absence of evidence of wrongdoing, Valencia drove to the Cárdenas municipality, where angry citizens reportedly had taken pollsters hostage.[14]

Despite the PRD's failure to provide proof, charges of dirty tricks filled the air in the wake of the November 20 election. Officials claimed that Madrazo had captured 56.1 percent of the ballots cast, to 37.74 percent for López Obrador and 2.53 percent for PAN standard-bearer Rodríguez Prats. The PRI-dominated State Electoral Tribunal (TEE) cavalierly rejected allegations of fraud and declared Madrazo the duly elected governor.[15] See Table 6 for these results.

In light of these "fictitious figures," López Obrador and his loyalists decided to organize a caravan to the D.F.; they reached the city on November 29. Once in the capital, they met with Moctezuma,

TABLE 6. *1994 Tabasco Gubernatorial Election*

CANDIDATE	PARTY	VOTES RECEIVED	%
Madrazo	PRI	297,365	56.10
López Obrador	PRD	200,087	37.74
Rodríguez Prats	PAN	13,410	2.53
Minor Parties	PPS, PFCRN, PARM, PDM, PT, and PVEM	6,636	1.25
Unregistered Parties		120	.02
Null Votes		12,524	2.36
TOTAL		530,142	100.00

SOURCE: Instituto Estatal Electoral of Tabasco.

who pledged to annul the election if they could prove substantial irregularities. At Moctezuma's request, IFE councilors Santiago Creel and José Agustín Ortiz Pinchetti prepared an analysis of the Tabasco election. Neither the TEE nor the local PRI cooperated with them.

On December 6 Tabasco's Congress ratified Madrazo's election. Two days later, Senator Auldárico Hernández Gerónimo and other PRD activists began blocking several hundred Pemex installations. Meanwhile, López Obrador and Cárdenas met with leaders of the Zapatista Army of National Liberation (EZLN). Subcomandante Marcos expressed sympathy for el Peje's plight but warned, "Here we have learned from Tabasco that you are a very hunted deer and you must watch your step."[16]

Cárdenas also led five thousand dissidents to protest Madrazo's swearing in. Three days before the inauguration, authorities violently expelled demonstrators from the atrium of the cathedral.[17] With great difficulty, the state government installed Madrazo as governor at El Teatro Esperanza Iris on January 1, 1995. Some three thousand armed soldiers and law enforcement agents were on hand to ensure the transfer of power. They were equipped with helmets, shields, bulletproof vests, and teargas pistols. There were also reinforcements at the Villahermosa airport, which, since December 19, had become a virtual military base because of the Zapatista threat.[18] In response to this armed presence, López Obrador disparaged the Zedillo administration, which, he claimed, "rather than opt for democracy . . . decided to continue the authoritarian model; we are moving from a soft dictatorship to an open dictatorship."[19]

Protestors continued to swarm into the capital's central square, impeding entry into the buildings housing the executive, legislative, and judicial branches of government. Hundreds of policemen and military personnel surrounded the Government Palace and the Quinta Grijalva, the governor's residence, which became known as the "bunker." Madrazo limited his appearances to a few ceremonial events and occasional trips to Mexico City, where he met with Moctezuma, whom Zedillo had placed at the head of the Government

Ministry. The PRD was convinced that Madrazo's head would roll. The only question was when.

During the second week of January 1995, PRD activist Javier González Garza, a confidant of Cárdenas, requested a meeting with Valencia. When the latter arrived at Carlos & Charley's restaurant in the D.F.'s Colonia Roma, he found that González Garza was accompanied by PRD president Muñoz Ledo. González Garza's message to Valencia was simple: "Why don't you do yourself and us a favor and put López Obrador in jail?"[20] While the proposal was ridiculous in light of the economic crisis, it demonstrated the animus that some *perredistas* harbored toward the Tabascan messiah.

PRD and the PRI representatives held talks at the Government Ministry to hammer out an end to the conflict. Madrazo sought to propitiate his opponents by promising a "frontal attack against corruption, dissembling, impunity, and injustice," and offered to form "a government of assured change" that might include a PRD member in his administration.[21] The zealous López Obrador quickly quelled such offers. "They think that our struggle is based on personal ambitions, that it is enough to offer us good-sized bones," he said. "They are wrong. Our struggle is for legality and democracy, for new elections."[22] He went on to condemn Madrazo's cabinet as "the same old gang" of individuals with shady backgrounds. "With Madrazo, things are bad, with the cabinet it gets worse, because these officials should spend 300 to 400 years in jail," he averred.[23]

The PRD also upset the local establishment by publishing a "blacklist" of Madrazo's supporters who had not paid their property, water, or electricity bills. Among the twenty accused, who owed some 177 million pesos, 6.8 percent of the state budget, were three well-known PRI state legislators.[24] López Obrador and his colleagues, who announced a boycott of the cited businesses, insisted that the delinquents "had accumulated wealth through business transactions paid for by the public treasury." A local magnate called the revelation "a lack of respect for those who wish to improve the economic situation of the state."[25] To demonstrate solidarity with López Obrador, additional customers stopped paying their electric bills, a practice that found 230,000 of 454,000 customers still not compensating the electricity company for services in early 2006.

ZEDILLO BOYCOTTS MADRAZO'S INAUGURATION

Tabasco's contested election posed the second political challenge to Zedillo, who had pledged to govern democratically. A week after his December 1, 1994, swearing in, the PRI's Eduardo Robledo Rincón won a highly dubious victory in Chiapas, where the EZLN had announced its "revolution." Meanwhile, López Obrador was engaged in negotiations with Moctezuma, even as the feisty Tabascan harshly criticized the chief executive for failing to move against

Madrazo. "Ernesto Zedillo was supposed to inaugurate a new stage in this country; he was to launch a democratic initiative. He has decided to continue with the authoritarian model."[26]

Neither Zedillo nor Moctezuma had extensive political experience. For instance, on December 19 the staff of Defense Secretary Enrique Cervantes Aguirre notified Los Pinos that the EZLN was blocking roads in Chiapas. Before departing for a visit to the north, Zedillo ordered his government secretary to open the federal highways and enforce the law. Moctezuma failed to follow through, possibly because he was arranging a meeting with Marcos. This inaction gave credence to the false claim that the Zapatistas controlled thirty-eight rather than four municipalities in the southern state.[27] A member of Zedillo's inner circle said that in late 1994 and early 1995, Moctezuma appeared to be acting more like the government secretary in Chiapas and government undersecretary in Tabasco than the head of the Government Ministry.[28]

The volatile situation in Tabasco reinforced Zedillo's resolve to break with tradition—commenced by Echeverría in 1970—and absent himself from gubernatorial inaugurations.[29] This move widened the gap between the new president and PRI stalwarts, who already looked askance at the technocratic Zedillo because he lacked a seasoned team, was hostile to Salinas, and met with opposition parties even as he maintained a "healthy distance" from the PRI. From Zedillo's perspective, however, greater competition meant that electoral outcomes were often disputed—sometimes with violence. He did not want his attendance at ceremonies to convey the idea that he was taking sides in a dispute between political forces and thereby compromise his legitimacy as the president of all Mexicans.

Moctezuma asked Liébano Sáenz Ortiz, the president's personal secretary, to inform Madrazo's staff of the president's decision. On December 30 Madrazo phoned to ask the reason and was told by Sáenz, "I have no more information, but Esteban is here if you want to talk with him."[30] In another telephone conversation, outgoing governor Gurría urged the chief executive to attend the event, but Zedillo adamantly refused.[31] With the exception of several *tabasqueños,* among them Arturo Núñez, federal officials followed the president's example.

Nonetheless, ten *Salinista* governors flocked to the ceremony: Aguascaliente's Otto Granados Roldán, Campeche's Jorge Salomón Azar, Chiapas's Robledo, Guerrero's Rubén Figueroa Alcocer, Michoacán's Ausencio Chávez Hernández, Oaxaca's Diódoro Carrasco Altamirano, Puebla's Bartlett, Tamaulipas's Manuel Cavazos Lerma, Veracruz's Patricio Chirinos Calero, and Yucatán's interim governor, Federico Granja Ricalde.

Valencia arrived for the event at Madrazo's personal invitation. When his escort from the airport suggested that he meet with the governor-elect, the visitor protested that Madrazo would be "too busy." Nevertheless, they drove directly to the hotel, where the Tabascan leader was having breakfast with some fifteen individuals, including the PRI's secretary of elections. Much to Valencia's dismay, Madrazo led him to a separate table, where they talked alone for forty-five minutes. Valencia later realized that his host was highlighting the presence of at least one member of Zedillo's entourage at his swearing in.[32] In addition, he could have been sending a message to Mexico City about the approval he enjoyed from state and national PRI notables.

During his inaugural speech, Madrazo introduced various guests. The governors received warm applause, and when he mentioned Robledo, the crowd shouted, "tough, tough, tough!"—encouraging his own battle to retain the governorship of Chiapas. In contrast, deafening silence met the new state executive's erroneous reference to Valencia as "Zedillo's representative."[33] Valencia felt a palpable coolness toward him at a small postinvestiture reception. Bartlett was especially hostile. Indeed, Valencia perceived that the Puebla strongman (whose father had once governed Tabasco) was attempting—in league with Guerrero's Figueroa—to organize hard-line governors against the president, with Madrazo as their "favorite son."[34] So uncomfortable was Valencia that he returned early to Mexico City, where he stopped by Moctezuma's home to pass along his concerns about a possible anti-Zedillo front.

TABASCANS FACE DOWN THE PRESIDENT

The situation in Tabasco and Chiapas, which included the Zapatista wild card, complicated Zedillo's efforts to garner PRD support for electoral reforms. To facilitate parleys with opposition parties, Zedillo promised to settle the two electoral conflicts. Muñoz Ledo continued to demand Madrazo's ouster, a move that appealed to Moctezuma and Zedillo. It would rescue the administration from a predicament and remove a formidable obstacle to reaching agreement on badly needed political changes.

In early December Moctezuma asked Valencia, who had become the adviser to the Government Ministry, to consult a first-rate lawyer he knew about how Madrazo might be removed. The attorney reported that no legal way existed unless the governor requested a leave of absence.[35]

Without applying pressure, Zedillo explained to Madrazo the dilemma he was facing. A serious economic crisis beset the nation even as he was trying to renovate the antiquated political regime. What was Madrazo's view of things?[36] Although the governor did not want to leave office, he entered into negotiations with the government secretary—in part because he wanted to buy time to maneuver, in part because he did not want to refuse the man whose word had been law in Mexico's political system, and in part because he could not determine whether the little-known Zedillo would take a page from Salinas and force his resignation. Madrazo was well acquainted with the PRI's hardball tactics, having been the point man in the 1992 Michoacán contest, in which his party's presumed victor was booted from the statehouse in the wake of a "second round" of postelection demonstrations.

Local support for Madrazo notwithstanding, the army had thousands of troops in Tabasco to carry out orders from Los Pinos. Moreover, in his January 15 meeting with Moctezuma, Marcos had agreed to prolong their truce in exchange for new gubernatorial elections in Chiapas. Governor Robledo cooperated. He promised that, after taking his family on an extended European vacation, he would request a leave of absence. He kept his word and was named ambassador to Argentina. Zedillo had no Machiavellian plans to remove elected governors as Salinas had done. Still, Madrazo kept his options open by having his confidant, Ángel Buendía, draft a leave of absence request in mid-January.[37]

Moctezuma was behaving as if a new political culture had crystallized. For his part, Madrazo was adhering to the old rules of the game. The cabinet official interpreted Madrazo's readiness to bargain as proof of his willingness to step down, and so informed the president. After all, protests convulsed his home state to the point that Madrazo could not even enter his own office or travel without a sizable security detail. He appeared to have been rejected by thousands of Tabascans, and he might harm a promising career by repressing those he governed.

If Madrazo could obtain a cabinet post, Moctezuma reasoned, he would win Zedillo's gratitude and position himself to become the PRI's national president en route to Los Pinos in 2000. Moctezuma claimed that after days of discussions, Madrazo had agreed to accept the post of secretary of public education, replacing incumbent Fausto Alzati Calderón, whose days in office were numbered because he had grossly misrepresented his academic degrees.[38]

The politically naïve Zedillo and Moctezuma thought they had hammered out a compromise: Madrazo would voluntarily vacate the governorship in exchange for a powerful and prestigious cabinet position.[39] A wilier chief executive would have publicized Madrazo's appointment to the cabinet post. Zedillo neither made such an announcement nor asked for a written pledge. Also playing under new rules, he believed that two gentlemen had reached a good faith accord. In other words, Zedillo thought that that Madrazo was "playing fair."[40] Upon receiving the offer of the cabinet seat, however, the cagey Madrazo told a confidant who was waiting for him outside the presidential residence, "If I give up the governorship, they could toss me out of the administration in a few weeks. What would I tell the people of Tabasco?"[41]

While feeling pressure from all sides, Madrazo wanted to do what was best for his political career. He also hoped to remain on good terms with Zedillo if possible. Needless to say, the party's national president, María de los Angeles Moreno, Governor Bartlett, Hank González, and other *priísta* mandarins were furious at Moctezuma for challenging Madrazo's victory.[42]

RED LIGHTS IN TABASCO

On the night of January 16, Víctor Hugo Esquivel and Rubén Dario Rodríguez, allies of Jiménez Leon, president of the Governing Committee, known as the Gran Comisión, of Tabasco's Congress—received a phone call from a friend in the Government Ministry in Mexico City. He informed Hugo and Dario that a meeting had been held in the Casa de Barcelona, a ministry office, in which Madrazo had agreed to resign the governorship in return for a high-level position. This pledge formed part of the political reform agreed to by the nation's four major political parties that was scheduled to be signed on January 17.

The signatories committed themselves to a "definitive" overhaul of federal and state electoral statues, including laws governing fund-raising and spending. They also affirmed that opposition parties should have "full access" to the media and that the IFE, the election arbiter then dominated by the PRI, would be placed under nonpartisan control. Opposition parties avowed to abstain from "post-electoral actions that violate the legal framework of institutions." Federal authorities and the PAN, PRD, and PT leaders privately agreed to hold new elections within twenty-four months in the southern states of Chiapas and Tabasco, where the PRD had protested PRI triumphs.[43]

Jiménez León, a PRI veteran and former state party president who had served in numerous political posts, immediately set about blocking Madrazo's resignation, which would have compromised his own political fortunes. He first sought help from Félix Eladio Sarracino Acuña, the secretary of the Gran Comisión, which has responsibility when the legislature is not in session. Sarracino was reluctant to oppose Zedillo but said, "You are crazy, but count on me."[44] Then Jiménez León told the legislature's chief administrative officer to notify all PRI and PAN deputies that they must be in Villahermosa early the next day with suitcases packed with a week's supply of clothing. This was a credible request because Jiménez León often organized impromptu study trips with his colleagues.

At 7:30 A.M. on January 17, Jiménez León explained the situation and asked for support from the nineteen PRI and two PAN deputies—only three declined.[45] This meant that a majority, eighteen of twenty-five legislators, stood ready to reject the governor's resignation even before it had been received. PRI veterans recalled the removal of Governor Manuel Bartlett Bautista, the father of Manuel Bartlett, in the wake of protracted student protests in 1955.

Younger party members vividly remembered the purge of Neme. They were determined to prevent the removal of another local leader by Mexico City authorities. They knew that López Obrador, who had played but a secondary role in Neme's ouster, was quick to take credit for that purge and would display the same opportunism if Madrazo were tossed overboard.

PRD militants had blocked entrances to the congress. Thus Jiménez León persuaded the deputies and their alternates to take up residence in the José María Pino Suárez Library. He wanted to shield them from federal officials who might use information about suspect business deals, unpaid taxes, the size of bank accounts, and relationships with women to "persuade" them to change their positions.[46]

With his colleagues isolated from such pressures, Jiménez León went on the *Telerreportaje* radio program to report the "rumor" that, under pressure from the capital, Madrazo would seek a leave of absence. He emphasized that "in the hypothetical case that the governor sought a leave, the Congress would not recognize it." He added that the appropriate authorities had validated the November election and that any leave that was requested under duress would constitute a "nullity." Even as he was speaking on XEVA, legislative colleagues were echoing his message on other stations.

Medina Pereznieto, the state's director of social communication and a Madrazo confidant, proposed that he arrange an interview with Televisa at 10:00 that morning. Jiménez León waited in vain for the camera crew to arrive and finally concluded that Madrazo, who was negotiating in the D.F., had dissuaded Medina Pereznieto from contacting the TV giant.[47]

At 1:00 P.M. on January 17, Madrazo's entire cabinet convened in house of Government Secretary Tellaheche. The group was split down the middle on what action to take. Tellaheche, a bland political independent, opposed fighting Los Pinos, arguing that in Mexico "not even a tree moves without the president's consent." Supporting this position were Finance Secretary Leopoldo Díaz Aldecoa; Education, Culture, and Recreation Secretary Graciela Trujillo de Cobo; Comptroller General Patricia Isabel Pedrero Iduarte; and Government Undersecretary Andrade Díaz. Andrade, who would become governor in 2001, did not want to see a repetition of the ugliness that surrounded the ouster of Neme.

On the other side of the issue were the Coordinator of Advisers Georgina Trujillo Zentella, Health Secretary Lucio Lastra Escudero, Development Secretary Gustavo Rosario Torres, Coordinator of Advisors Jorge Abdó Francís, and Transit Director Jaime Echeverría.[48]

That night, Jiménez León met with business moguls in the home of Enrique Priego Oropeza. They had formed the Civic Front, led by Manuel Ordoñez Galán, head of a consortium of contractors, and Alberto Banuet Abhari, a prominent entrepreneur. Other business leaders backing Madrazo's continuation in office were Magali

Broca Calles, who represented restaurant owners; César Fernández Díaz, president of the Regional Union of Livestock Producers; Pedro Reséndes Medina; Oscar Casep Peralta; Aurelian Rabelo Cupido, cattle producer and publisher; Mario Trujillo, former governor and affluent landowner; Ignacio Cobo González, a one-time basketball player who married Trujillo's daughter and became an associate of billionaire Carlos Slim Helú; Arcadio León Estrada, alternate senator and cattleman; Francisco Rubio Solís, contractor; and Federico Jiménez Saénz and Federico Jiménez Paoli, proprietors of sugar mills.[49] Madrazo's allies barely concealed their contempt for Valencia, who was Moctezuma's representative at the conclave. Their message to León Jiménez was, "We are fully behind your struggle."[50]

They demonstrated this commitment by agreeing to participate in civil disobedience—a technique that their nemesis López Obrador had practiced so effectively. They allocated responsibility among the attendees for blocking the four main arteries into Villahermosa, halting the delivery of refrigerated meat to Mexico City, and supplying sandwiches and other food to those who were staffing the barricades.[51] Taxi service was discontinued, and the drivers took part in blockading the thoroughfares connecting the state capital with the rest of the country.[52]

In addition to political considerations, Valencia sensed that the businessmen were apprehensive about Tabasco's vulnerability to the EZLN, particularly if there was protracted strife over the governorship. Given the geography of the state, the Zapatistas had easier access to Tabasco via Palenque than they had to most of Chiapas. In early 1995 it was unclear whether the rebels posed a military threat or, as turned out to be case, were merely practicing guerrilla theater.

Civic Front activists also fretted over the question of an interim governor. The local press mentioned Luis Priego Ortiz, a member of the PRI who had good relations with López Obrador and others ex-*priístas,* as a possibility. His affinity for these dissidents made him a pariah to both Madrazo and Tabasco's power structure. While admitting that his name was being circulated, Priego Ortiz emphasized that he received no communication from the Zedillo government or its allies about his replacing the governor.[53]

Rosario Torres, a pivotal member of the state's economic elite, remained in constant communication with Madrazo and Buendía, who helped manage the events in his home state. The meetings and mobilizations on the governor's behalf enabled him to tell the president, in essence, "I want to help you, but the leaders and people of Tabasco won't let me leave office."[54]

In a display of solidarity, the business community closed down most of the commerce, industry, and services in Villahermosa on January 18. When radio stations aired federal bulletins warning that the resistance would chill investment and produce cuts in Tabasco's budget, a dozen prominent businessmen took over Radio

Acir, XEVA, and other stations as part of civil resistance "against the imposition from the Center."[55] Meanwhile, a local columnist wrote that "if the problem is Tabasco's, it must be resolved by *tabasqueños*."[56]

On January 18 Veracruz senator Manuel Ramos Gurrión showed up as the regional delegate of the national PRI. He asked to breakfast with Jiménez León and stated that he carried messages from the legislator's friend Zedillo and from Madrazo. Jiménez León replied, "I do not have time for breakfast, Zedillo is not my friend, and I am not accustomed to receiving messages from Madrazo." Any statement by the senator, he added, "should be directed to all the members of Congress, who were still encamped in the Pino Suárez Library."[57]

Ramos Gurrión asked those assembled, including several federal legislators and mayors, to acquiesce in Madrazo's request for a leave of absence. He attempted to mollify the group by assuring them that the president would be "responsible for your political careers."[58] Rather than accept this proposition, the group castigated the PRI's National Executive Committee (CEN) for its "pusillanimous" lack of support for Madrazo, adding that they were prepared to resign from the PRI to form a new party.[59] Upon learning of this action, the *veracruzano* "turned white as a sheet," observed one participant.[60] When the PRI's secretary of organization, Ochoa González, learned of the threat, he implored the Tabascans not to resign. Meanwhile, local politicians declared Ramos Gurrión persona non grata and gave him twenty-four hours to leave the state.[61]

Some of Madrazo's loyalists became concerned about the attention that Jiménez León was garnering and tried to counterbalance it in the media. Nicolás Haddad López appeared on *Telerreportaje* to urge residents to burn their voting cards and implied that Tabasco might separate from Mexico over the treatment of Madrazo. Other hotheads revived the idea of proclaiming Tabasco, Chiapas, and Campeche an independent territory known as "TACHICAM."[62]

Jiménez León realized that such irresponsible rhetoric could hand the Senate an excuse to declare the state "ungovernable" and place federal authorities in charge—an action that had preceded Governor Bartlett's removal four decades earlier. Jiménez León also knew that destroying voting credentials would put the PRI at a disadvantage in the event of a new election. He quickly phoned the program to reiterate that the local protesters supported the Mexican federation. "Our dispute is with the central government," he affirmed as he discouraged the burning of voting cards.[63]

Before leaving the state, Senator Ramos Gurrión asked Jiménez León to join him at the Hyatt Hotel, where they would read jointly a statement to the media from PRI president de los Angeles Moreno. Before agreeing, the Tabascan asked to read the document, which stated in effect that "the PRI's National Executive Committee recognized Madrazo's victory as governor, but respected his right to ask for a leave of absence." Exclaiming, "I am not an "ignoramus" (*pendejo*), Jiménez León refused to participate, "because like Pontius Pilate, the CEN is trying to wash its hands of the Madrazo affair."[64] He believed that Madrazo was ready to accept a cabinet post.

On the evening of January 17 Madrazo asked Valencia to accompany him to Villahermosa the following day. Moctezuma recommended that Valencia go but not inform the governor until the next morning. When Valencia called early on January 18, Madrazo said they would fly from Toluca airport around 9:30 A.M., after Madrazo had visited Los Pinos.

The besieged Tabascan did not arrive until 1:00 P.M. because he had talked by cell phone from his Suburban with Manuel Gurría after leaving the presidential residence. Gurría, who avows that he gave his protégé no advice, told Madrazo, more or less, that "it is unfortunate that the Zedillo administration is seeking to have you leave your elected post."[65] During the previous days, Madrazo had also talked with Hank González.

With the words of Gurría fresh in his mind, Madrazo headed for the airport. Once aboard the aircraft, along with his confidants Ulises Ruiz and Buendía, the governor inquired of Valencia, "How do I ask for a leave of absence?" Valencia responded that that it was not an esoteric matter. Madrazo, who earlier in the day had carried a yellow folder with the text of the request for a leave of absence, argued that the situation was thorny because a majority of the legislators were holed up in the Pino Suárez Library and would not entertain his request.

Upon landing at the Villahermosa airport at 3:48, Madrazo took a helicopter to the Quinta Grijalva. Madrazo's personal secretary, Feliciano Calzada Padrón, and later another longtime private secretary, María Luisa Pequeño, called Jiménez León to invite him to meet with their chief. When the congressional chief informed them that he was too busy, Madrazo himself phoned. Jiménez León told the governor that the legislature would not accept his request for a leave of absence. Following that brief conversation, Valencia called to emphasize that Madrazo's decision to step aside was his own. Jiménez León replied that Moctezuma should meet with local lawmakers. "If he can talk with masked Zapatistas, he can meet with members of Tabasco's Congress who don't wear masks," Jiménez said, before abruptly hanging up.[66]

Later that afternoon, Madrazo, whom events had overcome, met with a group of businessmen in the dining room of the Quinta Grijalva. The only outsiders were Ulises Ruiz, Javier González, and Valencia. The Tabascans severely criticized Zedillo and said, in essence, "We have invested too much in you to do this. We are not going to permit it." Former governor Trujillo even invoked the name of Carlos A. Madrazo: "[If] your father could see you, he would be ashamed."[67] One participant claimed that Madrazo seemed frightened, even stupefied.[68]

Alarmed by the ugly turn of events, including virulent attacks on Zedillo, Valencia tried to contact Moctezuma but could not reach him. In a phone conversation with Zedillo, Madrazo said that the local discontent was understandable and that all would be calm by the next day. The last thing Zedillo, who was negotiating a financial bailout, needed was a political upheaval in Tabasco. Valencia regrets not having called the president directly to advise him of the real conditions in the state.[69] After meeting with the businessmen, Madrazo's mood changed. "Now I have made *my decision*," he said. "Tomorrow morning I will be in my father's office."[70]

On the morning of January 19, Jiménez León again called *Telerreportaje* to reiterate that the state lawmakers were not going to compromise Tabasco's sovereignty by permitting Mexico City to remove its governor. He even threatened that if Madrazo continued asking to step down, lawmakers would take legal action against him for violating the state constitution, which permitted such a leave only for "serious cause" (*causa grave*) and stressing that no such condition existed.[71]

Meanwhile, de los Angeles Moreno stressed that the national PRI "completely respected the decision that the Tabascans take in exercising their sovereignty."[72] The unanimous vote of PRI senators in favor of Madrazo's retaining his post made clear that federal authorities would not intervene in the state. Moreover, the PRI-run legislatures of Guanajuato, Aguascalientes, Michoacán, and Zacatecas proclaimed solidarity with Tabasco's Congress.

In the early afternoon, local PRI leader Evaristo Hernández, along with Vicente Morales and Manuel Ordóñez Galán, spearheaded the removal of thousands of anti-Madrazo demonstrators from the Plaza de Armas, which had been christened "the drunk," or *la borracha,* because it was "always being taken by demonstrators." The hoodlums also pummeled Senator Auldárico Hernández Jerónimo and his comrades, who were blocking traffic at the city's Taabscob intersection.

Although Moctezuma forbade his returning to office, at 9:55 P.M. Madrazo went into the Palacio de Gobierno. Upon entering, he told Jiménez León, "It is an honor to enter into the Palace with you." To those who welcomed him, he could only repeat the famous words of Mexican singer and film legend Pedro Vargas: "I thank you, I thank you, I thank you."[73] According to *Proceso,* he said: "I wish to tell you that I am here as a result of a popular mandate expressed on November 20. I want to thank the great people of Tabasco . . . that there is certainty in our state. Many thanks." Five minutes later he left the building.[74]

The following day the undersecretary of government, Luis Aguilar Villanueva, flew to Villahermosa in the hope of making peace. On January 20 he and Valencia met with Madrazo, who agreed, as López Obrador had suggested, to hold a plebiscite on whether he should remain in office. "I have a commitment to history," he told them. "The teachings of my father live in me and every day I make a greater effort to honor his example."[75]

Meanwhile, Ovalle spoke alone with López Obrador at his home in Villahermosa. The PRD activist emphasized that he would not betray his people by capitulating. His visitor responded, "If you are convinced that you won the governorship and municipal presidencies, don't give up your fight."[76] When López Obrador demanded that Madrazo resign before holding a *consulta* and that an independent body count the ballots, the governor quickly jettisoned this proposal. Although talks over the future of the governorship proceeded in Teapa, a town near Villahermosa, they were entirely cosmetic. The federal government had no cards left to play.

At a March 4 speech to the PRI's National Political Committee, Madrazo received a prolonged standing ovation after being introduced as the person "who halted the political deals [*concertacesiones*] in Mexico." "He was treated as a hero," remembers Juan S. Millán, a senator from Sinaloa who was in attendance.[77] Party regulars cheered the Tabascan's refusal to relinquish the statehouse as Salinas had forced both governors and governors-elect to do in Guanajuato (1991), San Luis Potosí (1991), and Michoacán (1992). Of course, there was a major difference between those *concertacesiones* and the outcome in Tabasco: the former represented political deals that bore no relationship to electoral results; the latter involved credible evidence—later to become overwhelming—of widespread abuses. In any case, the Tabasco governor had defied the president, whose decisions, until then, had represented the will of God for *priístas*. The reception that party militants accorded Madrazo increased the likelihood that he would one day lead their party and even vie for the presidency of Mexico.

Zedillo smoked the peace pipe with Madrazo on May 14, 1995, when he took time out from a trip to Campeche to inaugurate the Tabasco Fair. As a courtesy, Zedillo's private secretary, Liébano Sáenz, phoned Madrazo several weeks before the event to ask whom he would like to represent the federal government at this springtime exposition begun by the anticlerical Governor Garrido to divert attention from Easter celebrations. The enormously large and expensive fair brings ranchers, elected officials, bankers, and notables from throughout the southeast to Villahermosa to cut business and political deals. Because of the importance of ranching and cattle production to the state, Madrazo requested Agriculture Secretary Labastida.

When Sáenz advised his boss of this preference, Zedillo asked, "What do I have scheduled on this date?" Sáenz answered that he had a meeting with governors from the Gulf of Mexico States Accord in Campeche, which is contiguous to Tabasco. The president asked him to wrap up this session early, and announced that he would inaugurate the Tabasco Fair.[78] In all probability, he kept the trip secret to avoid demonstrations in Villahermosa.

Zedillo, who attended this tense affair with several cabinet members, declared "an end to postelection negotiations," adding that all he asked of *tabasqueños* was that "respect for the law and the will of the majority prevail." Then, lifting his voice, he affirmed, "I am here to say, I am here to declare that Roberto Madrazo and I will work together until the year 2000."[79] A few days later, when the press asked about these comments and his relations with Mexico City, Madrazo insisted that after the president's visit to Tabasco, "there is little to say on this subject."[80]

Although Madrazo emerged the big winner, he quickly forgot his debt to Jiménez León, who not only had fought Mexico City on his behalf but also had managed his unsuccessful bid for the PRI nomination to succeed Zedillo in 1999. Madrazo reneged on his promise to back Jiménez León for governor in 2000, and allies of the outgoing state executive worked against Jiménez León when he sought a seat in the Chamber of Deputies.[81] In May 2002 he left the PRI to join Convergence for Democracy, a party that later backed el Peje's presidential bid.

ZEDILLO'S PREDICAMENT

Zedillo was facing the Zapatista insurgency as well as the worst economic crisis since the Great Depression. To add to the ferment, Cárdenas was calling for a broad-based "government of national salvation"; authorities had just revealed the identity of Marcos; and the Popocatepétl volcano overlooking Mexico City had began erupting in December and January.

In light of these challenges, Zedillo reluctantly accepted the sharpest political setback inflicted on a PRI president. He realized that if Madrazo ignored a public demand to resign, the chief executive would lose even more credibility. Moreover, if successful in unseating the governor, he would have ignored his promise to spurn his predecessors' heavy-handedness. Zedillo's real target was Salinas, a Madrazo confidant. But the face-off with the *tabasqueño* epitomized the contradictions of Zedillo's administration, which lacked a coherent political team in large measure because he was an "accidental president" catapulted to power by Colosio's assassination. In general, Zedillo promoted pluralism and democracy. At times, however, he attempted to cultivate, or at least propitiate, PRI dinosaurs. In the words of one news article, "Mexico's state governors—powerful overlords, whose fathers and grandfathers were often governors before them—represented the obvious ballast for the president's unstable ship."[82]

MOCTEZUMA REMOVED

Having mishandled the Madrazo affair, Moctezuma forfeited his job in late June. Zedillo had lost confidence in his ability to manage political affairs, and governors had come to regard him as a light-weight. June proved an especially trying month for the forty-year-old political ingénue. In addition to clashing with Madrazo, he had tried to appease the militant El Barzón debtors at a time when Finance Secretary Guillermo Ortiz Martínez was negotiating a sweeping rescue package. In June, El Barzón protestors laid siege to Bucareli 99, the Government Ministry's headquarters. From markings on the vehicles that brought them to the capital, it appeared that Edomex governor Emilio Chuayffet Chemor and Guerrero governor Figueroa had inspired the twenty-six-hour demonstration.

Moreover, despite Moctezuma's dramatic meeting with Marcos the previous December, negotiations with the EZLN had atrophied. Relations with the dioceses of San Cristóbal de las Casas, which had hosted the Zapatista government talks, deteriorated after the Ministry of Government inexplicably expelled three foreign priests from the country. To make matters worse, the PAN and the PRD walked out of the political reform negotiations that had begun on January 17. In addition, the government secretary had been unable to find a consensus president for IFE.

Zedillo replaced the young, inexperienced Moctezuma with a man considered his antithesis. He selected Chuayffet, a political apparatchik who boasted extremely close ties to Salinas, Hank González, the fabled Atlacomulco Group, and most of the PRI establishment.

FUNDS FLOW INTO TABASCO

Now that Madrazo enjoyed Zedillo's formal blessing and Madrazo's ally was the government chief, the federal government lavished resources on Tabasco. For instance, Pemex made available 7.3 million new pesos[83] to support high-priority health programs and 488.3 million new pesos to help fishermen in the Centla municipality buy new equipment. The Solidarity and Regional Development Program (Sedesol) contributed 256.6 million new pesos for scholarships, job creation, and transportation.[84] On a per capita basis, Tabasco and Guanajuato, then governed by Fox, received more funds under Zedillo than any other state.

Zedillo also cooperated with Madrazo on federal candidacies. In 1997 the president acquiesced in the Tabasco governor's choice of Mayans Canabal as the PRI Senate nominee, though the chief executive preferred Rodríguez Prats.[85] When Mayans joined the "Galileo Group" of legislators who criticized his policies, Zedillo lamented, "Madrazo cost me two senators: Prats and Mayan."[86] Madrazo also persuaded the president to back César Raúl Ojeda Zubieta, principal owner of Villahermosa's Hyatt Hotel, for a seat in the Chamber of Deputies. After Madrazo lost the PRI presidential nomination to Labastida in late 1999, Zedillo again invited him into his cabinet as secretary of health. Madrazo, no doubt angered by the president's support of Labastida in the primary, declined, saying, "I want to return to Tabasco."[87]

Unlike Zedillo, López Obrador was not about to accommodate himself to a Madrazo administration. True to form, he launched yet another march—this time the "Exodus for Dignity and National Sovereignty," or simply the "Second Exodus," which left Villahermosa for Mexico City on April 23, 1995. López Obrador had become a national figure and received publicity throughout the country, shown in both the name of his exodus and his new demands. Although he still sought to remove Madrazo, he also presented a countrywide agenda. His proposals included naming a new presidential cabinet; revising the handling of the nation's external debt; earmarking 10 percent of the federal budget for Indians; halting the firing of public employees (especially in Pemex); confiscating the illicitly acquired wealth of Salinas and his associates; resolving the Chiapas problem; repealing the increase from 10 to 15 percent in the value-added tax (IVA); and renouncing the privatization of Pemex.[88]

López Obrador and hundreds of sympathizers encamped in the Zócalo, using the historic plaza as a launching pad for demonstrations in front of buildings that symbolized the perceived evils of the neoliberalism. The *exodistas* began with a twelve-hour fast in front of the modern, twenty-four-story Bolsa, or, in López Obrador's words, the "cathedral of financial speculation in the country."[89] During their protest, el Peje claimed, without offering evidence, that "the firms that traded on the Bolsa witnessed their profits grow 600,000 percent." "The voraciousness of the speculators," he added, "fed by the government, has driven peasants from their lands . . . [while] the purchasing power of workers is lower than in 1935 and social justice is only a rhetorical artifice for the authorities."[90]

There is little evidence to substantiate the allegations of fraud that frequently besmirch Mexican elections. One PRD activist was skeptical about wrongdoing in the 1994 Tabasco contest. Unlike the 1988 and 1991 elections, there were few discrepancies between official tallies and those compiled by the PRI's foes.[91] Still, López Obrador inveighed against electoral corruption.

CLOAK-AND-DAGGER EPISODE

Before sunrise on June 5, 1995, a cloak-and-dagger episode transformed what had been a nondescript demonstration into a cause célèbre. López Obrador's operatives claimed that two strangers awakened them with the promise that they had something "very important for the democratic movement in the country." That something turned out to be boxes jammed with ledgers, invoices, canceled checks, and receipts that, according to the PRD, proved that Madrazo had spent nearly $72 million to capture the governor's palace.[92] This sum, more than sixty times the legal ceiling on campaign expenditures in Tabasco ($1.2 million), amounted to $250 dollars per vote received by Madrazo, twice the figure that Zedillo had reported having spent to win the presidency. In any case, $72 million exceed the $61.8 million in public funds allocated to the U.S. Democratic and Republican nominees to wage their presidential campaigns in 1996, and the population of the United States was nearly 160 times larger that that of Tabasco. It appeared that Madrazo had followed Hank's dictum that "in politics all that you can buy with money is cheap."

The documents showed that alleged money launderer Cabal Peniche, owner of Banco Unión, contributed heavily to the PRI campaign. He had given $25 million to PRI candidates: $15 million to Colosio, $5 million to Zedillo, and $5 million to Madrazo.[93] The banker later fled to Australia when the government charged him with failing to pay $461 million in taxes. In 2001 he was extradited to face the charges and was subsequently exonerated.

The putative PRI outlays shocked few Mexicans. After all, access to a trove of money from regime beneficiaries had helped the official party dominate the country since 1929. On February 23, 1993, Salinas presided over a $25 million per person "small dinner party" at the home of former finance secretary Antonio Ortiz Mena. The dining room in his Polanco mansion was decorated with sixteenth-century French furniture and works by famed muralists Diego Rivera, David Alfaro Siqueiros, and José Clemente Orozco.[94] Party president Genaro Borrego had arranged the event with the assistance of two tycoons, construction baron Gilberto Borja and banking magnate Roberto Hernández. In addition to his organizational and financial support, Hernández also had the food prepared by the Paris-trained culinary team from Banamex. The purpose of the "billionaires' banquet" was to raise a $500 million war chest for the upcoming presidential race.[95] One of the twenty-nine high rollers reportedly said, "I have earned so much money in these [Salinas] years that I [will] commit myself to a greater amount."[96] The government showed its appreciation by awarding him sixty-two new television channels in 1993.

The surprise over the so-called Madrazogate came in the compelling evidence. It was the political version of archeologist Alfons Caso's 1932 discovery of Monte Alban, the ancient Zapotec capital in Oaxaca, or Howard Carter's 1922 unearthing of King Tut's tomb in Egypt.

On June 9, 1995, López Obrador disclosed the documents in the scandal in the presence of IFE counselors Creel and Ortiz Pinchetti and a group of reporters. Even the PAN president joined with his PRD counterpart to demand Madrazo's resignation. This was not a pact, he said, but a "common stance" to help the political system "die well."[97] A highly respected journal called the materials both "the exhumation of the expressions of subterranean politics of the authoritarian system" and "objective elements of the entrails of a perverse monster [the PRI]."

Who blew the whistle? The key player was Rafael López Cruz, a socially active lawyer for the poor, a founder of the Tabasco PRD, a López Obrador confidant, and later the state party president. He received a phone call from Félix Herrera Sánchez, a friend and neighbor in Villahermosa's Colonia Indeco. Herrera claimed to have seen a trove of articles, presumably ballots, being carried into a semiabandoned house in their community. The home belonged to Ana Berta López Aguilar, director of accounting and the top aide to Gastón Viesca, the state PRI's undersecretary of finance, who handled the money for Madrazo's campaign.[98] Because he frequently distributed cash, Viesca became known as one of Madrazo's two "bagmen" (*hombres de la maleta*).[99]

López Cruz recruited three young men to remove the material from López Aguilar's home on or about June 2. Pedro García Salazar found a friend with a van who would drive himself, Ernesto Hernández Ramos, and Mario Humberto "Chayotito" González to their destination at the corner of Mártires de Río Blanco and Andador del Dibujante. Originally they had planned to accomplish their task at night. López Cruz convinced them, however, that they would minimize suspicion by making their pickup in broad daylight. Upon finding the door locked, the men summoned a locksmith, assuring him that it was García Salazar's home, that his keys had been stolen along with his car, and that he needed assistance to gain entry. The locksmith obliged, but soon scurried away when the men began to lug boxes from the house.[100]

López Cruz encountered the young men later in the afternoon at the PRD headquarters on Juan Escusia Street, where they had taken the load of purloined goods. They were noticeably disconsolate, saying: "There is not even one ballot or list of results in the boxes. They are useless."[101]

López Cruz reached a different conclusion. The very first box he opened contained receipts for monies paid to the Concamin and Canacintra chambers of commerce, which had organized the highly touted "fast counts" that favored Madrazo. The deeper López Cruz dug, the more evidence he found of illegal outlays. Fearful of a raid on the PRD headquarters, García Salazar took the treasure to the home of Romero Oropeza, who was in Mexico City. Without asking their contents, the maid allowed the boxes to be left in the house.[102]

Armed with photocopies of checks and other incriminating documents, López Cruz hopped a bus to the D.F. to inform López Obrador of the discovery. When he arrived in the capital, the marchers were in Ciudad Nezahualcóyotl, and he could not catch up with the PRD leader until 5:00 P.M. the following day, June 3.

He told him, "I must speak with you! It's urgent! It's a matter of life or death!" Preoccupied with the march, el Peje told his persistent friend to "give it to Octavio [Romero]." López Cruz refused, handed the folder to el Peje (who passed it on to Romero), and went off to get some sleep. When he rejoined the Tabascans at midmorning on June 4, Pérez Mendoza said, "Stay right here. López Obrador wants to see you at once. Don't move."[103]

El Peje promptly showed up and, as the two men walked around the Zócalo, he asked López Cruz about the boxes. López Cruz made two stipulations: first, that he could not give the names of the men who obtained their contents, and second, that the PRD chief send legislators with armed guards to bring the documents to Mexico City. López Obrador consented, saying, "I want to congratulate you on all that you have done for your party."[104] He later praised those who had obtained the boxes as "heroes of democracy."[105]

López Obrador placed Romero Oropeza, Deputy Julieta Uribe, and Senator Hernández Jerónimo in charge of transporting the parcels to the capital. The exposé garnered enormous publicity for López Obrador nationwide and in the PRD. He disclosed the contents of only fourteen of the forty boxes, perhaps to avoid embarrassing political allies.[106]

At first Madrazo and his loyalists suggested that the PRD had forged the papers, but the quality, scope, and complexity of the material refuted this self-serving accusation. They next offered the lame excuse that they had raised the money at dances, raffles, and *tianguis*. Then Madrazo, in what seemed like a warning to Zedillo, widely proclaimed that the monies had flowed mainly to the resource-short presidential campaign, which had printed materials and produced media items focused on the late Colosio. While no apologist for Madrazo, even renowned scholar Luis Rubio suggested that the Tabascan may have been wrongly blamed for handling funds that were largely intended for the chief executive's race.[107]

ATTORNEY GENERAL'S INVESTIGATION

López Obrador requested that the Attorney General's Office (PGR) probe Madrazo's extraordinary expenditures. Antonio Lozano Gracia, a PAN stalwart whom Zedillo had appointed attorney general, met with López Obrador four or five times. On several occasions, the highly respected, Harvard-trained, politically experienced attorney Samuel del Villar accompanied the Tabascan to these sessions. López Obrador insisted on meeting directly with Lozano Gracia inasmuch as two key undersecretaries—Fernando Córdoba Lobo and Manuel Galán Jiménez—belonged to the PRI. López Obrador even advised the removal of these men because of their political affiliation. Lozano Gracia rejected this suggestion on the grounds that they were consummate professionals and that he did not want to "politicize" the PGR by basing his appointments on partisan affiliation. Madrazo did attempt to communicate with the undersecretaries, but Lozano Gracia is convinced that they never accepted his invitations for meetings.[108]

Lozano Gracia explained that he could bring charges if he found violations of federal tax law or the misuse of federal funds. PGR agents compared the bank documents provided by López Obrador to bank statements obtained in Tabasco and determined that they were similar enough to justify a thorough investigation. The PGR said that PRI officials would be summoned to the D.F. to clarify the origin and purpose of the resources spent.[109] Then the PGR would determine whether there was a crime. Although Madrazo hinted broadly that the PRI payments had benefited the presidential race, Zedillo never interfered in Lozano Gracia's investigation.[110]

Tabasco's PRI leader, Haddad López, denounced "the markedly partisan position" of Lozano Gracia, whom he implored to stop meddling in Tabasco's affairs and to "suspend his militancy in the PAN."[111] For his part, Madrazo filed a lawsuit with the nation's Supreme Court (SCJN) in which he tried to frame his action as a constitutional dispute between Tabasco and the opposition-led PGR. "We are sure that the Attorney General is not competent to proceed in this matter," Madrazo said.[112]

THE KIDNAPPING OF MADRAZO?

In what appeared to be a melodramatic ploy, Madrazo claimed that he had been kidnapped for seven hours on August 17 when driving alone between Cuernavaca and Mexico City. He insisted that his three abductors, who also beat him, belonged to the Federal Judicial Police (PJF), an agency under the attorney general's jurisdiction. The PGR denied this assertion. It seemed curious that Madrazo, who usually had a chauffer, was traveling alone on the criminal-infested federal highway between Cuernavaca and Mexico City.[113] While the alleged kidnapping sparked questions, Lozano Gracia confirmed that the badges of the officers described by Madrazo could have been those of the notoriously corrupt Morelos judicial police.[114]

Lozano Gracia turned the tax issue over to the Treasury Ministry (SHCP), whose lawyers concluded that no fiscal crime had been committed. Finance Secretary Guillermo Ortiz was a *priísta* and a leading proponent of economic liberalization. Lozano Gracia speculated that his ministry's decision may have hinged on "politics."[115] It was widely believed that Pemex funds had found their way into the PRI's coffers, just as in 2000. Yet the PGR could not prove such transfers, largely because campaign workers made cash deposits— sometimes in amounts totaling 20 million pesos.

Lozano Gracia ultimately determined that the major issue was the possible misappropriation of state funds. This crime lay within the jurisdiction of state authorities. On June 5, 1996, he turned the evidence over to his counterpart in Tabasco, Patricia Isabel Pedrero Iduarte, whom he urged to investigate "the possible existence of electoral crimes."[116] Moreover, as he had promised López Obrador, he revealed the sum that the PRI in Tabasco had allegedly spent on the 1994 campaign. State authorities wasted no time in sweeping the matter under the rug.

The Supreme Court ruled in favor of the PGR on the question of jurisdiction. However, inasmuch as Lozano Gracia believed he had no grounds to pursue the case, Madrazo erroneously stated that the court had found him innocent of all charges.[117]

Legal matters aside, international factors may have dissuaded the government from delving more deeply into Madrazogate. The Zedillo administration had just negotiated a bailout agreement with the United States and other countries, and Los Pinos was reluctant to stir up a firestorm over electoral shenanigans, or to convey the idea that the president was not in full control of the nation. Another factor may have been the use of funds in the presidential contest.

Completely disillusioned with a political system that tolerated obscene corruption as fiercely as it resisted reform, López Obrador would remain in the D.F. For him, Madrazo—like the despised Salinas—used treachery to obtain power; both made mockeries of Juárez's republican austerity and Lázaro Cárdenas's social and nationalistic agenda; and both took advantage of neoliberalism to enrich themselves. As PRD president, he would work miracles in building an organization committed to uplifting the poor in the spirit of revolutionary nationalism espoused by the PRI before technocrats and opportunists hijacked the party. In this pursuit, the man who started out as an idealistic admirer of Carlos Pellicer evolved into a Machiavellian messiah.

PRD PRESIDENT: A "MIRACLE WORKER"

As PRD national president from 1996 to 1999, López Obrador showed himself to be a miracle worker. He did not feed five loaves and two fishes to the crowd gathered by the Sea of Galilee, but he did multiply both the number of votes received by the PRD and the ranks of his party's officeholders. His feats were all the more awesome when one considers that he inherited a party convulsed by personal, ideological, and policy strife. He increased the PRD contingent in the Chamber of Deputies from seventy-one in 1994 to 126 in 1997, doubled the number of senators from eight to sixteen, worked actively for the election of Cárdenas as mayor of the D.F., and recruited candidates who captured the PRD's first three statehouses, while joining alliances that elected two more governors. In performing these wondrous acts, el Peje displayed both messianic zeal and political pragmatism. His achievements as party chief eclipse those of his predecessors—Cárdenas, Roberto Robles Garnica, and Muñoz Ledo—whose performances introduce this chapter.

CUAUHTÉMOC CÁRDENAS

Cárdenas showed little interest in converting his 1988 electoral support into a coherent political party. As Kathleen Bruhn has pointed out, making the transition from "emergence" to "party consolidation" requires the construction of stable norms and expectations for mutual cooperation, decision making, and conflict resolution in five major areas: (1) among activists, (2) with voters, (3) with groups in civil society, (4) with other parties, and (5) with the state.[1]

Cárdenas ran the new organization in a personalistic, top-down manner, reflecting his father's leadership style and his three decades as a PRI activist. He was said to have "employees" instead of "allies," and viewed the new party as the vehicle for catapulting himself into the presidency. Cárdenas became the PRD's exalted chief because of his bold departure from the PRI, his defiance of the hegemonic regime, his ability to attract crowds, and his magical names—"Cuauhtémoc" and "Cárdenas." In a pro forma show of modesty, he voted for López Obrador, his protégé, as the first PRD national president.[2]

Cárdenas resembled a Banyan tree whose shoots grow down into the soil and take root to form secondary trunks. So thick is the tree's foliage that nothing can grow in its shadow. To overshadow other leftist politicians, Cárdenas seemed determined to fracture the coalition that had thrown its weight behind his presidential candidacy.

Three of the FDN constituent parties—the PPS, the PARM, and the PFCRN—failed to affiliate with the PRD, even as some of their members individually joined the new party. Although they backed Cárdenas's candidacy, these parties stood for different things. The PARM preached anticommunism; the PPS identified itself as "Marxist-Leninist, reformist, and anti-imperialist"; and the PFCRN became synonymous with its opportunistic, devious, and corrupt leader, Aguilar Talamantes. In the wake of the disputed presidential showdown, the Salinas administration spared no effort to return the PARM and the PPS to their satellite status. The government used money, jobs, and political posts to entice the stray sheep back into the fold. "There is a strategy of buying people, of bribing leaders and grassroots members," stated Heberto Castillo.[3]

Cárdenas used the registration of the Mexican Socialist Party (PMS) to found the PRD.[4] He took over its headquarters at Calle Monterrey 50, along with its accumulated debts. Having been born into a PRI that boasted support from the labor, peasant, and popular sectors, as well as unlimited resources and a monopoly on electoral victories, he had never worried about organizing a party. Despite the PMS's contribution to the PRD, Cárdenas treated it like a ragged stepsister; in part he resented PMS candidate Heberto Castillo's waiting until just before Election Day in 1988 to endorse him, and in part he regarded Castillo, his former professor and employer, as a threat to his unquestioned leadership.

The sixty-eight-year-old Castillo had gained notoriety as head of the UNAM professors group who made common cause with rebellious students in 1968, a stance that had landed him in jail for two years. Imprisonment stamped a badge of honor on the chest of the successful civil engineer, who, upon his release, founded the

Mexican Workers' Party (PMT). In 1987 it merged with the Unified Mexican Socialist Party (PSUM) to form the Mexican Socialist Party. Despite PRI pressures to remain in the race to divide the Left, Castillo withdrew in favor of Cárdenas, even though he, unlike the FDN aspirant, had been nominated in a primary.[5] In contrast to the sycophants who surrounded Cárdenas, Castillo had no qualms about speaking his mind. He greatly admired Lázaro Cárdenas and helped coordinate the former president's National Liberation Movement. Nevertheless, Castillo had misgivings about the intolerant, younger Cárdenas's commitment to agrarian reform, democracy, and social change. Like many members of the Left who had suffered under the heel of the PRI regime, Castillo favored negotiations and dialogue rather than hierarchical control. Castillo also advocated individual membership in a mass party based on the principle of equality. In contrast, Cárdenas preferred the groups and social movements whose leaders would have direct links to a powerful party chief prepared to reward allies and punish foes.[6] He showed no interest in opening the party to rank-and-file participation.

PRD President:
A "Miracle Worker"

In light of their differences, why did the PMS leadership allow itself to be manhandled by Cárdenas? Castillo, Ramón Sosamontes Herreramoro, Alejandro Encinas Rodríguez, Pablo Gómez Alvarez, Gilberto Rincón Gallardo, and other stalwarts had witnessed Cárdenas's attacks on fellow FDN allies and did not want to suffer the same abuse. They also feared being marginalized as Cárdenas led what appeared to be the Mexican Left's first "revolutionary force"; thus they sought to invigorate this movement, not weaken it.[7] As one former PMS insider told me, "we went to Cárdenas on our knees, begging to be forgiven for waiting so long to jump on the FDN bandwagon."[8]

Cárdenas gave short shrift to former PMS members, awarding them only three seats on the PRD's first National Executive Committee (CEN). The lion's share of the positions went to his devotees, many of whom had belonged to the Democratic Current (CD). These ex-priístas infused no fresh blood into the PRD. Although they had exchanged the three colors of the PRI for the yellow and black of the PRD, these men clung to the corporatist politics they had learned while serving under Echeverría and López Portillo.

Ricardo Pasco Pierce and other members of the Trotskyite Workers' Revolutionary Party (PRT) also joined the PRD.[9] Having clashed ideologically with the communists, the Trotskyites abhorred the rigid bureaucracy of the Mexican Communist Party (PCM), the PSUM, and the PMS. Thus, they valued direct access to the chief of a new, relatively amorphous organization.

The michoacano assiduously dominated the PRD by playing its several components off against each other. To this end he discouraged horizontal linkages between the factions. These practices militated against unifying the different constituencies. The competition among the party's "currents" prevented the development of a grassroots organization, or provided a convenient excuse for the lack of it. Cárdenas's experience in 1988 convinced him that by merely showing up in a city square or university hall with a band and banners he could marshal a mass audience. During his race for the presidency in 1994, he said, "I trust that the full plazas we are seeing mean full ballot boxes."[10] Why, then, did he need a rank-and-file structure? Instead of crafting sophisticated institutions, the PRD boss preferred assembling large crowds, or *plazismo*. While such rallies boosted Cárdenas's ego, they tended to attract admirers and did little to bring new members into the party's fold.

In addition, Cárdenas kept a tight grip on the party's resources, insisted on serving as the interlocutor with other parties in Congress, and disdained alliances that might jeopardize his control and policies. His approach was that of "democratic intransigence."

Such intractability manifested itself in Cárdenas's attitude toward the Salinas administration. Although he maintained contacts with Los Pinos until 1991, he opposed the president's electoral reform, warned that the chief executive was intent on privatizing the oil industry, and deplored the proposed free trade accord with the United States and Canada as another move to compromise the nation's sovereignty. He proposed instead a nebulous bloc of Latin American nations that, if united, could stand up to Washington.

Cárdenas also blasted the PRI's entrenched corruption, but he made no reference to the multimillion-dollar landholdings and business interests that his family had acquired during and after his father's presidency. The younger Cárdenas vilified the ruling party and its president without offering constructive alternatives. Amid his acidic attacks, he held a secret session with Salinas in the home of PRI leader Manuel Aguilera Gómez with Camacho present. Upon learning of the meeting years later, Muñoz Ledo accused Cárdenas of "double dealing" and engaging in a "historic lie."[11]

Cárdenas was no Puritan, yet he self-righteously decried the *concertacesiones*, or "Holy Alliances,"[12] that Salinas made with the PAN. He no doubt would have preferred that the president pursue pacts with the PRD. The PAN entered into these accords for several reasons: it supported his market-centered policies, backed a rapprochement between Mexico and the Roman Catholic Church, endorsed political reforms, reviled the Left, and was eager to obtain key political posts. After his questionable 1988 election, Salinas lacked the two-thirds majority in Congress required to amend the constitution, precipitating negotiations with a reliable party.[13] The president also feared that the PRD could evolve into a challenger, while the PAN's growth potential appeared limited to cities and suburbs. "It can't win votes beyond the asphalt," was a constant refrain.

Cárdenas's indifference to party building meant that only on his home turf of Michoacán did the PRD have committees in all municipalities. Elsewhere the PRD exhibited a significant presence in states that constituted just one-fifth of the national population: Chiapas, Guerrero, Hidalgo, Oaxaca, Tlaxcala, and Zacatecas.

Muñoz Ledo endeavored to expand the party's base by running for governor of Guantajuato in August 1991. Even though the PRD candidate lost, he recruited new followers in a state where it previously had few members. He joined with PAN nominee Fox in condemning the PRI's "fraudulent" victory. On the night of the election, he hoisted Fox's hand as if the *panista* had just knocked out his foe in a championship boxing match. Escalating protests and incessant charges of vote tampering prompted Salinas to force the governor-elect to step aside in favor of a PAN interim governor. The president, who despised Fox for having ridiculed him in Congress, selected León Mayor Carlos Medina Placencia as provisional state executive.[14]

In 1991 the PRD joined the Potosino Democratic Coalition (CDP) in backing the unsuccessful candidacy of Dr. Nava Martínez for the statehouse in San Luis Potosí. As in Guanajuato, postelection demonstrations prompted the president to remove the new governor, whom he replaced with Gonzalo Martínez Corbalá, the man who launched Salinas's career. Cárdenas labeled this initiative "the first opportunity to effectively unify the political forces of the opposition and . . . achieve democracy."[15] But he did not pursue this situational alliance by either seeking to integrate the CDP into the PRD or exploring cooperation with Nava in the 1994 presidential race.

In addition to ignoring structural questions, the self-absorbed Cárdenas devoted little time to candidate recruitment. While electoral officials accorded him 31.11 percent of the ballots cast in 1988, the PRD's portion of the vote declined to 20.50 percent in the 1991 congressional elections. An overlooked element of his tenure was the flight from the PRD of intellectuals who opposed Cárdenas's dogmatism, favored a more conciliatory approach toward the regime, and, after the fall of the USSR, embraced "socialism with a human face."[16] Among these so-called *mapaches*[17] was José Woldenberg Karakowky, a scholar who later won accolades as IFE's president from 1996 to 2003.[18]

In the words of one close observer, Cárdenas was a "disastrous" leader; the better organized Mexican Socialist Party—from which the PRD formally emerged—"would have fared better in elections."[19] Castillo echoed similar sentiments when he lamented that "the strong bossism [*caudillismo*] of the PRD national presidents had prevented the party's becoming institutionalized and achieving internal democracy and a greater electoral presence."[20]

ROBERTO ROBLES GARNICA

On February 28, 1993, with his eye on the 1994 national campaign, Cárdenas passed the PRD leadership to confidant Roberto Robles

Garnica. The interim leader's main chore was to protect Cárdenas from his growing number of PRD detractors, including Muñoz Ledo, Castillo, and Rincón Gallardo. Although in office only five months, the more moderate Robles Garnica encouraged talks with the PAN and sent delegations to the Government Ministry to explore major changes in the nation's electoral law.

PORFIRIO MUÑOZ LEDO

In mid-1993 Muñoz Ledo (41.6 percent) defeated Mario Saucedo Pérez (23.6 percent), Heberto Castillo (21.8 percent), and Pablo Gómez (3.7 percent) to win the PRD presidency. Although Cárdenas had promised not to meddle in the contest, he backed his Democratic Current ally. This was evident when Cárdenas's mother, Doña Amalia, signed a manifesto on behalf of Muñoz Ledo. The *cardenista* support did not arise from enthusiasm for the brainy if disorganized Muñoz Ledo, with whom Cárdenas often disagreed. For example, Muñoz Ledo had endorsed an all-out attack on the government after the July 1988 electoral fraud; Cárdenas favored conciliation. Muñoz Ledo advocated a broad center-left coalition; Cárdenas insisted on intransigence. In addition, Muñoz Ledo, who had been the more important figure when both men belonged to the PRI, and had functioned as the FDN's principal strategist, resented playing second fiddle to Cárdenas in the PRD.

Even though Cárdenas viewed Muñoz Ledo as a competitor,[21] he was concerned that Castillo, who finished first in balloting for a Senate seat in 1988, posed a greater threat to his hegemony. Muñoz Ledo enjoyed the backing of the "Rainbow Coalition" (*Coalición Arcoiris*), composed of various elements of the traditional Left[22] and such former PMS members as Amalia García Medina, Raymundo Cárdenas, Rincón Gallardo, and Alejandro Encinas.

Although supported by moderates, Muñoz Ledo had never developed a team of loyalists within the PRI during his extensive service as secretary-general of the Mexican Social Security Institute (1966–70), secretary of labor (1972–75), national president (1975–76), secretary of education (1976–77), and Mexico's permanent representative to the United Nations (1979–82). He continued to play the "lone ranger." This tendency sprang from arrogance, confidence in his vaunted intelligence, a mercurial temperament, and his recognized ability to persuade others of the correctness of his position. Consequently, Cárdenas's allies dominated the CEN during Muñoz Ledo's tenure as party president.

The new leader exhorted his colleagues to embark upon a "new stage" in the party's development and become a party of "long pants," meaning that its leaders should abandon vapid rhetoric and present well-reasoned proposals that would make the PRD a serious, center-left alternative to the PRI. In accordance with that view, he disdained contacts with the Zapatistas. Instead, he sought to build alliances with the PAN on the grounds that its new president, Carlos Castillo Peraza, was not "a prototypical reactionary *panista*, but a person with a social commitment."[23] In October 1993, however, Castillo rejected a PAN-PRD alliance in the 1994 election on the grounds that "it is practically impossible to work with this party, because it is a body with two heads and two hundred mouths that can never agree."[24]

In accord with his conciliatory approach, Muñoz Ledo replied to a congratulatory letter from Salinas, marking the first time that the PRD had recognized the PRI leader's 1988 victory. This exchange opened the way for the party's participation in preparing a new Federal Code for Electoral Institutions and Procedures (Cofipe). Muñoz Ledo insisted that such a reform include impartial electoral bodies, voting rights for Mexicans abroad, reliable electoral credentials, trustworthy registration rolls, proportional representation in the Senate, the direct election of Mexico City's mayor, the awarding of legislative seats to parties based on the number of votes they received, and abolition of the so-called governability clause.[25]

In the wake of Cárdenas's humiliating loss to Zedillo in the 1994 presidential election, many *perredistas* believed that López Obrador's confrontational tactics were preferable to the political bargaining contemplated in the Cofipe-style reform. Nevertheless, at the mid-1995 PRD Congress, Muñoz Ledo persuaded the party faithful to embrace institutional change. "Dialogue is not just one method of struggle," he thundered. "Our challenge is to rebuild the state as a democracy, not to destroy it irresponsibly."[26] He also defied Cárdenas, who, in a speech in the Zócalo on March 18, 1994, virtually commanded the PRD to oppose Cofipe. Most officials sided with Muñoz Ledo, some because they believed in a political opening, others because they craved the public monies that would give the PRD resources never before enjoyed by Mexico's Left.

In addition, Muñoz Ledo departed from Cárdenas's authoritarianism to involve non-CD activists like Mario Saucedo and Pablo Gómez in charting the party's direction. In the same vein, he invited six members of the Current of the Democratic Left (CID) to hold leadership positions. This faction, discussed below, emerged from popular organizations formed by René Bejarano, his wife, Dolores Padierna, and young activist Martí Batres Guadarrama after the 1985 earthquakes. Muñoz Ledo also named three lieutenants of Pablo Gómez to the party's CEN and cooperated with allies of Castillo.[27]

Unlike the parochial Cárdenas, Muñoz Ledo had a sophisticated understanding of world affairs. He had traveled widely, lectured at the University of Paris, advised UNESCO, and served as his nation's envoy to the United Nations. This background was evident when he spearheaded the PRD's entry into the Socialist International, a worldwide organization of social democratic parties in which

Spain's prime minister, Felipe González, was a vigorous spokesman for globalization.

ANDRÉS MANUEL LÓPEZ OBRADOR

At the request of Cárdenas, López Obrador sought the PRD presidency in early 1996. His principal opponent was Amalia García. She enjoyed the backing of Muñoz Ledo, who regarded López Obrador as a capricious "tropical import" and Cárdenas's instrument to preserve his hammerlock on the party.[28] The outgoing PRD chief also believed that López Obrador would promote Cárdenas as the party's 1997 candidate for mayor of Mexico City—a position Muñoz Ledo coveted. Castillo offered himself as a third contender.

The candidates agreed on maintaining state ownership of Pemex, promoting democracy, and advancing human rights. Nonetheless, the primary contest reflected ideological nuances within the party. Like Cárdenas, López Obrador, now forty-three, had taken an intractable stance, as evidenced by his militant reaction to the outcome of the 1994 Tabasco election. In his campaign for party leader, he attempted to project a more centrist image. He downplayed the intransigence that had catapulted him from Tabasco into the national arena, muted the radicalism of his antigovernment message, and virtually ceased to mention his fondness for mass mobilizations and extrainstitutional protests. Instead, he spoke of his readiness to engage in dialogue and abide by the rules of the institutional game. This change, he explained, was a response to national conditions that were different from those that prevailed in his home state. In addition, he selected as his running mate for secretary-general Jesús Ortega Martínez, a leader of the moderate "Chuchos," whose name derives from the presence of several men named Jesús in the faction's leadership.

For her part, former communist Amalia García, forty-five, shared Muñoz Ledo's commitment to forging a left-center coalition to defeat the PRI. In addition, she was a robust advocate of women's rights. An attractive personality complemented her effectively articulated views, prompting one admirer to label her "the tranquil force," after the brand of socialism practiced by France's François Mitterand.[29]

Senator Castillo had unsuccessfully battled Muñoz Ledo for the party's presidency in 1993. A distinguished professional and greatly admired leftist leader, Castillo took direct aim at López Obrador when he declared that the PRD should abandon its image as a party of "protests" and become a party of "proposals."[30]

On July 14, 1996, el Peje captured 358,274 votes (74 percent), smothering Castillo (49,279 votes, or 13.62 percent), and García (44,100 votes, or 12.38 percent). Amid a 71.63 percent abstention rate, the victor defeated his rivals in twenty-seven states and the D.F.[31]

López Obrador's reputation as a fighter reflected the views of his party's rank and file. In an early July 1996 survey, the newspaper *Reforma* found that 58 percent of respondents believed that the defense of social causes was more important than winning elections; only 12 percent assigned greater weight to electoral success. More than half of those interviewed wanted the PRD to be a "leftist" party; one-third backed a centrist posture.[32]

PRD President: A "Miracle Worker"

Once in office, López Obrador simulated uniting the fragmented party. He devised a broad-based "consultative council" composed of Cárdenas, Muñoz Ledo, Castillo, economist Ifigenia Martínez, and others. He wanted to give the impression of bringing harmony to the PRD's various groups, while attenuating the personality cult that Cárdenas had fostered as the party's presidential candidate and its unofficial "moral leader." In fact, the council was more ornamental than substantive.

As depicted in Table 7, López Obrador selected a CEN that included the party's major currents. Nonetheless, he named loyalist Romero Oropeza as chief administrative officer. In a subsequent reorganization, the party president selected another Tabascan, Oscar Rosado Jiménez, as the PRD's treasurer. Both men would serve as his apostles when el Peje captured the D.F. mayorship in 2000.

López Obrador's decision to create five secretaries for social affairs (women, Indians, workers, youth, and a popular movement) reflected his devotion to corporatism. The scheme drew criticism from leaders such as Angelica de la Peña and Senator Rosalbina Garavito, who labeled the gambit an example of "neocorporatism" reminiscent of the PRI's organization. Rosario Robles, the new secretary of organization, backed López Obrador's move. She denied that the positions constituted a corporatist structure, because participation in these areas would be individual and voluntary.[33]

STANCE TOWARD THE GOVERNMENT

Once el Pejelagarto had addressed the party's organizational challenges, he concentrated on changing the PRD's image, emphasizing that party members were "opponents," not "enemies," of the Zedillo administration. He repeatedly disavowed violence and agreed to meet with the president. In late August, López Obrador, Secretary-General Ortega Martínez, and the PRD's legislative coordinators went to Los Pinos. At this meeting they stressed their hope that he would resolve the Tabasco situation, because "no one can govern without political legitimacy and moral authority." In addition, they urged the president to demilitarize Guerrero, where elections would soon be held, bring the Zapatistas into the country's political life, ensure state ownership of Pemex, and prevent tax monies from flowing to PRI nominees in upcoming local elections. Through his spokesman, Zedillo indicated his eagerness

TABLE 7. *López Obrador's First National Executive Committee*

APPOINTEE	POSITION	BACKGROUND	RELATIONSHIP TO LÓPEZ OBRADOR*
Amalia García Medina	Alliances and Political Relations (Relaciones Políticas y Alianzas)	Partido Comunista Mexicano (PCM)	3
Raymundo Cárdenas Hernández	State Reform (Reforma del Estado)	Partido Comunista Mexicano	3
Rosario Robles Berlanga	Organization	UNAM Student Movement	1
Alejandro Encinas Rodríguez	Political Training (Capacitación Política)	Partido Comunista Mexicano	2
Eloi Vázquez López	Secretary of the National Council (Secretario del Consejo Nacional)	Partido Comunista Mexicano	3
Pablo Gómez Alvarez	Electoral Action (Acción Electoral)	Partido Comunista Mexicano	2 or 3
Mara Robles Villaseñor	Youth Affairs (Convergencia Juvenil)	Partido Comunista Mexicano	1
Raquel Sosa Elízaga	Election Inspector (Escrutador)	Partido Comunista Mexicano/ López Obrador	1
Octavio Romero Oropeza	Chief Administrative Officer (Oficial Mayor)	PRI/López Obrador	1
Ramón Sosamontes Herreramoro	Legislative Coordinator (Coordinación Legislativa)	Heberto Castillo	2 or 3
Laura Itztel Castillo	Communications	Heberto Castillo	3
Eduardo Espinosa Pérez	Municipal Affairs (Asuntos Muncipales)	Heberto Castillo	2
Eduardo Prieto	Vice President of Consejo Nacional	Heberto Castillo	3
Carlos Navarrete Ruiz	Planning (Planeación)	Partido Socialista de los Trabajadores/Partido Mexicano Socialista (PST/PMS)	2

* 1 = closest, 2 = middle, 3 = most distant

TABLE 7 *(cont'd).* *López Obrador's First National Executive Committee*

APPOINTEE	POSITION	BACKGROUND	RELATIONSHIP TO LÓPEZ OBRADOR*
Pedro Etienne Llano	Chamber of Deputies Coordinator	Partido Socialista de los Trabajadores (PST)	1
Héctor Sánchez López	Senate Coordinator	Coalición Obrera, Campesina, Estudiantil del Istmo (COCEI)	1
Rafael Hernández Estrada	Undersecretary (Subsecretario)	Partido Mexico de Trabajadores (PMT)	?
Erick Villanueva Makul	Undersecretary (Subsecretario)	Partido del Frente Cardenista de Reconstrucción Nacional (PFCRN)	2
Martín Longoria Hernández	Indigenous Affairs (Asuntos Indígenos)	Movimiento Revolucionario Popular (MRP)	1
Carmelo Enríquez Rosado	Undersecretary (Subsecretario)	Movimiento Revolucionario Popular (MRP)	2
Saúl Escobar Toledo	Labor Affairs (Asuntos Laborales)	Organización de Izquierda Revolucionaria (OIR)	1
Ricardo Pascoe Pierce	International Affairs (Asuntos Internacionales)	Partido Revolucionario de los Trabajadores/Movimiento al Socialismo (PRT/MAS)	1
Mario Saucedo Pérez	Senate Coordinator	Asociación Cívica Revolucióna Nacional (ACRN)	1
Leticia Ramírez Amaya	Election Examiner (Escrutador)	Radical Teachers' movement	1
Rosa María Márquez	Women's Affairs (Secretaría de la Mujer)	From Puebla; close to René Bejarano's group; Partido Comunista Mexicano (PCM)	1
Manuel Ortega Martínez	Social Movements (Movimientos Sociales)	Local politician from Zacatecas	1

SOURCE: For assistance with this table, I am indebted to Saúl Escobar Toledo, interview by author, March 7, 2005.

to keep open the channels of communication, "because he considers it important that the PRD be an active party that reflects the point of view with respect to problems facing significant sectors of Mexico's citizens." Pedro Etienne, the head of the *perredista* faction in the Chamber of Deputies, called the meeting a new stage in PRD-presidential relations.[34]

Such overtures aside, López Obrador opposed the sweeping Cofipe statute that Muñoz Ledo had boldly endorsed. This proposal strengthened IFE, gave citizens control over organizing elections, counting votes, and determining winners, and ensured public funding of political parties. When Government Secretary Chuayffet asked López Obrador to support the legislation, the PRD leader demurred. Congruent with his belief in "republican austerity," he objected to parties receiving government funds because this would give a bad impression to the public and could contaminate the recipients. At the same time, he revealed his contempt for democracy, saying, "I don't believe in transformations made by laws," and arguing that democracy would only come to Mexico "by staging mobilizations, not tinkering with legislation."[35] "How can we be sure that the gains achieved through mobilizations will be effective if there are no laws?" Chuayffet responded.[36] Led in the Chamber of Deputies by Ortega Martínez, PRD legislators quietly rebelled against López Obrador. They voted against or abstained on its financial provisions but generally supported other elements of the successful legislation.

USE OF COFIPE MONIES

López Obrador again showed his Puritanism when the IFE dispersed funds under the new law. Many PRD activists urged the acquisition of a larger building, installing up-to-date communications, and purchasing new computers. Yet el Peje insisted on spending the monies on free textbooks in PRD-governed areas, on pensions to the widows of an estimated five thousand party members who had died during PRI rule,[37] and on scholarships to the victims' children. This stance reflected not only reflected the Tabascan's asceticism but also his determination to keep the party weak to enhance his personal dominance.

ELECTORAL SUCCESSES

While he did nothing to strengthen party structures, López Obrador vowed to double the party's vote percentage in 1997. In pursuit of this objective, he traveled continuously, arguing, "We will recover the democratic ideals of Madero, the justice of Zapata, and [the values] that represented the popular government of Lázaro Cárdenas."[38] He also made clear that, as he had attempted in Tabasco, the party would select its nominees through direct, open contests in which strong "external candidates" could compete only if they adopted the PRD's goals. He repeatedly turned to current or ex-PRI politicians. A PRD founder said that "López Obrador allowed *priístas* to take over the PRD just as the Romans took over Christianity in the fourth century."[39] El Peje may have bolted the PRI, but his outlook was that of a PRI militant of the 1970s and 1980s when he was a party activist.

In accord with this orientation, he began to meet with Camacho, the former PRI secretary-general with whom he had butted heads over the 1988 gubernatorial election in Tabasco. López Obrador discussed with Camacho, who had exited the PRI after being passed over for the 1994 presidential nomination, the possibility of forming a broad democratic front. He also endorsed the use of polls to select strong standard-bearers, promised to disburse funds where they would have the greatest impact, and vowed to upgrade the efficiency of campaign workers. To this end el Peje encouraged Deputy Rosario Robles to mobilize votes for the PRD by sending paid activists, known as Sun Brigades (*Brigadas de Sol*), door to door in key neighborhoods.

López Obrador did not have to wait long to test his new strategy. On August 10 voters selected state and local leaders in Guerrero. Despite some electoral slippage, the revolutionary party preserved majorities in the seventy-six municipalities and the forty-six-member legislature. This outcome reflected the revolutionary party's strong grip on the state.

Things turned out differently on November 10, 1996, when citizens in México State, Hidalgo, and Coahuila went to the polls amid the worst economic downturn since the Great Depression. After the dust had cleared, the PRD emerged with 44 victories in the municipal showdowns: 34 of 122 municipalities in México State, 9 of 84 in Hidalgo, and 1 (Ocampo) of 38 in Coahuila. Especially impressive were the gains in México State, which not only boasts the largest number of voters in the country but also curls around the D.F. For instance, the PRD captured the huge municipalities of Texcoco, Tejulpilco, and Ciudad Nezahualcóyotl, which lie cheek by jowl with the capital. These triumphs provided López Obrador's party with beachheads from which to contest the D.F. mayoral election in 1997. The PRD chief gave a sermon to these mayors-elect. He admonished them to abandon PRI practices and display moral rectitude by having only "one car, one home, and one wife."[40] While *mariachis* boomed out *¡Viva Mexico!*, Robles exclaimed that "we definitely exceeded our expectations."[41]

Next, López Obrador focused on Campeche, which would elect a state executive in 1997. In search of a strong PRD gubernatorial candidate, he negotiated extensively with Senator Layda Sansores San Román, a prominent figure in the state and daughter of ex-governor Carlos Sansores Pérez, a former PRI national president. The discussions paid off when Sansores left her party to accept the PRD's candidacy in the mid-1997 contest. Though the hard-charging senator failed to win, she garnered 41.6 percent of the votes in a five-way race. Thus the PRD secured a toehold in a PRI bastion where the only leftist presence had been a few ex-PSUM stalwarts.

In 1998 Amalia García obtained López Obrador's tentative support for nominating the former attorney general, Ignacio Morales Lechuga, for governor of Veracruz. The proposal died, however, when Cárdenas publicly opposed it.

SUCCESSES AT THE STATE LEVEL

At the state level, the party president recruited disaffected *priístas* as PRD candidates. López Obrador's gravitation toward Romero Oropeza and other PRI activists in Tabasco demonstrated his attachment to his old party. The first major success for el Peje's recruiting practices came in Zacatecas, where Ricardo Monreal Ávila, a deputy and vice coordinator of the PRI's legislative bloc, had launched his campaign for the PRI nomination, believing the selection process would be above board. Instead, he encountered stiff opposition from former governor Genaro Borrego Estrada, who succeeded in marginalizing the popular legislator to obtain the candidacy for one of his cronies. Upon having the rug yanked from under him, Monreal wasted no time in forming the Citizen Alliance for Democracy and Dignity. The PRD promptly named him its gubernatorial candidate and the tireless Monreal handily defeated Borrego's dauphin.

The next breakthrough came in Tlaxcala. On May 9, 1998, the PRI nominated Joaquín Cisneros Fernández, who captured only a third of the votes cast in a seven-way primary. Cisneros neither propitiated the losers nor comprehended the agenda of ex-governor Beatriz Paredes Rangel, a powerhouse in this PRI rotten borough and a mayoral candidate in the D.F. in 2006. Paredes did not want Cisneros to challenge her dominance in the state and began working behind the scenes for PRD candidate Alfonso Sánchez Anaya—a former state PRI president and one of the losers in the party primary—who won the contest as the PRD's standard-bearer.

The following year, López Obrador was ready to take advantage of an internecine battle within the PRI in Baja California Sur. When Leonel Cota Montaño, ex-mayor of La Paz and a former deputy, lost the PRI gubernatorial nomination, he called the PRD president. López Obrador invited him to be the PRD candidate.[42] Cota Montaño won the election, emerged as a disciple of el Peje, and ascended to the PRD presidency in 2005.

In 1999 López Obrador similarly benefited from a PRI rift in Nayarit. When the revolutionary party turned its back on Antonio

Echevarría Domínguez, a coalition of the PRD, PAN, PT, and PRS threw their support to the multimillionaire, who won handily. Even though the new governor cast his lot with the PAN in 2001, the PRD boosted its presence in this PRI citadel and narrowly lost the statehouse four years later.

As party chief, López Obrador gave impetus to negotiations among a half-dozen parties with respect to the Chiapas governorship. Seven parties eventually threw their weight behind independent Pablo Salazar Mendiguchía, who narrowly defeated the wily PRI contender to capture the nation's most turbulent state.

Despite his growing success, López Obrador also suffered setbacks, not the least of them in his home state in 1997. The PRI's leadership was reeling from losing its majority in Congress and the mayorship of Mexico City earlier in the year. Governor Madrazo was determined not to repeat this performance in the October municipal and state legislative contests in Tabasco. Taking advantage of the shortcomings of several PRD mayors, the PRI seized the offensive. As a result, it swept all seventeen municipal presidencies, while winning twenty seats, including all eighteen directly elected contests, in the thirty-two-member state legislature. On the basis of proportional representation, the PRD picked up eleven seats and the PAN one seat. Madrazo emerged from the landslide as the PRI's hero. What the party could not accomplish nationally, he succeeded in doing on his own terrain.

State party president Rafael López Cruz accepted responsibility for the defeat and tendered his resignation on October 22. El Pejelagarto blamed the setback on Madrazo's vote manipulators and declared that this was no time for retirements. The PRD State Council promptly rejected López Cruz's offer to step down. López Cruz admitted some role in the blowout, but the PRD had managed the campaign from the D.F., sending in Sun Brigades and other outsiders. The newcomers, who were paid, contributed to the loss because they knew little about Tabasco and failed to work with volunteer local party committees.

López Obrador's conciliatory words aside, some members of the national PRD wanted López Cruz's scalp. They demanded that the eleven PRD deputies give up their legislative seats lest they validate the "monumental electoral fraud" of October 19, 1997."[43] López Cruz refused to direct them to comply, on the grounds that his party members deserved the positions and that the presence of PRD legislators in the front lines of demonstrations often dissuaded the police from employing violence.

At this point, Romero Oropeza launched a stealth attack. He secretly convened a rump meeting of the PRD State Council in his home, alleged that López Cruz and Electoral Action secretary Armando Padilla Herrera had "arbitrarily" changed the list of candidates, charged that López Cruz had made libelous statements against the party's CEN, and spearheaded a vote to oust him. In addition, the national party expelled the eleven PRD deputies who refused to vacate their seats, including Heredia Damián, one of López Obrador's first supporters. López Cruz and Padilla Herrera are convinced that Romero Oropeza took the action because the PRD local deputies were not members of his team. López Cruz, who had obtained the material that demonstrated Madrazo's outrageous expenditures in 1994, was embittered by López Obrador's toleration of Romero Oropeza's clandestine actions against him.[44]

Meanwhile, López Obrador sought to have the Federal Electoral Tribunal (TEPJF) annul PRI victories in Guerrero (February 15, 1999), Hidalgo (February 22, 1999), and Quintana Roo (February 22, 1999). On behalf of his party, he stated that it should recognize "no spurious elected officials and no one who had not been chosen in free and clean elections." He accused the Government Ministry of mobilizing Guatemalans to vote in Quintana Roo for the PRI's shady nominee, Mario Villanueva Madrid.[45] With respect to Guerrero, López Obrador implored Zedillo to "clean up" the election, "to prevent eliminating the electoral route as the peaceful option for the renovation of elected officials, because if he did not do so there would be no peace in either the state or in the country."[46]

AMLO CHALLENGES FOBAPROA

As party chief, López Obrador became obsessed with the Banking Fund for the Protection of Savings, known as Fobaproa.[47] In 1990 the government created this agency to administer deposit insurance as part of the bank privatization program. During the financial crisis of 1995–96, Fobaproa took over $12 billion of bad loans from seven failed banks (of the eighteen that were privatized), encouraged foreign institutions to become minority investors in other shaky banks, and accepted some of the worst loans from the stronger banks' balance sheets. Assumption of a bad loan meant that Fobaproa allowed the bank to write off 25 percent of the value of the asset in exchange for government paper worth 75 percent of its original value. "The portfolio bought by Fobaproa was acquired with discretionary powers of government officials and coziness between bank owners in officials," according to PRD deputy Carlos Heredia Zubieta.[48]

Fobaproa's inexperienced staff, which hoped to cover a major share of the government's exposure by auctioning off assets, found that guaranteed loans garnered no more than seventeen cents on the dollar. Zedillo needed legislative approval to assume more than $65 billion in bad loans, the equivalent of 14 percent of GDP. After protracted debate, a majority of PRI and PAN legislators endorsed this deeply flawed measure in late 1998. They justified their votes on the grounds that it was imperative to prop up the nation's wobbly banking system to prevent another economic debacle.

Muñoz Ledo, the PRD leader of the lower house, decried the legislation as "fascist-style trickery."[49] López Obrador also lambasted the congressional action.

IMPACT OF OPERATION CASABLANCA

Why did el Peje latch onto this issue? To begin with, PRD activists and citizens alike were outraged at U.S. involvement in the 1998 "Operation Casablanca," which disclosed linkages between the Cali and Juárez drug cartels and twelve of Mexico's largest banks. U.S. undercover agents lured Mexican bankers to the United States, arrested twenty-two of these officials, and seized six tons of illegal drugs and $35 million in suspected drug money. Washington raised hackles by failing to notify Mexican officials of the venture until shortly before Attorney General Janet Reno held a news conference.[50]

This clandestine move encouraged Alfonso Ramírez Cuellar, leader of El Barzón debtors' movement that was gravitating into the PRD's magnetic field, to examine the Fobaproa bailout closely. Also probing this initiative was Marcelo Ebrard Casaubon, an independent deputy who would become the PRD's successful candidate for D.F. mayor in 2006. The two provided information to López Obrador, who began to excoriate the plan, which Zedillo—with PRI and PAN votes—had hoped to move quietly through the Congress.

In mid-1998 Javier Moreno Valle, a tennis-playing friend of Salinas who ran a financial boutique, hosted a dinner at his home in Lomas. The purpose of the soirée was to pressure the PRD president to mute his criticism of Fobaproa. In addition to López Obrador, Mayor Cuauhtémoc Cárdenas and his son Lázaro were among the guests. Also on hand was Javier's brother, General Rafael Moreno Valle—a prominent PRI politician who had served as a senator, governor, cabinet member, and head of the Mexican Red Cross. Javier Moreno Valle proposed striking a deal with the PRD: approximately twenty-five people might be prosecuted for financial crimes, bankers would take back some of their bad loans, and the government would assume the rest of their obligations. After listening for a while, López Obrador casually stood up to light a cigarette and, while looking for an ashtray, said, "[The bankers] want everything, don't they?" before leaving the house.[51]

To prove that his position had popular backing, el Peje organized an unofficial referendum on August 30, 1998. More than 95 percent of the nearly 3.5 million citizens who participated in this poll opposed the use of public monies to rescue the banks. The results confirmed López Obrador as the number-one critic of Fobaproa.

Foes castigated the balloting, which one scholar called "equivalent to Soviet style elections or plebiscites organized by Saddam

Hussein to boast that he counted on the support of 102 percent of the Iraqi population."[52]

Despite the tally, in late 1998 PRI and PAN legislators approved the replacement of Fobaproa with a new banking regulatory agency, the Institute for the Protection of Bank Savings (IPAB). The PAN obtained two concessions for its support. It blocked former finance secretary Guillermo Ortiz and Eduardo Fernández, ex-head of the National Banking and Securities Commission (CNBV) from sitting on the IPAB board. They argued that both men held office when Fobaproa shouldered the burden. The government also agreed that Fobaproa's liabilities would not automatically become public liabilities. Each year, Congress would have to authorize bonds to refinance Fobaproa's debt.

Enactment of the legislation did nothing to quiet López Obrador. To the contrary, he continued to scorn the evils of Fobaproa with the fervor of a fundamentalist preacher railing against sin. A number of factors explain his position.

First, while bashing Pemex enabled López Obrador to recruit a broad following in Tabasco, and while the revelation of the PRI's prodigious spending in 1994 further increased his visibility, Fobaproa presented him with an opportunity to transcend state matters to capitalize on a major, complex national issue. He placed himself in the tradition of Lázaro Cárdenas, who had used nationalistic rhetoric to condemn the predatory actions of foreign oil interests in 1938.

Second, this extremely complicated issue was unfathomable to the average person. This allowed the PRD chief to explain it in black-and-white terms (corrupt men were being rewarded for irresponsible behavior; the people, or "victims," were being exploited). He also gave vivid examples of alleged abuses by Fobaproa's pampered beneficiaries. He claimed that the shareholders of Grupo Sidek—a construction giant and the largest benefactor of the scheme—had rented a medieval castle with four stone towers, a flower-filled garden, and a cave filled with exquisite wines. They stayed at this citadel outside Paris en route to African hunting safaris.[53]

Third, the issue allowed el Peje to present himself as a champion of the people determined to put an end to backroom deals between self-serving neoliberal politicians and jowly rich bankers. The Zedillo administration claimed that bank secrecy statutes prevented it from providing legislators with specific information about debts and debtors whose loans had been transferred from the banks to the rescue fund. López Obrador disagreed, calling for public accountability, full disclosure of wrongdoing, and compensation for the medium-sized and small debtors who had been victims of the economic crisis.[54] To drive home his point, in 1998 he caused an uproar by publicizing the names, obtained by a computer hacker, of thousands of individuals and firms believed to have profited from Fobaproa.

Fourth, the controversial bailout permitted the political messiah to show a trail of wrongdoing in conspiratorial terms. Because former Banco Unión president Cabal Peniche and other tycoons who profited from the bailout had contributed lavishly to the PRI, el Peje alleged that Madrazo and his party had used these funds to win the 1994 elections. In exchange, the government threw a lifeline to mismanaged banks.

Fifth, Fobaproa's many dimensions meant that there were issues to raise and culprits to skewer in multiple press conferences, as discussion of the proposal dragged out over several years. Opposition legislators demanded that the rescue package include an independent audit of the bailout fund and selected Michael Mackey, a Canadian certified public accountant, to carry out the task. In the words of Pulitzer Prize–winning journalists, his audit uncovered "a system riddled with fraud and incest."[55] Loans of some $4.4 billion were made by one bank to another bank and its customers; illegal loans totaled $638 million; and irregular loans amounted to $7.7 billion. Mackey encountered severe resistance from the government, which would not allow him to examine Cabal Peniche's fund in one of his banks that supposedly funneled secret contributions to the Zedillo campaign.

López Obrador had a field day decrying the cost of the scheme, originally estimated as $65 billion and later elevated to $150 billion. He pounced on the subsequent purchase of the banks by foreigners, once they had jettisoned their bad loans: Citigroup acquired Banamex; Banco Bilbao Vizcaya Argentaria bought Bancomer; Scotiabank took over Inverlat; Banco Santander purchased Serfín; and HSBC bought Bital.

Sixth, that most lawmakers had voted for the legislation gave López Obrador a chance to tar the PAN and the PRI with the same brush. Both parties, he averred, were responsible for the "holdup" of the Mexican people.[56] López Obrador continually linked Fox with the "sinister, obscure forces of neoliberalism"—overlooking the fact that as governor of Guanajuanto, the future president had blasted the action.

Seventh, Fobaproa served as an all-purpose whipping boy. In early September 2004, for example, the mayor reminded journalists at his morning news conference that the federal government would commit 100,000 million pesos in its next budget to pay the interest on Fobaproa, debts accumulated by the energy sector, and funds borrowed to take over failed privatized toll roads. This amount, he insisted, was twice the budget of the D.F. and six times that of UNAM.[57] He used Fobaproa to oppose all tax increases.

Eighth, Fobaproa exploded at a time when "globalization schemes began to crack."[58] The Asian (1997) and Russian (1998) financial crises had taken place, and Nobel Prize–winning economist Joseph Stiglitz and others were slamming the "Washington Consensus," whereby Western nations, the IMF, and the World

Bank extolled the virtues of free trade and economic liberalization. Criticism focused on the hefty stipends that developed countries lavished on well-heeled farmers who competed with their less efficient counterparts in the developing world. Stiglitz observed that the U.S. government provided $4 billion a year to cotton producers whose output was worth only $3.5 billion.[59] Such arguments lent credence to López Obrador's attacks on Salinas and the other technocrats who had hitched Mexico's fortunes to the global economy.

Ninth, Fobaproa allowed el Peje to present himself as the savior of masses vis-à-vis Salinas and his self-serving cronies. He ridiculed his evil adversaries for deriding public expenditures on the poor as "populism or subsidies," while they considered channeling resources to the elite as "development or [a necessary] rescue."[60] He attacked neoliberals in the same way that Jesus drove the moneychangers from the temple. Later, as mayor, he refused to provide security to banks even amid a contagion of robberies.

Finally, he brandished Fobaproa like a whip with which to lash other controversial proposals, such as deferred payments for energy projects under the Pidiregas plan and the autonomy of the CNBV and other financial institutions.

SELECTING AMLO'S SUCCESSOR

López Obrador left the party presidency before his term expired. His official reason was that he wanted to prevent the need to elect the new PRD chief at the same time that the party was nominating its presidential standard-bearer. In fact, he was mulling over his third bid for governor of Tabasco. Even as he lashed Fobaproa, el Peje was conducting the contest for his successor. His insistence on fair elections as PRI president in Tabasco vanished during the intramural contest for the PRD's top position. Fraud abounded in the race among Amalia García, Ortega Martínez, Mario Saucedo, Senator Garavito, and six minor contenders.[61]

All told, the party's electoral oversight committee found irregularities in 1,613 of the 5,800 voting places. The most flagrant violations were changes in the location of polling places, substitution of officials, falsification of tallies, and incomplete documentation. As a result, the party's CEN annulled the election. Rather than take responsibility for the disaster, López Obrador spoke about the "risks of a political opening." "A democratic principle that we will also practice is rectification; if errors are committed, we are going to rectify them openly because this is a self-critical, transparent, and open party," he added.[62] He struck the same self-serving theme in his last speech as party chief: "The decisions at the top—the bargaining among political and bureaucratic elites—may result in a consensus, but [this] is not participatory democracy. Don't forget that democracy is the power of the people, and we don't

TABLE 8. *Comparison of PRD Presidents, 1989–1999*

PRD PRESIDENTS CATEGORIES	CUAUHTÉMOC CÁRDENAS (1989–93)	PORFIRIO MUÑOZ LEDO (1993–96)	ANDRÉS MANUEL LÓPEZ OBRADOR (1996–99)
LEADERSHIP STYLE	Authoritarian, Messianic	Lone Ranger, Impetuous, Arrogant	Authoritarian, Messianic
IDEOLOGICAL ORIENTATION	Revolutionary Nationalism	Center-Left Democratic Socialism	Zealous opposition to Fobaproa and support for the poor
PARTY FINANCES	Controlled finances through his loyalists		Benefited from public financing of parties, but sharply increased debt
ALLIES (INDIVIDUALS)	Michoacán: Leonel Godoy, Cristóbal Arias, Robles Garnica, Francisco Kuri Pérez; N.L.: González Garza Lucas de la Garza; SLP: Moises Rivera D.F.: Samuel de Villar; and Joaquín "La Quina" Hernández Galicia	David Ibarra, Flores Olea, Carlos Fuentes, Jorge Castañeda	Cárdenas (at first), Rosario Robles, René Bejarano, Dolores Padierna, Tabasco group (Octavio Romero Oropeza); Camacho Solis and other ex-PRI activists
ALLIES (GROUPS)	Corriente Democrática; ex-PRT members who formed MAS; CEU-OIR university radicals (Carlos Imaz Gispert; Imanol Ordorika, Rosario Robles, Armando Quintero); Oil Workers Union; CNC (Veracruz)	Los Amalios (ex-PMS); Los Chuchos (ex-PMT)	La CID; and grassroots organizations like El Barzón, Asamblea de Barrios, Frente Popular Francisco Villa
ENEMIES (WITHIN PARTY)	Heberto Castillo, Rincón Gallardo, Muñoz Ledo, Martínez Verdugo	Cárdenas, López Obrador	Cárdenas, Muñoz Ledo, Amalia García, Demetrio Sodi Tijera
ENEMIES (OUTSIDE PARTY)	Most of PRI		Madrazo, Carlos Hank González, traditional *priístas*
RELATIONS WITH PARTY'S "CURRENTS"	Sought to divide and conquer them	Less personalistic than Cárdenas; more conciliatory with respect to strategy, but uncompromising on tactics	Decided preference for la CID
RELATIONS WITH OTHER PARTIES	Skeptical to hostile	Advocated coalition building to create a social democratic force	Eager to reconstitute the PRD as a traditional PRI

TABLE 8 (cont'd). Comparison of PRD Presidents, 1989–1999

PRD PRESIDENTS CATEGORIES	CUAUHTÉMOC CÁRDENAS (1989–93)	PORFIRIO MUÑOZ LEDO (1993–96)	ANDRÉS MANUEL LÓPEZ OBRADOR (1996–99)
RELATIONS WITH PRD LEGISLATORS	Sought to give them marching orders		Left legislative matters to Muñoz Ledo
RELATIONS WITH THE GOVERNMENT	Bad (although he met with Salinas)	Good; worked with Zedillo government on Cofipe	Confrontational; opposed Cofipe; vehemently opposed Fobaproa, the epitome of neoliberalism
INTERNATIONAL RELATIONS	Traveled abroad to maintain his stature as a serious presidential contender; critical of economic globalization	Spearheaded the party's joining the Socialist International	Minimal
INTEREST IN PARTY'S STRUCTURE	Minimal—except to the degree the structure could advance his presidential ambitions	Minimal—more concerned with sweeping national reforms	Minimal—weakened party by paying Brigadas de Sol for campaign work previously done by volunteers; bypassed party activists to recruit non-PRD candidates
QUALITY OF THE CEN	Mixed; largely subservient to Cárdenas	Mixed; controlled by cardenistas	Apparently broad-based but tightly controlled by López Obrador
ELECTORAL SUCCESS	Dramatic losses in the Chamber of Deputies from 138 in 1988 to 41 in 1991	PRD lost ground in presidential contest but increased its number of deputies from 41 to 65	Major advances in (1) Mexico City, where Cárdenas won the mayorship; (2) the Chamber of Deputies (65 to 125); (3) the Senate (8 to 16); and (4) governorships—Zacatecas, Baja California Sur, Tlaxcala (and alliances in Nayarit and Chiapas)
LEGACY	Divisions that meant the PRD was more a collection of tribes than a united organization	Ensured the party increased resources via Cofipe; demonstrated statesmanship; and took PRD into the Socialist International	Provided the party with a competitive presidential candidate

want 'kratos' without 'demos'; we do not want power without the people."[63] In a second election on July 25, García Medina defeated Félix Salgado Macedonia (55 percent to 26.7 percent) and seven other aspirants. Tables 8 and 9 highlight the traits of PRD presidents between 1989 and 1999 and depict the currents in the party in 2006.

PRD President: A "Miracle Worker"

López Obrador lifted the PRD, a political Lazarus, from the dead. He made even more miraculous advances at the national level than those achieved in Tabasco. He reconstituted his party as a haven for converts from the PRI who captured governorships in Zacatecas, Tlaxcala, and Baja California. He also spurred unprecedented PRD gains in Congress, while assisting Cárdenas's successful race for the D.F.'s city hall. His messianic impulses manifested

TABLE 9. *Major PRD Currents in 2007*

CURRENTS	LEADERS	ORIENTATION
Foro Nuevo Sol—FNS (Amalios)	Amalia García Medina, Raymundo Cárdenas Hernández, Eloi Vázquez López, Juan José García Ochoa (D.F.)	Moderate; social democrats
Nueva Izquierda—NI (Chuchos)	Jesús Zambrano Grijalva, Jesús Ortega Martínez, Carlos Navarrete Ruiz, Guadalupe Acosta Naranjo, Isaías Villa González	Moderate; social democrats; best structure among the currents
Izquierda Democrática Nacional—IDN	René Bejarano Martínez, Dolores Padierna Luna, Agustín Guerrero, Javier Hidalgo Ponce, Agustín González Cázares, Alejandra Barrales Martínez, Alfredo Hernández Raigosa, Aleida Álvarez Ruiz, Manuel Oropeza	Leftists; focused in Mexico City and composed of grassroots organizations like the Frente Popular Francisco Villa, the Sindicato Independiente de Trabajadores del GDF Valentín Campa, and the Asociación de Transporte Metropolitano; supporters of López Obrador Pro-Cárdenas
Unidad y renovación—UNiR	Pablo Gómez Álvarez, Armando Quintero (formerly grupo IDEA), Deputy Gilberto Ensástiga Santiago	
Izquierda Social—IS	Martí Batres Guardarrama, Alejandra Barrales Magdalena, Susana Manzanares Córdoba	Radical allies of López Obrador who have bolted the IDN
Associación Cívica Nacional Revolucionaria—ACNR (Cívicos)	Mario Saucedo Pérez, Deputy Francisco Saucedo Pérez	Radical; small leftist group
Red de Izquierda Revolucionaria—Redir	Pablo Franco Hernández, Camilo Valenzuela Fierro (obtained almost one-quarter of vote when challenging Leonel Montaño Cota for the PRD presidency on March 20, 2005)	Radical; small leftist group

themselves in the disdain for the law that he expressed when asked to support the Cofipe political reform. He paid members of the Sun Brigades rather than rely on uncompensated grassroots militants to deliver votes, and he passed over PRD stalwarts to select ex-*priístas* who appeared to be stronger candidates. In 1997 he even permitted Romero Oropeza to purge the PRD in Tabasco, a stinging slap in the face to longtime allies.

In so doing, he again demonstrated his effort to create a yellow-and-black facsimile of the PRI. He pursued a divide-and-conquer strategy, encouraging disputes among the party's currents that would fortify his power and authority as PRD leader. He became the most virulent critic of Fobaproa, a program that he believed embodied all the iniquities of neoliberalism at home and abroad. Yet López Obrador overlooked the domestic and international ramifications of the collapse of the nation's banking system. By pursuing these self-serving interests, el Peje gave momentum to his redemptive mission. He reiterated his faith in the "will of the people" after the fraudulent 1999 intraparty election; and, although he still toyed with a race in Tabasco, he was ready to leave the provinces for Mexico's Jerusalem, the D.F.

THE NEW JERUSALEM

Just as Jerusalem was the Roman command center in Palestine, contemporary Mexico City functions as the main base of the neoliberal legions. Not only did Salinas and his market-oriented successors rule from Mexico City, but the capital also served as the home of the Stock Exchange, the Bank of Mexico, the Finance Ministry, major financial institutions, subsidiaries of multinational firms, and other agents of the abhorrent economic strategy.

In addition, Mexico's capital city functioned as the PRI's amphitheater, where the ruling party flaunted its power and national spectacles were staged before audiences of *defeños,* as the capital's residents are called. Political players dramatized perceived injustices in the D.F. Poorly paid teachers from Oaxaca, disgruntled peasants from Chiapas, UNAM student malcontents, anti-Pemex protestors from Tabasco, and other dissatisfied troupers engaged in street theater in the Zócalo, where they attained press notices, if not cheers, for their cause. Political actors hoped that if they heralded their grievances, high-level impresarios would pay attention to their plight.

Trade unions have been especially active over the past several decades in Mexico. In February 1959 Demetrio Vallejo, a brash, baby-faced communist, led a strike of railway workers that paralyzed the National Railways, the largest of thirteen separate railroad lines. The administration of Adolfo López Mateos (1958–64) quickly agreed to Vallejo's demand for a $28 per month pay increase, but when the union firebrand called a second work stoppage over the government's refusal to extend the settlement to other lines, the army savagely rang down the curtain on his show. Police and military units smashed the strike, killed some union members, arrested hundreds more, and allowed the state company to fire thousand of "radicals." In 1963 authorities sentenced Vallejo to a sixteen-year prison term under the nation's antisubversion law. He was released eight years later.

In 1965 doctors launched a strike to protest low pay and what they called the "proletarianization" of their profession. The health-care providers believed that their interests were being neglected inasmuch as blue-collar workers outpaced them in social benefits. When hard-line President Díaz Ordaz (1964–70) balked at these demands, Ernesto Uruchurtu, whose bravura performance made him one of the most popular "regents"[1] in D.F. history, agreed to sign individual contracts with the strikers.[2]

Hopes for administrative solutions to the problems of political thespians were dashed on October 2, 1968, when Díaz Ordaz's subordinates ordered troops to fire on unarmed civilians gathered in the Plaza de las Tres Culturas. The president was determined to have peace for the Olympic Games, which Mexico was hosting in November 1968, and he tried to justify the massacre, which snuffed out hundreds, possibly thousands, of lives, by invoking the menace of "armed provocateurs" and "communist subversives." The chief executive believed this excuse would seem credible in light of the U.S. anticommunist war in Vietnam and the violent actions of French university students. Evidence mounted that there was no external threat in Mexico, that the protesters were students and other citizens with legitimate complaints, and that the regime had laid plans to crack down on its detractors. Documented accounts of a giant funeral pyre for the dead and the widespread torture of prisoners further darkened the ruling party's image.[3]

The October 1968 bloodbath radicalized students, intellectuals, journalists, opposition party members, non-PRI trade unionists, and others, who joined or founded organizations to depose the ruling party. It also affirmed the importance of the Federal District as a venue for alternative political scenarios. At least one guerrilla movement, the 23rd of September League, made its debut at this time.[4] Various social democratic, Anarco-Syndicalist, Maoist, Christian, and nationalist ideologies infused the nonviolent groups and gave rise to a new generation of antiestablishment performers.

During Hank González's 1976–82 term as mayor, the construction of Line 3 of the metro and Ejes Viales Norte 1 and 2 sparked protests. These paled in comparison, however, to those that burst forth several years after the flamboyant *profesor* left city hall.

Although the capital remained the primary arena for rallies and protests, the nation's linkage to the global economy diminished the ability of the PRI's city and national leaders to solve domestic problems. Anonymous decision makers—often scrutinizing computer screens thousands of miles away—increasingly determined capital flows, exchange rates, and primary product prices. A prime example of this reliance on the international system occurred as Mexico became a major oil exporter in the late 1970s. President López Portillo depended heavily on petroleum revenues to fund the extravagant spending of a government redolent of corruption. Mexico's foreign debt skyrocketed, and the fizzling of the oil boom in 1981 drove the nation to the brink of bankruptcy.

Only a $10 billion rescue package, assembled in August 1982 by the Reagan administration in concert with other industrialized nations, the IMF, the Bank of International Settlements, and private banks, kept Mexico solvent. The twenty-eight-year-old López Obrador regarded these international financial obligations as illegitimate. After all, bankers from the United States, western Europe, and Japan had lavished loans on Mexico during the halcyon days of the late 1970s. Such credit enriched domestic banks and the corporations they controlled. The Tabascan deplored kowtowing to self-serving financial elites and, as mentioned earlier, advocated a plebiscite to allow the people to determine whether the foreign commitment should be honored.

Although López Portillo did not renege on the debt, he too was infuriated by the bailout, which compromised Mexico's sovereignty. He sought to burnish his nationalistic credentials by expropriating the country's banks on September 1, 1982. In his last state of the nation address, he justified this action on the grounds that, "in the last few years, a group of Mexicans who were led, advised and backed by private banks . . . extracted more money from the country than all the empires since the beginning of our history."[5]

Meanwhile, de la Madrid, who had assumed the presidency three months later, began to whittle away the benefits that had accrued to the public. Among other things, he raised the price of energy, dietary staples, and transportation. The rapidly deteriorating conditions chilled foreign investment, diminished the peso's value, boosted the inflation rate, and expanded unemployment. The national crisis fell especially hard on shopkeepers, white-collar workers, lower-level bureaucrats, and middle-class professionals such as doctors, teachers, and government workers. Economist Carlos Tello found that between 1982 and 1985 real salaries declined 65 percent, joblessness rose from 5 to 15 percent, and housing shortages reached a new high.[6] By early 1985 the National Coordinator of the Popular Urban Movement (Conamup) had begun to attack the government. Groups representing small industries and commerce in the capital joined with popular neighborhood organizations to demand a change in macroeconomic strategy. The antiregime sentiment manifested itself in the 1985 elections, in which the PRI garnered only 42.63 percent of the ballots cast in the D.F.—almost 6 percent less than six years before and twenty-two points below its national level. The abstention rate, which approached 45 percent citywide, reached 50 percent in some highly mobilized areas.[7]

On September 19, 1985, "a mighty blow from hell"[8] struck Mexico City in the form of an earthquake that registered 8.1 on the Richter scale; a second major tremor hit the capital area the following day. De la Madrid's vacillation in response to this disaster cost the PRI dearly in the D.F., particularly in the devastated thirteen-square-mile central zone. It undermined the legitimacy of the chief executive and the single-party apparatus over which he presided. The paternalistic regime failed to take care of its people in their greatest moment of need, and the PRI's approval level took a nosedive.

Mayor Ramón Aguirre Velázquez and his entourage minimized the loss of human lives and property. Secretary of Urban Development and the Environment Guillermo Carrillo Arena claimed that "the only serious damage is to the telephones." Several days later, with thousands of homeless people living in the open, the Sedue chief asserted that "there are no disaster victims in the streets. The real disaster is the collapsed buildings."[9] No doubt he and the mayor were trying to curb panic, but to many denizens of ravaged areas, the government seemed engaged in a "perverse effort to belittle their losses."[10]

The earthquakes killed at least ten thousand people and left tens of thousands homeless. In the wake of this disaster, any ward politician worth his patronage allotment would have clamped on a hard hat, rolled up his sleeves, and waded into the smoking debris. Yet, as Mexicans from every walk of life organized to rescue family members, neighbors, and fellow workers, de la Madrid struck one diplomat as more of an "accountant scrutinizing a balance sheet" than a concerned patriarch of a tormented national family. The president appeared neither at a press conference called after the first quake nor, after the second shock, on the balcony of the National Palace to offer sympathy and succor to grieving families assembled below in the Zócalo.

Soon he became the butt of bitter jokes. "Why did de la Madrid make only twelve visits to devastated sites?" According to cynical survivors in the hard-hit Tlatelolco neighborhood: "Because he owns only a dozen leather jackets"—a snide reference to the sartorial elegance displayed during televised appearances in afflicted zones. In addition, the chief executive failed to activate his own political party. "The vaunted organizational talents of the PRI were nowhere in evidence. The party's labor and agrarian wings, which on numerous occasions had convoked hundreds of thousands of trade unionists and peasants for political rallies, failed to mobilize anybody to aid the earthquake victims."[11]

Colorless technocrats on de la Madrid's team lacked either popularity or well-cultivated ties to the people, and many old guard leaders proved incompetent. This may explain their refusal to allow the army to implement its 188-page DN-III emergency plan in response to *El Grande,* as the earthquakes were known, even though the scheme had worked well in the 1982 eruption of a volcano in distant Chiapas. The army shuffled into the streets several hours after the earthquake, yet Mayor Aguirre refused to deploy troops in the rescue efforts for fear that he would "lose control of the city." De la Madrid shared this concern and limited the armed forces' role to preventing looting. The president may have feared either that the military was ill prepared for an urban crisis or that an effective performance in the media-infested capital would have whetted the appetite of the ever-more professional army for a larger political role.[12] Meanwhile, the navy's reputation sparkled, as the collapse of its headquarters brought forth sweaty, grimy, blue-uniformed officers relentlessly hunting for survivors in the ruins of their own and nearby buildings.[13]

In the aftermath of the catastrophe, the PRI administration continued to lose favor. For instance, law enforcement officers extracted bribes from victims who wanted to cross security lines and search through rubble for loved ones and possessions. These actions, along with the theft of musical instruments of dead mariachis from a collapsed apartment building near Garibaldi Plaza, contributed to the erosion of public confidence in the willingness and ability of law enforcement personnel to assist the city's distressed. "The tortured bodies of prisoners were found in the wreckage of the Federal District's Attorney General's office," according to muckraking writer John Ross. Rather than investigate Attorney General Victoria Adato de Ibarra, authorities systematically thwarted an inquiry into the scandal, and the president promoted her to the National Supreme Court of Justice (SCJN).[14]

De la Madrid's vacillation had political repercussions. These tumultuous events illuminated the incompetence and corruption of PRI officials. Not only had they failed in their efforts after the quake, but their missteps before the catastrophe had exacerbated the suffering. They and their allies had built many of the crumbled edifices, cutting corners on building materials and construction standards. Observers were incredulous over the collapse of the twenty-five-building IMSS National Medical Center, Latin America's most sophisticated hospital. Even the highly regarded Cardiology Hospital broke apart, killing seventy doctors, nurses, and other staff members. Throughout the complex, several hundred patients were smothered or crushed, and thousands had to be evacuated.[15]

Two journalists claimed that Carrillo Arena, an arrogant PRI stalwart, had approved construction plans for the Juárez Hospital, which fell like a house of cards. How, they asked, did a government official like Arena accumulate the 15 billion peso fortune set forth on his disclosure statement? Before the earthquake, the comptroller-general had already begun investigating him for suspicious land dealing in Acapulco.[16]

A product of the old school, Carrillo Arena indulged in the fantasy that the revolutionary party could regain the people's esteem through traditional machinations. For instance, the PRI substituted its own nameplates on thirty-six housing units constructed by the International Red Cross for earthquake survivors. So intense was the antigovernment sentiment that the army surrounded Los Pinos to prevent attacks on the compound.

Mexico City residents had to cope with the crisis with minimal official help. Taxis became ambulances, ham-radio operators configured a communications network, and agile young people—known as "moles" or *topos*—dug through the rubble with their hands looking for victims. "We realized for the first time that we could help each other without relying on the government," remembered one community activist.[17]

Even though de la Madrid had first refused offers of American help, President Reagan sent his wife, Nancy, as a visible symbol of empathy for the sufferers. Accidentally separated from her security detail, the First Lady was trying to comfort victims when a huge smoke-blackened figure suddenly materialized from the ruins and threw his arms around her. It was tenor Placido Domingo, who was clawing through the rubble in hopes of finding family members buried in the wreckage of the Tlatelolco housing complex. Given such a lack of official aid, the importance of grassroots organizations—later crucial to López Obrador's success—increased greatly in the wake of the tragedy.

GRASSROOTS ORGANIZATIONS

Although bands of citizen activists had existed in the past, they exhibited neither the numbers nor the strength of the associations that surfaced after the earthquakes. Most of these groups laid aside their political affiliations to work cooperatively on behalf of the tens of thousands of victims. The glue that held them together was their growing hatred of the socially indifferent PRI and the Mexican state.[18] On October 24, forty groups joined forces in the Unified Coordination of Victims (CUD), which became the intermediary between neighborhoods and the government. Among its founders were Dr. Cuauhtémoc Abarca Chávez, a spokesman for tenants in the devastated 103-building Tlatelolco project; Armando Ramírez Palomo, director of the Union of Neighbors in the Colonia Guerrero; Alejandro Varas Orozco, head of the September 19 Union of Neighbors and Victims (UVyD-19), which represented residents of the Roma neighborhood; Miguel Angel Armas, leader of the Neighborhood Union of the Colonia Morelos; and Ernesto Jiménez Olín, chief of the Valle Gómez People's Union.

Guillermo Flores Velasco, a key advisor to Dr. Abarca, spearheaded the incredibly efficient reconstruction accomplished by the Neighborhood Union of the Colonia Doctores. He was aided by Ernestina Godoy Ramos and the National Association of

Democratic Lawyers. Working together, they provided the victims in their neighborhood with housing, food, and clothing, as well as free legal, medical, and childcare services. Also visible was Marco Rascón Córdoba, head of both the Coordination of the Tlatelolco Buildings (Coordinadora de Cuartos de Azotea de Tlatelolco) and the Committee of Struggle for the Tenants of the Center (Comité de Lucha Inquilinaria del Centro). Rascón, who adopted the sobriquet "Superbarrio" and donned tights and a cape to complement the role, recruited not only legitimate renters for his group but also poor people to whom managers had illegally rented living space in laundry rooms and storage areas in the crumbled Tlatelolco structures.

Latecomers to the CUD were teacher-activist René Bejarano and his politically astute wife, Dolores Padierna, who would later serve as apostles of López Obrador. The couple, along with allies like student leader Martí Batres Guadarrama, mobilized the homeless and street vendors through a supposedly nongovernmental organization, New Tenochititlán Popular Union (UPNT). They were especially prominent in la Morelos, el Centro, la Lagunilla, Garibaldi, and other neighborhoods, or *colonias,* in the downtown Cuauhtémoc borough.

By early 1986 the CUD spoke for fifty thousand sufferers from the center of Mexico City. For the first time, a nongovernmental entity had united large numbers of middle- and working-class citizens. Before the tragedy, the PRI had orchestrated mass rallies of party members. "The mobilizations after the earthquakes, by contrast, were initiated from below, and not sanctioned by the state."[19] Scarcely a day passed without a protest, and if the government failed to respond, CUD leaders threatened to disrupt the World Cup soccer matches scheduled to begin in May 1986.

MANUEL CAMACHO'S ROLE

The president selected Manuel Camacho to take charge of the reconstruction. Having earned a reputation as a trusted troubleshooter for de la Madrid, he assumed responsibility for handling the mounting agitation in the metropolis after the earthquakes. As undersecretary for regional development in the Ministry of Budget and Planning (SPP), he had accompanied the president on trips around the country. In addition, he negotiated a truce between Education Secretary Jesús Reyes Heroles and STPRM boss Hernández Galicia, who wanted to name the director of the federal technical institute in his hometown. In the mid-1980s Camacho had defused a move by radical teachers to seize the building in which the president and the state governor were meeting in Tuxtla Gutiérrez, Chiapas; and he served as a conciliator when San Luis Potosí governor Carlos Jonguitud Barrios withheld education funds from Salvador Nava, the anti-PRI mayor of the state capital.

Scorned by Camacho, Mexico City regent Aguirre Velázquez fell out of favor with the president in light of his blundering response to the disaster. He also had poor relations with SPP secretary Salinas, who was emerging as the strongman of the cabinet. Thus, de la Madrid and Salinas placed responsibility for rebuilding devastated parts of the city in the hands of Camacho, then an ardent Salinas ally who believed that he was destined to become president.

In April 1986 Camacho received a call from de la Madrid's private secretary, saying that his boss wanted to see him at once. The SPP undersecretary thought that the chief executive might offer him the ambassadorship in Washington, as rumor had it that Jorge Espinosa de los Reyes would be stepping down from that post. Instead, "he invited me to become part of his cabinet," Camacho recalled, replacing Carrillo Arena at Sedue. While he was prepared to serve as the president saw fit, Camacho responded that he "knew nothing about architecture and engineering." De la Madrid asked him how he might be of help. The young man responded that he had a background in political negotiations and an interest in the environment. "Why do you think I summoned you?" the chief executive shot back.[20] Upon accepting the position, Camacho was determined to accomplish a 180-degree change in the government's policy. Instead of giving orders, he said, "I would listen to the people."[21]

Salinas circumvented Aguirre Velázquez and the PRI president in the capital to provide funds directly to Camacho. He in turn relied on engineer Guillermo Guerrero Villalobos to oversee technical matters, Jorge Gamboa de Buen to take charge of financial affairs, and Manuel Aguilera to serve as the intermediary with social groups.

In contrast to the authoritarian Carrillo Arena, the new Sedue chief spent up to nineteen hours a day, seven days a week, listening to the problems, needs, and complaints of average citizens, who did not hesitate to garnish their views with vulgar language, especially when referring to the PRI.

After several false starts—an ill-considered expropriation gambit, an attempt to move center-city victims to the periphery of the D.F., and the victims' resistance to small, cookie-cutter houses—the reconstruction began. In view of the PRI's emphatic lack of credibility, Camacho and Aguilera set up a parallel structure constituted largely of groups representing earthquake victims. In 2000 these organizations provided the base for López Obrador's successful mayoral campaign—once again underscoring the earthquakes' impact on reconfiguring the D.F.'s political landscape.

NEGOTIATIONS PAY DIVIDENDS

After weeks of negotiations that involved more than a hundred groups, Camacho persuaded the CUD to sign a Pact for Democratic

Agreement on Reconstruction, which established the ground rules for rebuilding the devastated zone. For new housing, the World Bank provided a loan of $400 million, an amount matched by Mexico's government. Meanwhile, most of the $50 million contributed to a National Reconstruction Fund and the $14 million donated from abroad were earmarked for rebuilding hospitals and schools.

Not only did Camacho have to address the needs of half a million homeless people, he had to take into account their attachment to their devastated neighborhoods. In downtown Guerrero and Morelos, many people lived in fetid, crowded tenements but resisted relocating to the suburbs. Some of these victims were among the hundred thousand people who inhabited camps of makeshift shacks.

By the first anniversary of the crisis, the government had satisfied the needs of 28 percent of the homeless—with the promise to take care of the rest of the victims by year's end. The crowd greeted de la Madrid with boos, however, when he entered the Azteca Stadium to inaugurate the World Cup. Still, Camacho's endeavors yielded success, for only one demonstration took place during the competition: a footrace organized by the victims in support of rebuilding their communities.[22]

After reaching an accord with the victims' organizations, Camacho sought to enlist the participation of the Civic Solidarity Center. This organization, founded by José Barroso Chávez, was composed of major business chambers and conservative Catholics who sought to channel relief supplies to the disadvantaged. At first, center members recoiled from affixing their signatures to a document to which the radical leftists had agreed. The tide turned when Lorenzo Servije, the multimillionaire head of the Bimbo food conglomerate, said, in effect: "If this young man has been able to convince the Left to agree and wants us to be part of this success, we have an obligation to do so." Once he signed, his colleagues followed suit.[23]

Camacho began his work in the city with excellent ties to de la Madrid and Salinas but with no political base of his own. In a few years, the urban popular movement and the leading members of these organizations would advance his own political agenda in the D.F. Thanks to their ties to Camacho's team, CUD activists like René Bejarano, Dolores Padierna, Javier Hidalgo Ponce, Alejandro Vargas, René Arce Islas, Ramirez Paloma, and Rascón were involved in decisions about the design and location of new housing, who would live in these units, and which merchants could sell their wares on streets and lots cleared of rubble. They also developed links with successful companies that participated in the reconstruction and reportedly acquired fortunes in the process.[24] Years later, 180 families in the Tláhuac neighborhood alleged that Centro Construction Company, a New Tenochititlán affiliate, had provided them with defective housing for which it would not take responsibility. "To obtain our homes, we had to give our support to Dolores and René in all of the marches and meetings that they organized," and to back the candidacies of many *perredistas* who, "after they won election, forgot about us," complained a spokesman for group.[25]

All told, Sedue sponsored the erection of forty-eight thousand prefabricated housing units in the Centro and other stricken areas.[26] In addition, Rascón, who later organized the Neighborhood Assemblies (*Asamblea de Barrios*), persuaded the Commerce Ministry to provide him with five thousand tanks of cooking gas, which he distributed to residents for a fee.[27]

Camacho claims to have shunned the violence-prone Francisco Villa Popular Front (FPFV), which concentrated on areas outside the devastated zone. This radical group, led by Eli Homero Aguilar Ramírez, illegally occupied a portion of Tlalpan, a key ecological enclave that absorbs much of the city's rainwater. It justified this seizure on the grounds that real estate companies were seeking to develop the sensitive area. When the government displaced the invaders, the FPFV staged a demonstration of more than three thousand people in the Zócalo. After protracted negotiations, authorities gave the group land in El Molino zone of Iztapalapa, where the organization now concentrates its activities.[28] As mayor, López Obrador drew elements of the FPFV into his orbit.

Camacho cultivated the press, giving rise to a plethora of favorable news items about his accomplishments. His enemies took umbrage at this sympathetic treatment and privately criticized him for "buying articles" and "using the catastrophe" to pave a road to Los Pinos. While the Sedue secretary basked in the positive coverage, he worried about overshadowing the president. He became acutely concerned when Rogelio Naranjo, *El Universal*'s prize-winning satirist, published a cartoon depicting a crumbling statute of de la Madrid being held up by Camacho's scaffolding. The young man phoned Los Pinos to apologize for the caricature and to assure him that he knew nothing about it beforehand. The president curtly thanked him for calling.[29]

UNIVERSITY ACTIVISM

No sooner had Camacho begun to register success with earthquake victims than he found himself confronted with a strike by UNAM students in late 1986. Spearheaded by Carlos Imaz Gispert, Imanol Ordorika Sacristán, Martí Batres Guadarrama, and Antonio Santos, the University Student Council (CEU) opposed a move by the rector, Jorge Carpizo McGregor, to "elevate educational excellence." By this he meant eliminating automatic admission to UNAM from its network of preparatory schools, raising the absurdly low tuition rate, and giving the administration greater control over the institution's governance. After twenty-two days Carpizo was forced to retreat. Years later, many of these activists cast their lot with el Peje.

1988 PRESIDENTIAL CAMPAIGN

CUD affiliates, which had helped Camacho distribute housing and quell unrest, were divided over whether to cast their lot with Cárdenas in the presidential showdown with Salinas. Armas, Ernesto Jiménez, Javier Hidalgo, and Flores Velasco urged backing the FDN standard-bearer, while Varas, Abarca, and Palomo opposed such support, possibly because of their allegiance to Camacho. The cunning Bejarano, who had received financial support from the city's PRI regime, also backed Cárdenas. This division spurred the CUD's breakup. Still, Cárdenas captured 49.2 percent of the vote, including thirty-nine of the city's forty electoral districts. The FDN won only one congressional seat, though, because its member parties failed to form coalitions for legislative posts.

Following the acrimonious election, Camacho skillfully negotiated with opposition parties to ensure that Congress—which acted as an Electoral College in presidential elections—validated Salinas's victory. Once in office, the new chief executive, who had garnered only 27.2 percent of the ballots cast in the capital, appointed Camacho as regent of the D.F., then a cabinet post. His agenda included continuing the rebuilding initiative, cultivating neighborhood organizations, preserving stability, and laying the groundwork for a PRI rebound in the 1991 midterm contests. To assist his ally, Salinas lavished resources on the capital.

CAMACHO AS REGENT

Camacho proceeded to build a coherent team. His top lieutenant was Marcelo Ebrard, whose boyish face and ruthless behavior earned him the nickname "Chucky," after Hollywood's serial killer doll. In 2006 Ebrard succeeded López Obrador as mayor. Other members of Camacho's entourage included Manuel Aguilera as secretary-general of government; Juan Enríquez Cabot as director of Metropolitan Services of the Federal District (Servimet); and Roberto Campa Cifrián, a young PRI stalwart who had served as deputy delegate in Iztapalapa and ran for the presidency in 2006.

They spent $3 billion monitoring emissions and lowering the level of pollution, thanks in part to the introduction of the "Day Without Driving" program. They restored the Xochimilco gardens, expanded the metro, promoted tourism, and began rehabilitating the historic zone. They reduced the number of robberies and broadened the tax base of a city that had depended on the federal government for 20 percent of its revenue.

More important, they took advantage of the Representative Assembly of the Federal District (ARDF), which began operations in 1988. Camacho said "the Assembly . . . was a laboratory in which to develop political agreements and not a battering ram against the regime."[30] Although it was an advisory body, the ARDF afforded elected members a chance to voice their grievances and blow off steam. Significantly, it provided an arena for the mayor, who was preparing to seek the presidency, to cultivate the Left at a time when Salinas was repressing the PRD. The mayor also used his loyalists in the assembly to attack political enemies such as the director of the city's antidelinquency department.

Although Salinas remained anathema to the PRD, he greatly improved his public standing through bold actions. In January 1989 he imprisoned the supposedly "untouchable" STPRM leader Hernández Galicia. He also ousted Carlos Jonguitud Barrios, chieftain of the venal 1.2-million-member National Union of Educational Workers (SNTE), replacing him with Elba Esther Gordillo Morales, who was destined to play a visible, controversial, and decisive role during the 2006 presidential campaign.

In mid-February, in order to demonstrate that labor leaders were not the only government targets, authorities charged stockbroker Eduardo Legorreta Chauvet, a member of a prominent banking family, with securities fraud and trading in bogus treasury certificates. Later in the year, a Mexican court convicted two drug kingpins of masterminding the murder of U.S. Drug Enforcement Administration agent Enrique Camarena.

NATIONAL SOLIDARITY PROGRAM

Salinas shrewdly took advantage of Pope John Paul II's May 1989 visit to Mexico to launch the National Solidarity Program (Pronasol). This antipoverty venture, commonly called "Solidarity," germinated from interviews that Salinas had conducted in the Mexican countryside while preparing his Harvard thesis in the mid-1970s. He discovered that grassroots leaders favored projects when they and their neighbors—not bureaucrats in Mexico City—identified local priorities and helped to accomplish desired goals.[31]

The disbursement of funds from the capital to beneficiaries bypassed local politicians and other corporatist big shots, even though huge outlays poured into PRD strongholds. Yet Salinas designed the venture to foster a new constituency composed of the hundred thousand local committees indebted to the president who had improved their lives. One analyst noted that "Pronasol point[ed] the way to a kind of neo-corporatism which could modernize clientelism by giving it roots not only in the trade unions, as in the past, but also at the territorial level and by giving political weight to the new social actors who have emerged from the neighborhood associations."[32]

The PRI took advantage of the popularity of the Pronasol program. "If Pronasol were pork, the PRI owned all the pigs," observed scholar Kathleen Bruhn. Bruhn also recounts an exchange between two Mexicans. One complained that the PRI was using Pronasol to buy votes; the other responded, "Well, finally the vote is *worth* something!"[33]

Salinas also viewed Solidarity's social infrastructure as a possible trampoline from which he might vault to the presidency in 2000, provided his successor managed to change the Constitution's ban on re-election. At one point he remarked to Camacho, "The only thing we lack is re-election."[34]

While propitiating the masses with Pronasol, Salinas made headway on his neoliberal agenda. He overruled PRI president Colosio to recognize the PAN triumph in the July 1989 gubernatorial race in Baja California, the first statehouse conceded to the opposition. He also proposed political reforms to improve Mexico's image north of the Rio Grande and announced his intentions to explore a free trade accord with the United States. NAFTA drew fire from revolutionary nationalists like Cárdenas and el Peje.

Although the economy was flat as a tortilla during the 1980s, national income growth, which reached 3 percent in 1990, approached 4.5 percent in 1991. At the same time, a labor-business-government stability pact reined in inflation, which had soared to triple digits the year Salinas took office. While hostile toward politicians in general, Mexicans came to admire the bold leadership of a man called the "Atomic ant." He boasted a 62 percent approval rating in early 1991, with only 16 percent of respondents voicing a negative opinion.

Salinas was determined to convert his popularity into a landslide in the upcoming local and congressional elections. He wanted to sweep away the lingering cloud over his 1988 "victory" and enhance his legitimacy as chief executive. When advisers proposed that the PRI should aim for 56 percent of the vote, he ripped up the document that bore this figure and instructed them to use all the resources at the party's and government's disposal to obtain 67 percent. Camacho, who believed this goal was madness (*una locura*), angered the chief executive by telling him that employing traditional methods in the D.F. would turn the clock back to the pre-1985 period and risk a possible social explosion.[35] Camacho refused to introduce Pronasol in Mexico City because he did not want Colosio, the program's director and his rival for the PRI presidential nomination, to benefit from its success.

Still, both men had a vested interest in returning the capital to the PRI column. Even as Colosio was gaining stature, Camacho was convinced that Salinas would select him as the PRI's presidential standard-bearer. Rather than rely on the corporatist sectors in the city, the party introduced "vote promoters," who went door to door and used "everything from bribes to more plausible offers of assistance with legal problems and benefits from government programs" to win votes for the PRI.[36] The PRI even dusted off a ploy called "Operation Tamale," which entailed feeding breakfast to voters before escorting them to the polls. Camacho also recruited the radical peasant group Antorcha Campesina into the PRI and promoted the growth of the Green Ecological Party of Mexico (PVEM).[37]

Thanks largely to Salinas's achievements and, to a lesser degree, to Camacho's work, the PRI made a sharp comeback in the 1991 local and congressional elections in Mexico City, boosting its share of the vote from 27 percent (1988) to 46 percent. Nationwide, the ruling party garnered almost 63 percent of ballots cast. It increased its number of deputies from 260 to 320, while the PAN lost ground (its deputies decreased from 101 to 89), and the PRD made nominal gains (34 to 41). Nationally, the PRI captured all but one of the thirty-two Senate seats that were up for grabs, as well as statehouses in all six states that held gubernatorial contests. This strong showing made López Obrador even more hostile to the president's promarket policies. El Peje would move heaven and earth to oust the PRI from the neoliberal citadel.

GRASSROOTS OUTGROW THE PRI

A medley of factors—the activists' political savvy, their links to the mayor, their ample resources, and their control of tens of thousands of poor people—enabled the New Tenochititlán Popular Union, the Assembly of Neighborhoods, the Francisco Villa Popular Front, and sister organizations to become power brokers. Bejarano, Padierna, and Batres created the Current of the Democratic Left (CID) as the political arm of New Tenochtitlán. The CID, which later affiliated with the PRD, replaced the PRI as the strongest grassroots power in city politics and became a staunch ally of its political and economic benefactor, Camacho. The CID was prepared to join the mayor's quest for Los Pinos. The mayor built another bridge to the Left with his cultivation of Ramón Sosamontes Herreramoro and Jorge Martínez Rocillo.[38]

Then came the political fratricide. On November 28, 1993, the president enraged Camacho by selecting the less experienced Colosio, secretary of social development, which directed Pronasol, as the PRI presidential contender. As a *New York Times* reporter observed, "In the ritual world of Mexican politics, there is no death more horrible than the one Manuel Camacho Solís suffered on Nov. 28. That Sunday . . . Salinas buried a dagger in the life's dream of his old friend."[39] Incensed by this betrayal, Camacho threatened to quit the government, but Salinas convinced him to stay on as foreign secretary.

Camacho was politically reborn a month later when the EZLN rebelled. The foreign secretary criticized Salinas's deployment of the army against the guerrillas. He threatened to resign his cabinet post and join the antigovernment protests unless the president began negotiations with the masked insurgents—with Camacho serving as the peace commissioner. He warned Salinas that only he could prevent the Zapatistas' allies from igniting a social conflagration in Mexico City. In this way the mayor-turned-foreign secretary attempted to enhance his reputation in the hope of displacing Colosio as the PRI's nominee. Camacho's ability to manipulate the popular forces in the D.F. illustrated the potency of these networks.

Frictions had begun to complicate relations between Colosio and the chief executive, who vetoed the candidate's selection of Carlos Rojas Gutiérrez as his campaign manager. In the words of one close observer, there was a "campaign against the campaign," and negative information about Colosio seemed to be issuing from Los Pinos.[40] Nonetheless, Salinas was so irate at Camacho's assertiveness that the foreign secretary asked a close friend to take his children to the U.S. embassy for protection if he did not return from his meeting with the chief executive.[41] With the threat of mass mobilizations, Salinas reluctantly named Camacho peace negotiator. In this role he helped bring about a ceasefire and parleys between the government and the rebels.

VICTORY OF CÁRDENAS, 1997

Further weakening the PRI in Mexico City was the decision to have nonpartisan neighborhood elections in 1996. If candidates ran as individuals, *priístas* would oppose *priístas* in some areas, sharpening personal conflicts and weakening party ties. The practice also sent the message that the PRI was ashamed of its party name.[42] Many future CID-PRD leaders emerged from these contests, including delegation heads in Coyoacán (Miguel Bortolini Castillo) and Cuajimalpa (Ignacio Ruiz López) in the 2003 to 2006 period.

Moreover, in 1997 the PRI's National Political Council decided to nominate its D.F. mayoral candidate on the basis of public opinion polls. President Zedillo, who succeeded Salinas, placed Campa Cifrián in charge of conducting a fair selection process. The potential candidates were Alfredo del Mazo González, former México State governor (1981–86) and former secretary of energy, mines, and decentralized state industries; Antonio González Fernández, former federal deputy and D.F. attorney general (1995–97); and Manuel Jiménez Guzmán, ex-federal deputy and representative to ARDF. The three firms hired to conduct surveys found that del Mazo enjoyed the highest name recognition, with approximately 60 percent, followed by González Fernández, with 30 percent. As it turned out, the pollsters had asked questions that focused on the contenders' past performance rather than on how well they might govern the capital.[43]

Disunity and incompetence afflicted del Mazo's campaign. To make matters worse, street violence, which surged during the 1994–96 recession, continued to plague the PRI because of its ties to corrupt policemen and other lawbreakers. Compounding del Mazo's problems were charges of egregious fraud leveled against incumbent PRI mayor Oscar Espinosa Villarreal.

For its part, the PAN nominated Castillo Peraza, an ex-federal deputy and former party president (1993–96), and a sharp-tongued intellectual from Yucatán. Although he began the race with a robust lead, his populist approach seemed a product of political marketing. Residents of poor neighborhoods and university students often jeered the candidate, even as he began to trade insults with an increasingly antagonistic press corps.

PRD NOMINATION

Cárdenas vied with Muñoz Ledo for the PRD's mayoral nomination in 1997. The Michoacan native obtained the bid as a result of several factors: ubiquitous name recognition, two previous presidential races, support from López Obrador, and, above all, control of the PRD machinery.

The PRD candidate emerged as the number-one critic of Zedillo's economic policy. In the aftermath of the 1994–95 devaluation, he had called for the president's resignation and proposed a "government of national salvation." Such a pluralist, broad-based administration, the PRD leader argued, would spur employment through public works. He also proposed renegotiating Mexico's foreign debt, controlling prices, increasing salaries, and lowering interest rates. His supporters claimed that Cárdenas could provide the leadership that the incumbent lacked. Zedillo rejected this overture and managed to pull the country out of its economic trough by 1997. Still, citizens were eager to punish the PRI for the severe recession. They vividly remembered watching their savings disappear, losing their jobs, paying exorbitant credit card interest rates, and having their automobiles repossessed.

As a consequence, Cárdenas overwhelmed his opponents, winning 47.14 percent of the vote to 25.08 percent for the PRI's del Mazo, 15.27 percent for PAN's Castillo Peraza, and 10.5 percent for a mélange of small parties. The CID contributed to Cárdenas's victory. Despite an earlier clash with Bejarano over an education issue,[44] Cárdenas named Bejarano director-general of the city's government; Padierna became a federal deputy and secretary-general of the PRD in the D.F.; and Batres assumed the leadership of the PRD faction in the ALDF.

Voters also manifested their anger in the midyear congressional balloting. Led by López Obrador, the PRD took advantage of the anti-PRI backlash and, to a lesser degree, Cárdenas's coattails, to register sharp advances. Its numbers increased from 71 to 125 members to become the second-largest party in the Chamber of Deputies. The PRI captured 239 seats and the PAN won 119—with the PT and the PVEM winning seven and five seats, respectively. Even more significant than the PRD's advances was the fact that the PRI lost its legislative majority for the first time since its founding in 1929.

Cárdenas, the first elected mayor of the capital since 1834, entered office as a virtual vice president. Even Zedillo congratulated his antagonist, saying, "this July 6, Mexico took a historic, definitive, and irreversible step toward democratic norms."[45] In the words of journalist Miguel Ángel Granados Chapa, Cárdenas "assumed the post of mayor as if it were a parallel presidency. The enormous expectations that he unleashed upon his arrival in the capital's government constitute an enormous challenge. Never in Mexican history has so much interest been aroused by the inauguration of someone who was not president."[46] Described by Julia Preston and Sam Dillon as a man possessed of a "granitic personal integrity," Cárdenas seemed like a mayor who could combat the rampant crime wave, promote social justice, and provide economic opportunities for the masses. Success in the capital would catapult him into the presidency, where he could reverse or curtail the despised neoliberal initiatives.

At his swearing in on December 5, 1997, the new city leader promised to attack the Herculean problems facing the D.F. He pledged to institute "a new way of governing." He promised to act at once, saying, "The offerings and commitments of the new government will have to be seen and felt in everyday life immediately. We cannot wait to squeeze change from this capital, because if we are passive, better times will never come."[47]

Above all, he promised to halt the frightening level of crime that had engulfed the capital, where some 628 felonies were reported every day. "We are going to take this city away from criminals," he said at his austere swearing-in ceremony. He also took aim at the rampant corruption that had characterized the regime of his predecessors. Under Espinosa, it was alleged that 10 percent of municipal employees were "aviators"—that is, they did no work but flew in twice a month to pick up their paychecks. Bribes, job selling, covert payoffs, and scores of other scams were as ubiquitous as the smog that clouded the city's air. Years later, the former mayor was convicted of embezzlement, sentenced to seven and a half years in prison, and ordered to pay $26 million in reparations. "Corruption will not be tolerated, not in any form," the dour Cárdenas affirmed. He promptly launched a purge of corrupt law enforcement agencies and promised a new dialogue with representatives of the poor and homeless.

A poll published in the newspaper *Reforma* revealed that 71 percent of city residents thought that life would improve under his rule. In spite of his good intentions, Cárdenas underestimated the scope of wrongdoing he faced. For instance, garbage haulers who belonged to the hundred-thousand-member Single Union of D.F. Government Workers (SUTGDF) demanded tips before they would pick up trash. Union bigwigs also owned factories that sold the garments that city employees were required to purchase. When Chief Administrative Officer Ricardo Pascoe Pierce refused to continue buying union items, he became the target of death threats and a kidnapping attempt.[48]

Twenty-two months after entering city hall, Cárdenas stepped down to make his third race for Los Pinos. In all fairness, he took modest steps to fight crime and corruption, combat pollution, curb bureaucratic delays, improve transportation, and bestow more power on the sixteen borough chiefs. Scholars Peter M. Ward and Elizabeth Durden have compared his regime to the "curate's egg" that proved "good in places." They point to improved administration and decentralization as areas where he achieved the most profound advances. At the same time, they note that Cárdenas was "something of a part-time mayor," functioning as his party's principal eminence and devoting many hours each week to his upcoming presidential race. After all, he remembered the 1988 fraud and wanted to prepare himself for a difficult contest in 2000. Ward and Durden also stress that his stern demeanor, behind-the-scenes governing style, and failure to publicize achievement worked to his disadvantage.[49]

Despite his noble aspirations, the outgoing mayor failed to convince the public that he had accomplished major changes, and crime remained a nightmare. The TV networks pilloried him after the June 1999 murder of popular comedian Paco Stanley. "I hold you responsible, Governor Cárdenas, because you haven't delivered what you promised," snarled TV Azteca anchor Jorge Garralda as he glared into the camera amid shouts of "enough already!" and "resign!" from those in the studio.[50] The media paid far less attention to the comic's cocaine habit and his ties to narco-traffickers.

To make matters worse, Cárdenas's former ally, Muñoz Ledo, accused him of having diverted approximately $16 million in city funds to his presidential campaign. The absence of evidence did not prevent Muñoz Ledo from alleging that he had abused his public office more than any other presidential aspirant to promote his electoral position.

Cárdenas had aroused hopes he could not satisfy. When he finally handed over the mayor's post to Rosario Robles in September 1999, a poll revealed that 53 percent of *defeños* were disappointed in his performance and only 41 percent approved. Cárdenas had not rescued the city, and voters did not believe that he could run the country. He finished a distant third behind the PAN's Fox and the PRI's Labastida in the 2000 presidential showdown.

Meanwhile, Interim Mayor Robles dazzled the public by zipping around the city in a cherry-red Jeep, vivaciously mixing with community groups, curbing demonstrations by anarchic students, and confronting Zedillo when he proposed cutting the city's budget. She also launched a pricey media campaign to enhance her image and readily took credit for programs begun by her predecessors. She left office with a 66 percent approval rating.

From the perspective of López Obrador's supporters, Cárdenas was an inept savior. He had temporarily occupied enemy territory in claiming the Federal District for the PRD, yet he had not concentrated enough power in his hands and those of his loyalists to solidify his position. Even worse, he had played by the illegitimate rules of the game, retained PRI technocrats in the bureaucracy, delegated responsibilities to borough chiefs, neglected to toot his own horn, failed to implement popular social programs, and treated the office as a stepping-stone to Los Pinos. This was not the man to banish the hated neoliberalism.

López Obrador would not make these mistakes. He fortified his ties to Camacho, an inveterate Salinas hater with whom el Peje had negotiated in the past, basked in pro-PRD TV spots, and relied upon the popular organizations that Camacho had nurtured to forge a base for his own mayoral race—the messianic politician's next step in redeeming Mexico.

THE MAYOR OF
MEXICO CITY

After his extremely successful tenure as PRD president, López Obrador yearned to renew his crusade for the Quinta Grijalva. To attain this goal, he had developed an extensive grassroots constituency composed largely of Indians, peasants, and fishermen. Equally important, el Pejelagarto had fashioned a potent two-pronged message to unite his followers: he would redeem the masses and he would force Pemex to compensate individuals and families who suffered from its activities. While keeping one eye on the statehouse, the messianic politician became increasingly aware of an opportunity to obtain a much more prominent post than the governorship. The miracles that he had wrought as PRD chief and his attacks on Fobaproa had thrust him into the national limelight. Several opinion polls showed that López Obrador and the PAN's Diego "el Jefe" Fernández de Cevallos, the PAN's unsuccessful presidential candidate in 1994, were the most popular politicians in the D.F.[1] Challenges had never deterred him, but el Peje would have had an uphill battle in Tabasco, where Governor Madrazo had strengthened the PRI's structure, cadres, and finances.

While López Obrador was contemplating his future, Cárdenas, the inept savior of Mexico City, was preparing another run for the presidency. To reach Los Pinos, he would need an impressive turnout in the vote-rich capital. Despite his losses in 1988 and 1994, the PRD's "moral leader" was convinced that, just as he had captured the mayorship in a landslide, he could defeat the increasingly unpopular PRI in 2000. Hoping they could reinforce each other's candidacies, he sought to convince Muñoz Ledo to run for mayor. But the bombastic federal deputy had tired of deferring to Cárdenas and was determined to seek the nation's top office in his own right. He left the PRD to accept the PARM's nomination.

Thus Cárdenas prevailed upon López Obrador to forego the Tabasco contest in order to attain the second-most prominent position in the nation. Interim Mayor Robles also urged López Obrador to enter the race, as did Bejarano and Padierna, whose CID controlled the PRD's machinery in the D.F. Before committing himself, however, López Obrador made a dramatic show of obtaining the "authorization" of *tabasqueños* for the race. In paternalistic fashion, he toured his home state's seventeen municipalities, ostensibly to ask permission from the PRD flock to run in Mexico City rather than in Tabasco.[2] His supporters claim that he visited a thousand towns, after which he held a referendum in which the participants unanimously endorsed his decision.[3] As the champion of the downtrodden, he relied on the "people's will" to legitimize his quest for greater power to use on their behalf. "He sounded out people in Tabasco; he wanted to be governor of the state," said a close collaborator. "But he also took into consideration the interests of the party, and perhaps it needed him more in the Federal District."[4]

The PRD selected its standard-bearer in a primary. In addition to López Obrador, this face-off drew four contenders: D.F. city councilman and former deputy Demetrio Sodi de la Tijera; 1968 UNAM student activist and deputy and former communist Pablo Gómez; Asamblea de Barrios founder "Superbarrio" Rascón; and leftist economist and former senator Ifigenia Martínez.

The contest raised an embarrassing question for López Obrador: was he eligible to serve as mayor? Article 122 of the Constitution stipulates *inter alia* that a contender who was born outside the city "must have lived in the D.F. continuously for five years before his election."[5] Electoral officials required that el Peje fill out a special registration form inasmuch as his name did not appear on the voters' list at his local polling place. Even his voter identification card carried a Villahermosa address.[6] Detractors alleged that López Obrador had established his domicile in the capital in 1996, when he was elected the PRD's national president, and not in 1995 as he asserted. "It's simple," wrote Pablo Gómez, who succeeded el Pejelagarto as party president, "he moved to Mexico City in July or August of 1996. So he's not eligible for the post. If he becomes the candidate, it'll turn into a catastrophe."[7]

Yet legal niceties never prevented this providential man from doggedly pursuing his mission. Besides, Cárdenas was in his corner. In the November 14, 1999, primary, López Obrador (77 percent) trounced Sodi (8.4 percent), Gómez (7.4 percent), Rascón (3.8 percent), and Martínez (3.4 percent) to win the PRD's nomination.

As the PRD nominee, López Obrador had to walk a fine line. On the one hand, he was committed to delivering city residents from the ravages of neoliberalism. On the other hand, he could not blatantly criticize the shortcomings of the administrations of Cárdenas and Robles. His strategy involved using Fobaproa as a weapon that he could fire at all issues. Why was the city short of resources? Because the bank scheme had diverted monies from the D.F. How could the capital obtain more revenue? Require Fobaproa's beneficiaries to pay back the bad debts they had foisted on the taxpayers. "We are going to use the open documents to demonstrate publicly that the [PRI and PAN] . . . are in reality crooks," he said.[8] While lambasting Fobaproa, he relied on the CID and the Sun Brigades to mobilize grassroots support.[9]

The Mayor of Mexico City

López Obrador's stock began to rise after he bested the redoubtable Fernández de Cevallos in a TV debate on March 7, 2000. The encounter was less a debate than an exchange of insults. El Peje emerged victorious not because of his rhetorical prowess but because he flung more dirt that stuck to his opponent.[10] The triumph over Jefe Diego was no mean feat. Known for his oratorical prowess, PAN candidate Fernández de Cevallos had made mincemeat of Cárdenas and Zedillo in the first televised debate ever held among presidential aspirants in 1994.

One week after the face-off with el Jefe, López Obrador got another boost when independent deputy Marcelo Ebrard, mayoral candidate of the small center-left Center Democratic Party (PCD), cast his lot with the PRD nominee. This endorsement meant that López Obrador was backed by six parties that constituted the "Alliance for the Federal District."[11] Ebrard helped knit even tighter ties between el Peje and the CID.

OVERCOMING THE FIRST SERIOUS CHALLENGE

A poll taken by *Reforma* in early April showed López Obrador (31 percent) leading the PRI candidate, Jésus Silva Herzog (27 percent), and the PAN nominee, Santiago Creel Miranda (25 percent), with minor party contenders trailing the pack.[12]

On April 15, 2000, the PRI filed papers contesting López Obrador's eligibility to run. The PAN joined the PRI in mounting a highly publicized challenge to the legality of his mayoral candidacy. They presented a document that purportedly showed that López Obrador had registered to vote in Tabasco in 1996.[13] Jorge Alcocer Villanueva, who was working with presidential candidate Labastida, exuded confidence that the decision would turn against el Peje, even though the PRD-dominated ALDF had selected the electoral judges in a process that bristled with controversy and bitterness.[14] Alcocer was heard to say, "We are not going to permit López Obrador to do the same thing to President Labastida that Boris Yeltsin did to Mikhail Gorbachev."[15]

López Obrador produced housing documents and affidavits from neighbors to buttress his residency claim.[16] The PRD borough chief in Coyoacán, where he lived, also submitted an official paper on his behalf. Moreover, in keeping with his image of an embattled crusader fighting for the have-nots against neoliberal demons, he charged his foes with attempting to penalize him because he gave voice to the plight of the downtrodden. "I've moved into the lead, and they know when I'm mayor I won't favor the ruling clique," he said, raising a clenched fist before enthusiasts in a downtown hall draped with red hammer-and-sickle flags. "So now Zedillo and the mafia around him are trying to shove me aside. This isn't a legal challenge. This is just another dirty trick."[17] In other words, he was not the lawbreaker. To the contrary, he was the target of the same wrongdoers who had concocted Fobaproa and now strove to block his candidacy. López Obrador, always on the lookout for a conspiracy, accused the PAN and PRI of cutting a secret deal. In return for allowing Creel to triumph in the D.F., the PAN would acquiesce in Labastida's winning the presidency, he alleged.[18]

Meanwhile, in accord with his devotion to the people's will, López Obrador held an unofficial poll on whether he should be allowed to stay in the race. More than 96 percent of the 413,272 voters in this informal *consulta* backed el Peje's right to run; 14,565 voters, or 3.5 percent, opposed his candidacy.[19] Silva Herzog condemned the results as "a sleight of hand" and urged his own supporters to join his "Army of Triumph."[20]

Mexico City's electoral authorities concurred with the outcome of the *consulta*. On March 11 the Electoral Institute of the Federal District (IEDF) approved López Obrador's registration by a 4–3 vote. The PRI and the PAN then appealed this ruling to the Electoral Tribunal of the Federal District, which affirmed the IEDF's decision by a 3–2 vote, with judges selected by leftist parties constituting the majority. In fact, the swing vote was cast by Juan Martínez Veloz, whose brother was a PRD deputy.

Silva Herzog reacted to the decision, saying, "It would be better if he stopped playing the victim . . . and discussed his proposals."[21] In retrospect, Silva Herzog admitted, "we made a big mistake in attacking López Obrador's credentials . . . because he came out of the controversy bathed in publicity and with a sharpened image as a man ready to fight the establishment. We made him a martyr."[22]

Aguilera Gómez, then PRI president in the D.F., disagreed. He believed that the PRI mayoral candidate had erred in not taking his challenge all the way to the Electoral Tribunal of the Federal Judiciary (TEPJF)—the nation's highest electoral court.[23] The ultimate decision on PRI strategy was made by the Labastida camp. Alcocer, however, who had misjudged the outcome of the earlier challenge, had lost his credibility, and the party decided not to pursue the matter lest the dispute give further impetus to el Peje's rise in the polls. The PAN was split. Fernández de Cevallos advocated taking the case to the TEPJF; party president Luis Felipe Bravo Mena and Creel turned thumbs down, and no further action was taken.[24]

THE PRI STANDARD-BEARER

At the beginning of the year, many observers believed that PRI candidate Jesús "Chucho" Silva Herzog would be the man to beat. A graduate of Yale University, the sixty-five-year-old economist had held a number of key posts, including finance secretary, ambassador to Spain, tourism secretary, and ambassador to the United States. Jesús Reyes Heroles, Chucho's successor as envoy to Washington, and other PRI leaders had even proposed that Silva Herzog seek the mayorship in 1997, but Silva Herzog demurred.[25] In 1999 the affable Chucho expressed his desire to run for mayor to his longtime friend and tennis partner Labastida, with whom he had served in Salinas's cabinet. Labastida acquiesced in this request, shoving aside senator and former party president de los Angeles Moreno, Finance Secretary Gurría Treviño, Campa Cifrián, and several other party bigwigs.[26] Many observers believed that Silva Herzog, a man of distinction not closely identified with the PRI, would attract independent voters.

Still, Aguilera Gómez had misgivings after he sensed the antipathy of the press toward Chucho. Reporters agreed to attend a breakfast for the mayoral aspirant only after the PRI leader assured them that he, not Silva Herzog, was the host. Before the primary, Aguilera warned Zedillo that Chucho would lose and that de los Angeles Moreno would make a stronger nominee. The president responded, in effect, "You must take that up with Labastida."[27] In fact, Zedillo preferred candidates who—like del Mazo in 1997 and Silva Herzog in 2000—were anti-Salinas, even if they were not his allies.[28]

Silva Herzog did receive an unexpected and spirited challenge from Campa Cifrián, a savvy veteran of D.F. politics whom Zedillo encouraged to seek the nomination at a meeting in Los Pinos. Campa reportedly asked the chief executive if he planned to get involved in the campaign. Zedillo replied, "No, but I will walk you to your car so that the press can see us together."[29] Campa, who was serving as head of the Office of Federal Attorney for Consumers, criticized Silva Herzog for having once disavowed PRI membership, for being the establishment's favorite, and for being out of touch with the needs of *defeños*. In a TV debate Campa presented himself as a man with the stamina of youth. "In five years," he said, "I will be only forty-seven years old, while Silva Herzog will be seventy." "It's not that I do not respect experience, but I think that youth is necessary to confront the grave problems facing Mexico City," he added.[30]

Although Silva Herzog ran ahead in opinion polls, Campa did well in "focus groups." After the handful of specially selected participants in these sessions viewed videos of the aspirants presenting their programs, they ranked Campa as highly as, if not more highly than, his competitor. Still, some members of Silva Herzog's camp treated Campa's candidacy as if it were obscene to challenge the establishment's choice. Ex-deputy Oscar Levín Coppel, the PRI's secretary-general in the D.F., told Campa, "if you oppose Silva Herzog, we will go after you with all of the party's resources that we can muster."[31]

Approximately eight hundred thousand people participated in a well-run primary on November 7, 1999. They gave 51.2 percent of their votes to Silva Herzog and 40.3 percent to Campa, with a third candidate winning 8.5 percent.[32] On election night, Aguilera Gómez averred that the open contest marked the end of the *dedazo*. Meanwhile, Levín Coppel called for a "healing operation," promising that the PRI would apply "vitacilina ointment, mercurochrome, iodine to all those who feel wounded by this contest."[33]

After his triumph, Herzog failed to offer even a Band-aid to the losers. In fact, he rubbed salt in their wounds by selecting the irascible Levín Coppel to manage his general election campaign. This inexplicable move further alienated Aguilera Gómez and Campa.[34] The latter became Labastida's D.F. coordinator but gave short shrift to the mayoral nominee. The feud with Campa was only the beginning of headaches for Silva Herzog, who emphasized his honesty and decades of distinguished public service. This recitation of an impressive résumé did not excite young voters or the poor, most of whom had never heard of Silva Herzog. He held public events with such unpopular PRI constituents as street vendors and the violence-prone Antorcha movement. Still, his lackadaisical style, which found him campaigning only a few hours a day and playing tennis on weekends, failed to energize the PRI's 850,000 hard-core members (*voto duro*).

In all fairness, Silva Herzog did offer a five-point platform that emphasized fighting crime, spurring development, improving public services, combating corruption, and reorganizing the capital's government.[35] Still, he failed to make these general goals relevant to the average voter.

In late March, he and the PRI got a black eye when former mayor Espinosa was accused of embezzling 420 million pesos ($46 million) during his 1994–97 tenure. Espinosa, whom Zedillo appointed secretary of tourism, had earlier run afoul of the redoubtable Robles. In January 2000 she released her financial statement and called upon Espinosa to do the same. When Robles agreed to his terms, Espinosa still refused to make any disclosures.[36] He subsequently fled the country rather than face embezzlement charges. He was extradited from Australia in 2001 and convicted in mid-2005.

NEW CAMPAIGN COORDINATOR

Silva Herzog's failure to gain traction spurred Zedillo to place Fernando Lerdo de Tejada, the president's spokesman, in charge of the campaign in early May. The chief executive sought in vain to halt the internecine fighting within the D.F. party so that its activists would rally behind Silva Herzog. Lerdo de Tejada's presence did not prevent the PRI candidate from faltering in the May 30 televised debate. In a postdebate survey of 1,114 citizens, López Obrador (44.9 percent) vanquished Creel (22.8 percent), Silva Herzog (15.4 percent), and two minor-party contenders.[37]

While not avoiding joint appearances with Silva Herzog, Labastida's entourage was dismayed by the mayoral nominee's lethargy, and problems sometimes arose when the two men campaigned together. For example, the PRI was fined when the candidates playfully spray-painted "Vote for Pancho [Labastida] and Chucho [Silva Herzog]" on the wall of a school in Iztapalapa. Silva Herzog's prospects were so grim that de los Angeles Moreno, a PRI institution in the city, left for a meeting in Europe several days before the election. Table 10 shows the standing of the contenders in the run-up to the mayoral election.

THE PAN'S CONTENDER

Presidential candidate Fox convinced Santiago Creel that he should seek the PAN's candidacy at a nominating convention on November 27, 1999. Scion of an aristocratic family and a highly respected

TABLE 10. *Polls in Run-Up to the 2000 D.F. Mayoral Election*

CANDIDATE	PARTY	SURVEY DATES					
		June %	*May* %	*April* %	*March* %	*February* %	*January* %
Creel	Alliance for Change	25	27	28	30	31	34
López Obrador	Alliance for Mexico	46	44	41	37	31	27
Silva Herzog	PRI	25	27	30	32	34	34
Other Candidates	PSD and PARM	4	2	1	1	4	5

SOURCE: *Reforma*, June 21, 2000, 1A. The results derive from personal interviews in the homes of 1,109 adults. The margin of error is usually ±3 percent.

attorney, Creel had served as an IFE councilor before winning a seat in Congress. Even though he had joined the PAN only in mid-1999, he captured 59.9 percent of the ballots cast, defeating Fernando Pérez Noriega (23.9 percent) and Salvador Abascal Carranza (16.2 percent).[38]

López Obrador kept his distance from Cárdenas, and Labastida often appeared in the D.F. without Silva Herzog. In contrast, Creel joined himself to Fox's hip. "We are going to campaign together when Vicente is in the Federal District; we form part of the same strategy," he told a reporter.[39] On April 4, Fox served as official witness of Creel's registration as a candidate, and the two men appeared together in more than twenty events to take advantage of the "Fox effect." As the campaign progressed, Creel began to deliver his message in a more hard-hitting style, à la Fox. Fox and Creel gained momentum simultaneously, as independent voters migrated to their candidacies.

MAYOR ROBLES SPENDS LAVISHLY

Interim Mayor Robles played a crucial role in López Obrador's success. As mentioned in the previous chapter, she turned in a sparkling performance at city hall. A product of radical UNAM politics, Robles had held a congressional seat before López Obrador recruited her to head the Sun Brigades. Spokesmen for the rival PAN alleged that she ran up a $77 million advertising and marketing bill during her short time in office—double what the city budget had allotted.[40] Her lavishly financed advertisements, which extolled the achievements of the city government, rehabilitated the PRD's status in the D.F. In all probability, el Peje could not have won had the uninspiring Cárdenas still occupied the mayor's chair.

López Obrador, who employed the innocuous slogan "Let's win the city again," proved a master at obtaining free media coverage for his twenty-item agenda. His program included running an honest and austere administration, halting poverty, improving public security and providing protection to citizens, promoting education, and governing with the participation of all the capital's residents.[41] While Silva Herzog spoke in generalities, López Obrador pledged that in his first year in office he would construct twenty thousand housing units, earmark 5 billion pesos to help the poor, and improve transportation by providing cheap credit for the acquisition of microbuses.[42]

The only candidate with campaign experience, López Obrador held final rallies in each of the D.F.'s sixteen *delegaciones,* as well as in forty PRD strongholds within these boroughs. He also benefited from the party's extensive get-out-the-vote apparatus, which he had promoted when he was PRD president. In addition, PARM candidate Alejandro Ordorica virtually withdrew from the race, awarding his meager support to López Obrador.

So confident was el Peje of victory that as early as five weeks before the election he spoke of his potential cabinet, which would be composed of men and women who were "honest, imaginative, talented, hardworking, and possessed of social sensitivity." He implied that at least two members of Robles's cabinet exhibited these characteristics and would be invited to retain their posts.[43]

López Obrador's victory in the face of the PRD's crushing defeat for the presidency provoked backbiting from Cárdenas loyalists. They criticized el Peje for using the excuse of a "supersaturated" schedule to justify his absences from Cárdenas campaign functions in the city. They even floated the canard that the Tabascan had struck a deal with Fox, maintaining a low profile in the weeks before the election to help Fox increase his vote in the capital. "And clearly Andrés Manuel hurt us," argued *cardenista* Julio Moguel. "He was so confident that he stopped campaigning three months ago. He didn't understand that it is one thing to be popular and another to have the electoral structure well moored." El Peje brushed off these accusations, saying, "you can expect anything from the 'celestial court'"—a reference to Cárdenas's inner circle.[44]

Contributing to the bad blood between Cárdenas and López Obrador was the latter's behavior on election night. Believing that Fox had won the presidency, the mayor-elect suggested that Cárdenas prepare a concession speech. This advice led to a vitriolic exchange between the PRD leaders. The two men got over their contretemps and went together to the Zócalo, where López Obrador lauded Cárdenas as "the principal precursor of the democratic changes that we are living." He went on to berate the "antipopular and sell-out regime represented by the president of the Republic," adding, "We are going to defend the right of workers to a decent salary; we are going to continue demanding an increase in pension; we are going to continue opposing fully the privatization of education, of our cultural patrimony, of our oil and electricity sectors; we are going to continue defending our agenda for the nation."[45]

As if to throw a wet blanket over the enthusiastic gathering, Cárdenas took the microphone to remind López Obrador that he was still a candidate and that some TV analysts were calling the race a "technical tie." Striking a more conciliatory note, the doom-sayer added, "We do not agree to think the same thing here; here the winner was the candidate supported by various parties and it is a decision that we must defend."[46] (See Table 11 for the results of the mayoral election.)

After this dose of sour grapes, the two men were permanently estranged; the protégé had supplanted his master as the top figure in the PRD. This antagonism appeared not only during el Peje's mayorship but also when Cárdenas threatened to cast his lot with

TABLE 11. *Results of 2000 D.F. Mayoral Election*

CANDIDATE	PARTY	NO. OF VOTES RECEIVED	%
Santiago Creel Miranda	Alliance for Change PAN + PVEM	1,460,931	33.4
Andrés Manuel López Obrador	Alliance for Mexico City	1,506,324	34.5
Jesús Silva Herzog	PRI	998,109	22.8
Teresa Valle	PSD	43,660	3.3
Alejandro Ordorica Saavedra	PARM	15,939	0.4
Other Candidates	PT, PCD, PSN, PAS, Convergencia	168,642	3.8
Invalid Votes		77,896	1.8
TOTAL VOTES		4,271,501	100

SOURCE: Instituto Electoral del Distrito Federal, http://www.iedf.org.mx/PEL2000/EJG_RD.

another party and run against PRD candidate López Obrador in the 2006 presidential contest. Cárdenas abandoned this quixotic venture. El Peje had deposed a failed redeemer who proved unable to take charge of the holy war against the iniquities of neoliberalism. A true messiah had arisen.

"REPUBLICAN AUSTERITY" AND *MAÑANERAS*

Had López Obrador not thrown himself into politics, he could have excelled as an evangelist. He is amazingly astute in establishing rapport with audiences, identifying himself with average people's concerns, creating his own bully pulpit for disseminating ideas, and presenting himself as the champion of the victims of neoliberalism. His modest living style has invested him with enormous legitimacy in his quest to win converts. Although the masses might have approved of the policies and personae of previous PRD mayors, they could not identify with their lifestyles. Cárdenas—whose family has a fortune—resides in upper-middle-class Polanco. Even the energetic Robles lives comfortably. López Obrador successfully portrayed his "oneness" with the people through his 6:15 A.M. news conferences, known as *mañaneras*—a punning reference to early morning lovemaking by peasants too fatigued for nighttime intimacy.

The predawn press sessions allowed the mayor to distinguish himself from the elite. While they were sleeping, he was on the job, just like hundreds of thousands of working-class Mexicans. While they inhabited expensive homes, he lived in a tiny house in Copilco. While they drove (or were driven in) luxury automobiles, he arrived at city hall in a well-worn Tsuru. While they decorated their speeches with fancy phrases, he spoke in the idiom of the common man. While they strutted about in tailored suits, he bought his attire off the rack. While they adorned their wrists with Rolexes, he donned a simple metal watch. While they hid behind communications directors, he faced the press every morning—

seven days a week. While they made excuses for the paralysis besetting Congress, he announced generous programs for poor and working-class families. López Obrador projected the image of a "poor Christ" who renounces creature comforts to pursue his vocation of service. In the words of television producer and media expert Federico Wilkins, "Subliminally he capitalized on the . . . message: 'we are still [on our way to work] . . . and Andrés Manuel is already working.' Thus, Andrés Manuel converted himself into one who made great sacrifices, a 'poor Christ.' Very much to the left, he epitomized the vocation of service by leaders who devote twenty-four hours a day to their mission. He had no [personal] life because he lived for the people."[1]

ORIGIN OF THE *MAÑANERAS*

A native of hot, humid Tabasco, el Peje has been an early riser all his life. When campaigning for mayor, he pledged to hold crack-of-dawn cabinet meetings. The day after he swore the oath of office, a TV journalist and a newspaper reporter staked out the neoclassical Ancient Palace of the City Government (Antiguo Palacio de Ayuntamiento) that served viceroys in the early eighteenth century and now functions as city hall. Cynical about the fulfillment of campaign promises, these ardent members of the fourth estate were eager to learn whether the new executive would be as good as his word.

The journalists had to run a gauntlet of office seekers and poor citizens camped out in the hope of obtaining a job, housing, money, assistance in cutting red tape, or some other form of aid. Often people with problems slept on makeshift bed covers outside city hall so as to be on hand for the *mañanera*. Once in a while, López Obrador listened to petitioners himself, but his staff usually attended to them. Leticia Ramírez Amaya, head of the General Direction of Constituent Service, and her deputy, Rocío Bárcenas Molina, a former activist in the radical CNTE teachers' union and an ally of Robles, directed supplicants to the public offices related to their needs. Although it was part of the mayor's attempt to reach out to the disadvantaged, his staff's attentiveness to such people did not escape the attention of the press.

As promised, el Peje arrived early on December 6, 2000. Word of his schedule spread and the number of newsmen awaiting his arrival increased. Upon entering the building, he soon found himself deluged with questions from the sidewalk—a practice known as *banqueteras*. The first exchanges took place in the predawn chilliness, until the mayor's staff invited the reporters to pose their inquiries in the building's ornate hallway; several weeks later, they migrated to a small room adjacent to the mayor's first-floor office. On May 31, 2001, the interchanges became more formal still when they were moved to a ground-floor room that had once housed a walk-in vault. César Yáñez Centeno Cabrera, who succeeded Ana Lilia Cepeda de León as communications director, christened this twenty-five-square meter venue the "Francisco Zarco Press Room" in memory of an advisor to Juárez who had championed freedom of the press.

In the four and a half years after López Obrador's inauguration, he held sessions nearly every day, including weekends. The death of his wife in early 2002 and his own occasional illnesses explained several failures to appear. In addition, he did not hold *mañaneras* on the day before and the day of the July 6, 2003, election, to avoid violating the D.F.'s legal restrictions on public acts during political contests. He missed several days in observance of Holy Week each year, and in late 2004 he began to make out-of-town trips to promote his book and political platform. When the mayor was away, Government Secretary Encinas took his place at the conferences.

After Congress voted on April 7, 2005, to strip the mayor of his political immunity in the El Encino case, which is analyzed in Chapter 14, he passed the reins of government to Encinas, who conducted the early-morning briefings. Meanwhile, López Obrador met the press in the Hugo B. Margáin Park outside his home, waiting until 8:00 A.M., as a courtesy to his neighbors, to convene these sessions. On April 25, 2005, he returned to the mayor's office and recommended press meetings. These continued for three months until he resigned to hit the campaign trail. Between May 31, 2001, and April 9, 2005, el Peje held some 1,316 morning conferences and missed only ninety-one days (see Table 12).[2]

On a typical day as mayor, López Obrador rose at 4:30 A.M., dressed, and ate a light breakfast before Nicolás "Nico" Mollinedo Bastar drove him from the south of the city to his office. Along the way he read annotated news stories that Yáñez and information director Manuel Moreno Domínguez had gleaned from the Internet the night before. He also listened for late-breaking items

TABLE 12. *López Obrador's Mañaneras: May 31, 2001–April 9, 2005*

YEAR	CONFERENCES	LÓPEZ OBRADOR NOT PRESENT	% NOT PRESENT
2001 (after May 31)	211	4	1.90
2002	356	9	2.53
2003	343	22	6.41
2004	328	38	9.68
2005 (through April 9)	78	18	23.08
TOTAL	1,316	91	6.91

SOURCE: Dirección General de Comunicación Social, GDF, "Numeralia de las conferencias matutinas," http://www.comsoc.df.gob.mx/; and Manuel Durán, "Érase una vez la 'mañanera,'" *Reforma*, April 10, 2005, http://www.reforma.com.mx/.

on the radio. He usually entered city hall through a side door on Avenida 20 de Noviembre and discussed with Yáñez and Moreno critical stories, probable questions, and the names of the reporters who had gathered. Although he was prepared to begin the news conferences at 6:15 A.M., el Peje waited for his logistics aide, Pedro Aguilar Cueto, to inform him when a critical mass of journalists has assembled. If the number was deemed too small, he began his remarks later.

Upon entering the improvised press room, the mayor made a beeline for the old bank vault, now known as *la bodeguita*. In this storage room, which is no more than four square meters in size, he found a press summary, an array of newspapers, information cards, and toiletry items. There he sipped coffee and perused the papers before taking his place behind a small podium bearing the capital's official shield. On the wall behind him was emblazoned the slogan "Government of the Federal District of Mexico: The City of Hope," next to which stood national and city flags. Then he greeted the crowd with a simple "buenos días."

Often he delivered a brief opening statement, though sometimes he asked D.F. officials to address the group. For instance, on the Sunday before public schools opened in 2003, several public safety officers outlined measures that had been adopted to promote the safety of children.[3] On another occasion he introduced the secretaries of social development, economic development, and tourism, who reported on the progress of their agencies.[4] In a session in mid-2003 he gave a PowerPoint presentation on a new housing initiative.[5] After such preliminaries he invited questions, and reporters showed no hesitation in quizzing him. The only topics off limits were intramural activities of his PRD and the presidential race (before he announced his candidacy in early 2005).

El Peje proved to have a deft touch at evading awkward questions. He simply changed the subject, responded indirectly, grimaced, fenced with the reporter, or unobtrusively raised his index finger to signal that he did not intend to answer. Sometimes he complemented this negative gesture with the phrase, "See what my finger says," or "I am not going to involve myself in this." A showman before the cameras, he deflected unwelcome inquiries with jokes. At times he explained his refusal to answer a question on the grounds that it would be in "bad taste" (for example, when reporters asked for his assessment of López Portillo's regime the day after the controversial ex-president died). He declined to answer questions about his relations with a woman he had dated. He also ducked inquiries about the Giuliani brothers' report on how to combat crime, a subject discussed in Chapter 11.

López Obrador claimed that his "batting average" was .900— that is, that he responded to 90 percent of reporters' queries.[6] Many reporters disagreed. In August 2003 he dodged 176 of 943 inquiries, for an average of .813.[7] *Reforma* journalist Fernando del Collado, who attended five *mañaneras* between February 17 and February 22, 2004, calculated that the mayor avoided 38 of 131 questions, for an average of .710.[8]

SCANDALS

With the eruption of scandals in early 2004, questions on local subjects became much more salient than those involving national issues. The first of these was known as "Nicogate," the revelation in January that Mollinedo Bastar, the mayor's chauffeur, received almost 62,000 pesos per month, equal to the salary of a city cabinet undersecretary. El Peje immediately defended his employee, claiming that in addition to driving an automobile with 62,000 miles on the odometer, Mollinedo served as his "security chief and logistical coordinator." The Tabascan chided the press for blowing the matter out of proportion. The attack was launched to cut his high approval ratings, he averred. The perpetrators were a right-wing "gang" who regarded López Obrador's antineoliberal strategy as "pure poison for its interests."[9]

No sooner had Nicogate subsided than *Reforma* reported that the D.F. had traded twelve parcels of land in the booming Santa Fe area to the giant Cemex and Apasco corporations. In exchange for the property, valued at 640 million pesos, the government had received 125,000 square meters of cement. Critics questioned the swap in view of soaring land values in Santa Fe, a newly developed area where corporate offices, gated communities, and condominiums coexist with slums. López Obrador justified the trade on the grounds that the D.F. needed huge amounts of concrete for public works.[10]

Then the *videoescándalo* broke. The first element of this brouhaha featured videos of D.F. finance secretary Gustavo Ponce puffing on a cigar while playing high-stakes blackjack at the swanky Bellagio Casino in Las Vegas. Journalist Joaquín López Doriga revealed bills from the casino that showed a minibar charge of $2,200. Ponce was also known as a generous tipper.[11] The mayor immediately fired Ponce, and Yáñez insisted that the other officials knew nothing of the former secretary's addiction to gambling. The communications director explained that Ponce had made multiple trips to the U.S. West Coast in 2002 and 2003 to visit his sister, who was seriously ill.[12]

Even as authorities were trying to find Ponce, René Bejarano, el Peje's right-hand man, found himself at the epicenter of the furor. On March 3, 2004, PAN deputy Federico Döring Casar appeared on Televisa's popular *Mañanero* show. He provided Trujillo, the popular clown-attired host, with a video of Bejarano receiving cash from Carlos Ahumada Kurtz, a wealthy businessman whose Grupo Quart had dozens of city construction projects in the works.

Upon airing the incriminating video, Trujillo immediately phoned Bejarano, who had just been discussing urban problems on the competing TV Aztec network. Caught off guard by the unexpected inquiry, Bejarano avowed that the monies were contributions for a candidate running in the 2003 city election. "I gave the money to the borough leader," he said. "It should be on file as a cash donation. . . . I have nothing to hide."[13] In a nighttime program on March 3, Bejarano was shown meeting with Ahumada on July 29, 2003, almost two months after the exchange recorded in the morning video.[14] Bejarano immediately took a leave of absence from the ALDF and temporarily resigned from the PRD. Two other figures—Tlalpan borough chief Carlos Imaz Gispert and PRD official Ramón Sosamontes Herreramoro—also stepped down.

Ahumada, a business tycoon who also owned the newspaper *El Independiente* and the Santos Laguna soccer team in Coahuila, had been working with PRD administrations for years. In fact, his constant companion in the early 2000s was the party's president, Robles, an archenemy of Bejarano. In early 2002 a meeting took place in city hall for the announced purpose of allocating public works projects for the year. An observer at this session remembers that "Señor Carlos Ahumada arrived and in a matter of fifteen minutes, he indicated to all of the directors of public works [of the boroughs], one by one, to what firms they must award all the projects on the table at the moment. Clearly, all the companies belonged to the Quart Group. Ahumada alone decided upon the allocation of resources of at least 300 million pesos in a matter of a half-hour."[15]

Bejarano gained his release from prison in mid-2005, when a federal judge found that there was insufficient evidence to convict him of money laundering. He was subsequently exonerated of the lesser crime of violating electoral laws.

Rather than concentrate on why high-level officials were taking money from a businessman with a plethora of city contracts, López Obrador brushed aside the affair as an attack by conspirators who would use whatever "missiles" necessary to damage him and his ideas. "I have information that the plot was hatched by the federal government, PAN members Diego Fernández de Cevallos and Federico Döring, and quite probably Carlos Salinas de Gortari."[16] Ever the victim, he said, "it hurts me . . . that they raise doubts about my principles, convictions, and integrity."[17]

JOURNALISTS

The informal December 2000 sidewalk press conferences attracted approximately ten media outlets, including journalists from *Reforma*, *El Universal*, Radio Red, and Televisa. After a few weeks, the ranks of reporters grew to thirty or forty, with all of the major newspapers, radio stations, and television networks represented.[18] The explosion of the *videoescándalo* in early March 2004 led to even greater numbers of attendees.

The journalists were generally twenty-five to thirty years old, came dressed casually in blue jeans and comfortable shoes, and had received professional training in communications. Unlike highly structured White House news conferences, the *mañaneras* were short on decorum. Rather than raise their hands and wait to be called on, reporters often shouted their questions. They sometimes asked tough questions but seldom followed up if the mayor began to dodge and weave. An esprit de corps characterized the journalists, who helped each other flesh out notes, lent one another batteries for tape recorders, and explained to each other the background of certain issues.

With few exceptions, López Obrador received sympathetic treatment from the city hall press corps. Most of the journalists liked the mayor's David versus Goliath stance on social and economic issues, and most admitted that they and their newsroom colleagues favored the PRD. The leftist, mass circulation *La Jornada* has been the most favorable to el Peje. Although the nationalistic and prestigious *El Universal* often bashed him, it also gave his views and projects as mayor a full airing. The highly regarded *Reforma*, which is owned by Monterrey's affluent Junco family, has expressed strong opposition to many of López Obrador's ventures. Still, its editorial pages offer a variety of views and feature essays by both backers and detractors of el Pejelagarto. Ahumada's *El Independiente*, until it closed 2004, was more critical. But el Peje's most outspoken critic has been *La Crónica*, a paper of anemic circulation that is closely associated with Salinas. At his *mañaneras*, the mayor even referred sarcastically to Alejandro Sánchez, a young reporter from *La Crónica*, as "Carlos Salinas."[19]

The weekend news conferences were more relaxed. There were fewer reporters, they were often junior and less experienced, and their questions were not as probing as those of the regulars who covered city hall.[20] In addition, the weekend sessions began later, and López Obrador often wore a casual shirt and leather jacket rather than a coat and tie. Following the Sunday press sessions and cabinet meetings, he usually played the impresario's role for his programs in the Zócalo.

On August 17, 2003, for example, he gave each of 219 senior citizens fifteen thousand credits with which they could make down payments on new red-and-white taxis, which they drove away. The Program for the Substitution of Taxis was designed to replace old vehicles with newer ones that generated less pollution. During his administration, López Obrador promised to provide two thousand cars to individuals who, because of their age, could not obtain bank financing. Although the mayor presided over the event, the Nacional Financiera development bank, automobile manufacturers, and the Mexico City Chamber of Commerce helped finance the initiative.[21] "This is a very noble program," he said, "because its helps people who are working, struggling to make ends meet, and they are doing so in legal and dignified manner. In addition, it is a means of reactivating the economy."[22] As López Obrador edged toward a presidential candidacy, more and more foreign journalists began showing up for the *mañaneras*. These included reporters for the *Washington Post, New York Times, Boston Globe, Houston Chronicle, Dallas Morning News, Wall Street Journal, Financial Times, El País,* and *Le Monde*.[23]

Domestic and international attendance increased after controversial actions such as the TV broadcast of the video showing Bejarano receiving money (March 1, 2004), the U.S. Treasury Department's decision not to share financial information with the Mexican government because of leaks (April 23, 2004), and the megamarch against insecurity (June 27, 2004). On May 24, 2005, López Obrador held a meeting exclusively with foreign correspondents in the Hotel Sheraton Centro Histórico in downtown Mexico City.

At first blush, the predawn assignments seemed to be highly undesirable, and some reporters admitted to difficulties in adjusting their schedules. Nevertheless, the mayoral beat offered definite advantages. First, on a personal level, the journalists did not have to fight rush-hour traffic to get to the Zócalo by 6:15 A.M., and, in the case of reporters from financially sound newspapers and stations, the early-morning obligation allowed them to leave work in midafternoon.

Second, they usually reported the first story of the day, which, in the case of radio and TV journalists, would be played repeatedly during morning drive time and even in the afternoon. Without the *mañanera*, the mass media would have had to rely heavily on a rehash of news from the night before. The radio and TV reporters had different clips of the mayor's comments to vary the message delivered to listeners and viewers during the day.

Third, the reporters formed part of the "the source" (*la fuente*) that covered one of the country's top newsmakers, a man who, to control his message and save time, seldom granted interviews to reporters during the day. He told journalists who wanted to pose inquiries to show up at the early-morning sessions. (In mid-2005, this practice changed when he began barnstorming the country.)

Fourth, their access to the mayor was unfiltered by spokesmen or press secretaries. Yáñez and Moreno maintained a low profile. They were available to distribute transcripts of the conference, to supplement the mayor's statements, and to chat with reporters.

Fifth, el Peje embossed his presentations with colorful, quotable language. On one occasion he admitted, "I have to throw different pitches at my opponents—a fast ball, a curve, or a screwball." After

Mexico's foreign secretary supported the U.S. bombing of Iraq in 2003, he said, "If his father were alive—with all due respect—he would spank Foreign Secretary Castañeda."[24]

Sixth, the journalists could obtain comments from other key officials who were present for government and security cabinet meetings that followed the *mañaneras*. To facilitate these interviews, Yáñez had his staff set up microphones at the base of the several stairways that curl from the ground floor to the first floor, where the offices of the mayor and his key cabinet members are located. This enabled reporters to conduct interviews immediately after the *mañaneras*. The reporters found Encinas, who became interim mayor upon López Obrador's departure, especially generous with time and information, but on any given morning they found Attorney General Bernardo Bátiz, Public Security Secretary Joel Ortega Cuevas, and other officials prepared to respond to questions. Before they assumed other posts, Batres (who moved from undersecretary of government to PRD president in the D.F.) and Ebrard (who moved from public security secretary to social development secretary to mayoral candidate) were often on hand to answer questions. "There really are three or four press conferences each day," said a veteran reporter.[25]

Finally, the journalists developed a personal bond with the man who seemed likely to become the nation's next chief executive. After years of interaction, López Obrador knew the majority of reporters by name. At times he would publicly chide a journalist from a hostile medium—reporters for *La Crónica* bore the brunt of criticism. More often, he joked with them. On one occasion a Televisa reporter tried to hand him a western-style "wanted" poster—featuring a picture of el Peje, who was "wanted" for the presidency—that had been designed by the mayor's supporters. At first, the mayor playfully spurned the offering; then he started to take it, then drew his hand back, and finally exclaimed, "give it here . . . as if I didn't want the thing." Seven TV cameras covered the action as the room erupted with laughter.[26]

STOCKHOLM SYNDROME

The "vulnerability" of his media audience enhanced López Obrador's effectiveness. In most cases, the young journalists had just gotten up, had not read the day's newspapers, and had not yet been to the newsroom, where editors and colleagues might suggest questions to ask or breaking stories to probe. They literally drank their first cup of coffee with the city executive on his turf.

El Peje often lavished praise on his interrogators. He also treated the newsmen as if they were involved in a collective endeavor. On August 4, 2003, he noted that "the give and take makes the press conferences attractive. Here there is no news release, no monologue, no prohibition on questions. Here there is absolute liberty."[27]

"And because of the hour, it is normal that they identify with Andrés Manuel [and] . . . that a kind of 'Stockholm Syndrome' emerges," in the words of one expert.[28] The mayor's team fortified this prisoner-guard relationship or, in the case of the *mañaneras*, the journalist-politician bond, by giving reporters dominant access on a nearly exclusive basis. During his first thousand days in office, López Obrador granted only four one-on-one interviews to print journalists. In light of the broad reach of radio and television, however, he gave forty-nine "exclusives" to the electronic media averaging ten minutes long. In addition, he allowed noted journalist José González Vivó to interview him every three months on Radio Monitor. As of mid-2004, 198 reporters had covered at least one *mañanera*. Should reporters arrive late, Yáñez's aides provided them with a hastily prepared transcript of the news conference. Later, an edited version appeared on the D.F.'s official Web site. The "syndrome" was so strong that some editors sought to avoid clientelism by changing reporters who covered the mayor. During the conferences, *Reforma* had half a dozen different journalists on hand; *La Crónica* had four.[29]

López Obrador did not confine his courting of the media to beat reporters. He lunched each month with Emilio Azcárraga Jean and Ricardo Salinas Pliego, the majority owners of Grupo Televisa and Grupo Televisión Azteca, respectively. His administration also propitiated the press by proposing legislation to curb libel suits.

SEND IN THE CLOWNS

El Capitán Guarniz, who wore a leather flying helmet and muttered in gutturals as if he were drunk, occasionally showed up for the press sessions. Guarniz "reported" for *El Mañanero,* which was hosted by Víctor Trujillo, who once dubbed the voices for Richard Chamberlain and Robert de Niro in Spanish-language versions of American films. The clever, versatile Trujillo, who assumed the role of "Brozo, the Gloomy Clown" on the popular television show, boasted an audience of 7 to 8 million viewers. The program derived its success from Brozo's mordant, iconoclastic black humor, which he often directed at public officials. The scantily clad "intern" (*la Becaria*) played by Evelyn Robles added a titillating dash of sex to the program. Prominent political figures such as First Lady Marta Sahagún, Cuauhtémoc Cárdenas, government secretary Santiago Creel, Senate leader Enrique Jackson Ramírez, and dozens of other notables frequently appeared on the show. Brozo often added editorial comments to news, weather, and traffic reports with facial expressions and gestures. During an item about the alleged March 2004 assassination attempt of Governor José Murat, Brozo said nothing, but jabbed his finger into his arm, possibly to suggest that the Oaxaca leader had injected himself.

Brozo's time slot—his program aired from 6:00 to 10:00 A.M. daily on Televisa's channel 4—allowed him to provide ample coverage of López Obrador's morning press conference. The Gloomy Clown often used issues raised at these briefings as the grist for ranting commentaries and questions to guests. While he did disseminate el Peje's ideas, Brozo was no sycophant, as evidenced by his having broken the Bejarano story.

Following the death of his wife, Trujillo ended the program in early June 2004. One week later, Government Secretary Encinas accused Televisa, the network that carried *El Mañanero*, of conspiring against López Obrador. He said that the "campaign" was spearheaded by the PAN and its ultra-right-wing Yunque allies, many of whom worked in Los Pinos.[30]

PRESS TEAM

Until he left the government to join López Obrador's campaign, César Yáñez headed the twenty-one-member staff of the General Directorate of Social Communication (DGCS). Born on June 2, 1962, in Colima, Yáñez earned a degree in social communication from the Autonomous University of Mexico. He began his career in the Ministry of Commerce and Economic Development, analyzing news coverage of the secretary and his associates. Yáñez participated in Cárdenas's 1988 and 1994 presidential campaigns and served as information chief for "el Inge," Cardenas's nickname, when he ran for mayor in 1997, a post that he retained after the PRD candidate won the city's top spot. As an indication of his professionalism and flexibility, Yáñez worked for twelve months in 1994 and 1995 for PRD party president Muñoz Ledo. Yáñez also handled communications for López Obrador during el Peje's tenure as party president from 1996 to 1999.

The deputy information secretary, Manuel Moreno, was Yáñez's right-hand man. One or both could usually be found at the mayor's side. Meanwhile, Socorro Aubrey held the post of deputy for broadcasting. A Veracruz native and former federal deputy of the PRD, Aubrey, forty-nine, had a background in the electronic media. Aguilar Cueto looked after logistics for the *mañaneras*. The Social Communications Office employed approximately two hundred people. The 180 unionized workers arrived at 9:00 A.M. and left at 3:00 P.M., which meant that some twenty men and women showed up early and stayed late to accommodate the mayor's demanding schedule.[31]

Before López Obrador's administration, each major city department had its own communications section. Not only did this situation breed redundancy, waste, and confusion, it also gave rise to the dissemination of competing messages as officials engaged in one-upmanship with political competitors. Zealous agency heads also authorized the payment of stipends to journalists so as to buy favorable coverage of their actions.

The new mayor put an end to the multiple communication streams emanating from government offices. On February 13, 2002, he published Decree 4 in the *Gaceta Oficial del Distrito Federal*. This measure eliminated all social communication departments in various agencies and established the General Directorate of Social Communication. The DGCS was invested with full powers to "regulate general policies related to actions involving publicity, propaganda, broadcasting and information." Decree 4 also stipulated that information should pertain to the "strategies, priorities, and objectives of government programs," and not be used for "promoting the image of public servants, political parties, or candidates for elected positions."[32] The only agencies to have their own press offices were the Ministry of Public Security, whose head is a presidential appointee, and the Attorney General for the Federal District, which prizes its autonomy.[33] This reorganization of social communications complemented the *mañaneras* in enabling the authoritarian mayor to control the flow of information and ensure that his administration was speaking with a single voice.

IMITATORS

As PAN's president in the D.F. from 2001 to 2003, José Luis Luege Tamargo sought to steal some of the mayor's thunder by holding his own weekday press conferences.[34] For these sessions, which began in early 2003, he chose the ornate Gran Hotel de la Ciudad de México, a historic landmark just half a block from city hall. As an added inducement to attract journalists who had covered "the source," the PAN provided a tasty breakfast. The mayor even cooperated with Luege, telling the reporters, "Get your news here and then go over to the PAN briefing for breakfast."[35]

At first the dynamic, well-spoken Luege attracted many of the *mañanera* reporters: some went in search of food, a few were attracted by the novelty of the event, and others actually showed up for news. The number of participants gradually declined, however, until the PAN discontinued the briefings before the national elections in mid-2003. Luege frankly admitted that his audience had dwindled. He added that "a party president simply cannot generate the interest commanded by a key elected figure who had the ability to make policy every day."[36]

Luege's effort also suffered from a lack of coordination with the president. Fox's schedule was not always known to the PAN, which limited Luege's ability to respond to questions regarding the chief executive's appearances. Luege, who at the outset said he would not hold conferences if there were no items to discuss, finally abandoned the sessions. As he put it, "mi hacen los que al viento a Juárez."[37] In other words, it was no skin off his nose. Although quite dynamic, the prickly and conservative Luege could not forge the ties with youthful reporters in the masterly way of el Peje.

Even though the PAN did not recommence its morning news conferences after the mid-2003 elections, two of the party's ALDF members—Gabriela Cuevas and Jorge Lara—filed suit against the city government when it denied them access to the *mañaneras*. The PAN had tried before to have a PAN militant attend the mayor's *mañaneras*, but Yáñez would not grant him a credential.[38]

Former government secretary and presidential aspirant Creel, who lost the PAN nomination to Felipe Calderón, increased his number of press briefings but did not attempt to emulate el Peje by having one at a specific time every day. In mid-2004 Fox appointed Rubén Aguilar Valenzuela his presidential press spokesman. His task was to minimize the number of off-the-cuff controversial remarks made by the chief executive and to minimize public squabbling between cabinet members. But Aguilar Valenzuela raised the hackles of the press when he wrote, "It is not desirable in a democracy that political journalism increasingly relies on sensationalism and the trivialization of politics."[39] He also complained about the information disseminated about the lives of political figures and expressed his support for reform of the Federal Radio and Television Law, including incentives to improve reporting.

ADVANTAGES FOR LÓPEZ OBRADOR

Even as Aguilar Valenzuela struggled to deliver a coherent message from Los Pinos, López Obrador emerged as the hands-down winner of the communications battle. The *mañaneras* fed material to the information-starved media, enabling him to dominate the morning news cycle nationwide. Responses to his statements frequently highlighted the afternoon cycle and enabled him to effectively set the news agenda. He made front-page news throughout the country with his strident condemnation of Fobaproa, the generous retirement benefits afforded ex-presidents, tax increases, and privatizations in the energy field. After the mayor introduced an issue, journalists immediately asked other politicians their opinions on his populist stances. Often the reporters phrased their inquiry along the lines of "have you stopped beating your wife?" or "do you support the multibillion-dollar rescue of rich bankers?" This made it extremely difficult for reasonable respondents to answer succinctly—in a thirty-second sound bite—without coming across as apologists for neoliberal initiatives. At one press conference López Obrador held up half a dozen newspapers, all of which carried major articles about the subject of the previous day's session. El Peje invariably came out on the side of purported victims.

He even used the question of Daylight Saving Time to appeal to the downtrodden, criticize Fox's pro-American posture, and capitalize on public wariness of government initiatives. This "is just part of a desire to automatically imitate the United States and Canada," claimed an editorial in the PRD newspaper *Fuerza*.[40] Other politicians asserted that turning the clock ahead would increase early-morning muggings, while disrupting citizens' sex lives. López Obrador urged the president to hold a national referendum on the subject. Some observers criticized the mayor for what they called blatant demagogy. López Obrador "has his eye set on the 2006 elections," wrote Mexico City author and columnist Germán Dehesa. "He wants to create this pretty myth of himself as El Zorro, the prince of democracy fighting against arbitrary decisions of Fox."[41] Whatever el Peje's motives, the Supreme Court of Justice struck down his move to prevent the adoption of DST in the capital.

The press events also gave the Tabascan an opportunity to fend off attacks by offering an alternative explanation of events. When reporters discovered that his chauffeur earned a large salary, he spoke in terms of the many hours the man put in each day and the number of functions he performed for the mayor. When the *videoescándalo* arose, he blasted the "conspirators," who he said were out to destroy him because of their contempt for his alternative economic strategy.

Wilkins praised the mayor's ability to employ artifice to exert "total control" over the conferences. He set the rules of the game for participants, avoided off-the-cuff statements that might have diverted him from his message, lowered his voice to project a sense of peace, security, and certainty, and added drama to his presentations with long pauses. It is even said that when Tabascans argue, the first one to pause loses the dispute. López Obrador managed to slow his rat-tat-tat, *tabasqueño* speaking style, although he still used phrases that abound in his home state. For "to the marrow," he used *hasta el cogoyo*. He called big shots *zangamilotes*.

El Peje pooh-poohed the suggestion that he had taken acting lessons, but he obviously labored to develop an effective delivery. He employed the Tere Struck y Asociados public relations agency to help him craft his messages, speeches, and slogans. Teresa Struck, the firm's owner, suggested that he preface his lapidary phrase "First the Poor," (*Primero los Pobres*) with "For the Good of All" (*Por el Bien de Todos*).

The *mañaneras* enabled the mayor to forge a personal relationship with his viewers. As Marshall McLuhan observed more than forty years ago, television is a "cool medium" that people watch in the comfort of their homes (in contrast to the "hot" medium of radio, which they may listen to in their cars or in the workplace). Thus, in contrast to the tub-thumping of candidates and the droning recitations of legislators, López Obrador's soft, conversational tones allowed him to establish a rapport not only with journalists but also with many TV viewers, to whom he became a virtual member of the family.

Unplanned, or apparently unplanned, activities linked to the press conferences added to the mayor's image as a down-to-earth, approachable individual. When he arrived at city hall on November 13, 2003—his fiftieth birthday—he found a group of residents from Cuajimalpa prepared to celebrate the event.[42] The group, composed largely of poor women, had arrived at 5:00 A.M., bringing along a large cake, *atole,* a corn-based chocolate drink, Oaxacan-style tamales, a bouquet of flowers, and a hand-knitted scarf. Also on hand were mariachis, who serenaded him with "Las Mañanitas," "El Rey," and other sentimental favorites. When asked to make a birthday wish, López Obrador hesitated. A woman suggested, "Ask for 2006!" When a journalist inquired how it felt to be fifty years old, he replied that "it is hardly fifty centavos" ("es apenas un tostón").[43]

At 5:00 A.M. on May 26, 2005, the Ultravisión musical group, made up of the visually impaired, arrived at the Ancient Palace of the city government to play "Las Mañanitas" and other songs to celebrate López Obrador's saint's day. Meanwhile, a group of transvestites delivered an invitation, asking the mayor to attend a play entitled *Confesiones de una güera oxigenada.*[44]

Just as Jesus often assumed the role of teacher, López Obrador reveled in giving lessons to those gathered around him in the Francisco Zarco Press Room. For an entire week he tutored his listeners on the intricacies of Fobaproa and how the program benefited the rich and battered the poor. In March 2004 he used questions about the video scandals to embellish his argument that his programs had made him the target of a conspiracy. In June 2004 he presided over a five-day seminar called the "Seminar-Workshop on the Manipulation of the Law for Political Purposes: The Encino Case."

While Jesus spread his gospel by word of mouth, "maestro" López Obrador relied heavily on television to reach his flock through carefully managed news conferences. Like Christ, the mayor instructed by example, accentuated his rejection of the material world, stressed action over knowledge, declaimed the worth of the learner, and emphasized character above content.[45] The *mañaneras* allowed an unassuming, self-proclaimed "little ray of hope" to endear himself to people across the country. At the same time, he delivered his vision for the nation, and his readiness to make any sacrifice necessary to deliver social justice, through journalists, who sometimes behaved as if they were communicants receiving the truth from the master. He would promote the cause of the masses, he proclaimed, despite venal conspiracies to destroy him and his plan to liberate the people from the abomination of neoliberalism.

THE LOAVES AND
THE FISHES

In his December 2000 inaugural speech, the man who had minis-
tered to the Chontales and led exodus marches again aligned himself with the masses with his mantra, "For the Good of All, Above
all the Poor." He infused his message with attacks on neoliberalism:
"We will not accept the artifice of labeling as populism or paternal-
ism the little that is allocated to the poor and define as development or bailouts the much greater resources delivered to the privileged."[1] He pledged to follow Juárez's principle of austerity and
called for an anticorruption campaign with "zero impunity." Once
López Obrador completed his speech, he quickly left the ornate
Legislative Assembly building and, like a latter-day Christ, sought
out the common people in nearby Alameda Park—where old men
hunched over checker boards and traded tall tales about their
youthful exploits. "I will not let you down," vowed the Tabascan
amid a sea of admirers, many wearing T-shirts bearing the faces of
socialist icons Fidel Castro and Che Guevara.[2]

NEOCORPORATISM

After thirty-five years in the PRI, el Peje realized the importance of
organizing constituencies around common purposes and reciprocal
interests. Even as the PRI's corporatist fabric frayed, López Obrador began to weave a new tapestry of groups forgotten or neglected
by the revolutionary party. He started with senior citizens.

Senior Citizens

Soon after taking office, el Peje discouraged references to "old people," preferring instead "people of the third age." He ordered the distribution of a plastic card to every person age seventy or older. The de facto credit cards carried a value of approximately $62 (later increased to $72) and could be used in supermarkets, pharmacies, restaurants, and most establishments an individual would wish to patronize. The cards made an impact on families as well, as grandparents praised the initiative to their children and grandchildren. Assistance to older people often diminished the burden placed on younger relatives. By January 2006 the city reported the distribution of more than four hundred thousand cards.[3]

López Obrador shrewdly asserted that recipients had earned the entitlement. "The work of older citizens has contributed to the greatness of the city. Nothing that we have today in the city could have been achieved without the work of previous generations."[4] He condemned those who criticized the program's expense. Although Mexico's wealth had been plundered, and ubiquitous corruption had impeded the effective use of its riches, he said, the country still had tremendous wealth in resources like petroleum. As a result, "a few have everything and the majority lacks the most indispensable items. Thus, we must continue to defend their social rights."[5]

Single Mothers

In 2001 the D.F. introduced a plan to help single mothers by providing monthly $62 stipends to their children.[6] These "scholarships" were designed to promote school attendance of youngsters between the ages of six and fifteen and prevent the disintegration of the family. The money could be used for food, clothing, and other necessities. The families' needs as well as children's school attendance were verified. To be eligible, a family had either to have lived in a "zone of medium, high, or very high marginality" or to have earned no more than one "minimum salary"—46.80 pesos. In 2005 the city awarded scholarships to 138,000 children of single mothers.

Milk for Babies

Other city and federal programs assisted poor mothers of newborns. For example, they could take advantage of Liconsa, a subsidized milk program that benefited 621,500 low-income families. In mid-2001 the increased cost of imported powdered milk forced the Fox administration to raise the price of the milk from 3 to 3.50 pesos per liter. López Obrador denounced the move and said the D.F. would help the needy. The mayor was then informed that Liconsa, the milk supplier, was barred from accepting city funds in exchange for maintaining the lower price. They failed to support the poorest segment of the population, he charged, while "providing every kind of fiscal and financial opportunities to privileged groups."[7] In the wake of this decision, the D.F. distributed vouchers so that families could offset the fifty-centavo price hike.

The Disabled

The Federal District also launched an initiative to assist the disabled poor. At the outset of López Obrador's term as mayor, the city began giving "scholarships" to 40,333 people who met the following requirements. They had to be under age seventy, live in a poor or marginal neighborhood, earn less than two minimum salaries, and have one or more disabilities. By mid-2005, this program had served sixty-eight thousand people.[8]

Preparatory Schools

El Pejelagarto made good on his promise to open new preparatory schools that were free to poor children. During the 2005–6 academic year, 13,676 students attended these fifteen schools, which had 840 faculty members.

Autonomous University of Mexico City

In the face of shrill opposition, the mayor also established the first public institution of higher learning in the capital since 1974. He opened the Autonomous University of Mexico City (UACM) in the poor, crime-plagued Iztapalapa borough. At the ceremony he observed that enrollment in the capital's private universities had surged 168 percent over the preceding eighteen years, while matriculations in public institutions had grown only 6 percent. Denouncing the "strategy of exclusion," López Obrador argued that "the state has not met its responsibility to provide free quality education for everyone."[9] Eight hundred students were randomly selected from two thousand applicants to begin study on September 4, 2001. By 2005 there were 6,100 students—a figure that would rise to ten thousand in 2006, according to the university's rector. Allegations of job selling and low standards aside, the university now has four locations. The pro–López Obrador orientation of most of the 840 professors and the students' social backgrounds ensure that UACM graduates will be el Peje's janissaries in his fight against the elite.

Public School Children

In December 2003 the ALDF passed the Law to Provide Free School Supplies. Eight months later the city government launched the program for public school children for the 2004–5 academic year. Once parents obtained vouchers, they could pick up the boxes of materials for each grade from kindergarten through high school. The undersecretary for educational services for the D.F. established twenty distribution centers.[10] The large Gigante retail store in Iztapalapa alone provided ninety thousand packets.[11] In 2004 the government gave out 2,776,000 packets of school materials to 1.4 million students at a cost of 140 million pesos. Since late 2000 the city has also distributed 4.5 million free textbooks and served 70.8 million school lunches.

Housing

López Obrador highlighted the city's housing problems in both his inaugural address and in Informational Decree No. 2 as well as in his Housing Policy Pact. He pledged to attend to the requirements of the poorest segments of the capital's population and attract people back to the central boroughs (Cuauhtémoc, Benito Juárez, Miguel Hidalgo, and Venustiano Carranza), because the population had disproportionately increased in the southern and eastern parts of the city. He also emphasized the need to construct twenty-five thousand new housing units in 2001 as part of an effort to address the D.F.'s substantial housing shortage.

The lead agency for accomplishing these goals was the D.F. Housing Institute (INVI), whose director-general was architect David Cervantes Peredo, a former city and federal legislator who is a leader of the pro-PRD Asamblea de Barrios–Patria Nueva.

In theory, the criteria for obtaining a housing credit were that one must have lived in the D.F. for at least three years, head a household, be between eighteen and sixty years of age, have dependents or be married, and have an income of no more than 4.7 times the minimum salary. Hundreds of people flocked to the INVI at the crack of dawn every weekday morning in the hope of being granted the "miracle" of a new home. The number of applicants mushroomed after storms and flooding.

According to Cervantes, the López Obrador regime awarded approximately 70,000 credits valued at 3.8 billion pesos to enable recipients to improve or enlarge their homes. Of the 64,000 requests received for 2004, 32,000 credits were given in amounts ranging from 20,000 to 68,000 pesos, with a twelve-year repayment period. While some 25,600 applicants met the criteria, insufficient funding meant that 6,400 qualified applicants did not receive credits. INVI focused its resources on 840 poor neighborhoods in Iztapalapa, Gustavo A. Madero, Alvaro Obregón, and Tlalpan.

City Farmers

In view of its striking buildings, broad thoroughfares, urban sprawl, and shantytowns, it is easy to overlook Mexico City's rural areas. Not López Obrador, however. In early June 2004 he initiated a 13-million-peso program for the D.F.'s small farmers. This Community Fund for Fair and Sustainable Development made loans to producers in the boroughs of Xochimilco, Milpa Alta, Tlalpan, Tláhuac, and Magdalena Contreras.

Microcredits

In mid-March 2001 López Obrador began distributing microcredits to individuals who wanted to start family businesses known as *changaros*. He made awards totaling $220,000 to 630 heads of household, 90 percent of whom were women. The mayor took advantage of this event to lambaste Fox's own microcredit program. "They have spent more on publicity than what they are going to give to the people [in the federal program]," the mayor asserted. In June 2004 he bestowed credits of 9,902,000 pesos on 2,127 beneficiaries as part of his six-year plan to promote self-employment for 150,000 men and women. He explained that the city required no type of guarantee; the recipients' word would secure the credit. His approach in the D.F. mirrored the *creditos a la palabra* that he had awarded to Chontales twenty-five years before.

Street Vendors

At the beginning of his term, López Obrador promised to relocate street vendors from the city's center, where they hawk items ranging from pirated videos and New York Yankee baseball caps to phony Rolex watches. These peddlers, who specialize in contraband, often operate in front of the stores of merchants who expect protection in return for purchasing business licenses, paying taxes, and bribing municipal inspectors. As part of the downtown renovation, the city evicted some fifteen hundred street vendors from streets leading into the Historic Center.

When discontented peddlers gathered to protest the mayor's relocation policy, he vowed that he would not give in and allow them to operate in prohibited areas. "We must seek a permanent solution," he averred. "There are many vendors in public areas because the economy has not functioned for a long time, and many of those assembled here probably voted for Salinas in his time . . . and the PRI, and we are paying the price for those votes that they gave to bandits."[12]

López Obrador moved to assist another type of street merchant: prostitutes. In mid-2005 he established a retirement home for older ladies of the night, who continued to ply their trade in exchange for food or a few pesos. Their new residence, called Xochiquetzal after the Aztec goddess of the earth and love, provided medical and psychiatric care and job training.[13] If Christ could mingle with prostitutes, could not the mayor of Mexico City provide them with a decent home?

CORPORATISM OR NOT?

The mayor's team insisted that the social programs of the government of the Federal District (GDF) bore no relationship to the PRI's corporatist constituencies. Recipients were under no obligation to join a political party or engage in political activity; they received stipends as individuals, not as group members. And the government conferred benefits on the basis of objective criteria. For instance, all Mexico City residents age seventy or older were eligible to receive $62 per month. In addition, the programs were not aimed at people in certain occupations in the same way that the PRI's sectors focus on peasants, blue-collar workers, and public employees. Finally, there was no quid pro quo. Older citizens received a stipend because they had contributed so much to the city; and poor youngsters got scholarships to advance their education.

Such reassurances aside, citizens insisted that access to public housing in the D.F. came with political strings attached. Even though applications were accepted from individuals, home seekers quickly learned the importance of affiliating with a pro–López Obrador organization, lest their applications be ignored. Of the 21,358 credits that INVI granted for new houses between 2000 and 2003, 12,498 (58.5 percent) were issued to eighty-one organizations linked to the PRD.[14] Among the successful groups were Cervantes's Asamblea de Barrios–Patria Nueva; CID; El Arenal Daybreak (Amancer del Arenal), which boasted ties to Ruth Zavaleta Salgado, PRD borough chief from 2003 to 2006; and the Francisco Villa Popular Front.

Meanwhile, INVI awarded only 2,015 credits to thirteen organizations with bonds to the PRI (9.4 percent), 683 to groups affiliated with the leftist Workers Party or PT (3.2 percent), and 102 to organizations associated with the PAN (.48 percent).[15] Three beneficiaries explained that years of political work preceded their obtaining credits. "Everything is based on grades . . . that is, the type of apartment that each person has is congruent with the grade he receives for attending meetings, showing up at rallies, participating in marches, and always being ready to give money when asked."[16] Cervantes insisted that INVI had no information about the political affiliation of its clients.[17]

Its rhetoric aside, the city also entered into a tacit alliance with the leaders of vendor groups. Although there were fewer sprawling flea markets in the Zócalo area than in other parts of the city after López Obrador left office, the number of the capital's sidewalk peddlers increased from 354,600 in 2001 to 482,400 in 2004, according to a national employment survey.[18]

El Peje and his entourage understood that street vendors had political muscle and could mobilize votes. The newspaper *Reforma* reported that government officials had turned a blind eye to these organized forces, which were believed to have links to crime syndicates. The PRD, like the PRI before it, regarded these well-organized vendor associations as a richer mine of votes than middle-class shopkeepers. When Fox moved to oust el Peje from office, some two thousand peddlers waving "No al Desafuero" signs rallied to his defense near the Tepito market.[19]

Similarly, the government paid lip service to the desirability of clearing the streets of illegal taxis, known as pirates. Soon after entering city hall, López Obrador promised a group of registered cab drivers that he would not permit the continued operation of undocumented taxis, and his secretary of public security announced that he would "hunt down" lawbreakers. Not only did pirates represent unfair competition to authorized taxis, but assaults and robberies often took place in their vehicles. Owners of these vehicles were believed to pay politically well connected leaders of illegal taxi groups a total of some 4.5 million pesos per week.[20] In August 2005 the secretary of transportation and public roads gave up the chase, saying that the city had higher priorities.[21] By the GDF's own figures, the number of illegal taxis doubled between 2002 and 2006, reaching thirty thousand.[22] The head of the powerful and corrupt Pantera pirate taxi organization then endorsed Marcelo Ebrard, López Obrador's heir apparent.[23]

Francisco Javier Hernández Garduño served as president of the PRD Transport Commission, which includes his G-4 organization, Águilas Metropolitanas, Unión la Montaña, Grupo Metópoli, and ten other illegal taxi groups. He pledged that his members would transport ten thousand families to an early August "informative assembly" that López Obrador held in the Zócalo to demand a vote-by-vote recount of ballots cast in the presidential contest. He also said that his commission would serve as the "strong arm" for acts of the "For the Good of All" coalition, including using their vehicles to prevent authorities from dismantling the encampment installed in downtown Mexico City. Its slogan was, "In the struggle there are no irregular or pirate [cabs], for we must all join hands with the agenda of López Obrador."[24]

TAKING THE PUBLIC'S PULSE

Even though López Obrador acted in an authoritarian manner, he called himself an instrument of his several constituencies, who made up "the people." He used surveys, telephone polls, and referenda to project this image. In late January 2001 el Peje hired three polling firms to sample public opinion on the regulation of marches through the capital. A majority of respondents approved the use of force to break up blockages of major arteries. The following month he conducted the city's first "telephone poll" on whether the city should switch to Daylight Saving Time. The vast majority of the 318,000 people who called in agreed with the mayor in opposing the time change.

In late November 2001 the mayor invited citizens to take part in a similar survey on metro fares. Of some forty-eight thousand respondents, 59 percent supported raising the fare from 1.5 to 2 pesos. Even with the increase, the D.F. fares remained among the lowest in the world. Despite the low turnout, el Peje said he would respect the outcome, which showed the "responsibility and consciousness" of city residents.

The next referendum addressed the construction of second decks on the heavily traveled Viaducto and Periférico highways. Residents near the proposed public works organized a petition drive against a project that would exacerbate traffic, noise, and pollution. On January 19 and 20, 2002, 80,870 citizens voiced their opinion, more than 70 percent (58,577) expressing approval. Turnout fell below the 33 percent threshold, which meant the outcome was not binding. Still, the mayor called the balloting a success and moved ahead with construction.[25]

In December 2002 López Obrador encouraged citizens to express their views on whether he should complete his six-year term. If they turned thumbs down on his performance, he pledged to leave his future in the hands of the ALDF. Of the 691,619 residents who took part in this telephone poll, 95.28 percent believed that the mayor should remain on the job; only 32,624 said he should resign. "There's no guarantee whatsoever this poll is clean," stated Professor Pablo Becerra. "It's frankly alarming that such a strong potential candidate for the presidency would embrace such a nondemocratic measure," he added. El Peje praised the vote as "another step" in Mexico's democratic transition.[26]

POLITICAL BENEFITS OF *CONSULTAS*

In addition to "involving" the public in decision making, the *consultas* gave legitimacy to the mayor's actions. They also expanded the mayor's database of names. To cast his "vote," a caller had to enter his twelve-digit voter registration number plus his age. These data allowed the city to sort respondents by name, age, address, and issue preferences.

Even as López Obrador employed the informal surveys for political purposes, he had twenty-seven city employees continually taking scientific polls. During the four years and ten months that he was in office, his team measured his popularity 254 times, an average of once a week. The monthly salaries for the surveyors totaled 164,000 pesos.[27] (See Tables 13 and 14 for details.)

TRADE UNIONS

The corporatist orientation of the López Obrador administration also evinced itself in the role of trade unions. Labor organizations fell into three categories with respect to their posture toward the city government. There were dyed-in-the-wool supporters, some of whose leaders enjoyed positions in the GDF; groups that shared the mayor's views but occasionally opposed him; and affiliates of the PRI-linked Confederation of Mexican Workers (CTM), who

TABLE 13. *Referenda and Polls Conducted by López Obrador's Administration*

SUBJECT OF REFERENDUM	DATE	"YES" VOTES	%	"NO" VOTES	%	% INVALID, BLANK, OR DON'T KNOW VOTES	NO. OF PARTICIPANTS	COST OF REFERENDUM
Should GDF Regulate Marches?*	January 27–28, 2001	2,163	86.5	247	9.9	3.6	2,500	375,000 pesos
Should D.F. adopt Daylight Saving Time?**	February 24–25, 2001	78,867	24.8	239,437	75.2	None	318,304	N.A.
Should metro fare be raised by 50 centavos?**	November 24–25, 2001	28,078	58.70	19,797	41.30	None	47,835	N.A.
Should "double deck" be constructed on Viaducto and Periférico?**	January 19–20, 2002	58,577	72.43	22,293	27.57	0.12	80,970	500,000 pesos
Should "double deck" be constructed on Viaducto and Periférico?***	September 22, 2002	274,606	65.30	142,384	33.86	0.84	420,322	4.8 million pesos
Should López Obrador remain in office?**	December 7–8, 2002	654,795	95.28	32,289	4.72	N.A.	681,004	3 million pesos
Should López Obrador remain in office?†	December 18–19, 2004	531,771	95.52	24,956	4.48	N.A.	556,727	N.A.

* Based on surveys conducted by three polling firms, Arcop, Consulta Mitofsky, and ISA.

** Telephone consultations.

*** Election supervised by the Instituto Electoral de D.F. (IEDF).

† Telephone poll conducted by the Coordinación Técnica team of the city government.

SOURCES: Dirección General de Comunicación Social, GDF, "Consultas realizadas por el GDF," http://www.comsoc.df.gob.mx/; "Escasa participación en primer plebiscito en historia del país," *EFE News Service*, December 9, 2002, http://wwwefenews.com/; Bertha Teresa Ramírez, "Dan capitalinos a López Obrador un aval que rebase expectativas," *La Jornada*, December 9, 2002, http://www.jornada.unam.mx/; Jonathan Roeder, "Mayor Defends Referendum on Hiking Cost of Public Transit Costs," *News* (Mexico City), November 17, 2001, http://www.thenewsmexico.com/; Jennifer Dorroh, "Voters Approve Double Decks but Turnout Too Low to Be Binding," *News* (Mexico City), September 24, 2002, http://www.thenewsmexico.com/; and Bertha Teresa Ramírez, "Refrenda 95% de consultados el mandato de López Obrador," *La Jornada*, December 20, 2004, http://www.jornada.unam.mx/.

TABLE 14. *Benefits Conferred on Constituent Groups in* D.F.

CONSTITUENT GROUP	BENEFITS	NUMBER OF BENEFICIARIES (2006)	COST OF PROGRAM
Older Adults	Monthly stipend of 668 pesos	390,500	3.3 billion pesos
Single Mothers with Children	Monthly stipend of 688 pesos	17,804	15.4 million
Families	Subsidized milk	621,500 families (2005)	N.A.
Disabled People	Monthly stipend of 688 pesos	70,690	61.3 million pesos
Poor Children Attending Fifteen Preparatory Schools		13,647	N.A.
Poor People Seeking University Training (UACM)		7,886	300 million pesos in infrastructure
Families with Children in Public Schools	School supplies to public school students (*útiles escolares*)	1.4 million children (GDF prepared 1,190,747 packets of supplies in 2005)	97,200 million pesos
Public School Children	Free secondary school textbooks	488,760 (2006–7)	13 million pesos
Public School Children	Free school breakfasts	114.37 million to 674,339 children	
Public School Children	Counseling for anti-social youngsters	22,500 (2001–6)	
Microcredits to the Self-employed	Grants of approximately 5,004 pesos apiece	19,937	99.78 million pesos
Those in Need of Housing	New housing	8,342 (2005) (150,000 projected for 2001–6)	
Those in Need of Housing Repairs	Repairs	1.336 million families	
Credits to Farmers		1,731	10.8 million pesos
Día del Niño (April 30, 2005)	150-peso vouchers (*vales*) to children of police officers	53,000	7.950 million pesos
Total Social Spending	Various programs	9,995,000	32 billion pesos (government figure)

SOURCE: Fabiola Cancino, "Descarta AMLO suspender conferencias matutinas," *El Universal*, June 22, 2004, http://www.el-universal.com.mx/; Bertha Teresa Ramírez, "Una realidad las *prepas* del GDF," *La Jornada*, August 31, 2004, http://www.jornada.unam.mx/; and Bertha Teresa Ramírez and Mirtha Hernández, "Preparan operativo para dar los útiles," *Reforma*, August 17, 2004, http://www.reforma.com/; Mirtha Hernández, "Faltan dar 70 mil bolsas de útiles," *Reforma*, August 31, 2004, http://www.reforma.com/; Jorge Alberto Pérez, "Regala SSP local vales por día del niño," *Reforma*, April 30, 2005, http://www.reforma.com/; GDF, "Primer informe trimestral del quinto año de gobierno de Andrés Manuel López Obrador," http://www.comsoc.df.gob.mx/documentos/; GDF, "Quinto informe de gobierno de Alejandro Encinas Rodríguez, en la Asamblea Legislativa del Distrito Federal," http://www.comsoc.df.gob.mx/documentos/.

regarded el Pejelagarto as the anti-Christ. Table 15 depicts the several alignments.

The Tabascan curried even greater favor with the Left by allowing peasants, bureaucrats, and groups like the Zapatistas to hold demonstrations in the capital, and sometimes assisting them in this. The most persistent and most violent group, however, was the National Coordination of Educational Workers (CNTE), a rival to the extremely wealthy National Union of Educational Workers (SNTE). López Obrador's swearing in flashed a green light to the CNTE's most radical locals that they could bring their grievances to the capital. At first, López Obrador welcomed the CNTE rabble-rousers, who praised the new mayor. He may even have helped finance their bus trips to the capital. On December 11, 2000, CNTE extremists, accompanied by the General Strike Committee (CGH) student firebrands, forced their way into the Chamber of Deputies to disrupt the presentation of Finance Secretary Francisco Gil Díaz.[28]

In mid-May 2001 CNTE demonstrators tried to batter down the main door of the Ministry of Gobernación. When no city policemen showed up, federal law enforcement agents stepped in. Two weeks after this *portazo*, CNTE teachers again assaulted the ministry, forcing Secretary Santiago Creel to carry out his duties from a satellite office.[29]

Authorities took seriously a recommendation by New York mayor Rudolph Giuliani to prevent the protesters from disrupting the president's September 1, 2003, state-of-the-nation address, known as the *informe*. The Federal Preventive Police, city police, riot police, and agents of the presidential general staff dispersed throughout the D.F. to prevent demonstrators from reaching Congress.

Although the September 1 events came off smoothly, CNTE became one of several major forces in uniting violence-oriented groups in opposition to the Fox regime. Its unofficial partner is the extremely bloated Mexican Electricians Union (SME), which fears that electricity reform would reduce its numbers, income, and influence. Other organizations that make common cause with the CNTE and SME include unions representing workers at the IMSS, ISSSTE, UNAM, the Francisco Villa Popular Front, el Barzón, and the CGH.

Although these groups use and condone violence, the GDF under López Obrador provided them with portable toilets, drinking water, lodgings, police protection, and a sympathetic reception. López Obrador's permissiveness nourishes the belief that mobilizations, confrontations, and violence are an effective way to influence policy.

In messianic fashion, el Peje placed his interpretation of the people's will above laws crafted by a regime he deemed illegitimate. He complemented his informal polls with regular scientific surveys

TABLE 15. *Organized Labor and López Obrador in 2006*

PRO–LÓPEZ OBRADOR	LEADER	SITUATIONAL AGREEMENTS WITH LÓPEZ OBRADOR	LEADER	ANTI–LÓPEZ OBRADOR	LEADER
UNAM Workers' Union (Sindicato Único de Trabajadores de la UNAM—STUNAM)	Agustín Rodríguez Fuentes	National Union of Workers (Union Nacional de Trabajadores—UNT)	Francisco Hernández Juárez	Confederation of Mexican Workers (Confederación de Trabajadores de Mexico—CTM)	Joaquín Gamboa Pascoe
Single Union of D.F. Government Workers (Sindicato Unico de Trabajadores del Gobierno del D.F.—SUTGDF)*	Enrique Hanff Vázquez			National Union of Educational Workers (Sindicato Nacional de Trabajadores de Education—SNTE)	Elba Esther Gordillo Morales
Union of Flight Attendants in Mexican Aviation (Asociación Sindical de Sobrecargos de Aviación en Mexico—ASSA)	Arturo Aragón Sosa, Alejandra Barrales Magdaleno	Union of Telephone Workers of the Mexican Republic (Sindicato de Telefonistas de la República Mexicana—STRM)	Francisco Hernández Juárez	Federation of Unions of Workers at the Service of the State (Federación de Sindicatos de Trabajadores al Servicio del Estado—FSTSE)	Joel Ayala Almeida
Mexican Electricians Union (Sindicato Mexicano de Electricistas—SME)	Martín Exparza Flores			Revolutionary Confederation of Workers and Peasants ((Confederación Revolucionaria de Obreros y Campesinos—CROC)**	Isaías González Cuevas

* Just as the federal government has courted unions that resonated to López Obrador, Mexico City mayor Marcelo Ebrard has used the influence and resources of his office to cultivate the SUTGDF.

** On June 21, 2006, the CROC shifted its support from the PRI's presidential candidate to López Obrador. The labor body broke this alliance five weeks later when el Peje's post-election demonstrations in downtown Mexico City devastated the hotel and restaurant sector in which many CROC members are employed.

TABLE 15 *(cont'd).* *Organized Labor and López Obrador in 2006*

PRO–LÓPEZ OBRADOR	LEADER	SITUATIONAL AGREEMENTS WITH LÓPEZ OBRADOR	LEADER	ANTI–LÓPEZ OBRADOR	LEADER
National Coordination of Educational Workers (Coordinadora Nacional de Trabajadores de Educación—CNTE); Locals 9 and 10 (D.F.); 14 (Guerrero); 18 (Michoacán); 22 (Oaxaca); and 40 (Chiapas)	Feliciano Romero (Local 8); Blanca Luna (Sec'y, Local 9); Humberto Alcalá Betanzos and Alejandro Leal (Local 22)				
IMSS National Union (Sindicato Nacional de Trabajadores del IMSS—SNTSS)	Roberto Vega Galina			Union of the Metropolitan Mass Transit System (Sindicato Metropolitano del Sistema de Transporte Colectivo—SMSTC)	Fernando Espino Arévalo
National Pilots Union (Asociación Sindical de Pilotos Aviadores—ASPA)	Jesús Ramírez Stabros				
National Union of Nuclear Workers (Sindicato Único de Trabajadores de la Industria Nuclear—SUTIN)	Arturo Delfín Loya				
National Finance Development Bank Union (Sindicato Único de Trabajadores de Nacional Financiera—SUTNAFIN)	María Luisa Velázquez G				
Revolutionary Workers Confederation (Confederación Obrera Revolucionaria—COR)	Joel López Mayren				

to determine attitudes toward him and his initiatives. Such information enabled him to develop organized support within the capital by providing bread and circuses to the masses. The distribution of social benefits—his version of loaves and fishes—won him overwhelming approval from the people. López Obrador's PRD loyalists strengthened their grip on pirate taxis, street vendors, informal parking attendants, and other grassroots groups that were once dominated by the PRI. The D.F.'s zealous mayor assiduously collected the names and addresses of participants in referenda and beneficiaries of his social programs. This allowed him to create his own clientelist structure as he propagated a D.F. version of revolutionary nationalism, which he promised to implement throughout the country as an alternative to the despised policies of neoliberalism.

"LA CIUDAD DE LA ESPERANZA"

Just as López Obrador strove to gain legitimacy through social programs, he was eager to perform more miracles by transforming the chaotic capital into the City of Hope, beginning with the Historic Center. To obtain resources for this wondrous work, he vowed to reorganize the city's administration to reduce the redundancy of functions, the surfeit of personnel, and the blatant corruption that beset the GDF.

Even though his predecessor Robles had played a crucial role in his election, the crusading executive implicated her in the fraud that allegedly suffused the city. He claimed that some $10.5 million was missing from the treasury; the press reported his criticism in terms of Robles having a "piggy bank" (*cochinito*)—a crudely effective way of depicting wrongdoing. This followed an accusation by a Publicorp executive that the city had overpaid his advertising agency by 42.5 million pesos and a statement that it had returned these monies to Robles's political activities. She denounced her accuser as an alcoholic and drug addict,[1] and in September 2001 the city's attorney general closed the case without charging the former mayor.

REPUBLICAN AUSTERITY TAKES SHAPE

If López Obrador could live modestly, why could city bureaucrats not follow his example? Accordingly, he reduced salaries of key officials and restricted travel, access to credit cards, the availability of telephones and computers, and the purchase of new automobiles. El Peje did not limit these mandates to entities with bloated budgets like public works, transport, and law enforcement. *Reforma* reported that he even extended his ukase to a small, fifty-employee agency that had daily contact with the public. Its personnel were allocated only eight pencils, two erasers, six pens, and two jumbo rolls of toilet tissue each month. The legislation spelled out criminal and civil penalties for individuals who failed to abide by the regulations.[2]

"Compaction" became a slogan for the mayor's watchdogs. For instance, before López Obrador's changes, several agencies involved themselves in women's affairs. Not only was such duplication expensive, but women seeking municipal services often found themselves shunted from one office to another. To merge activities and make services more accessible, el Peje created a single Women's Institute. He also reformed programs for senior citizens, transportation, and healthcare. And he vowed to hold the line on metro fares, opposed tax hikes, and urged more federal funds for the D.F.[3]

HISTORIC CENTER RESTORATION

Mexico City was the New World's greatest metropolis when New York was a mélange of crude huts, muddy streets, and primitive fortifications. The center of this magnificent city began to deteriorate after the Great Depression. A rent freeze in the 1940s exacerbated decay by allowing tenants, who paid a pittance for a home or apartment, to make the same monthly payment until 1998, when the measure was finally repealed. Many renters and landlords allowed properties to disintegrate. Between 1970 and 1995 the population of the center dropped from 142,000 to 77,000. The 1985 earthquakes bequeathed what *The Economist* magazine called "the Beirut look" to the area.[4] Even before the catastrophe, the Historic Center had become an enclave of garbage-strewn lots, empty buildings, sleazy night clubs, pushy vendors, and criminals.

López Obrador enlisted powerful partners to rejuvenate the area: President Fox, Cardinal Archbishop Norberto Rivera Carrera, and Carlos Slim, who had become Latin America's wealthiest man in the 1990s. They established an executive committee to rescue the Historic Center. The renovations were concentrated in two major tourism corridors: the Zócalo to the Alameda to the Petroleum Fountain on Paseo de la Reforma; and the Metropolitan Cathedral to the Basilica of the Virgin of Guadalupe.

"Slimlandia"
Slim also created the Historic Center Trust of Mexico City, a private foundation that has poured $150 million into the rehabilitation

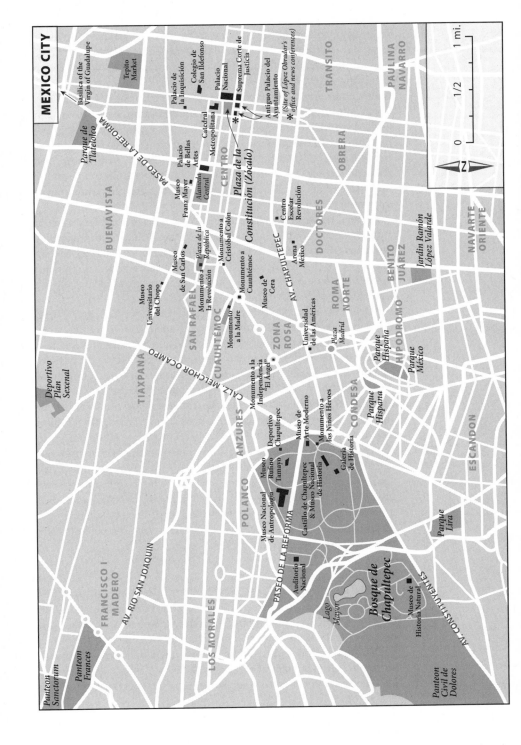

MEXICO CITY

Panteon Sanctorum

Panteon Frances

Panteon Civil de Dolores

Deportivo Plan Sexenal

FRANCISCO I MADERO

AV. RIO SAN JOAQUIN

LOS MORALES

Museo Nacional de Antropología

Castillo de Chapultepec & Museo Nacional de Historia

POLANCO

Auditorio Nacional

PASEO DE LA REFORMA

Bosque de Chapultepec

Lago Mayor

Museo de Historia Natural

AV. CONSTITUYENTES

Parque Lira

Museo Rufino Tamayo

Deportivo Chapultepec

Museo de Arte Moderno

Monumento a los Niños Héroes

Galería de Historia

CONDESA

ANZURES

CALZ. MELCHOR OCAMPO

TLAXPANA

Museo Universitario del Chopo

SAN RAFAEL

Museo de San Carlos

Monumento a la Revolución

CUAUHTÉMOC

Monumento a la Madre

Monumento a la Independencia "El Ángel"

ZONA ROSA

Universidad de las Américas

Plaza Madrid

ROMA NORTE

Parque Hispaña

Parque México

HIPODROMO

Parque Hispaña

ESCANDON

AV. CHAPULTEPEC

BUENAVISTA

PASEO DE LA REFORMA

Parque de Tlatelolco

Basilica of the Virgin of Guadalupe

Tepito Market

Plaza de la República

Monumento a Cristóbal Colón

Monumento a Cuauhtémoc

Museo de Cera

Museo Franz Mayer

Palacio de Bellas Artes

Alameda Central

Catedral Metropolitana

CENTRO

Plaza de la Constitución (Zócalo)

Palacio de la Inquisición

Colegio de San Ildefonso

Palacio Nacional

Suprema Corte de Justicia

Antiguo Palacio del Ayuntamiento

(Site of López Obrador's office and news conferences)

Centro Escolar Revolución

Arena México

DOCTORES

OBRERA

TRANSITO

PAULINA NAVARRO

Jardin Ramón López Valarde

BENITO JUÁREZ

NAVARTE ORIENTE

N

0   1/2   1 mi.

of what he labeled "the economic, political, cultural, academic and artistic heart of this country." Taking advantage of sharply reduced property taxes and water tariffs, the affluent entrepreneur attracted other investors, who restored or constructed office buildings, apartment complexes, restaurants, cafés, and hotels. In an article about "Slim Land," a journalist alluded to the entrepreneur's commercial, communications, and financial holdings: "Diners at one of Slim's hundreds of chain restaurants can use a Slim wireless service to connect to Slim's Internet provider to do online banking at Slim's bank, or pay off credit cards for Slim's department stores."[5] When detractors accused Slim of "privatizing" the Historic Center, he responded that "the private sector is giving impulse to the restoration of properties that are the patrimony of humanity."[6]

When representatives of the poor criticized the eviction of squatters from public lands, el Peje showed that he did not play favorites. In late 2002 he forced Margarita López Portillo, the sister of the ex-president, to return to the city one thousand square meters of protected parkland that had been annexed illegally for her luxury residence in the 1980s.[7]

Other entrepreneurs involved themselves in construction and renovation projects. Siahou Sitton Guindi spent more than $80 million on the 457-room Sheraton Centro Histórico. Canadian businessman Paul Reichmann erected the fifty-five-story Torre Mayor—now Latin America's tallest skyscraper—on Reforma at a cost of almost $3 billion. For every peso that the city invested in the historic zone, businesses contributed 22 pesos, according to the GDF. Since 2000, foreign investors have poured $30.8 billion into the city, which represented 57 percent of capital flowing into the nation from abroad. Cooperation between the private and public sectors directly or indirectly created 658,000 new jobs. Between January and November of 2004 the city added 89,611 jobs—the greatest expansion in the country. While the national economic growth had averaged 1.6 percent since 2001, the city's figure was 3.6 percent. Meanwhile, real tax collections rose 3.2 percent each year, the D.F. government claimed.

The Cardinal's Role

Cardinal Rivera applauded López Obrador's development ventures, especially the construction of the Mariana Plaza adjacent to the Basilica. Launched in October 2003, the three-hectare project will be larger than Rome's St. Peter's Square. There have been numerous delays, but if the plaza is completed, it will contain a colonnade with a hundred thousand recesses for human ashes, a public market, the San Juan Diego evangelizing center, and parking spaces for 560 automobiles.

When Pope John Paul II visited Mexico City in mid-2002, López Obrador welcomed him to the city, introduced him to his ailing wife, Rocío, and gave him a cape made by six peasant artisans. John Paul II then conducted a mass to canonize the Indian Juan Diego, who claimed to have witnessed appearances of the Virgin of Guadalupe in 1531.

El Peje, who has reiterated his respect for "all religious currents," propitiated Cardinal Rivera. In addition to rehabilitating church properties, the mayor worked with the ALDF to table a bill giving same-sex partners rights similar to those of married heterosexuals. Had the proposed "Law for Society Living Together" passed, the mayor said he would not have implemented it without its approval in a plebiscite. In his presidential campaign, López Obrador refused to stake out a position on either abortion or euthanasia, legalization of which is strongly favored by many PRD activists. The church came to the Tabascan's defense at the time of the *desafuero*, stating that "the political rights of the citizens of Mexico City who legitimately elected him have been violated."[8]

President Fox Lends a Hand

López Obrador shrewdly drew the president into his Historic Center initiative. He praised Fox for supporting the city's rejuvenation. In the same vein, the chief executive said that the two governments were fulfilling "the basic commitment of a democratic regime where there is no place for sterile confrontations."[9] Before subscribing to these accords, Fox did not consult local PAN officials, who gagged at the political benefits that the mayor would derive from federal projects, including the erection of the new twenty-two-story building for the Foreign Relations Ministry.

Public Works Projects

Even as he was adding luster to the Historic Center, the mayor embarked upon eye-catching transportation ventures to speed traffic flows. His major projects involved feeder roads, bridges linking Santa Fe to the southern part of the city, and various tunnels and overpasses. For years, architect David Zarur had tried to convince the capital's mayors that they could alleviate congestion by adding second tiers to heavily traveled thoroughfares. No one took this idea seriously until López Obrador entered city hall.[10] When the mayor publicized plans for the double decking, critics scoffed. In response, he allowed citizens to phone in their views on the subject in January 2000. When a solid majority approved the move, el Peje placed environment secretary Claudia Sheinbaum Pardo in charge of the project. By the time López Obrador left office to pursue the presidency, the city had constructed second tiers, bridges, tunnels, underpasses, and access roads that totaled forty-three kilometers. Also under construction were seventy-five kilometers of bicycle paths. In 2005 the city launched the Metrobús service. New buses travel in special lanes, picking up and dropping off passengers at thirty-five stations along Avenida Insurgentes, which bisects the city.

Fun and Recreation

Taking a page from the Roman emperors who appealed to the masses with bread and circuses, López Obrador sought to court Mexico City residents with family-friendly entertainment, which included performances by the Hermanos Vázquez Circus in the Zócalo in mid-2002. The mayor explained that the city was sponsoring the circus to benefit families with limited resources who could not afford to visit the beach or Disney World.[11]

Crime

Since the severe recession of the mid-1990s, crime has constituted the number-one concern of the city's residents. Security firms are prospering, private police patrol bank entrances, and wealthy families often travel in armor-plated vehicles. Denzel Washington's 2003 film *Man on Fire* dramatically depicted an affluent family's attempt to rescue their ten-year-old daughter, who was kidnapped in Mexico City. In Latin America, only Colombia exceeds Mexico in the number of abductions each year. Criminals increasingly engage in "express kidnappings": they force victims to make withdrawals from ATM machines or bank accounts as a condition of being released. Citizens report only one-fifth of such crimes[12] because they lack confidence in the D.F.'s several police forces, whose members are known to engage in illicit activities or work hand in hand with felons.

In October 2001 López Obrador attracted international attention when he invited the Giuliani Partners, headed by former New York City mayor Rudolph Giuliani, to provide advice on reducing crime levels. Slim and other moguls paid the $4.3 million fee charged by the U.S. consultants. On March 1, 2004, Ebrard unveiled a revised version of Giuliani's proposals, which included creating a comprehensive database that matches law enforcement resources to crime-prone areas. Also proposed was combining the Preventative Police, which patrol neighborhoods, and the Judicial Police, which carry out investigations. The foreign firm advised establishing an organized crime unit, setting up a fast-track judicial process to handle open-and-shut cases, and investing state judges with greater discretion over crimes that should be prosecuted. Other ideas included cracking down on petty crimes as a means of gaining the confidence of citizens, thus encouraging them to cooperate in the apprehension of big-time felons. Such a "broken windows" approach entailed tougher penalties on petty drug dealers, enforcing antigraffiti laws, and curbing informal parking attendants and windshield washers. Also recommended were placing "panic buttons" on buses, preparing a registry of bus drivers, and eliminating pirate taxis.

Ebrard, who said that half of Giuliani's suggestions had already been implemented, extolled the placement of more plainclothes policemen on the streets. He noted that a five-month "Operation

Polanco" had been accompanied by a reduction of muggings from eight to two a day and a decrease in car thefts from ten a week to just two.

In contrast to Ebrard's upbeat attitude, however, spokesmen for the poor argued that many street peddlers, beggars, car-window washers, and prostitutes were victims of failed economic policies and should not be harassed by the police.[13]

On March 21, 2005, López Obrador asserted that the number of crimes reported during his administration had declined to 466 per day, down from 654 between 1995 and 1997. He also cited a fall in homicides and car thefts compared with previous periods.

EVALUATION OF LÓPEZ OBRADOR'S ADMINISTRATION

The prudent use of resources is desirable, but such restrictions as those imposed on middle- and lower-level public servants at times proved counterproductive. When five or six employees must rely on one telephone, the ability to serve citizens often suffers. A scarcity of computers can delay obtaining important information and communicating with colleagues; and the failure to reimburse employees for the use of their personal vehicles or for taxi fares may mean that sanitation or building inspectors simply remain in their offices.

In addition, thousands of dismissed civil servants have taken their cases to labor courts, arguing that the government did not adhere to proper procedures when firing them. If, as anticipated, complainants win a majority of these cases, Mayor Ebrard will be forced to dole out millions of dollars in back pay and other compensation. Still, López Obrador took Fox to task for having allowed the salaries of federal bureaucrats to shoot up 40 percent on his watch.[14]

The renovation of the Zócalo and its environs is an impressive achievement. Yet even as the city rehabilitated two tourism corridors, San Ángel, Coyoacán, Tlalpan, and other historic zones were marred by peddlers, graffiti-defaced buildings, clogged metro stations, traffic bottlenecks, and irregular parking patterns.

Moreover, while el Peje reported a reduction in car thefts and homicides, these self-serving statistics did not take into account the capital's rapid population growth and the failure of citizens to report crime. Missing from his final report as mayor were data for such felonies as kidnappings, assaults, and bank robberies. The controversy over crime figures aside, 57 percent of *defeños* interviewed by *Reforma* said that he had not succeeded in the area of public safety. Only 21 percent gave him favorable marks on this issue, down from 38 percent at the beginning of his administration.

In terms of his transportation agenda, López Obrador paid little attention to subway service, which is so important to the poor.

The ALDF slashed 2.25 billion pesos from the 2004 city budget, with the subway system losing funds even though it carries 5.5 million riders each day and is the tenth-largest in the world. Several factors explain this cut: underground construction is expensive, and a PRI activist heads the Metro Workers' Union. But there was also a blatantly political element: above-ground public works are highly visible, while digging in the bowels of the capital attracts little attention.

Middle-level city officials readily admit that substantial cost overruns have afflicted the second tiers and other key projects. In an act of political theater, el Peje implored the ALDF to audit his transportation initiatives, but the PRD-dominated assembly voted to postpone such scrutiny until after the 2006 election. When opponents cried cover up, the outgoing mayor said, "It is possible to say many things about me, it is possible not to like my style . . . but no one can accuse me of being a criminal because I do not lust for money or power for power's sake."[15]

López Obrador helped kill a $2.3-billion airport in the San Salvador Atenco municipality in nearby México State. In so doing, he aligned with machete-waving protesters. "With my proposal [to enlarge the existing airport], the air traffic problem would be solved and it also wouldn't endanger the communal lands," he said.

LÓPEZ OBRADOR'S OBJECTIVES

Despite budget machinations and an inability to diminish crime, López Obrador proved himself to be a man of action. While Fox and the PAN found most of their legislative initiatives stymied, and the PRI struggled to live down its legacy of corruption, López Obrador increased his activism. He left office as the most popular mayor in modern history, with an unprecedented 76 percent approval rating and with more achievements than Uruchurtu (1952–66) and Hank González (1976–82). He ran second to Tirana's Edi Rama as "World Mayor 2004" in a nonscientific competition organized by *City Mayors* magazine.[16]

In addition, the mayor infused life into the Historic Center. His staging of circuses, concerts, dances, and other events signaled to the poor as well as the middle class that it was safe to return to the heart of their city. At the same time, the new restaurants, cafés, hotels, and office buildings brought people back to the Zócalo and other tourist spots.

His efforts to revive the city enabled him to forge ties with business moguls. While Carlos Slim was his most conspicuous comrade, he also worked with real estate guru Reichmann and such tycoons as Adrián Vargas, Carlos Hernández, Diego Quintana, and Bernardo Riojas. He developed ties with members of the small but influential Jewish community through the Daniel Brothers construction company.

López Obrador used his cooperation with Slim, Rivera, Fox, and other notables to change his image from rabble-rouser to statesman. How radical could he be if he was rubbing elbows and cutting ribbons with the wealthiest man in Latin America, the city's cardinal archbishop, and the nation's chief executive? If he could successfully manage an ungovernable city, he was ready to take the reins of the nation. By inviting foreign investment and hiring the Giuliani Partners, he sent a message to international markets that, as president, he would extend a welcoming hand, not a menacing fist, to responsible investors from abroad.

Even as he hobnobbed with the rich and famous and pursued capitalist economic policies, el Peje reinforced his reputation as protector of the humble by denouncing the erection of a new airport that would have displaced a few hundred peasants in México State. And he unveiled a "popular" economic strategy—featuring public works, job creation, and a leaner bureaucracy—as an alternative to the "bankrupt" neoliberal approach.

In addition, López Obrador burnished his image as an honest official by cutting the resources available to the bureaucracy. Meanwhile, he claimed ignorance of shady dealings within his entourage, even though Ponce's and Bejarano's money grabbing made a mockery of the mayor's self-righteous devotion to republican austerity. Yet his personal frugality and popular initiatives won favor with a public that longed for a redeemer.

Finally, by rechristening the D.F. the City of Hope, he identified himself with a transcendental value. If the crumbling core of the capital could be revived, might it be possible to rehabilitate your impoverished village in Guerrero? Your own household? Just as Christ offered the prospect of eternal life to believers, López Obrador's work in the D.F. disseminated the glad tidings of hope to his followers.

APOSTLES, DISCIPLES, AND MAGDALENAS

"Diversity, compactness, and pluralism" were López Obrador's overarching criteria for his cabinet. "Politicians would make the decisions and functionaries would obey," according to an associate.[1] El Peje perceived that his predecessors had sought to manage existing resources, whereas "he wanted to build new things."[2] In fact, as a political messiah, López Obrador surrounded himself with individuals who demonstrated walk-through-fire loyalty. With the exception of several technical areas, the expertise of cabinet members meant less than their commitment to el Peje and his mission.

LÓPEZ OBRADOR'S TEAM

From the beginning of his career in Tabasco, López Obrador had been a loner—distrustful of others and determined to work with an extremely small team. This characteristic appeared in his governance of the D.F. Accordingly, he placed trusted *tabasqueños* in several of the most sensitive positions. Alberto Pérez Mendoza and Octavio Romero Oropeza have been López Obrador's closest apostles. A confidant since the Tabascan's first gubernatorial campaign, Pérez Mendoza was Governor Rovirosa's press secretary when el Peje headed the INI. Later, Pérez Mendoza edited the antiestablishment *Corre la Voz*, helped found the pro-PRD newspaper *La Verdad del Sureste*, and worked closely with López Obrador when he headed Tabasco's PRD. In the D.F. he served as director-general of the city's Real Estate Holdings (*Patrimonio Inmobiliario*), which manages hundreds of millions of dollars' worth of government land, buildings, and other assets.[3]

Romero Oropeza was born in Jalapa, Veracruz, in 1959. He obtained a degree in agricultural engineering and subsequently taught mathematics, worked for the Banco Serfín, and made broadcasts on his family's radio station in Villahermosa. In the mid-1990s he became active in the PRD, serving in various party posts, including as president of the state executive committee after the surreptitious ouster of López Cruz. El Peje invited former *priísta* Romero Oropeza to run for the Chamber of Deputies on the PRD ticket in 1994. During López Obrador's tenure as national party president, Romero functioned as the party's chief administrative officer and followed his boss to city hall in the same capacity. The apostle also acted as a troubleshooter, helping identify subordinates on whom to blame the El Encino imbroglio if the *desafuero* ended up in a courtroom.

Oscar Rosado Jiménez should not be considered an apostle, but he is another insider from Tabasco. Born in Comalcalco in 1961, he succeeded Romero as the national party's chief administrative officer in 1998. He then functioned as coordinator of administration and finances in the mayoral campaign of el Peje, who named him treasurer of the D.F.

While not apostles, other prominent *tabasqueños* in the ex-mayor's entourage include Rafael Marín Mollinedo (Teapa), director-general of Urban Services in the D.F.'s Ministry of Public Works, who has been close to el Peje since he ran for governor of Tabasco in 1988. His upper-middle-class family helped finance López Obrador's first political crusade. Nicolás "Nico" Mollinedo Bastar (Teapa), the mayor's coordinator of logistics, who picked up his boss in the mornings, remained at his side during the day, and returned him home at night is another. Luz Elena González Escobar, general director of the Passenger Transport Network (RTP), is a third prominent member of el Peje's cadre. Before assuming this post in mid-2003, she was executive director of Political Integration and Institutional Coordination of the D.F.'s Ministry of the Environment.

While René Bejarano claimed to have retired from politics after his release from prison in July 2005, he is still a López Obrador apostle, as is his wife, Dolores Padierna. In light of the *videoescándalo*, Bejarano might be judged the "Judas" among el Pejelagarto's closest followers. However, he only embarrassed the Tabascan by taking cash from Ahumada. López Obrador never condemned him, claiming the videotape had been edited. Bejarano also functioned as director-general of the D.F.'s government from 1998 until 2003. He was López Obrador's private secretary and confidant before capturing a seat in the ALDF, where he became that body's leader.

López Obrador's youngest apostle is the highly disciplined ex-PRD president in Mexico City, Martí Batres Guadarrama. He comes from a militantly leftist family,[4] and cut his political teeth in UNAM student politics and in the New Tenochititlán movement. Although he was only thirty-one years old, he headed the PRD faction in the ALDF before assuming the same post in the Chamber of Deputies. A vegetarian who neither drinks nor smokes, Batres shares el Peje's zeal to drive neoliberals from power and became the leading spokesman for the Tabascan after the election of July 2, 2006.

In addition to his apostles, López Obrador gathered ex-PRI notables who backed his candidacy. The most prominent of these "converts" was Manuel Camacho, former Zacatecas governor Monreal, Deputy Socorro Díaz Palacios, and Senator Raúl Ojeda. They helped to coordinate a citizens' network to disseminate López Obrador's gospel, identify candidates for the 2006 congressional contests, and attract more followers to his mission. Another PRI convert—Cota Montaño—served as PRD president until mid-2007. These individuals applauded their paladin when he rejected Calderón's victory in mid-2006 and proclaimed himself the nation's "legitimate president." (See Table 16 for more details.)

MAGDALENAS

Just as females played a significant role in the life of Jesus, López Obrador attracted a group of latter-day Mary Magdalenes to help advance his cause. Hard work, fidelity to their leader, a readiness to shield him from attacks, and a thirst for social justice characterized all of these women. Among these loyalists was Environment Secretary Sheinbaum, a political independent who holds a doctorate in electrical engineering. Her versatility in handling different challenges and her ability to complete assignments promptly enhanced her standing with the extremely demanding and authoritarian mayor. She enjoyed el Peje's full confidence. Equally devoted was Culture Secretary Raquel Sosa Elízaga, a member of a well-to-do family, who became active in leftist parties and served as the city's social development secretary until early 2005.

Other "Magdalenas" were Health Secretary Asa Cristina Laurell, a Swiss-born surgeon; Economic Development Secretary Jenny Saltiel Cohen; Luz Rosales Esteva, who headed the D.F.'s Women's Institute; and Comptroller Bertha Elena Luján Uranga, former head of the anti-PRI Authentic Work Front, which vehemently opposed NAFTA. Critics claimed that under el Peje, Luján spent more time covering up abuses than ferreting out wrongdoing. When PAN deputies accused the Coyoacán borough chief of spending public funds to help Ebrard's campaign, Luján suspended the local leader for thirty days but exonerated the mayoral candidate. She also cooperated with Romero Oropeza in identifying and harassing one or more scapegoats in the El Encino case.

TABLE 16. *Key Positions Held by the National Democratic Left in the D.F., 2006**

GOVERNMENT D.F.	PRD CITY COMMITTEE	ALDF	DELEGATIONS	CHAMBER OF DEPUTIES
Marti Batres, Undersecretary of Government before becoming the PRD president in the D.F. (he later left the National Democratic Left to form his own Izquierda Social [IS] or "Social Left" faction); Francisco Garduño Yáñez, Secretary of Transport and Roads	Martí Batres Guadarrama, President Agustín González Cázares, Press Secretary	(1) Alejandra Barrales Magdaleno; (2) Francisco Chiguil Figueroa; (3) Alfredo Hernández Raigosa; (4) Andrés Lozano Lozano; (4) Juventino Rodríguez Ramos; (5) Aleida Alvarez Ruiz; (6) Elio Bejarano Martínez; (7) José Jiménez Magaña; (8) Adrián Pedrozo Castillo; (9) Maricela Contreras; (10) Rodrigo Chávez; (11) Emilio Fernández; (12) Juan Manuel González Maltos; (13) Alfredo Hernández Raigosa; (14) Rigoberto Nieto; (15) Adrián Pedrozo; (16) María Rojo; (17) Pablo Trejo; (18) Araceli Vázquez; (19) Gerardo Villanueva	Leticia Robles Colín **(Alvaro Obregón)**; Laura Velázquez Alzúa **(Azcapotzalco)**; Miguel Bortolini Castillo **(Coyoacán)**; Ignacio Ruiz López **(Cuajilmalpa)**; Virginia Jaramillo Flores **(Cuauhtémoc)**; Octavio Flores Millán **(Gustavo A. Madero)**; Héctor Chávez López **(Magdalena Contreras)**; Fátima Mena Ortega **(Tláhuac)**; Faustino Soto Ramos **(Xochimilco)**	(1) Dolores Padierna Luna; (2) Emilio Serrano Jiménez; (3) Guadalupe Morales Rubio; (4) Marcos Morales Torres; (5) Susana Manzanares Córdova; (6) José Luis Cabrera; (7) Nancy Cárdenas Sánchez; (8) Pablo Franco Hernández; (9) Bernardo Ramos Iturbide; (10) Édgar Torres Baltasar

* These politicians left office after the July 2, 2006, election, when the New Left or "Chuchos" replaced Bejarano's
National Democratic Left as the dominant PRD force in Mexico City. Led by Víctor Hugo Círigo, chairman of the
ALDF's powerful Government Committee, the New Left controlled 21 of the party's 34 seats in the 66-member city
council—with the remainder in the hands of the Bejarano's National Democratic Left (11) and Batres's Social Left (2).
The National Democratic Left maintained its grip on only four delegations: Azcapotzalco (Alejandro Carbajal González),
Cuajimalpa (Remedios Ledesma García), Cuauhtémoc (José Luis Muñoz Soria), and Tláhuac (Gilberto Ensástiga Santiago); members of the pro-Cárdenas Unity and Renovation wing (UNyR) held sway over Coyoacán (Antonio Heberto
Castillo Juárez), Iztacalco (Erasto Ensástiga Santiago), Magdalena Contreras (Héctor Guijosa Mora), and Tlalpan (Guillermo Sánchez Torres); the New Left headed Iztapalapa (Horacio Martínez Meza), Milpa Alta (José Luis Cabrera Padilla),
and Venustiano Carranza (Julio César Moreno Rivera). Batres's Social Left boasted the leadership of Álvaro Obregón
(Leonel Luna Estrada), Gustavo A. Madero (Francisco Chiguil Figueroa), and Xochimilco (Uriel González Monzón).
The PAN won the relatively affluent delegations of Benito Juárez and Miguel Hidalgo. Ricardo Ruiz Suárez, who is not
closely associated with a party faction, was elected the PRD's party president in the capital, and the UNyR's Carlos Reyes
Gámiz was chosen secretary-general.

While not Magdalenas, other devotees are Secretary of Housing and Urban Development Laura Iztel Castillo, former head of the Coyoacán borough and the daughter of the late Heberto Castillo; Citizen Attention director Leticia Ramírez, whose ten-member staff responded to tens of thousands of requests for food, housing, jobs, health care, and other items; and Deputy Attorney General María Estela Ríos González, a political independent and distinguished lawyer.

One of the most trusted women in López Obrador's entourage was Secretary of Tourism Julieta Campos. As part of a broader effort to encourage tourists to visit the City of Hope, Campos had responsibility for enhancing the attractiveness of the Paseo de la Reforma, which runs through the Zona Rosa tourist mecca and became a venue for the postelection encampment. After UNAM specialists devised a master plan, she collaborated with Public Works Secretary César Buenrostro Hernández on maintenance, sidewalk improvements, and beautification projects. A renowned poet, essayist, and novelist, Campos mixes easily with other intellectuals and used her literary skills to write and edit speeches for the mayor. Her fierce independence excludes her from the Magdalena rubric.

What explains the sizable number of women in el Peje's cabinet? First, López Obrador has stated publicly that women are "more honorable and responsible than men."[5] Indeed, the female traffic police officers in Mexico City have a better reputation for honesty than their male counterparts. The mayor exhibited his confidence in females by selecting five distaff officers from the city's Judicial Police for his security detail. Trained in martial arts, "the Gazelles"—known by the code names "Alejandra," "Leticia," "Norma," "Jessica," and "Araceli"—followed López Obrador in a white Tsuru similar to his vehicle and remained nearby when he mixed with crowds.[6]

Second, women seem better prepared to implement the social programs of a government that provides assistance to disadvantaged groups.

Third, the appointment of a substantial number of women played well with D.F. residents. In a November 2000 survey by *Reforma*, 81 percent of respondents said that it was "good" that there were more females than males in the cabinet; only 5 percent called it "bad."[7]

Fourth, the presence of women who are married to political actors helped solidify el Peje's entourage. For instance, Saltiel Cohen is the spouse of López Obrador adviser Ignacio Marván Laborde; Luján is married to prominent attorney Arturo Alcalde Justiniani; and Claudia Sheinbaum's husband is left-wing firebrand Carlos Ímaz Gispert, who was elected head of the D.F.'s Tlalpan delegation in mid-2003, only to step down after videos showed him receiving cash from Ahumada. Despite her offer to resign, López Obrador affirmed his full confidence in her.[8]

Fifth, el Peje wanted to outshine Fox in terms of placing women in prominent posts. The president named only four women to his cabinet, two of whom received important assignments: Marta Sahagún, director of communications, whom Fox married on July 1, 2001; and Josefina Vazquez Mota, secretary of social development, who later coordinated Calderón's successful presidential campaign.

Sixth, el Peje sought to enhance his appeal to women in the 2006 presidential contest. As it turned out, he won greater support from male (34.8 percent) than from female voters (29.4 percent).[9]

Finally, women around him assert that López Obrador is extremely *machista* and that, while he will not admit it, he appears to believe that women are more obedient and submissive than men. A key female cabinet member brushed off this assertion, saying that her distaff colleagues were not reticent about challenging the mayor's views.[10]

Although journalists have linked the Tabascan romantically with several women since the death of his wife in 2003, he showed no inclination to remarry before the election, although rumors swirled through the capital that he would marry Beatriz Gutiérrez Müeller the day after the contest. In 2005, observers of Mexico's social scene began writing about Müeller, a widow and former reporter for *El Universal de Puebla* and host of a radio music program.[11] The couple wed on October 16, 2006.

FOUR CABINETS

El Pejelagarto sought to shape, if not make, every key decision. To achieve greater control, he created four cabinets: Government and Security, Sustainable Development, Progress with Justice, and Administration and Finances.

Government and Security Cabinet

Government and Security was the most important of these bodies. It met after the *mañaneras* seven days a week and had responsibility for security issues, the judicial system, demonstrations, and political affairs. In late 2002 Encinas succeeded lawyer Ortiz Pinchetti as the head of this cabinet.[12] A highly competent administrator and former member of the Mexican Communist Party, the cherubic, bearded Encinas has twice won election to the Chamber of Deputies, has written books on peasant movements, and has served as the city's secretary of the environment (1997–2000). Earlier in López Obrador's administration, Encinas held the posts of secretary of economic development and undersecretary of government. He became interim mayor when López Obrador left office to campaign full time.

As public security secretary, Ebrard participated in the cabinet until he was shifted to Cultural Development. A few months later, he stepped down to seek the PRD nomination for mayor. Ebrard was active in the PRI from 1978 until 1995, serving as the party's secretary-general in the D.F. (1989–91). A protégé of Camacho, he held a deputy's seat for the Green Ecological Party of Mexico (PVEM) from 1997 to 2000 and, with Camacho, founded the center-left Center Democratic Party (PCD) in 1999. In addition to working with neighborhood groups, Ebrard had responsibility for the city's several police forces. Ebrard was actually appointed by the president, who has the constitutional mandate to fill this position. Fox dismissed Ebrard from the security post in November 2004 after an angry mob in the Tláhuac neighborhood brutalized and killed two federal agents.

Harvard-educated Attorney General Bernardo Bátiz, an extremely influential cabinet member, was a member of the PAN from 1965 to 1992 but resigned over the party's deals with Salinas. Legal counselor María Estela Ríos González and Chief of Advisers José Zamarripa de la Peña completed the makeup of this cabinet.

Sustainable Development Cabinet

The Sustainable Development Cabinet concentrated on public works, transportation, and environmental protection to enhance the city's ability to spur growth and create jobs. César Buenrostro, a civil engineer and ex-member of the PRI's Democratic Current, formally headed this cabinet. When he clashed with the mayor on the double-decking initiative, López Obrador placed the unswervingly loyal Sheinbaum in charge of the project. Not only did she take the lead on second tiers, she was placed in charge of the trust devoted to rehabilitating the Chapultepec Park area.

An equally important member was Francisco Garduño Yáñez, the tough-as-nails secretary of transport and roads. In this position, he operated in the murky, corrupt netherworld of transportation unions, microbus companies, and unlicensed pirate cabs. He left the government to serve as the "For the Good of All" delegate to Hidalgo State.

Other members of the Sustainable Development Cabinet were Campos, Itzel Castillo, and the directors-general of Civil Defense and the Fire Department.

Progress with Justice Cabinet

The Progress with Justice Cabinet had primary responsibility for social programs. Education is a federal responsibility in Mexico, which means that the D.F. has only an undersecretary of education. When appropriate, this cabinet coordinated matters with the Ministry of Public Education. It also handled scholarship assistance to youngsters, adult education, and the UACM. Sosa Elízaga chaired this cabinet until she became culture secretary. Sosa Elízaga's colleagues included Dr. Laurell, who was in charge of most programs for senior citizens.

Administration and Finance Cabinet
As its name indicates, the Administration and Finance Cabinet had administrative and budgetary responsibilities. The powerful Romero Oropeza presided over this body, which included Finance Secretary Saltiel, Comptroller Luján, and Treasurer Rosado.

TRUSTS

Under López Obrador, the city established several public-private trusts, known as *fideicomisos*. The most important of these concentrated on the historic zone and was headed by Ana Lilia Zepeda, who was well versed in politics as a former federal deputy and the ex-wife of President Echeverría's son. Her task was to raise public and private funds to restore the Historic Center. As mentioned earlier, Secretary Sheinbaum had responsibility for the Chapultepec trust, whose work concentrated on the area around the Chapultepec Palace, the Anthropology Museum, and the corridor that joins several of Mexico's largest hotels—the Nikko, the Marriott, and the Chapultepec Presidente. The Trust for the Improvement of Rapid Highways focused on the second tiers. Although formally headed by Rodríguez Rey Morán, the overall supervisor was the ubiquitous Sheinbaum.

AMLO'S MANAGEMENT STYLE

An unyielding taskmaster, López Obrador demanded that his subordinates achieve their objectives on time. He summed up his style in the aphorism "Friends are for playing dominoes."[13] He reiterated his philosophy in March 2004, after two members of the city government were accused of corruption. Friends and family did not matter, he said, because "I came here to serve and I am not going to betray the confidence that the people have placed in me."[14]

Like the Christian messiah, López Obrador chose trusted individuals as apostles, the majority of whom came from Tabasco. He recruited converts from the PRI to spread his popular, antineoliberal gospel, and Magdalenas who faithfully, unquestioningly, and effectively undertook tasks essential to running city government. Although four cabinets loomed large on his government's organizational chart, el Peje often departed from the structure to make decisions personally or give special assignments to his closest allies. He emphasized that neither family ties nor friendships would interfere with his sacred mission to vanquish oppressive neoliberalism.

CHALLENGING THE PHARISEES, SADDUCEES, AND SCRIBES

Jesus took issue with the excessively literal manner in which the Pharisees, Sadducees, and Scribes interpreted the Torah. He ultimately censured the clergy and made a physical assault on the temple. He did not provoke an uprising against the priestly caste, but he did chastise them. Matthew reports Christ as saying, "Woe unto you, scribes and Pharisees, hypocrites! For ye shut up the kingdom of heaven against men: for ye neither go in yourselves, neither suffer ye them that are entering to go in" (Matt. 23:13).[1]

In a similar vein, López Obrador pays lip service to operating within his nation's legal system, but he harbors contempt for the nation's judiciary and legislative bodies. His defiance of the law yielded dividends in Tabasco, where laying siege to oil wells enabled him to exact a danegeld from Pemex and use these resources to attract even more followers to his cause. He justified these acts because corruption suffused the PRI government, which catered to the elite at the expense of the poor.

In addition, he led marches to Mexico City, where his followers camped in the Zócalo or other public venues, a prelude to the encampments that he established after the July 2006 election. Demonstrators demanded "indemnities" for the supposed losses they had sustained in Tabasco. Mayor Camacho and other officials gave el Peje substantial sums to vacate the public spaces and return home. The documents that revealed the PRI's outrageously high expenditures in the 1994 elections accentuated the Tabascan's scorn for a venal regime. He expressed his disdain for democracy when he refused to support the Cofipe electoral reform.

As mayor, López Obrador refused to obey a court decision involving an alleged expropriation of private property. Two years before he was elected, a landowner sought 1.81 billion pesos in compensation for the city's "illegal" taking of a 298-hectare parcel, known as the Paraje San Juan, in Iztapalapa borough. The claimant won the suit, and in September 2003 a judge ordered the GDF to make full restitution. El Peje refused and urged the Supreme Court to form a commission to review the matter. The high court turned down his petition. In the meantime, Fox's secretary of agricultural reform discovered that Paraje San Juan was federal land and that the putative proprietors did not hold a valid deed. A vindicated López Obrador reacted to this information by admonishing judges "not to politicize matters and, above all, avoid using institutions to harm their adversaries." He called the case "fraudulent" and reiterated his view that "the people are fed up with corruption and shady political deals."[2]

The messianic López Obrador defines democracy as "government of the people" rather than statutes enacted by legislators or decisions rendered by judges. He has also asserted that the courts should not override "popular feelings" or the "human laws of people."[3] When an angry mob assailed two police officers in Tláhuac in late 2004, the mayor said this was a case of the real Mexico expressing itself through local "uses and customs" that should be recognized and understood.[4] The Tabascan's beliefs reflect those of many Mexicans: that the judicial system is rotten to the core, that the police are even worse, and that legislators care only about enriching themselves. Forty-nine percent of respondents to a 2003 *Reforma* survey believed they should not have to obey unjust laws.[5]

Later, the El Encino affair found Attorney General Rafael Macedo de la Concha attempting to strip López Obrador of his political immunity and prosecute him for flouting a judicial decree. In response to this move, the mayor argued, "If they are truly democrats, why don't they let the decision rest with the people so that the people may govern."[6]

LÓPEZ OBRADOR AND THE ALDF

López Obrador ran roughshod over the ALDF early in his administration. During the first three years of his term, the PRD held only sixteen seats in the sixty-six-member body, and just nine of these deputies were diehard supporters of the city executive.[7] These divisions enabled opposition parties either to pass bills that their deputies introduced or to impede the mayor's proposals.

The mayor showed no tolerance for his antagonists, treating them as the enemy, not the loyal opposition. When they refused to back his initiatives, he circumvented his detractors with "informative decrees" (*bandos informativos*), which he used to delay authorizing legislation. He also employed the pocket veto, refused to publish laws in the *Gaceta Oficial del Distrito Federal* so that they could take effect, and resorted to other devious practices. "He acted like a viceroy," said PAN leader José Luis Luege Tamargo.[8]

One of the earliest clashes arose when the representatives voted 55 to 1 to approve an electoral reform. The mayor resisted a provision to increase the ban on publicizing tax-funded projects from thirty to forty-five days before an election. As a crowd-pleasing ribbon cutter, el Peje objected to this move because trumpeting his ambitious construction program curried public favor for him, his allies, and his party. He also opposed lengthening campaigns by three months on the grounds that longer contests would cost more; in fact, he wanted to select his successor, and shorter races can enhance the influence a popular incumbent has over the outcome of the contest.

López Obrador vehemently objected to annulling ballots if voters marked the name of a candidate more than once. Citizens did this in the mayoral contest, when the Tabascan garnered the nomination of three entities: the Alliance for Mexico City (PRD, PT, Convergencia, PSN, and PAS), the Social Democratic Party, and the Center Democratic Party. People scratched an "X" next to his name at least twice on some two hundred thousand ballots, but the PAN did not protest the results because his margin of victory was a quarter-million votes.[9] Although Government Secretary Ortiz Pinchetti agreed to implement the electoral reforms at once, López Obrador executed a de facto pocket veto. Neither he nor many members of the PRD leadership wanted to make the elections more transparent, because this could thwart their ability to manipulate votes. In addition, the PRD draws support from the less educated, who are more likely to mark ballots incorrectly.[10]

As discussed earlier, one of his first mayoral decrees prohibited Mexico City from adopting Daylight Saving Time. The mayor accused the Fox administration of pandering to foreign interests: "In reality what exists are commitments between [the Mexican government] and the New York Stock Exchange so that markets will open at the same time." He also attributed the move as a means to help "yuppies in the financial industry who don't want to get up an hour earlier."[11] The Supreme Court disagreed and voided his action.

When ALDF passed the Metropolitan Urban Development Plan to disperse new housing around the city, the mayor struck back. In lieu of making the approved initiative law by placing it in the *Gaceta Oficial*, he published Decree 2 instead. His version concentrated living units in the capital's four central boroughs, which had been hemorrhaging population. Although el Peje justified his action as a means of curbing the rapid growth in the southern and western parts of the city, Luege accused him of catering to the pro-PRD New

Tenochititlán and other groups that were particularly powerful in the center of the capital, where they allocated new housing to their followers.

In late 2003 PAN deputy Patricia Garduño Morales drafted and attained approval for legislation establishing an Institute for Crime Prevention. Although the body exists on paper, it remains a dead letter because López Obrador would not create it.

Along the same lines, he refused to enforce legislation—passed 46–16, with one abstention—to require motorists with D.F. license tags to insure their automobiles. He proclaimed that auto owners who failed to comply would not be fined. He attempted to disguise this blatantly political move by insisting that the law was unjust and constituted a hardship for citizens.[12]

In addition, he warred with the ALDF over the 2003 financial code. Most members of the assembly's finance committee believed that water and property levies should be raised in order to expand the city's fiscal base. When word of this plan reached city hall, the mayor's loyalist, D.F. treasurer Oscar Rosado, rushed to the ALDF. There he convened a private meeting with PRD deputies to remind them that López Obrador had run on a "no-tax-increase" platform. He warned that López Obrador would work to defeat anyone who voted to increase taxes.[13] El Peje and his treasurer prevailed. The D.F. executive does not have a line-item veto; yet when the budget bill passed without the PRD's support, López Obrador eliminated particular projects by refusing to publish them in the *Gaceta Oficial*.[14]

LÓPEZ OBRADOR AND THE PRD IN THE ASCENDANCY

In the mid-July 2003 election, the PRD won thirty-seven of the sixty-six seats in the ALDF. This victory enabled López Obrador to achieve his goals through conventional methods without resorting to illegal and quasi-legal artifices. With tongue in cheek, López Obrador also characterized the ALDF as an "independent" entity. Yet the mayor emerged from the late 2004 session with an unbroken string of legislative victories. So striking was López Obrador's influence that PRI deputy Mauricio López called it "a legislative microwave into which the Jefe de Gobierno inserted his proposals and the *perredista* majority pressed the buttons to cook them."[15]

López Obrador's first measure to pop out of the oven was the Universal Pension Law. This measure gave full legislative status to the mayor's administrative program of providing stipends to D.F. residents age seventy and older.

The mayor also reconfigured the Access to Information and Transparency Law, which the ALDF had first approved by a 55–0 vote on December 17, 2000—with the eleven PRD deputies abstaining. The Tabascan refused to establish the Public Information Council of the D.F., which the lawmakers had authorized to administer the statute. He insisted that his personal honesty made the council unnecessary. After all, he was the first mayor to publicize daily the income and expenditures of the capital. Besides, he claimed, a new body would siphon money from social programs and constitute another layer of bureaucracy. "It is not possible that public officials always use the big spoon [to benefit themselves] while they make speeches about justice for the poor. . . . [I]t is pure demagogy," he said.[16] Furthermore, citizens who wanted information could address their requests to the relevant governmental agency. The mayor also observed that he had named two hundred "citizen accountants" to scrutinize contracts. Yet the press could find neither the names of these individuals nor any reports they had prepared.[17]

Despite el Peje's allergy to the council, the PAN took the matter before the Supreme Court, which, on November 14, 2003, ordered that López Obrador activate the body. The mayor grudgingly complied, although the council president named by the ALDF had resigned in September 2003 because of the lack of political support.

The new PRD-dominated Legislative Assembly diminished the council's influence by enlarging its membership, reducing the salaries of citizen members, and limiting their functions. It could only recommend—not require—that agencies provide information to citizens. Despite paying lip service to presiding over an open administration, López Obrador would not release (1) a list of the senior citizens, the disabled, and the single mothers who received monthly stipends; (2) the construction costs of the double decking of highways; (3) the number of GDF employees; and (4) the cost of forty-five rail cars purchased for the metro. PAN deputy Obdulio Avila Mayo was able to obtain a court order that directed the Collective Transport Network to furnish information about the cost and acquisition of the subway cars.[18] In October 2005 *Reforma* filed a freedom-of-information request to obtain the results of the extensive polling that the city had conducted during López Obrador's administration. (See Table 17 for the evolution of the capital's Access to Information and Transparency Law.)

The mayor also won support to modify the Electoral Institute of the Federal District (IEDF). After the PRD-dominated ALDF took office in September 2004, he advocated reducing the institute's members from five to three and cutting the agency's budget. He called the measure an effort to save money. In fact, López Obrador had long borne a grudge against the IEDF because of its refusal to award the PRD more seats (on the basis of proportional representation) than the thirty-seven that it won directly in 2003. Also vexing him and the PRD were fines imposed by the IEDF, as well as the institute's intrusion into the party's internal affairs. This "meddling" came in response to a PAN and PRI complaint that the PRD had violated the

TABLE 17. *Evolution of Mexico City's Transparency Law*

DATE	ACTION
December 17, 2002	ALDF approved the Transparency Law (Ley de Transparencia y Acceso a la Información Pública del Distrito Federal).
July 15, 2003	López Obrador filed a "constitutional controversy" (*controversia constitucional*) with the SCJN, challenging the composition of the information council that would administer the statute.
September 10, 2003	Leoncio Lara resigned as president of the Citizens Council.
November 14, 2003	The SCJN ordered the GDF to install the information council.
December 2003	The PRD-dominated ALDF severely modified and weakened the Transparency Law.
February 18, 2004	The ALDF's Public Administration Committee selected Gustavo Velásquez de la Fuente from 17 candidates as president of the information council.
March 2, 2004	Members of the information council were sworn in.
March 29, 2004	The mayor announced that he was disbanding the Transparency Council for Public Finances that he had created via Decree 15 on December 21, 2001. The members of this anticorruption body resigned on March 9 in the wake of the video scandals. They claimed that their opinions had no weight.
April 5, 2004	By a 2–1 vote, the information council selected Manual Galindo Tapia as its administrator.
March 10, 2005	In its annual report, the Transparency Council criticized the functioning of the Transparency Law, because anyone requesting information required an official identification document, and the GDF arbitrarily classified information on the grounds of "national security."
June 21, 2005	The ALDF discussed reforming the Transparency Law to give citizens greater access to information.
July 5, 2005	Council member Pérez-Jaén characterized some of the proposed reforms as "positive" but said that the real goal of the legislators was to dismantle the Transparency Council.
July 5, 2005	The Transparency Council announced that it would sponsor one- to five-minute radio spots to inform the public about the Transparency Law. The commercials would cost 84,438 pesos.

SOURCES: Manuel Durán, "Cancelan el consejo anticorrupción," *Reforma*, March 30, 2004; Ariadna Bermeo, "Falla transparencia en DF—Consejo," *Reforma*, March 11, 2005; Carolina Pavón, "Proponen abrir el DF al 100%," *Reforma*, June 22, 2005; and Carolina Pavón, "Proponen 'parchar' Ley de Transparencia," *Reforma*, July 15, 2005, all at http://www.reforma.com.mx/.

city's advertising law by plastering public spaces with propaganda in the run-up to the January 2003 selection of its candidates for borough chiefs, ALDF representatives, and federal deputies.[19] To add insult to injury, the IEDF later nullified this primary election on the grounds that it did not safeguard the rights of party militants. López Obrador failed to cow the IEDF. In May 2004 the institute fined the PRD 1.8 million pesos for the sloppy way it paid people who carried out political operations. Other parties also incurred penalties—the PAN, 45,000 pesos; the PRI, slightly more than 85,000 pesos; and the PT, 100,000 pesos—but the IEDF cited the PRD as having the poorest financial control and accountability.[20]

López Obrador endeavored to draw attention from this criticism by reviving the Fobaproa issue. He recommended that the ALDF establish a "truth commission" to detect unlawful acts and take legal action against those responsible for damages arising from the rescue of the banking system.

In addition, the ALDF passed, intact, his $20 billion budget, which—because of fewer pesos from the federal government—included lower outlays for public works, the Integral Family Development Institute or DIF (a social service and child welfare agency), water projects, security, assistance to delegations, and the subway system. With respect to reduced outlays on mass transit, José Medel, vice coordinator of the PRI deputies and head of the Subway Workers' Union, complained they were "an act of revenge against his [the mayor's] enemies." Such grumbling aside, the assembly not only approved the modifications but gave el Peje even greater flexibility in shifting funds from one program to another.

To avoid a conflict with the church, López Obrador prevailed on Bejarano to set aside the controversial Living Together of Societies and Civic Culture bills. The former would have banned discrimination based on gender; the latter would have amplified the government's power to crack down on graffiti, unruly behavior, begging, street vendors, and protesters. Also called the Ebrard Law, this measure represented an attempt to institute Giuliani's "zero tolerance" of minor crimes.

Even though López Obrador had lobbied for "autonomy" for the D.F., his allies in the ALDF seized control of the Chamber of Deputies to prevent approval of constitutional reform that would have relieved the federal government of paying the total cost of education in the capital. The local deputies vowed that they would remain in San Lázaro as long as necessary to prevent "an injustice against children, teenagers, and young students in this capital."[21] PAN coordinator Francisco Barrio castigated the action as a "disorderly incursion" and averred that the body would not succumb to pressure. In fact, the ALDF legislators, along with PRD federal deputies, continued to employ demonstrations to block the initiative. PRD leader Deputy Pablo Gómez justified the action, saying, "We toast our solidarity with the *asemblistas* who came to protest the deafness of the actors in the Chamber of Deputies. It is logical, when the path of dialogue is closed, to open [paths] of protest."[22]

El Peje disdains the decisions of appointed judges and bills passed by opposition lawmakers who form part of the neoliberal conspiracy against him. He regards the people's will as a higher law. His ability to interpret this will means that he reconfigured bills passed by the ALDF. His self-proclaimed honesty obviated the need for enforcement of a freedom-of-information law. He supposedly named anonymous citizen accountants to oversee contracts and projects. He backed force over debate to block actions in the national Congress. Like Jesus in his time, López Obrador regards court decisions and legislative actions as illegitimate unless he approves of them. This attitude became clear when he organized a civil resistance movement to protest the selection of Calderón as Mexico's new chief executive.

VICENTE FOX: LÓPEZ OBRADOR'S LAST NEOLIBERAL PRESIDENT

Having captured Jerusalem and ousted the occupying PRI forces—the equivalent of latter-day Romans—el Peje set his sights on the Eternal City of Mexico's neoliberals: Los Pinos. Only by capturing this fortress could he implement "the Alternative Agenda for the Nation" (*el proyecto alternativo de nación*) and transform Mexico in the way that Constantine reshaped the Roman Empire by embracing Christianity. At the same time that López Obrador worked incessantly to ensure that Fox would be the last neoliberal chief executive, he often complemented his severe attacks on Fox by proclaiming support for the "institution of the presidency." After resigning to campaign full time, however, the messianic Tabascan averred that "the economic policy of President Fox has been a complete failure. The same officials that have managed economic policy since Salinas's term continue governing."[1]

FOX'S SHORTCOMINGS

When movie producers make a film about the Fox administration, they will entitle it *El Sexenio Perdido del Marlboro Man* in reference to the six-year presidential term and the chiseled good looks of Mexico's previous leader. Indeed, Fox's finest hour came five months before taking office. In mid-2000, as the joint PAN-PVEM nominee, he scored an upset victory over the revolutionary party. Given the double-digit advantage that the PRI enjoyed after its

November 1999 nominating primary, it can be argued that Francisco Labastida "lost" the election, not that Fox "won."

Even though the Marlboro Man knocked his adversary for a loop, the PRI still had breath in its dinosauric lungs. It boasted 208 seats in the 500-member Chamber of Deputies and 60 seats in the 128-member Senate. For their part, the PAN and Green Ecological Party of Mexico (PVEM) had 222 deputies and 51 senators in a Congress where constitutional reforms require a two-thirds majority. A skilled vote winner, Fox detested the tedious heavy lifting of coalition building required to move measures through Congress. He seemed to abhor politics and politicians. This hostility took shape during his several decades in the private sector, where he faced avaricious politicians seeking payoffs for helping to negotiate the labyrinth of excessive rules and regulations. (See Table 18 for the breakdown of the Congress.)

After his stunning triumph, the new president could have lunged for the throat of his nemesis by exposing the corruption that suffused the long-ruling party. In contrast, he could have offered a handshake in the hope that several dozen progressive *priístas* would back his vitally needed energy, fiscal, labor, and judicial reforms. Unfortunately for Mexico, the politically naïve Guanajuatan attempted both tactics. He denounced the PRI for funneling $90 million from the state oil company to its nominee, Francisco Labastida, in the "Pemexgate" scandal. He then turned around and urged the party's support for broadening the unpopular value-added tax. When its legislators balked, Fox pilloried them with TV ads designed to do the impossible: drum up grassroots support for higher taxes.

As a result of Fox's clumsiness and the selection of wheeler-dealer Roberto Madrazo as party chief, the PRI regrouped in 2002. It cooperated with the PRD to deny the peripatetic chief executive

TABLE 18. *Seats in Mexican Congress, 2000–2006*

PARTY	CHAMBER OF DEPUTY SEATS (2000)	CHAMBER OF DEPUTY SEATS (2003)	SENATE SEATS (2000–2006)
PRI	208	201	58
PAN	205	148	47
PRD	54	97	15
PVEM (Greens)	17	17	5
Convergencia	1	5	1
PT	8	6	0
PSN (Party of the Nationalist Society	3	0	0
PAS (Social Alliance Party)	2	0	0
Independents	2	26	2
TOTAL	500	500	128

permission to travel to the United States and Canada; the two parties cynically rejoiced when inept members of the "Montessori Cabinet"—so called because of their preference for self-expression over teamwork—botched the siting of a new Mexico City–area airport; and they thwarted Fox's legislative agenda. Meanwhile, the chief executive ricocheted from one "priority" to another—courting the Zapatista rebels, encouraging small businesses, fighting poverty, combating crime, and lobbying the White House for changes in U.S. immigration policy, among other things. This "flavor-of-the-month" approach yielded few results. And much to the chagrin of his own party, Fox's hyperambitious wife, Marta Sahagún, began to dabble openly in policy and stage-whispered her desire to seek public office, possibly the presidency.

Fox took office boasting a close relationship with George W. Bush. The "Dos Amigos" had known each other as governors, owned ranches, shared a fondness for cowboy boots, and had won their respective presidencies in the same year. Their friendship soured after Mexico sent mixed messages to Washington after the September 11 terrorist attacks in 2001. U.S. decision makers were especially vexed by Government Secretary Creel's reiterating his nation's pacifist tradition. A member of the U.S. National Security Council staff asked, "What's Creel up to? Is he a member of the Taliban?"

Bilateral affairs continued to worsen when Mexico's UN representative denounced America's invasion of Iraq. There has been cooperation on fighting Mexico's obscenely wealthy drug cartels. Yet the prospect of overhauling U.S. immigration statutes had become a nonstarter by the time Fox left office.

Apart from defeating the PRI, Fox's major achievement was economic stability. Finance Secretary Gil Díaz and Central Bank president Ortiz Martínez have skillfully crafted macroeconomic policy, with the result that inflation fell from 16.6 percent in 1999 to 4 percent in 2006. While income distribution remains brutally skewed, the living standards of the poorest Mexicans have risen slightly thanks to programs like "Opportunities" and "Popular Security." The GDP rose nearly 5 percent during the final months of Fox's sexenio.

To its credit, the government also respected decisions of the citizen-run IFE and the TEPJF, and these electoral bodies have grown in stature. Nevertheless, the country's traditional control mechanisms—trade unions, peasant leagues, law enforcement agencies, the presidency, political parties, and Congress—lost influence and legitimacy under Fox. This erosion of key institutions contributed to widespread urban violence, police corruption, political crises in states like Oaxaca, and narco-trafficking, including growing domestic drug consumption. Fox's welcoming the EZLN to the D.F. in 2001 conveyed a disturbing message to dissidents: "If you want to get the government's attention, arm a few hundred people, declare war against the state, and stage a march on the capital."

FOX'S BACKGROUND

Fox and López Obrador hail from completely different backgrounds. While el Peje was born into a lower-middle-class family in Macuspana, Fox grew up on his prosperous family's ranch in San Cristóbal, Guanajuato. He attended elite Jesuit schools before matriculating at the Jesuit-run Iberoamericana University in Mexico City.

In the 1960s, Coca-Cola had no Mexicans in top corporative jobs in the country. As a result, Monty Thomas, Coke's popular vice president for Latin America, visited the Iberoamericana campus to recruit potential executives. Among those whom he selected were Cristóbal Jaime Jáquez, Lino Korrodi, José Luis González, and Fox. Korrodi, an intrepid money raiser, and González, a marketing guru, later helped form the Friends of Fox political organization.

Fox's rugged good looks and vivacious first wife, Liliana de la Concha, made him popular with Americans. The spouses of American executives were attracted to the young man from Guanajuato, who became known as "Marshal," after Marshal Matt Dillon on the popular *Gunsmoke* television series.

Fox moved up the ladder until he became president of Coca-Cola for Mexico and Central America. Although he portrays himself as a successful businessman, the real risk takers in the soft drink industry are the bottlers. They must acquire land and buildings, invest in machinery, provide transportation, purchase bottles, construct storage facilities, hire a workforce, and buy ingredients for "the Real Thing" from the patent holder.[2]

After fifteen years, Fox left Coke to return to his family businesses in Guanajuato. He and his wife adopted four children and established a hospital for foundlings. Meanwhile, in his capacity as president of an export consortium, he made a speech before de la Madrid when the chief executive visited León. The undiplomatic businessman blasted the red tape that ensnarled exporters, using a Commerce Ministry manual crammed with bewildering regulations as evidence for his complaints.

In 1988 entrepreneur Manuel J. Clouthier, the PAN presidential nominee, recruited Fox to run for the Chamber of Deputies. Clouthier lost, but Fox won a three-year term. He also served as "secretary of agriculture" in Clouthier's "shadow cabinet," which he created to scrutinize the programs of the Salinas administration. Fox showed little interest in legislative affairs as he prepared to run for the statehouse in Guanajuato. Electoral authorities initially credited the PRI nominee as the winner of the August 1991 gubernatorial race. But after cries of fraud, Salinas elbowed aside his party's nominee and selected as "interim governor" Carlos Medina

Plascencia, the PAN mayor of León. In 1995 Fox took advantage of the anti-PRI backlash to the economic crisis and campaign reforms that had cleaned up elections to win his second bid for the governorship. He promised to spend only one day a week behind his executive desk in Guanajuato, the state capital, with the other days devoted to constructing dams and canals, building highways, rehabilitating a decrepit educational system, placing a computer in every school, and attracting new companies to locate in the poorer areas of the state. "I am going to hire a governor," he said in an interview, smiling. "I'm going to be a politician."[3]

Foes criticized his quest for *maquiladoras.* "On the agrarian front, Fox completed the transnationalization of the Bajío [central Mexico]—during his reign, Green Giant, Bird's Eye, Campbell, and Del Monte became dominant players in the field."[4] The state executive turned such criticism to his advantage, trumpeting his ability to promote investment and trade. He used this record to tout his qualifications for the presidency. He barnstormed the country and, with money and organizational help from some one million adherents to the Friends of Fox, obtained the PAN nomination in September 1999 without opposition.

LÓPEZ OBRADOR AND FOX

Beginning with his inauguration on December 6, 2000, López Obrador went out of his way to demonstrate that he—not the neoliberal president—had the best interests of the country at heart. Like the judo expert who uses his opponent's weight against him, el Pejelagarto often manipulated the chief executive to the mayor's advantage—with a view to promoting himself as the national alternative to Fox's market-centered approach.

The *mañanera* press sessions, which made López Obrador almost as well known as his rival in Los Pinos, became a forum for attacking the chief executive. When Fox proposed increasing the value-added tax, the city executive accused him of trying to "pick the pockets of the poor."[5] López Obrador also chided Fox for his frequent travel abroad, where the president and his companions hobnobbed with the glitterati. For his part, the ascetic "people's mayor" seldom left the D.F. before initiating his presidential bid. As noted earlier, el Peje first lambasted the transition to Daylight Saving Time. As a reporter said, the two men "are engaged in a modern-day version of ancient Mayan clashes over who controls time."[6] More important was the confrontation over control of Mexico's destiny.

An Eye on the Polls
In February 2001 *Reforma* pollsters found that 41 percent of Mexico City respondents liked the Tabascan's criticism of Fox—a figure

that had fallen to 33 percent by May.[7] This change forced López Obrador to rethink his "attacks" at a time when the people believed that Fox should be given a chance to effect the "change" that he had promised. Thus, el Peje began working with the chief executive on ventures beneficial to the D.F.

This shift became apparent after the revelation that Fox's staff had authorized the purchase of expensive towels ($443), sheets ($1,060), and curtains ($19,000) for the presidential residence.[8] Rather than pounce on an issue that he knew the press would play up, the mayor called a truce: "I am worried about the deterioration of presidential authority . . . things could become complicated, above all in economic matters."[9] The rapprochement took the form of a joint agreement in August 2001 to rehabilitate the city's Historic Center and collaborate in the fight against urban crime.[10]

Although the president and mayor clashed in February 2002 over the appointment of Mexico City's police chief, the "era of good feelings" continued into May 2003, when the mayor cut the ribbon on the San Antonio connector road in the presence of the chief executive. López Obrador compared his relationship to Fox with that between conservative Jacques Chirac, when he was mayor of Paris, and France's socialist president, François Mitterand. "They had different [ideological] positions . . . [but] they fought for the love of Paris. . . . In this constructive competition, Paris won," stated el Peje. Fox added, "To govern today requires constructing . . . accords, not accentuating the differences over solutions for Mexico. Negotiation is an obligatory practice to ensure that the country advances."[11]

Six months later, the mayor termed "unjust" Fox's proposal to impose a 10 percent value-added tax on all items, including food and medicine. Instead of "hurting the poor," the city executive advised the government to tighten its belt, combat corruption, diminish the payments for Fobaproa, and reduce tax evasion from 50 to 30 percent.

On December 4, 2003, López Obrador called Fox "a good man" who had shown tolerance, while alluding to the government's "chiaroscuro" aspects. The dark hues were Fox's inability to spur economic growth, create jobs, and combat poverty.[12] The Marlboro Man responded on December 5: "I don't know if he is thinking about the next election. . . . Today the important thing for the Mexican people is to act responsibly."

López Obrador and Fox recommenced their verbal sparring in early 2004. At his January 9 session with the press, the mayor offered blistering criticism of the federal government for its wrong-headed economic policy, which, he said, had increased unemployment and was indifferent to average people. The level of mutual vituperation soon escalated—with Nicogate, the video scandals, and El Encino exciting controversy.

El Encino

The definitive break between Fox and López Obrador took place over a parcel of land known as El Encino (see Table 19 for a chronology of events). On November 9, 2000, more than three weeks before el Peje became mayor, the city government expropriated thirteen thousand square meters in the Santa Fe area to construct an access road to the prestigious ABC Hospital. On March 14, 2001, a federal judge approved the property owners' request for an injunction and ordered the city to halt any public works project on the land. When the judge discovered that the D.F. was continuing to build the road, he directed the PGR to investigate the possible abuse of authority. On January 23, 2002, an administrative court determined that the city chief had violated the judicial order. Later, another court ordered the PGR to conclude its investigation and make a finding. In mid-May 2004, Attorney General Macedo de la Concha requested that Congress strip the mayor of his political immunity.

Transparent Threats

In the wake of the attorney general's action, López Obrador said that he would hold a referendum later in 2004 so that the people could "decide what I should do" (see Table 20 for the public response). He pledged to ask city voters whether he should remain in office or run for the presidency.[13] In a transparent threat, the mayor urged his loyalists to suspend plans to launch marches on his behalf. "My recommendation is that there are no mobilizations . . . that we reflect on the situation, which has been converted into an eminently civic . . . even spiritual issue."[14] While sounding like a statesman, the Tabascan intimated that there could be widespread protests and a return to a "wild Mexico" if the *desafuero*—a virtual *golpe del estado*—succeeded.

The PRI's Role?

The naïve Fox might be excused for undertaking the *desafuero*, but why did Madrazo and the PRI join an enterprise that burnished López Obrador's image as an embattled savior? On March 8, 2005, the PRI chief met with a dozen leading researchers in the home of pollster María de las Heras. During a four-hour dinner, Madrazo got bad news: if López Obrador continued to gain momentum, he would be the odds-on favorite to capture the presidency. Madrazo and his colleagues, who seemed trapped in a time warp, continued to think in terms of competition among the PRI, PAN, and PRD, overlooking López Obrador's tremendous messianic appeal. Thus Madrazo opted to attack el Pejelagarto on the legal front in the hope of barring him from the following year's race. As a result, on April 7, 2005, PRI deputies joined forces with the PAN for a 360–127 vote to strip the mayor of his political protection. Much

TABLE 19. *Chronology of El Encino Process*

DATE	ACTION
November 9, 2000	City expropriated 13,000 square meters in the Santa Fe area to build an access road to the new ABC hospital.
December 4, 2000	The property owner, Promotora Internacional Santa Fe, sought injunctive relief against the expropriation.
March 14, 2001	Federal Judge Alvaro Tovilla León ordered city to halt construction on access road.
August 28, 2001	Tovilla found that the city had continued construction and directed the PGR to investigate.
January 23, 2002	The Seventh Administrative Court (El Séptimo Tribunal Colegiado en Materia Administrativa) determined that the mayor had violated the judge's injunction.
February 16, 2004	The Fourth Penal Court (El Cuarto Tribunal Colegiado en Materia Penal) directed the PGR to resolve the inquiry previously initiated against López Obrador.
May 17, 2004	The PGR determined there was probable cause to strip the mayor of his immunity so he could stand trial for "abuse of authority," a crime that carried a sentence of one to nine years in prison.
May 18, 2004	The PGR delivered request for *desafuero* to the Congress's Permanent Commission. In the name of the commission, Senator Enrique Jackson said that any such petition must be delivered to the Chamber of Deputies.
May 18, 2004	Government Undersecretary Martí Batres vehemently defended López Obrador.
May 20, 2004	The PGR delivered the *desafuero* petition to the Chamber of Deputies.
May 27, 2004	By a 3–1 vote, the chamber's investigating committee (Sección Instructora) determined that the PGR had presented sufficient evidence to warrant a full review by the committee.
June 3, 2004	The investigating committee formally notified López Obrador of its action; the committee turned over the case to a jurisdictional committee (Comisión Jurisdiccional) composed of sixteen members, seven from the PRI, five from the PAN, three from the PRD, and one from the PVEM.
June 3, 2004	At his early-morning news conference, López Obrador began the first of five "seminar workshops" on El Encino.
June 3, 2004	City PRD secretary-general Isaías Villa requested that party deputies and bureaucrats contribute a day's pay to López Obrador's defense fund.
June 5, 2004	In Iztapalapa, López Obrador reiterated his determination to hold a plebiscite, saying that only the people could decide his fate.
June 10, 2004	The mayor took out full-page ads in the nation's leading newspapers, defending himself by asserting, "This is political maneuvering. They are twisting the law because they want to block us for 2006."
June 10, 2004	In his response to the investigating committee, López Obrador charged that a "mediocre government" in league with the "most sinister persons" was prosecuting him not for violating the law but for his proposals for the "future of our country."

to their chagrin, a judge decided two weeks later that López Obrador had not committed an "imprisonable" offense and that the PGR could not arrest him. On April 24, hundreds of thousands of López Obrador's supporters swept through the capital's streets in a "silent march" to denounce the *desafuero*. Fox then announced the resignation of Macedo de la Concha, and the attorney general's

TABLE 19 *(cont'd).* *Chronology of El Encino Process*

DATE	ACTION
June 14, 2004	The city began distributing 2.2 million comic books, known as *historietas,* explaining the "whole plan of attack" against López Obrador's administration.
June 23–July 6, 2004	The investigating committee began a thirty-day period of gathering evidence in order to make a recommendation to the entire Chamber of Deputies.
August 7–10, 2004	The investigating committee made its preliminary "findings" (*expediente*) available to the complainant.
August 11–13, 2004	The investigating committee made its preliminary findings available to the accused.
August 14–19, 2004	The parties prepared their responses.
September 1, 2004	The investigating committee began its deliberations.
April 1, 2005	By a 3–1 vote, the investigating committee concluded that there was enough evidence for the Chamber of Deputies to decide whether to strip the mayor of his immunity.
April 7, 2005	The PAN and the PRI joined forces to vote 360–127 to strip the mayor of his immunity.
April 8, 2005	López Obrador stepped down from the mayor's office to await arrest; in a speech to supporters crowding the Zócalo, he urged "peaceful civil disobedience."
April 21, 2005	López Obrador refused the $180 bail posted for him by two PAN deputies and said he would seek the presidency from behind bars.
April 22, 2005	The court said that the PGR could not arrest the mayor because he had committed no "imprisonable" offense.
April 24, 2005	Hundreds of thousands of López Obrador's followers participated in a "March of Silence" to protest the *desafuero.*
April 25, 2005	López Obrador reassumed his duties as mayor.
April 27, 2005	Fox dismissed Attorney General Macedo de la Concha.
May 3, 2005	In a radio interview, López Obrador announced that he would probably leave the mayorship in July to launch his presidential bid, adding that it would be "unethical" for him to campaign while still one of the nation's top officeholders.
May 4, 2005	New attorney general Daniel Cabeza de la Vaca announced that the government was dropping all charges against the mayor.
May 6, 2005	Fox and López Obrador met for eighteen minutes in Los Pinos.
July 29, 2005	López Obrador resigned to seek the presidency.

SOURCES: Manuel Durán, "López Obrador anunció que participará en el proyecto alternativo de nación que impulsará su grupo político para lograr un cambio en el 2006," *Reforma,* May 18, 2004, http://www.reforma.com.mx/; "López Obrador: Fox Backtracks and Drops Prosecution," *Latin America Regional Reports: Mexico and NAFTA Report,* May 17, 2005, http://www.latinnews.com/.

successor vouchsafed that the federal government would not pursue the case against el Peje, who had already communicated his intent to seek the presidency.

Why did Fox throw in the towel? No doubt the remarkable public rally influenced his decision, as did the mayor's growing standing in opinion polls. Equally important was an effort by Fox, concerned about his reputation abroad, to practice damage control. Newspapers from the *Austin Statesman* to the *Wall Street Journal* took Mexico's chief executive to task for "acting in a high-handed

TABLE 20. *Public Response to Move to Strip López Obrador of Political Immunity*

QUESTION	RESPONSE	FEDERAL DISTRICT (%)	NATIONAL (%)
Is the move to strip López Obrador of his political immunity . . .	A Political Maneuver?	70	65
	A Strictly Legal Action?	22	19
	Both?	8	8
	Don't Know	4	4
Should he be stripped of his immunity?	Yes	32	34
	No	61	51
	No Opinion	7	15
Will López Obrador run for president in 2006?	Yes	71	61
	No	22	31
	Don't Know	7	8
What's your opinion of López Obrador?	Very Good	74	57
	Very Bad	17	18
	Don't Know	9	25
What's your opinion of the attorney general's office?	Very Good	36	32
	Very Bad	51	36
	Don't Know	13	32

SOURCE: Grupo Reforma, "Ven maniobra política acción apegada a la ley," *Reforma*, May 20, 2004, http://www.reforma.com/.

fashion" and pursuing a punishment that was "out of all proportion to the crime." As a presidential contender, López Obrador used this favorable coverage to promote a comparison between himself and Franklin Delano Roosevelt. "López Obrador's economics team has developed a blueprint for what they call the 'Mexican New Deal.' Their modern version of Depression-era populism is an ambitious program to create millions of jobs and stem migration by undertaking huge public works projects, including a railroad network, vast housing developments, ports and timber replanting," wrote a journalist for the *Washington Post*.[15]

Before the *desafuero*, attentive audiences abroad had paid little attention to López Obrador. In a maladroit move to eject him from the presidential race, Fox and Madrazo unwittingly introduced the mayor to the world as a paladin of the downtrodden who was under siege by self-serving powerbrokers. In so doing, they turned a popular politician into a martyr who would use the disqualification attempt as proof that the sinister forces of neoliberalism were conspiring against him and his crusade to uplift the masses they had oppressed.

THE ELEVEN COMMANDMENTS

The Ten Commandments given to Moses 1,445 years before the birth of Christ were central to Jesus' message and remain a code of conduct for Christians. Likewise, the messianic López Obrador enumerated his own postulates, which he promised to adhere to if elected president. Although offered as the "50 Commitments to resuscitate the nation's pride,"[1] they can be reduced to eleven tenets, which are analyzed briefly in this chapter.

1. Thou shalt not exploit the poor and disadvantaged.
2. Thou shalt not tolerate high unemployment.
3. Thou shalt neither spend lavishly on public officials and ex-presidents nor permit corruption.
4. Thou shalt not show disrespect to the branches or units of government.
5. Thou shalt not tolerate criminal activity, corruption, or abuse of sovereignty.
6. Thou shalt not remain dependent on other nations.
7. Thou shalt not curb freedom of speech, freedom of religion, and human rights, while we shall promote culture and well-being.
8. Thou shalt not neglect the nation's infrastructure, agriculture, and natural resources.
9. Thou shalt not compromise the autonomy of the central bank but grant concessions to regional banks that promote development.

10. Thou shalt not privatize the oil or electricity sectors, but strive to achieve more value added to petroleum.
11. Thou shalt not raise taxes.

The political redeemer insisted that adherence to these moral precepts would enable him to vanquish the sinister forces of neo-liberalism in order to bring peace and prosperity to Mexico's downtrodden. Just how realistic are his commandments?

1. THOU SHALT NOT EXPLOIT THE POOR AND DISADVANTAGED

One of the PRD candidate's top priorities reflected his experience in Tabasco. He expressed his commitment to the San Andrés Larráinzar Accords, which were negotiated with the Zapatistas in 1996. They allow indigenous municipalities to govern themselves by "uses and customs." These municipalities would presumably benefit from plans to promote education for youngsters from remote areas, just as el Peje did in the Chontal community in Nacajuca. In addition, López Obrador aimed to extend the "loaves and fishes"—stipends to senior citizens, the poor, the disabled, and single mothers that *defeños* now enjoy—to the entire country. He also pledged to furnish free health services to the needy, ensure minimum wage increases, and improve the care and pensions provided by IMSS and ISSSTE. He would distribute supplies to all public school children at no cost, provide free lunches and scholarships to disadvantaged youngsters, and create two hundred preparatory schools and thirty public universities. In short, he promised to create programs to protect people "from cradle to grave."[2]

While sounding benign, bestowing local autonomy on Indian communities could enable the strong to suppress the weak in Chiapas, which is convulsed by a myriad of feuds: the EZLN versus its foes; Protestants versus Catholics; conservative Catholics versus progressive Catholics; landowners versus the landless; and Chiapans versus Guatemalan refugees. Moreover, self-determination can precipitate a "state within a state," as localities demand collective control of minerals, timber, and water resources located within their boundaries. It could be asserted that these assets belonged to the Indians before Cortés reached Veracruz or Mexico declared independence three hundred years later.

There is also the thorny question of "race." Could people of mixed heritage choose between abiding by national statutes and adhering to traditional laws in Indian communities? Would EZLN leader Subcomandante Marcos, a mestizo residing in an Indian village, be subject to the Indian law, or would he fall under the state and federal legal systems? Would autonomy in Chiapas provoke cries for similar treatment in the nine other states where Indians constitute at least 14 percent of the population? If so, implementing the accords could lead to "Balkanization"—a major reason why the government rejected the proposal in the 1990s. Economist Manuel Suárez Mier has observed that President Juárez emphasized that the only way for Mexico to exist as a nation was under a system that treats all Mexicans equally, regardless of their ethnicity.[3] Acceptance of the San Andrés pact would also exacerbate the subordinate status of women, especially in villages where men have multiple wives, practice incest, and even sell their daughters to other men or exchange them for animals. Above all, the adoption of Indian uses and customs could find elders dictating how villagers vote at a time when Mexico is advancing toward democracy.[4]

El Pejelagarto was right to call for improving the delivery of medical services by IMSS and ISSSTE and even suggesting adjustments in retirement ages. Yet both systems are struggling under enormous operating deficits, as their unions have negotiated high pay and generous pensions for members, reflected in the joke that "a potential IMSS professional does not seek to become a physician but to become a retiree." Although modifications were agreed to in late 2005 for sixty-five thousand new hires, a family doctor who earned 285,590 pesos annually enjoys a yearly retirement stipend of 307,852 pesos. Expert Alejandro Hope placed the unfunded pension liabilities of IMSS at approximately $65 million. In the face of such problems, López Obrador advocated the expansion of free healthcare.

When IMSS employees threatened a strike in October 2005, the PRD candidate lamented the "satanization" of the labor officials. In contrast, he thundered against the highly respected outgoing IMSS director, "because [Santiago] Levy is a dogmatic, intransigent, right-wing technocrat."[5] Rather than slap Band-aids on cancers, Mexico's leader should consider consolidating the public healthcare and pension schemes that include IMSS and ISSSTE, as well as separate schemes for Pemex, Banobras, Bancomex, Nafin, the Bank of Mexico, the armed forces, and major universities. In March 2007, Calderón signed a reform of ISSSTE that created individual pension accounts with defined contributions, while gradually raising the retirement age for government workers.

2. THOU SHALT NOT TOLERATE HIGH UNEMPLOYMENT

El Peje advocated public-private partnerships in infrastructure, public works, and housing to stimulate the economy. He promised to construct 856,000 new houses each year—a venture that would invigorate the construction industry and thirty-seven other sectors.

He also stressed the importance of tourism, which he encouraged in the D.F. He recommended converting the Islas Marías—a notorious Pacific Ocean penal colony founded by Porfirio Díaz in

1905—into an Isla de los Niños (Island of Children) that would feature ecotourism. The Tabascan endorsed industries that would boost employment, curb imports, and reduce the outflow of foreign exchange. He envisioned incentives to keep *maquiladora* owners from moving their assembly plants to China or Central America. At the same time, he advocated low-interest loans to small businesses "through simple mechanisms" that involve minimal red tape.

López Obrador's enthusiasm for subsidies suggested that his administration would be able to "pick winners" better than market forces can. Meanwhile, he failed to take a position on breaking the growth-retarding monopolies and oligopolies that flourish in the transport, television, building materials, food-processing, cement, and communications sectors. This silence may have sprung from his not wanting to offend moguls like Carlos Slim, whose Telmex owns the lion's share of the nation's telephone land lines. While good rapport with the tycoon was crucial to the candidate's credibility in economic circles, el Peje delayed signing the "Chapultepec Accord," which Slim promoted and which called for tax, energy, and legal reforms to strengthen Mexico's weak domestic economy. Although López Obrador assured "honest businessmen" that they would have no worries if he won, he did not convince Coparmex president Alberto Núñez Esteva and other business leaders that he would obey the law. Núñez noted that the candidate's rhetoric clashed with his record. "He speaks of corruption, insecurity, transparency, debt reduction and many other things. . . . Here [in the D.F.] are the cases of Ponce and Bejarano . . . increased public debt, widespread insecurity [and] incomplete public works everywhere."[6] Moreover, the Tabascan seldom if ever mentioned "competition."

As for López Obrador's ability to accelerate business openings, in 2005 it took fifty-eight days to vault bureaucratic hurdles in the D.F., compared with forty-three days in Nigeria, thirty-nine days in Torreón, Durango, thirty-two days in Veracruz, five days in the United States, and two days in Australia.[7]

3. THOU SHALT NEITHER SPEND LAVISHLY ON PUBLIC OFFICIALS AND EX-PRESIDENTS NOR PERMIT CORRUPTION

López Obrador stressed that, as chief executive, he would demand republican austerity and honesty of public officials. He promised to accept only 50 percent of the $173,016 annual salary earned by Fox, spurn living in Los Pinos in favor of more modest quarters in the National Palace, and minimize the use of the aircraft available to the president. He called excessive the annual earnings of federal lawmakers ($122,565) and Supreme Court justices ($159,904), vowing to cap these salaries at $83,333 (900,000 pesos). He also vowed to eliminate the pensions of ex-presidents.

During his *sexenio*, bureaucrats would no longer live off the taxpayers, he vowed. "If the government is changed, those who think they can make money in public service will be subjected to the strict application of the law [and] they will go to jail."[8]

The pay reductions anticipated by el Peje could have boomeranged. He would have had difficulty recruiting the best and the brightest with salaries that are far below those in the private sector and many state and municipal governments. How many talented technocrats would continue in public service under a president who deprecated their backgrounds and accomplishments? A proposal to hire functionaries on the cheap makes a good sound bite, but it may encourage public servants to work a second job or accept bribes. The cases of Ponce, Bejarano, and Imaz cast doubt on el Peje's readiness to combat corruption in his own entourage. Furthermore, despite his promises to eliminate them or diminish their ranks, illegal vendors, contraband sellers, prostitutes, and pirate cabs flourished during his term.

4. THOU SHALT NOT SHOW DISRESPECT TO THE BRANCHES OR UNITS OF GOVERNMENT

López Obrador deserves credit for advocating civility among the various branches and units of government. A lack of tolerance militates against cooperation between the president and Congress, impedes the passage of reforms, divides political parties, and raises questions about the independence of the judiciary. He also promised to poll people midway through the presidential term to determine whether they wanted to revoke his mandate.

El Peje might have been more believable in this area if, as mayor, he had not continually and abusively attacked Fox, legislators, members of the judiciary, the Bank of Mexico, and the Finance Ministry. During and after his presidential campaign, he crudely belittled the Federal Electoral Institute and the Federal Electoral Tribunal and their officials. Holding a plebiscite on the president's performance sounds appealing, but Mexico's chief executive faces Herculean problems. Would not the prospect of a midterm vote encourage expensive, populist programs rather than politically difficult and badly needed fiscal, energy, competition, and labor reforms?

5. THOU SHALT NOT TOLERATE CRIMINAL ACTIVITY, CORRUPTION, OR ABUSE OF SOVEREIGNTY

Street violence is a plague for Mexico's many urban centers, including the D.F. and cities along the U.S. border. However, the PRD standard-bearer reiterated that fighting crime meant more than jailing wrongdoers: it meant fighting "unemployment, poverty, family disintegration, the loss of values, and hopelessness." Social development must be combined with ending police corruption with "intelligence, professionalism, firmness, and perseverance." El Peje suggested that the president, religious leaders, and media spokesmen disseminate positive values to youngsters during primetime broadcasts.

López Obrador praised the armed forces as a strong, loyal, and disciplined organization that has been the least penetrated by organized crime. He emphasized that he would broaden the military's role in the drug war, while it continued to defend Mexico's territory and sovereignty. He would not deploy soldiers to resolve social conflicts.

Mayor López Obrador lost his fight against crime in the D.F. The Giuliani Brothers provided a plethora of ideas, but their implementation proved politically and culturally unfeasible. Despite promises to clean up the police, corruption flourishes in the capital's law enforcement agencies. Exactly what did López Obrador mean by "keeping the armed forces out of social protests?" Should the EZLN again take up arms, would el Peje, as commander in chief, have ordered troops to stay in the barracks? Would they have obeyed?

6. THOU SHALT NOT REMAIN DEPENDENT ON OTHER NATIONS

In his marquee nationalist style, López Obrador sought to diminish Mexico's dependence on other nations by encouraging scientific research at home and reconfiguring NAFTA to protect domestic corn producers. Furthermore, he stressed nonintervention in the affairs of other countries and the peaceful resolution of conflicts to prevent foreign nations from interfering in Mexican affairs.

A product of Tepititán and Tabasco, López Obrador exhibited naïveté with respect to international matters. Nostalgia for the good old days aside, Mexico cannot insulate itself from the global economy. For instance, cutting-edge discoveries often spring from cooperative ventures by scientists and universities in several nations. For better or for worse, Mexico has already lowered barriers to corn imports from the United States and Canada,[9] and neither NAFTA partner will renegotiate the tripartite accord. While quick to defend Mexico's sovereignty, el Peje readily inserted himself into the policies of a neighbor. "In the agenda with the U.S. government, the principal issue will be migration and the labor and human rights of the Mexicans who, by necessity, cross the border to work in the United States."

7. THOU SHALT NOT CURB FREEDOM OF SPEECH, FREEDOM OF RELIGION, AND HUMAN RIGHTS, WHILE WE SHALL PROMOTE CULTURE

López Obrador committed himself to protecting "the culture of Mexico that has survived all of the disgraces of history." He stated his intention to assist creative artists of all kinds, encourage reading, and establish libraries and archives. At the same time, he wanted to expand the coverage of radio and television stations that engage in cultural broadcasting.

These proposals were congruent with his behavior as mayor. Although vague about the "disgraces" that have afflicted his nation's culture, he is a student of Mexican history who is eager to spread the ideas of nationalistic leaders. As head of government in the D.F., he sponsored book fairs, concerts, plays, and other events to bring average people into contact with their nation's creative works. He also selected as secretary of culture (2000–2005) the distinguished intellectual Dr. Enrique Semo Calev, who recorded major accomplishments despite the modest budget of his agency. In addition, he included in his entourage González Pedrero, Julieta Campos, and renowned author and diplomat José María Pérez Guy.

8. THOU SHALT NOT NEGLECT THE NATION'S INFRASTRUCTURE, AGRICULTURE, AND NATURAL RESOURCES

The PRD nominee excoriated neoliberal regimes for failing to invest in the primary sector. He vowed to reverse this trend by forging an "integral program" to promote agriculture and cattle production for home consumption, sales to the national market, and shipments abroad. He also advocated assisting the fishing industry to upgrade the conditions in riparian areas and spur the output of protein-rich food at low prices. To protect the environment and create jobs, he recommended planting 1 million hectares of lumber-producing trees in Veracruz and southeastern states, and he advocated a coherent approach to storing, managing, and distributing water.

Transportation projects loomed high on his priority list. He proposed creating two bullet trains that would operate between Mexico and the United States. In addition, he supported a new airport in Tizayuca, Hidalgo, with rapid transport to the D.F., and a rail bridge for containerized cargo across the Isthmus of Tehuantepec.

This commandment is full of good intentions, but it offers solutions to problems that existed forty or fifty years ago, when there were far fewer peasants and they could find opportunities on communal farms. Regrettably, most of the one-fifth of Mexicans who live in the countryside can scratch out only a meager living—with ever more dire prospects in light of the increased importation of grains. Small farmers will continue to suffer impoverishment unless there is a concerted effort to improve their healthcare and education so that they can find employment in modern sectors. Accomplishing such a transition represents an expensive challenge, which few governments have undertaken successfully. The upshot in most of the developing world has been escalating migration to industrialized nations, whenever possible.

The stewardship of Mexico's water resources is imperative. As mayor, however, el Peje devoted relatively few funds to the D.F.'s water system, whose old and leaky pipes mean that one-third of the city's water is lost between the source and the consumer.[10]

López Obrador's transportation proposals evinced his passion for expensive, high-visibility schemes of the kind he promoted as mayor. How, for instance, could he persuade travelers to take trains from Mexico City and Guadalajara to the border, when airline travel is less expensive? He was silent on whether there would be cost-benefit studies of the projects. Would there be transparent bidding? What would be the source of funding?

9. THOU SHALT NOT COMPROMISE THE AUTONOMY OF THE CENTRAL BANK BUT GRANT CONCESSIONS TO REGIONAL BANKS THAT PROMOTE DEVELOPMENT

López Obrador asserted that he would maintain the "macroeconomic equilibrium" achieved under Fox. He also vowed to pursue "an adequate monetary policy and exercise discipline in the management of inflation and the public deficit." These have been policies implemented by the Bank of Mexico and the SHCP. As a result, they have reduced Mexico's rate of inflation to 4 percent, down from 9.5 percent in 2000 and 16.6 percent in 1999. The $663 billion economy, Latin America's largest, grew by nearly 5 percent in 2006. At the same time, Mexico has lowered its public debt and increased its hard-currency reserves to an all-time high. These results have won accolades from the international financial community and have functioned as a magnet, attracting tens of billions of dollars of foreign investment. To gain credibility abroad, the PRD candidate endorsed the strategy of technocrats Ortiz and Gil Díaz.

Even as el Peje paid lip service to responsible economic principles, he berated Fox's finance secretary as "your supreme highness" because of Gil Díaz's support for bank secrecy and his ties to "the bankers of the past and the bankers of today." He also demanded the resignation of Ortiz. In light of his disdain for market-focused tenets, the candidate's commitment to sound monetary and fiscal policy looked like window dressing, all the more so because of his quirky management of D.F. finances. In addition, he called for concessions to regional banks that could provide development loans. The irresponsible provision of such credits by various government banks was a key factor in the inflation that provoked the December 1994 peso devaluation.

10. THOU SHALT NOT PRIVATIZE THE OIL OR ELECTRICITY SECTORS, BUT STRIVE TO ACHIEVE MORE VALUE ADDED TO PETROLEUM

Hydrocarbons lie at the heart of el Peje's economic development strategy. While Pemex would remain in state hands, he insisted that his longtime bête noire would have to undergo sweeping reforms, including the "complete elimination of corruption."[11] He called for more exploration and production to replace 100 percent of the nation's reserves consumed at home or sold abroad each year. He also advocated maintaining production at 3.4 million barrels per day while urging the construction and enlargement of refineries, which would operate near capacity, to process larger volumes of heavy crude. In accord with his nationalist principles, he planned to halt imports of natural gas, gasoline, and other petroleum products within three years and decrease the cost of gasoline.

Furthermore, he favored diminishing the demand for natural gas by using more fuel oil in electricity generation, as well as developing natural gas holdings in the Burgos Basin in the north, Veracruz, and his home municipality of Macuspana, Tabasco. As a final thought, he proposed developing alternative energy supplies.[12]

None of the Little Ray of Hope's commandments was more farfetched than this one. In 2003 Pemex replaced only 3 percent of its reserves; a year later, the restitution volume reached 18 percent. To restore reserves fully by 2007 would require the discovery of 7.427 billion barrels of oil. As former Pemex director-general Adrián Lajous has indicated, that volume would equal the accumulated production and remaining reserves of the major fields in the Campeche Sound in addition to those in the Tabasco littoral. The goal for new reserves would exceed the quantity of crude oil that still exists in Mexico's giant Cantarell complex. El Peje naïvely believed that simply drilling more wells would achieve his objectives, when in fact it is more important to determine where the search for hydrocarbons would take place. The monopoly faces a decline in reserves, an absence of major discoveries in recent years, mature and declining reservoirs, a decrease in output from existing wells, and increased costs of exploration and extraction.

Mexico may abound in undiscovered oil. Nonetheless, Pemex, which has a history and culture of dependence on large reservoirs, lacks the administrative and technical expertise to undertake the rigorous economic analysis that would boost secondary recovery from existing fields. In the same vein, the PRD nominee rejected cost-benefit assessments in proposing to use 100 percent of refining capability, eliminate the export of extralight Olmeca crude, and shift from natural gas to fuel oil whenever possible. For instance, Pemex has difficulty operating at 95 percent capacity without increasing the risk of major accidents. Failing to export Olmeca would constitute a financial setback, for this high-quality crude commands a premium price. Not only would the reconfiguration and building of refineries take much longer and be substantially more expensive than estimated, but producing more fuel oil to replace natural gas in electricity generation would substitute a polluting energy source for a clean-burning one. At a time when fuel oil consumption is declining because of environmental factors, Pemex would be turning out more of the product, and the Federal Electricity Commission would be forced to modify its gas-burning plants so that they could use this dirty fuel.

Meanwhile, subsidizing gasoline and other fuels would benefit well-to-do vehicle owners more than the poor; it would also lower Pemex revenues and distort prices throughout the economy. Moving away from market-based transfer prices among the monopoly's four divisions would blur accountability and open the door to more corruption and greater inefficiency. Finally, in light of declining reserves and the labor-intensiveness of oil production, future presidents must look to manufacturing—not Pemex—to power Mexico's growth, at least in the short and medium term.

11. THOU SHALT NOT RAISE TAXES

López Obrador asserted that he could fund billions of dollars' worth of social programs, agriculture, transportation, and infrastructure without raising taxes. He contended that he could achieve his goals by running an austere government, combating corruption, simplifying the fiscal system, and curbing ubiquitous tax evasion. Simultaneously, he would "definitely resolve" the issue of Fobaproa and other economic "black holes," like the rescue of private toll roads, Pemex's deferred financing of major projects (Pidiregas), and credits from the Development Bank. Moreover, he would "reorder" the public debt by publicizing the real amount owed rather than engaging in the "double accounting" that "implies paying a higher interest rate." He claimed that Mexico's debt had shot up from $80 billion in 1983 to $273 billion today.

The possibility of enjoying vastly greater benefits without paying a centavo more in taxes is seductive. The candidate correctly identified tax evasion as a severe problem: while citizens dislike forking over money to the government under any circumstances, ubiquitous corruption makes payment even more odious. It is one thing to promise to crack down on tax evasion and collect revenues more efficiently; it is another thing to carry out such pledges. For instance, one of the most difficult taxes for citizens to avoid is the value-added tax, or IVA, which el Peje denigrates as regressive—that is, lower-income people pay a higher percentage of their income in the IVA than do the wealthy. While there may be slight regressiveness in the collection of this tax, its expenditure is progressive inasmuch as a disproportionate amount flows to education, healthcare, public safety, environmental protection, and other programs that benefit the poor much more than the affluent. The former mayor lacked credibility in fiscal matters because he allowed the number of illegal street vendors and pirate cabs to mushroom in the D.F., to the detriment of merchants and owners of legal taxis, who must pay taxes and purchase various licenses from the city.

Launching a crusade against the black holes mentioned above could chill investment, diminish growth, and hamper job creation. In focusing on the government's debt, López Obrador mixed apples and oranges. The $80 billion figure represented the nation's foreign debt in 1983, while the $273 billion is domestic debt, financed at a low rate of interest. In addition, the $80 billion debt of the early 1980s equaled 100 percent of GDP, while today's $30 billion foreign debt constitutes only 10 percent of GDP.[13]

In Christianity, following the Lord's commandments enhances the believers' chances of fending off Satan en route to the Kingdom of God. El Peje offered his strictures as a passage to their salvation. If obeyed, the masses could overcome the hellish precepts of neoliberalism to enjoy a decent education, competent healthcare, well-paying jobs, and a comfortable retirement. He guaranteed access to a Promised Land on earth—free of personal sacrifices.

WINNING THE "PROMISED LAND"

To defeat the hated neoliberals, López Obrador realized that he would have to swell the ranks of his faithful as he had done in the D.F. The messiah understood that his PRD had an organization in only a half-dozen states, held just four governorships, and had won less than 17 percent of the votes in the last two presidential contests. His strategy to attain the "Promised Land" of Los Pinos involved five major elements:

- Presenting his new book in various parts of the country on weekends before he left city hall;
- Drawing independents and non-PRD activists—especially PRI defectors—into "Citizens Networks";
- Barnstorming the nation after he resigned as mayor;
- Relying on his party's operatives to mobilize votes in the D.F. and in states with PRD governors; and
- Attempting to convince international opinion leaders that he would be a responsible manager of Mexican affairs.

When it was suggested that he attend Luiz Inácio Lula da Silva's inauguration in Brasilia, el Peje said, in effect, "My obligation is to stay here and work for the people who elected me." The Tabascan also delighted in practicing republican austerity, while Fox made more trips abroad during his first three years in office than had his three predecessors combined. El Peje's "oneness" with the people kept him in the D.F.

On November 20, 2004, López Obrador began to travel throughout the country to unveil his *proyecto alternativo de nación,* the first iteration of his Eleven Commandments. All told, he presented his anti-neoliberal manifesto—dedicated to "all who have not lost hope"—in more than a dozen cities. During his literary and political excursion, he covered 4,299 kilometers and spoke before 20,700 people.[1] By June 1, 2005, the first rendition of his political creed had sold 37,000 copies, netting the author 476,599 pesos for his campaign.[2] To demonstrate that he was not using the income for creature comforts, el Pejelagarto released his income and expenditures for 2003 and 2004 (see Table 21).

In addition to propounding his doctrine, the mayor used these sessions to restore his image, which had been tarnished by various scandals, as well as his caustic remarks about the "Citizens March Against Crime" that brought some quarter-million, largely middle-class, people into the streets of Mexico City in late June 2004.

The book events gave him a chance to schmooze with local leaders, explore electoral alliances, and win converts to his cause. Among those who assisted in these activities were political confidants Manuel Camacho and Ricardo Monreal, economist Rogelio Ramírez de la O, Pérez Gay, adviser Ignacio Marván, former culture secretary Semo, communications director Yáñez, and private secretary Alejandro Esquer.

CITIZENS NETWORKS

Meanwhile, the mayor's brother, Pío López Obrador, and the PRD's secretary of labor and social movements, José Antonio Rueda, began organizing "citizen committees" distinct from the party. By September 2004 they had spawned such groups in a dozen states, mostly in the southern and central parts of the country.[3]

On December 5, 2004, López Obrador proclaimed that he was seeking to win 60 percent of the Mexicans. To achieve this goal, he announced the formation of "Citizens Networks" to broaden his

TABLE 21. *López Obrador's Income and Expenses, 2003–2004*

CATEGORY	2003 (PESOS)	2004 (PESOS)
Income	1,295,358	1,435,502
Expenditures on clothing	100,000	110,000
Expenditure on shoes	25,000	25,000
Expenditure on recreation	241,000	300,000
Expenditure on a housekeeper	72,000	65,000

SOURCE: Manuel Durán, "Obtiene $476 mil AMLO por su libro," *Reforma,* June 1, 2005, http://www.reforma.com.mx/.

political base. On its Web site, this "citizens' movement" stressed its commitment to "the full exercise of liberties, economic growth, greater justice, and strengthening our national identity."[4] He named as organizers five PRI converts and one independent. Each coordinator was responsible for creating and overseeing the networks in one of the nation's five political zones:

- Deputy Socorro Díaz Palacios (Baja California, Baja California Sur, Colima, Guanajuato, Jalisco, Nayarit, Sinaloa, and Sonora);
- Deputy Manuel Camacho Solís (Aguascalientes, Chihuahua, Coahuila, Durango, Nuevo León, Querétaro, San Luis Potosí);
- Former Zacatecas governor Ricardo Monreal Ávila (Guerrero, México State, Michoacan, and Zacatecas);
- Senator César Raúl Ojeda Zubieta, candidate for governor of Tabasco (Campeche, Chiapas, Oaxaca, Quintana Roo, Veracruz, Yucatán, and Tabasco); and
- Deputy José Agustín Ortiz Pinchetti, a successful attorney who had been López Obrador's first secretary of government (D.F., Hidalgo, Morelos, Puebla, and Tlaxcala)

Federico Arreola Castillo, the erstwhile executive vice president for publishing at the Multimedios/Milenio conglomerate, served as the organization's technical secretary. Among his responsibilities was raising and managing funds for the network, each of whose local committees was expected to be self-supporting. Although the organizational chart was flexible, to say the least, there were—below the coordinators and Arreola—national subcoordinators for each of the electoral zones and national delegates to each state's networks.

In late March 2005 Camacho claimed that the networks had formed 970 local committees—a figure that would soar to four thousand.[5] The networks appeared similar to the Friends of Fox, which had played a crucial role in Fox's victory. They had a malleable structure that could respond quickly to the needs of the leadership; were focused on a single individual; could raise money for their candidate; attracted independents who normally spurned partisan activities, as well as PRI activists disenchanted with Madrazo; depicted differences with their political foes in black-and-white terms; complemented the relatively weak PRD machinery just as the Friends of Fox complemented the PAN; and discouraged citizens adversely affected by neoliberalism from wasting their votes on other candidates—a variation on Fox's "valid vote" strategy to dissuade citizens from backing Cárdenas in 2000.[6]

These similarities aside, the networks differed from the Friends of Fox in several ways. Their leaders were politicians, not businessmen. These coordinators were searching for candidates who could run for Congress and state and local positions to amplify the turnout for López Obrador and lend credibility in his campaign. Had he captured the presidency, el Peje would have required as much support as possible to advance his legislative agenda. Miguel Valladares García typified the kind of nominee the networks were eager to attract. He was a prosperous businessman, a member of a well-known San Luis Potosí family, a generous backer of the Tabascan, and owner of the *Pulso de San Luis Potosí* newspaper, as well as TV and radio stations.

In late October 2005, one of the network counselors, Villahermosa mogul Ojeda Zubieta, garnered the PRD gubernatorial nomination for his home state. He told his supporters, "I am not going to launch a pre-campaign as candidate for governor; I am going to campaign for the President of the Republic."[7] El Pejelagarto yearned to hear similar encomiums from one end of the country to the other.

He was counting on a major fracture within the PRI to propel him to victory. Longtime PRI stalwart Arturo Núñez, a bitter Madrazo rival, joined the networks and became the PRD-backed Senate candidate in Tabasco. Another Madrazo foe—Deputy Roberto Campa—temporarily signed on with López Obrador before embarking on his own presidential campaign, and elements of the PRI's National Campesino Confederation (CNC) were drawn to his candidacy. Much to the dismay of el Peje's entourage, though, the PRI's internal fighting had not precipitated as many defections as hoped for by early 2006. Many of those courted by López Obrador had their futures behind them. These included Enrique Ku Herrera, former CNC secretary of organization in Yucatán; Alfonso Durazo Montaño, former private secretary of both Colosio and Fox; Enrique Ibarra Pedroza, a lawyer from Jalisco who had spent thirty-five years in the PRI; and Gabino Cué Monteagudo, an ally of former Oaxaca governor Diódoro Carrasco, who left the PRI to join the Democratic Convergence Party.

After the *desafuero* threat subsided, leaders of the Citizens Networks concentrated on the two dozen states where the PRD had an anemic organization or, even worse, where a handful of self-important leaders scuffled over the limited resources available to them. In the 2003 congressional races, el Peje's party failed to capture a directly elected deputy seat in twenty-four states—the majority of which lie in the populous north and center of the country. In these contests, the PRD (17.7 percent) ran far behind the PRI (36.5 percent) and the PAN (30.6 percent).[8]

In August 2005 the Businessmen's Networks emerged as an adjunct to the Citizens Networks. Another member of the campaign family was the National Youth Network, which sprang to life in early 2005. The latter joined the Sun Brigades to canvass for PRD candidates.

THE ROLE OF THE PRD

The messianic politician visited PRD-governed states but accorded governors of these entities an opportunity to demonstrate their effectiveness in mobilizing voters. He installed loyalist Cota Montaño as national party president. The former Baja California chief executive concluded electoral pacts with the Mexican Workers' Party and Democratic Convergence, while encouraging unity among the PRD's several currents. To promote harmony, el Peje and Cota Montaño propitiated the relatively well organized New Left (NI) faction of the party, also known as the "Chuchos."[9] In a show of solidarity with this current, they named Guadalupe Acosta Naranjo the party's secretary-general and Jesús Zambrano undersecretary of government in the D.F. The New Forum, called the "Amalios" after Zacatecas governor Amalia García Medina, tepidly backed the Tabascan.

Winning the "Promised Land"

Even though the Citizens Networks constituted a parallel structure to the PRD, their organizers denied they would supplant the party. Some PRD leaders called the organization essential for victory. Carlos Navarrete, a leading Chucho, rejected the danger of a clash. "We need to incorporate into our political project millions of Mexicans who are not in our ranks and who have not voted for the PRD in the last sixteen years," he said.[10]

Nevertheless, many *perredistas* worried publicly that the networks would displace their faction-ridden party. Cota Montaño attempted to assuage these concerns by insisting disingenuously that the party would be the "only entity" choosing nominees in the 2006 federal, state, and local contests.[11] In reality, the networks dangled candidacies before non-PRD politicians in hopes they would board el Pejelagarto's campaign train. Yet, to fortify linkages, his apostle Pérez Mendoza became the PRD's secretary of organization in September 2005 and took responsibility for mobilizing votes for the candidate.

López Obrador backed Martí Batres, a leader of the dominant National Democratic Left (IDN), for the party presidency in the D.F. Gilberto Ensástiga became secretary-general as a concession to the small pro-Cárdenas Unity and Renovation Coordination (UyR), while Lorena Villavicencio of the New Left assumed the leadership of the party's ALDF delegation.

López Obrador endorsed IDN member Marcelo Ebrard over Jesús Ortega shortly before the December 4, 2005, nominating primary for D.F. mayor. The D.F.'s director of citizen participation, Eduardo Cervantes Díaz Lombardo, turned out three thousand "promoters" in seven hundred territorial units on behalf of Ebrard. They took advantage of a database, broken down by territorial units, to mobilize senior citizens, single mothers, the disabled, participants in referenda, residents of public housing, loan recipients, scholarship holders, University of Mexico City students, and other beneficiaries of social programs.

Despite López Obrador's takeover of their party, most chiefs of the PRD tribes worked their fingers to the bone for their presidential aspirant. They regarded him as a "winner" and relished the possible rewards that would accrue from having a *perredista* in the presidency.

Among the PRD-controlled states, Michoacán represented the candidate's biggest challenge. After López Obrador met with its governor, Lázaro Cárdenas Batel, in October 2005, "Lazarito" said, "I have always been at my father's side . . . but he is not now a presidential candidate. I see [López Obrador] as the only candidate of the PRD."[12] El Peje then proposed a long-term alliance, which would include a Senate seat for the senior Cárdenas. Such an offer notwithstanding, neither el Inge nor his loyalists expressed enthusiasm for the upstart Tabascan, whom they reviled.

BARNSTORMING THE COUNTRY

No sooner had López Obrador resigned as mayor than he began to campaign nationwide. His first goal was to visit the nation's fifty-five largest cities and then, before the end of 2005, to make appearances in the remaining 245 congressional districts. He pledged that his would be a low-budget enterprise and that he would not air TV spots early in his campaign. "We don't have money; we are not going to run an ostentatious campaign; we are not going to run a campaign based on publicity, on marketing, because we are not going to introduce a product into the marketplace," he affirmed.[13]

The former mayor traveled by automobile in what became known as the "Pejetour." He contrasted his "ground" campaign to that of his opponents, who regularly used private aircraft. To enhance his image as the poor man's nominee, el Peje released a number—019008492656—that people could phone to contribute small amounts to his candidacy. He opened the lines in mid-October and reported receiving five thousand calls, generating three hundred thousand pesos, in the first week. Still, there was no public accounting of the gimmick, which was later abandoned.

The initial phase of his odyssey took him to areas where the PRD was weak. On August 11, 2005, he first stopped in La Paz, Baja California Sur. From there he proceeded to Baja California and Sonora, before making appearances in Sinaloa, Nayarit, Chihuahua, Coahuila, Nuevo León, Tamaulipas, and San Luis Potosí. He visited thirteen cities, contacting more than seventy thousand people, many of whom were from the middle class, according to Counselor Díaz Palacios.[14]

In his second swing, he held events in the states of Bajío (Guanajuato, Jalisco, Querétaro, and San Luis Potosí) as well as in Zacatecas, Aguascalientes, Michoacan, México State, and Morelos. During the rest of September, he focused on the south; in October he returned to the north and Bajío; November found him in Tamaulipas, Hidalgo, Edomex, and nearby states; and he came back to the D.F. in December.

His campaign often resembled a pilgrimage. In Magdalena de Kino, Sonora, he deposited a floral wreath and stood with Arreola as honor guards at the mausoleum containing the remains of the sainted Luis Colosio and his wife, Dana Laura. He implied that Salinas was behind the murder, saying that such a crime was difficult to solve, "because when there is a political assassination, it is extremely difficult to know the actual killer and, above all, the intellectual authors [of the crime]."[15]

In Tamaulipas the faithful distributed prayers that called on the Lord to protect el Peje from a fate similar to Colosio's. Although the Tabascan had relied on the Gazelles for security in the D.F., Nicolás Mollinedo hired industrial and bank police to protect him and his sons during the campaign.

While in Michoacán, the messianic candidate paid homage to the Cárdenas family. Before three thousand people in Morelia, he expressed his admiration for Cuauhtémoc Cárdenas, whom he compared to figures like Morelos and the late president Cárdenas. "We cannot forget the contribution of *michoacanos* for forging what was the beginning of democracy in Mexico," he proclaimed.[16]

In Culiacán he extolled the accomplishments of a late presidential contender and PAN demigod. "As a distinguished Sinaloan said . . . Manuel J. Clouthier, a builder of democracy in our country: there are people and a leader and they will not fail."[17]

López Obrador also sought out ranking clerics in the Roman Catholic Church, which, like him, condemned globalization. In Monterrey he had a cordial session with Archbishop Francisco Robles Ortega, whose predecessor, Suárez Rivera, is the uncle of Camacho's late wife. In Puebla he met privately with Archbishop Rosendo Huesca Pacheco. In such tête-à-têtes, the candidate stressed the themes of poverty and corruption and suggested that the church might be a good "arbiter" of the political transition in 2006. Other clerics publicly expressed concerns about the "populist tactics" used by some candidates.

INTERNATIONAL OPINION

As mayor, the messianic Tabascan sought to spread the word abroad that he would be a responsible chief executive. One way of doing this was to meet with foreign dignitaries. These included former Bogotá mayor Antanas Mockus Šivickas, Berlin's mayor Klaus Wowereit, former Paris mayor Bertrand Delanoë, German president Johannes Rau, and French foreign minister Dominique de Villepin. He would show them the Historic Center, discuss his prized public works, and describe his social programs. (Table 22 lists the foreign dignitaries who visited Mexico City.)

Jeffrey Davidow, who served as American ambassador to Mexico from 1999 to 2003, had little contact with López Obrador.

TABLE 22. *Dignitaries Who Visited Mexico City, 2003–2004*

DATE OF VISIT	DIGNITARY	POSITION	SIGNIFICANT OUTCOME
January 15, 2003	Rudolph Giuliani	Former Mayor of New York City	Discussed security concerns in the D.F.
March 24, 2003	Leoluca Orlando	Former Mayor of Palermo, Italy	
June 3, 2003	Bertrand Delanoë	Mayor of Paris	Signed agreements of cooperation
October 11, 2003	Antanas Mockus Šivickas	Mayor of Bogota	
October 13, 2003	Klaus Wowereit	Mayor of Berlin	
November 19, 2003	Johannes Rau	President of Germany	
January 24, 2004	Esteban Loaiza	Pitcher, Chicago White Sox	
February 16, 2004	José Bono Martínez	President, Region of Castilla la Mancha, Spain	
October 6, 2004	Dalai Lama	Head of Tibetan Buddhism	
May 30, 2005	Heinz Fischer	President of Austria	

I am indebted to Joseph H. Jenkins for preparing this table.

However, when Davidow took a group of Shriners to city hall concerning problems with the completion of a Shriners Hospital in the D.F., he found the mayor receptive. The session went well and the city government helped advance the project.[18]

On a less cordial note, in early March 2004 López Obrador alleged that the U.S. Drug Enforcement Administration (DEA) had a hand in the videos that showed Gustavo Ponce gambling in Las Vegas. The taping and receipts linked to the former finance secretary "required the collaboration of an organ of the government of the United States," he claimed.[19]

LÓPEZ OBRADOR AND THE UNITED STATES

Mexico City's mayor several times contemplated accepting invitations from his distinguished guests to reciprocate their visits. He intended to travel to Europe in the spring of 2004 before the video scandals and the *desafuero* made it impossible for him to leave the country.

His next scheduled trip was to California, to celebrate the Independence Day "Grito" with Antonio Villaraigosa, the Mexican American mayor of Los Angeles. Several days before his departure, IFE notified him that the electoral code forbade campaign activities abroad. Although he canceled his flight, he branded IFE a "sold-out umpire" intent on impeding his election.

Perez Gay, his foreign affairs adviser, had to call off sessions arranged for López Obrador with the editorial board of the *Los Angeles Times,* as well as with business groups. Plans had also been laid for el Peje to fly to New York in the fall to meet with the editorial board of the *New York Times,* the vice president of the Federal Reserve Bank of New York, the Council of the Americas, the Council on Foreign Policy, and the Tepeyac Association of Mexicans.[20] Even though IFE imposed a Christmas "truce" on campaigning, pro-Peje activists in California vowed to use this period to drum up support for their candidate in California.[21]

Key members of López Obrador's entourage believed that their candidate could not win if the White House opposed him. Thus, in interviews with the international press, the PRD standard-bearer presented himself as a pragmatist who would maintain the prudent macroeconomic policies of the Fox years. For instance, he ruled out any designs on renegotiating NAFTA, which he had often castigated. "We are talking about asserting our rights within the treaty. We aren't talking about attempting to change the treaty," he told the *Financial Times.*[22]

As noted in his Eleven Commandments, he cited the human and labor rights of Mexicans in America as the number-one element in bilateral relations. He insisted that the provisions of the tripartite pact should be broadened to include the free flow of labor, as well as U.S. and Canadian economic assistance to Mexico—the *foxista* idea of transforming the continental accord into a North American version of the European Union.

In addition, he strenuously attempted to dispel the "Manichean and facile" comparison between him and Venezuelan strongman Hugo Chávez. El Peje emphasized his lack of a military background and stressed that "each country has its own reality; leaders have our own history and processes; no two are alike; I have [my own] political trajectory."[23]

He lauded the credentials of his economic team as evidence that his administration would be responsible. Among his advisers were Arturo Herrera Gutiérrez, a Ph.D. candidate at New York University who specializes in social development and education and served as Ponce's successor as D.F. finance secretary; Gerardo Esquivel Hernández, a Harvard Ph.D. in economics who conducts research on fiscal policy and economic growth; José Luis Calvo, a prize-winning journalist who concentrates on rural development; Rogelio Ramírez de la O, a Ph.D. and internationally respected president of the Ecanal business consulting firm, which has clients in Mexico, the United States, and Europe; and Édgar Amador, a Colegio de México graduate and NAFTA critic who taught at Princeton and functioned as chief Latin American economist for the New Jersey–based Stone & McCarthy's Research Association, where he founded Portafolios.com.

Ramírez de la O, a fifty-seven-year-old graduate of Cambridge University, has ties to top executives. He sits on the board of Grupo Modelo SA, the country's largest beer producer, and insurer Reaseguradora Patria SA. He gained credibility with investors when he warned of the peso's overvaluation on the eve of the 1994 devaluation. Ramírez introduced the candidate to members of the investment community and assured Credit Suisse First Boston, J. P. Morgan, Goldman Sachs Group, and several dozen other financial institutions that López Obrador would control spending to keep the budget deficit within the goals set by the Fox government.[24]

In mid-2005 Herrera made a favorable impression when addressing the United States–Mexico Chamber of Commerce in New York City. Although not a member of the economic task force, Camacho actively advanced López Obrador's candidacy abroad. He traveled widely in the United States, meeting with Henry Kissinger and other past and present high-level U.S. officials.

As a former PRD president, López Obrador recognized the futility of relying on his party to reach the presidency. Consequently, he named an independent and five PRI converts to construct Citizens Networks whose mission was to supplement the PRD's work, raise money, and—above all—recruit attractive candidates. Although some PRD leaders regarded the new structure warily, they threw their support behind el Peje because he represented the first opportunity for a member of their party win. Even before formally stepping down as mayor, López Obrador left Mexico's Jerusalem to disseminate his Eleven Commandments in more than a dozen major cities. After resigning his post, he carried his message of redemption to the masses. Meanwhile, he sought to downplay his messianic zeal by naming relatively well known economic advisers, some of whom traveled abroad to assure U.S. elites that their candidate had nothing in common with Hugo Chávez and would govern in a sensible manner. During his campaign's early stages, the Tabascan messiah lavished praise on political saints and met with church leaders. While supporters begged God to protect him, prayers that PRI activists would rush to López Obrador's side went unanswered.

AN ELECTORAL SETBACK

López Obrador entered the final hundred days of the presidential campaign as the front-runner. Surveys showed him leading his nearest competitor, former energy secretary Felipe Calderón, who had defeated Santiago Creel for the PAN nomination, by ten to fifteen points. People responded to el Peje's pledge to accomplish a "real purification of public life," to spur "a change from top to bottom," and to end the travesty of "a rich government and an impoverished people." He also elicited cheers when he promised that "the next president of Mexico will not be a puppet of anyone"—a thinly veiled allusion to Fox's attempt to forge closer relations with Washington. When asked about his religious beliefs, he said, "I am Catholic, and fundamentally Christian because the life and work of Jesus fills me with passion. He, too, was persecuted in his time, spied on by the powerful of his era, and they crucified him."[1] Women holding aloft banners of the Virgin of Guadalupe occasionally showed up at his rallies, as if they sought to link the "For the Good of All" candidate to their salvation. Other supporters offered prayers for his safety and success even as they draped him with flower garlands and treated him like a conquering hero.

By late winter, business leaders seemed to have reconciled themselves to a López Obrador victory and shied away from criticizing him. The private sector had gotten used to the prospect of his triumph, according to Michael Lettieri of the Council on Hemispheric Affairs in Washington. "Most see him as pretty moderate," he added. "They are coming to realize he's not this terrifying communist bogeyman who is going to nationalize all kinds of sectors."

Yasmin Corona, an analyst at the Bursamétrica financial consulting firm in Mexico City, explained that "for now, everything is calm, but some of his statements, especially recently, have been exaggeratedly populist. There is fear in certain sectors."[2] Some business leaders were even enthusiastic about el Peje's candidacy. Arturo González, former president of Concanaco, ran for the Senate as a part of the "For the Good of All" alliance in Baja California. He also served as an intermediary to the local private sector. Such cases showed that "in some cases there is a process of rapprochement" between the Tabascan and the business community.[3]

FORTUNES TURN

El Peje's fortunes began to turn when he began attacking President Fox for his overt intrusion into the campaign. Under the nation's electoral law, officeholders are prohibited from engaging in political activity. Sitting chief executives could easily remain on the sidelines during most of the seventy-one years of PRI hegemony because the outcome of the election was ensured in advance. Fox, by contrast, did not hesitate to enter the fray. His administration filled the airwaves with "public service announcements" that trumpeted the successes of his government and stressed the imperative of selecting a responsible successor to maintain the momentum. "We can continue advancing if we persevere in our effort, if we put aside easy promises and false illusions, the demagoguery and populism," he thundered in one of his many jabs at López Obrador. He warned citizens about being seduced by "false messiahs" who promise government handouts and lower gas prices that would bankrupt future generations of Mexicans. Populists, he averred, "give us a sandwich today so that we can go hungry tomorrow."[4] In an interview with the *Los Angeles Times,* the chief executive stated, "We paid a high, high price because of populism, because of demagogic proposals and because of irresponsibility on the budget." "No Mexican wants to even smell" that type of government, he added.[5] Political scientist Denise Dresser told a reporter, "He's clearly worried that Andrés Manuel López Obrador will be president and the country's economic model will change."[6]

El Peje chastised Fox for such rhetoric, saying, "He can't go around bad-mouthing me. He can't walk around throwing indirect attacks." The Tabascan also alluded to the president's many promises and few achievements. "He already had his opportunity and the only thing he did was to betray millions of Mexicans that trusted him."[7]

On March 10 López Obrador publicly demanded that President Fox "shut up," sometimes berating the chief executive with colloquial language. This response opened the way for the PAN "war room" to link el Peje to Hugo Chávez, another harsh critic of

Fox. Calderón advised the Federal Electoral Institute that it should investigate "the existence of Bolivarian cells financed by the Venezuelans, by embassy personnel or by the government of Hugo Chávez." He echoed a report published in the anti–López Obrador *La Crónica* that "revealed" that "Bolivarian groups" and "*Chavista* cells" had sprung up among radical university students. The newspaper claimed to have evidence that a confidant of a former Venezuelan ambassador had funded these clandestine operations. The PAN nominee embellished this theory by questioning the "real" aims of Venezuelan assistance for a healthcare campaign in a PRD-run municipality in Yucatán.[8]

If these references were too subtle, the PAN accentuated the purported López Obrador–Hugo Chávez nexus in a fusillade of television commercials that ran for three weeks, beginning March 19, conveying the message that the Tabascan represented "a danger for Mexico." One spot took language from a diplomatic squabble in 2005, when the Venezuelan leader had cautioned his Mexican counterpart, "Don't mess with me, sir. You'll get stung." Then it cut to video footage of López Obrador saying: "Shut up, *chachalaca*"—a reference to a constantly twittering rare bird.[9] The ad concluded with the admonition: "No to intolerance."[10]

The campaign's top advisers fiercely debated whether to bombard López Obrador with negative advertisements. After all, both the 2000 effort to keep him off the ballot for mayor and the 2005 *desafuero* had backfired on its promoters. El Peje had emerged from both initiatives as a "victim," with even higher levels of support. However, the PAN nominee was trailing by 10 percentage points in early March. His "Passion and Values for Mexico" slogan and his emphasis on market economics was falling flat. "We had to make adjustments," said Juan Camilo Mouriño, a deputy campaign coordinator, who became President Calderón's chief of staff.

One of the most important architects of this new strategy was Antonio Sola, a young Spanish political consultant who had worked for former Spanish prime minister José María Aznar. He was officially employed by Docsa—Development and Operation of Campaigns, which was under contract to the PAN. Sola joined campaign coordinator Josefina Vázquez Mota, Camilo Mouriño, Germán Martínez Cázares, César Nava Vázquez, Deputy Juan Molinar Horticasitas, Juan Ignacio Zavala, and Maximiliano Cortázar as part of the nominee's inner circle.

When challenged on the veracity of these commercials, Calderón's camp compared them to PRD and PRI complaints about the appearance of former Spanish prime minister Aznar at PAN headquarters on February 21, when he urged Mexicans to vote for Calderón. Although the Electoral Tribunal Federal forced the withdrawal of the Chávez-el Peje advertisements on May 23, they proved successful in raising public concern about the Tabascan's political posture. In addition, though they may have misgivings about a particular incumbent, Mexicans respect the office of the presidency, which López Obrador was once again demeaning.

The Little Ray of Hope condemned the commercials and emphasized that he neither knew nor had ever spoken with Chávez. Yet he failed to respond immediately with a media counterattack that, for example, might have emphasized that the PAN was lying about his (nonexistent) links to Chávez because el Peje's commitment to uplift the poor threatened the Fox/Calderón agenda of business as usual.

Instead, he ran commercials in which Elena Poniatowska, a seventy-three-year-old prize-winning author and the cultural coordinator of his campaign, chided the PAN and PRI for the "calumnies" they had inflicted on López Obrador and demanded that they "play clean." While she was a prominent intellectual, Poniatowska was hardly a household name. Moreover, she committed a cardinal sin of politics, namely, repeating the opponent's charges. "Don't denigrate [el Peje]. López Obrador has nothing to do with Hugo Chávez," she said. Then she gratuitously raised another sensitive subject. As for the accusations that he had run up big deficits in the D.F., she said: "The stipend that our old people receive was done with honesty, savings, and good government."[11] Poniatowska's defense aside, the gap between el Peje and Calderón began to narrow in opinion surveys.

In a May 19 letter to Fox, López Obrador apologized for his *chachalaca* references but took the president to task for saying that Calderón was increasing his lead and had the "wind behind him."[12]

The first televised debate also affected López Obrador's standing. When the Tabascan enjoyed a commanding lead, he said that he would take part in only one debate because his foes would use such forums to gang up on him. When the presidential candidates faced off on April 25, there was an empty chair on the stage for the missing "For the Good of All" standard-bearer.

PRI candidate Roberto Madrazo relied heavily on notes and gave a wooden performance; Roberto Campa, nominee of the Gordillo-created Partido Nueva Alianza, devoted his time to attacking Madrazo for corruption; Patricia Mercado, candidate of the small Peasant and Social Democratic Alternative Party (PASC), performed well, focusing on her signature human rights issues.

The PAN contender emerged as the star of the evening. He came across as well prepared, competent, and thoughtful. A post-debate *Reforma* telephone survey of 405 voters showed Calderón (43 percent) defeating Madrazo (18 percent), Mercado (14 percent), and Campa (7 percent). The survey also revealed that 55 percent of respondents believed that el Peje's absence had cost him votes, compared with 39 percent who disagreed.[13]

Neither López Obrador nor his staff took part in the postdebate "spinning" among journalists. If you embody the truth, why should you attempt to manipulate media coverage? They were not on hand to reiterate the ex-mayor's reasons for not participating, to point out weaknesses in the arguments of his four foes, or to emphasize how his proposals to improve the lives of the masses differed from those articulated before the television cameras. By spurning the debate and the postdebate chicanery, López Obrador lost an opportunity to calm fears raised by the PAN's "guilt by association to Chávez" ads, allay the misgivings of financial experts at home and abroad, and reinforce his populist appeal.[14]

The PAN also benefited from favorable economic reports. Mexico's GDP grew 5 percent during the first quarter of the year, while inflation fell below 4 percent. A Zogby poll taken for a University of Miami report indicated that a surprisingly large number of respondents (64 percent) said they were now better off than when Fox assumed office in 2000 (see Table 23).[15]

DIFFERENCES IN CAMPAIGNS BECOME APPARENT

By early May, nearly all of the surveys began to indicate that either Calderón had overtaken the Tabascan or the election was a toss-up. Rather than admit that he had made mistakes and return quickly to his message of redemption for the "have-nots," López Obrador scorned the survey data. As the savior of the populace, only one thing could account for his purported fall in approval—"a conspiracy." Among the conspirators were pollsters, *Reforma,* the mass media in general, Elba Esther Gordillo, the Fox administration, and bête noire Carlos Salinas.

In making these attacks, he got "off message"—that is, he flailed at his opponents rather than hammer home his commitment to the downtrodden. El Pejelagarto's erratic pronouncements accentuated his irresponsibility and sharpened misgivings about him on the part of the business community and independent voters. While he had enlisted an impressive array of advisers, he relied heavily on his own political instincts, as evinced by his having Poniatowska respond to the "danger to Mexico" blitz and absenting himself from the first debate. His problem, according to political economist Luis Rubio, borrowing a page from Winston Churchill, "is not that he is ignorant, it is that he knows too many things that are not true."[16] Still, López Obrador claimed to hold a ten-point lead, although he would divulge neither the contents of the alleged poll nor the firm that conducted it.

In contrast to López Obrador, Calderón learned from his slow start on the campaign trail. By recruiting former secretary of social development Vázquez Mota to be his campaign coordinator, she brought direction and cohesion to a campaign previously dominated by bright but inexperienced young people.

He recognized that his campaign themes were not resonating with the public and he began to identify himself as the "Jobs

DATE	PUBLISHER	LÓPEZ OBRADOR (%)	CALDERÓN (%)	MADRAZO (%)
June 23, 2006	Reforma	36	34	25
June 23, 2006	El Universal	36	34	26
June 23, 2006	Ulises Beltran y Asociados	34	34	26
June 22, 2006	Milenio	35.4	30.5	29.6
June 22, 2006	GEA-ISA	36	41	21
June 22, 2006	Alducin y Asociados	34	38	24
June 22, 2006	Consulta Mitofsky	36	33	27
June 21, 2006	Indermerc	33	32	28
June 21, 2006	Marketing Político	34	37	26
June 20, 2006	Parametría	36.5	32.5	27
June 19, 2006	Zogby	31	35	27
June 14, 2006	Reforma	37	35	23
June 13, 2006	Milenio	34.2	31	29.6
June 13, 2006	Consulta Mitofsky	35	32	28
June 12, 2006	El Universal	34	37	22
June 11, 2006	GEA-ISA	35	39	23
June 6, 2006	El Universal	36	36	24
June 6, 2006	Parametría	35.5	34.4	27
June 5, 2006	BGC, Beltrán y Asociados	35	35	26
May 29, 2006	Milenio	33	33	30
May 29, 2006	Consulta Mitofsky	34	34	28
May 28, 2006	GEA-ISA	31	40	27
May 24, 2006	Reforma	35	39	22
May 19, 2006	Zogby	29	34	22
May 15, 2006	El Universal	35	39	21
May 8, 2006	Parametría	34	36	26
May 4, 2006	GEA-ISA	31	41	25
May 3, 2006	Consulta Mitofsky	34	35	27

President," while constantly emphasizing the Mexican people's need for greater security. In response to criticism that he appeared too stiff and formal on the hustings, he began campaigning without a tie, rolling up his sleeves, and seeking many more "photo ops" among average people. He realized that he had to do well among lower-middle-class families. To appeal to these so-called Wal-Mart voters, he assembled thousands of flag-waving enthusiasts along the main thoroughfare connecting populous outlying municipalities like Tlalnepantla to the capital. "The campaign supplied a caravan of souped-up Volkswagen Beetles, the signature vehicle of urban workers, and a truckload of midriff-baring dancers to keep the crowed entertained until Mr. Calderón wheeled by, waving from a confetti-strewn pickup."[17]

He did not hesitate to draw on a professional consultant in launching the "danger to Mexico" onslaught, which not only weakened López Obrador's standing among undecided and independent

DATE	PUBLISHER	LÓPEZ OBRADOR (%)	CALDERÓN (%)	MADRAZO (%)
May 3, 2006	*Reforma*	33	40	22
May 2, 2006	*Milenio*	33	36	28
April 23, 2006	Parametría	35	33	28
April 17, 2006	*El Universal*	38	34	25
April 6, 2006	*Milenio*	34	31	31
April 6, 2006	Arcop	33	36	29
March 27, 2006	Consulta Mitofsky	37.5	30.6	28.8
March 27, 2006	BIMSA	31.2	25.5	21.4
March 21, 2006	GEA-ISA	34	36	28
March 16, 2006	*Reforma*	41	31	25
March 13, 2006	*El Universal*	42	32	24
February 22, 2006	Consulta Mitofsky	39.4	29.8	27.5
February 21, 2006	GEA-ISA	34	27	22
February 21, 2006	*Reforma*	38	31	29
February 20, 2006	*El Universal*	30	27	22
January 23, 2006	GEA-ISA	35	35	29
January 26, 2006	*El Universal*	33	27	20
January 20, 2006	Parametria	35.7	27.4	26.2
January 20, 2006	TV Azteca	38	31	28
January 19, 2006	*Reforma*	34	26	22
January 19, 2006	*La Jornada*	39	27	22
January 18, 2006	Consulta Mitofsky	38.7	31	29.2
January 8, 2006	*Milenio*	28	30	25
December 5, 2005	Univision.com	34.8	28.8	30.4
November 21, 2005	*Reforma*	29	28	21
November 5, 2005	*El Universal*	34	22	18

SOURCE "Mexican General Election, 2006," http://en.wikipedia.org/wiki/mexican_general_election,_2006.
NOTE: Polls conducted by Arcop (published in *Milenio* and showing the first lead of Calderón over López Obrador), and Covarrubias (published in *La Jornada* and showing the largest lead of López Obrador), are internal polls and are generally not as reliable as the others.

voters but also drove the Tabascan to depart from his effective populist message.

El Peje attempted to recover in the second debate, which took place on June 6. Above all, he sought to disabuse the public of the notion that Calderón had "clean hands"—a symbol he had used to proclaim his honesty. López Obrador insisted that Diego Zavala Gómez del Campo, owner of the Hildebrando Group, had won $220 million in government contracts thanks to the influence of his brother-in-law, the PAN nominee. This accusation complemented TV ads claiming that eighteen companies associated with Hildebrando had obtained lucrative contracts with Pemex, the bank-rescue agency IPAB, and the Ministry of Social Development. The commercial closed with the sardonic line: "How lucky Zavala's companies have been, and how unlucky for other businessmen not to be related to Calderón."[18] López Obrador also scored points for keeping his famous temper under control and sticking to the line that his plans to help Mexico's millions of poor were nothing radical. Although Zavala, Calderón, and the candidate's wife, former deputy Margarita Zavala Gómez del Campo, vehemently denied the charges, they hurt the *panista* in public opinion polls. As a result, the two major candidates entered the last weeks of the campaign, when they had to vie for attention with World Cup games, in a virtual dead heat.

ELECTION NIGHT

At 11:00 P.M. on election night, Luis Carlos Ugalde, president of the Federal Electoral Institute, said that he was unable to name a preliminary winner because of the paper-thin difference that separated Calderón and López Obrador, according to the official "Rapid Count," a random sample of 7,636 precincts (out of 130,500 precincts). In a nationally televised speech, he urged the candidates and public to remain patient and await completion of the preliminary count on Wednesday. Fox also gave a brief speech in which he applauded Mexicans for their civic responsibility, while pleading with voters to heed the IFE's decision. "It's the responsibility of all political actors to respect the law," he said.[19] Meanwhile, government officials requested that the TV networks not disseminate the results of the polls they had in their possession. Some observers interpreted this move as censorship; others considered the action prudent in that disclosure of a Calderón advantage could have sparked rioting among the Tabascan's supporters in downtown Mexico City.

Nonetheless, López Obrador declared victory before addressing thousands of enthusiasts in the Zócalo. He claimed to have an "irreversible" lead of half a million votes, based on tallies from across the country. "I listened to the messages of the IFE president and of the president of the Republic; I am extremely respectful of institutions and the particular manner that the institute resolves issues; however, I wish to inform the Mexican people that, in accord with our figures, we won the presidency of the Republic!"[20] "This is not the era of fraud! This is not 1988! The people now are not going to accept it [fraud]," Martí Batres, the PRD's radical leader in the capital, proclaimed at the rally.[21] As early returns showed a tight race, cries of "*¡Fraude!*" echoed from the crowd, which had anticipated an easy López Obrador win.

Calderón responded to el Peje's triumphalism by revealing the exit polls of four firms (Arcop, contracted by the PAN, GEA-ISA, Ulises Beltrán, and Marketing Político) that indicated that he had won by two to four percentage points. These data remove "even the slightest doubt that we have won the presidential election and IFE will corroborate these figures," he said.[22]

On July 3 López Obrador accused the IFE of having "lost" 3 million votes in a move to deny him the presidency. Even though the ballots had not in fact disappeared, Ugalde grudgingly admitted that some 2.5 million ballots, which had been laid aside because of technical irregularities, had been omitted from the first rapid count report. These preliminary results had given the PAN nominee a 1.04 percent lead, prompting the domestic and international media to trumpet Calderón as the winner. When the additional ballots were included in the sample, the *panista*'s advantage dropped to 0.64. This legerdemain gave the increasingly militant Little Ray of Hope additional grounds for impugning a political system he deemed corrupt.

An Electoral Setback

At 8:00 A.M. on July 7, the IFE initiated its count of results from the three hundred district councils, which had tabulated precinct totals from their areas. The process took thirty-one hours; throughout Wednesday and early Thursday, López Obrador held a narrow but consistent lead. Many of his followers went to bed convinced that the savior would be their next president. At 4:01 A.M. the trend reversed in favor of Calderón—with the final tally showing him 243,934 votes ahead, out of nearly 42 million ballots cast. The explanation for the turnabout lay not in dirty tricks but in the late reporting of western and northwestern states, which are in different time zones and whose officials started their work later. In most of these states Calderón ran well ahead of the pack. Soon thereafter, President Bush and his Canadian, Spanish, and Colombian counterparts, among others, made congratulatory calls to Calderón.

For his part, López Obrador summoned his supporters to a July 9 "informative assembly"—the first of many sessions he held in the wake of the IFE's announcement. At these gatherings in the Zócalo, he spoke of his "commitment to history," his role as the "principal guardian" of effective suffrage, and a leader whose "principal obligation is to promote the free expression of the popular will."[23]

López Obrador filed an 836-page legal attack before the Federal Electoral Tribunal, which was a product of electoral reforms that López Obrador had opposed in the mid-1990s. The tribunal's "upper chamber" is empowered to resolve, definitively and irrevocably, challenges to the outcome of presidential elections.

The seven judges, called electoral judges, are prestigious jurists. They are among the twenty-two jurists selected unanimously by the Senate from a list of sixty-six nominees (the Senate unanimously elects fifteen other TEPJF judges who preside over five regional chambers during years in which federal elections are held). To avoid corruption, the judges are paid approximately $415,000 per year and are limited to a single ten-year term.

Despite desultory charges of partisanship, in the course of making more than twenty thousand decisions, the TEPJF has taken action adverse to the interests of all parties at one time or another. Below are several examples:

- Overturned the Chihuahua state electoral court's annulment of a PAN victory in the Ciudad Juárez mayor election held on May 12, 2002 (2002);
- Fined the PRI $89.2 million for illegally funneling money to its 2000 presidential candidate, forcing the party to mortgage its headquarters (2003);
- Fined the PAN $40 million and its PVEM coalition ally $10 million for illegal contributions made in 2000 to Vicente Fox by the Friends of Fox (2004);
- Required the PRD to reinstate Maricarmen Ramírez, wife of the outgoing governor of Tlaxcala, as the party's candidate in the race to succeed him (2004); and
- Required the PVEM green party to revise its statutes to make them more democratic (2005).

In three cases, the TEPJF relied on the amorphous concept of "abstract cause of nullification" (*causa abstracta de nulidad*). On December 29, 2000, the tribunal annulled the gubernatorial election in Tabasco, in which the PRI candidate had defeated his PRD opponent by 1.11 percent of the votes cast. In rendering their decision, a majority of judges cited "grave irregularities" such as vote buying and the greater coverage afforded the PRI standard-bearer by the state-owned television network. Judges Castillo and Reyes Zapata championed the broader constitutional precept that voters enjoy the right to select leaders in equitable contests. They enjoyed the support of three colleagues; Judges Eloy Fuentes and Navarro dissented in the decision.[24] In 2003 the tribunal threw out a PRI gubernatorial victory in Colima State on the grounds that the outgoing governor had intervened in the election of his successor.

López Obrador's lawyers concentrated on the nullification precedent to insist that their client did not get a fair shake and was entitled to "a vote by vote, precinct by precinct" recount of the ballots cast on July 2. To buttress their case, they pointed out that there was no PRD member on the IFE's General Council, that President Fox had blatantly promoted Calderón's candidacy with public funds, that SNTE leader Gordillo had connived with PRI governors to obtain votes for Calderón, that the IFE had manipulated the rapid count to Calderón's advantage, and that the business community had run postelection spots in favor of the IFE's initial figure. In addition, the attorneys argued that a software program had been employed to skew initial vote counts, and that there were irregularities in fifty thousand polling stations, including areas such as the middle-class Coyoacán borough of Mexico City, where PAN activists supposedly pressured citizens into voting for their nominee.

López Obrador complemented these legal maneuvers with attacks on Fox ("a complete traitor to democracy"), the IFE ("a pawn of the party of the right"), and PRD poll watchers who had vouched for the correctness of original tallies ("bought off" politicians).

On August 5 the judges called for a recount of approximately 9 percent of the ballots cast, which led them to annul more than 150,000 votes in hundreds of polling places. Still, changes in the overall results were minimal. In their final ruling on September 5, the judges concluded that Calderón had edged out López Obrador by only 233,831 votes out of 41.5 million ballots cast, a margin quite close to the IFE's early July number (see Table 24). In a unanimous decision, the seven-member court rejected López Obrador's arguments that the election should be voided because of Fox's interference in the campaign and because business leaders had spent millions of pesos on illegal negative advertisements to assist the PAN nominee. Several of the judges deplored the "black propaganda" that Calderón and some private-sector organizations had used against el Peje, depicting him as an ideological ally of Hugo Chávez, whose economic strategy would bankrupt the country. They also indicated that Fox's barrage of attacks on López Obrador had placed the validity of the election in jeopardy. Nevertheless, the judges ruled that the chief executive had not broken electoral statutes; and although the $19 million in advertisements or black propaganda paid for by business leaders had violated the law, the judges said they had not influenced the election enough to justify annulling the outcome. Alfonsina Bertha Navarro, who helped to write the 309-page ruling, said, "There are irregularities, some that were not proven, others that were not grave enough to put in doubt the veracity of the election."[25]

Why was the count so close? To begin with, Madrazo never emerged as a serious contender, partly because of his reputation as a ruthless, power-hungry "dinosaur," partly because as party president (2002–6), he failed to alter the PRI's image as a corrupt, self-serving patronage machine, and partly because he alienated important figures in his own party—Gordillo, former México State governor Arturo Montiel, most of the PRI governors, and Senate president Enrique Jackson. His failure to keep agreements made Madrazo persona non grata to a broad swath of the business community. The myth that the PRI's hard-core voters—the once almighty *voto duro*—would mobilize at the eleventh hour to propel Madrazo to victory proved to be a "political wet dream," in the words of one TV journalist.

TABLE 24. *Preliminary Results of 2006 Presidential Contest*

CANDIDATE	PARTY/COALITION	TOTAL VOTE	%
Felipe Calderón	National Action Party (PAN)	14,916,927*	35.89
		15,000,284	35.89
Andrés Manuel López Obrador	Por el Bien de Todos (PRD, Workers	14,683,096	35.33
	Party, and the National Convergence	14,756,350	35.31
	party)		
Roberto Madrazo	Alliance for Mexico (PRI and the	9,237,000	22.22
	PVEM Greens)	9,301,441	22.26
Patricia Mercado	Peasant and Social Democratic	1,124,280	2.71
	Alternative	1,128,850	2.70
Roberto Campa	New Alliance	397,550	0.96
		401,804	0.96
Unregistered candidates	Víctor González Torres, known	298,204	0.72
	as "Doctor Simi" because of his	297,989	0.71
	multimillion-dollar chain of cut-rate		
	pharmacies		
Invalid Ballots		900,373	2.17
		904,604	2.16
TOTAL VOTE		41,557,430	99.99
		41,791,322	99.99

* Bold figures represent the final results reported by the
Federal Electoral Tribunal; the second set of figures
represent preliminary results provided by the Federal
Electoral Institute (IFE). The participation rate of
registered voters was 58.55 percent.
SOURCE: Federal Electoral Institute (July 7, 2006); and Federal Electoral Tribunal (September 5, 2006), http://
electionresources.org/mex/index_es.html.

TWO MEXICOS

The marginalization of the PRI candidate turned the race into a clash of opposites. In contrast to López Obrador's modest background, Calderón, age forty-three, was a lawyer from a comfortable middle-class family and a conventional politician. He had grown up in the PAN, which his father had helped found nearly seven decades before. He had functioned as the party's youth leader, president, and gubernatorial candidate in his native state of Michoacán. In addition, he had won election to the D.F.'s city council, as well as two terms in the five-hundred-member Chamber of Deputies. There he headed the PAN faction from 2000 to 2003. Although much more astute than the politically tone-deaf Fox, Calderón pledged to continue, broaden, and deepen the incumbent's market-oriented policies. Inspired by social-Christian ideals, he also promised to combat the poverty that afflicts half of his nation's 107.5 million inhabitants. As indicated in Table 25, he proved attractive to women, young people, well-educated voters, party loyalists, individuals concerned about security, and lower- and lower-middle-class citizens. He also did well in the relatively prosperous north and west, in the business communities, with those who approved of Fox's performance, and with beneficiaries of social programs focused on the poorest of the poor.[26]

For his part, López Obrador appealed to men, low-income citizens, older people, citizens with primary and secondary school education, opponents of Fox's policies, and *perredistas*. El Peje attracted more votes from poorer southern states, while he and Calderón ran neck and neck in rural areas.

The Tabascan's messianic qualities enabled him to come within an eyelash of winning the presidency. These same characteristics, however, denied him the position. While Calderón learned from his mistakes and adjusted his strategy to overcome them, López Obrador—always the vessel of truth—refused to listen to others. As a result, he squandered a double-digit lead—first, by continuing to use *chachalaca* and other demeaning terms to castigate President Fox; second, by failing to participate in the first candidates' debate; and third, by blaming his fall in opinion surveys on outside forces—a move that not only raised questions about his reliability but also distracted him from affirming his popular "For the Good of All" message in the crucial days of the campaign.

In fact, the a messianic Tabascan could have overcome these faux pas had he not committed a bigger blunder in November 2005. During that month, Deputy Camacho Solís—a key AMLO adviser—approached fellow deputy Roberto Campa about the possibility of a meeting between López Obrador and Gordillo.

Campa's good friend, the head of the powerful SNTE teachers' union, agreed to talk with López Obrador. At that point, PRI leaders were considering her expulsion from the party and she was being courted by both Creel and Calderón, who were vying for the PAN's presidential candidacy. Campa relayed Gordillo's receptiveness to a meeting to Camacho. Several weeks passed and there was still no word from el Peje. Finally, Camacho informed Campa that López Obrador was not disposed to enter into parleys with la Profesora.

Why had Camacho made the overture if el Pejelagarto was opposed to meeting with the most powerful woman in Mexico? Could talks have prospered to the point that the SNTE would have thrown its weight behind the former Jefe de Gobierno del Distrito Federal?

The most likely answer to the first question is that Camacho was freelancing. A man who is skilled at bargaining, negotiating, and compromising, the former ally of Salinas may have thought he could ensure an el Peje presidency—and boost his personal political stock—by brokering a deal between López Obrador and Gordillo.

For his part, el Peje enjoyed a double-digit lead over his closest contenders. Moreover, it appeared that the weaker competitor—former government secretary Creel—would emerge from primary contests as the PAN candidate.

TABLE 25. *Characteristics of Voters for Presidential Candidates, 2006 Election*

CANDIDATE	MEN	WOMEN	VOTERS AGE 18–29	VOTERS AGE 30–49	VOTERS AGE 50 AND OLDER	PRIMARY SCHOOL	HIGH SCHOOL	PREPARATORY SCHOOL	UNIVERSITY OR ABOVE
Calderón	31.7	32.0	33.6	32.8	28.6	26.6	29.9	35.0	41.8
López Obrador	34.8	29.4	32.1	32.1	21.7	30.7	32.7	33.8	31.5
Madrazo	19.0	20.9	18.8	19.7	31.4	25.0	20.9	15.7	13.1
Mercado	1.8	3.4	4.3	2.3	1.5	1.3	2.6	4.5	3.7
Campa	0.8	1.0	1.2	0.8	0.7	0.7	1.2	0.9	0.8
No Response	11.9	13.3	10.0	12.3	16.1	15.7	12.7	10.1	9.1
TOTAL	100.0	100.0	100.0	100.0	100.0	100.0	100.0	100.0	100.0

SOURCE: Consulta Mitofsky, "Encuesta de Salida: 2 de Julio, elección presidencial," http://www.consulta.com.mx/interiores/11_elecciones/elec_ENCUSAL_presi/.

Gordillo had no love lost for López Obrador, who had gone out of his way to castigate her leadership of the SNTE. Still, she knew that the great majority of teachers resonated to the Tabascan, and generals prefer, whenever possible, to work in concert with their foot soldiers. As late as January 31, 2001, she stated that she would like to be a "friend" of the PRD candidate.

An Electoral Setback

After el Pejelegarto slammed the door on conversations with la Profesora, she gravitated to Calderón's candidacy. Indeed, he has her to thank for his July 2 victory. Gordillo urged SNTE activists to vote for candidates of PANAL, the party she had spearheaded, for Congress and for the *panista* for president. This gave rise to a chasm between the votes obtained by PANAL aspirants for Chamber of Deputies seats (1,876,443) and Roberto Campa (397,550), the party's presidential competitor in an election that Calderón won by only 233,831 votes.[27]

When the Federal Electoral Tribunal proclaimed Calderón the winner, the Little Ray of Hope refused to recognize the results. It was impossible for the beloved savior of the masses to lose. Once again, he railed against the corruption and spuriousness of the system that had defrauded him and called on his followers to hold a National Democratic Convention that would install a "legitimate government."

A SECOND COMING?

López Obrador continually reprised his Tabasco performances on the national stage. In both theaters, he preached the gospel of salvation. El Peje focused his message of redemption on the downtrodden; he surrounded himself with a small band of apostles; he relied on Magdalenes for key tasks; he recruited "converts" to his cause; he identified himself with prophets whose teachings influenced his life; and he spearheaded confrontations with the "illegitimate regime" that had defrauded him of victory.

LÓPEZ OBRADOR REPRISES ACTIONS IN TABASCO

López Obrador drew much of his postelectoral strategy from his experiences in the 1994 gubernatorial contest in Tabasco, where he emphasized his crusade for "democracy and truth." In the frequent "informative assemblies" that he convened in the Zócalo after the IFE issued its preliminary finding in July 2006, he stressed his "commitment to history" and presented himself as the "principal guardian" of the "popular prerogative . . . [with] a duty to facilitate the free expression of the popular will." Just as he claimed that Madrazo's victory in Tabasco was "morally impossible," he asserted that Calderón would be a "spurious president" who lacked "moral and political authority." In the same way that he castigated the "authoritarian model" in his home state, the Little Ray of Hope argued that the PAN president-elect confirmed that "a rapacious minority has kidnapped the [nation's] institutions and has imposed officials who will preserve and enhance their privileges."[1]

As discussed in Chapter 5, López Obrador protested Madrazo's alleged triumph by organizing a march from Villahermosa to Mexico City, which he called "The Exodus for the Dignity of National Sovereignty." Once in the capital, the *exodistas* set up camp in the Zócalo even as their colleagues in Tabasco occupied the Plaza de Armas in Villahermosa. A few days after the IFE released the presidential results, el Peje spearheaded a "National March for Democracy" that brought his faithful from the country's three hundred electoral districts to the D.F. to attend his first informative assembly on July 12, 2006. He scheduled a second march from the National Anthropological Museum to the Zócalo four days later.

Before riot police and thugs expelled them on December 31, 1994, López Obrador's followers had occupied the Plaza de Armas in Villahermosa. Following Madrazo's January 1 inauguration, they again laid siege to key government buildings in the state capital. Similarly, the Tabascan installed forty-seven encampments in the Zócalo, the Alameda, and along five miles of el Paseo de la Reforma to pressure the seven magistrates to launch a vote-by-vote, precinct-by-precinct recount of the nearly 42 million ballots cast in the showdown for chief executive. In mid-August several of his legislative allies also attempted to stage a sit-in in front of the San Lázaro Palace, where the Chamber of Deputies meets. One reason that el Peje demanded a national recount was that he knew it was an academic question. In June 2006, anticipating a photo finish, Chief Judge Leonel Castillo told *Milenio Semanal*, "Some may ask for a total recount, but when that petition arrives, we're going to say no."[2]

The faithful lived in sturdy tents and, thanks to the generosity of the D.F. government and the PRD, enjoyed access to toilets, showers, water, electricity, and food—all of which were lacking or in short supply in the villages of many peasant participants. They recited poems, played cards, watched television, strummed on musical instruments, sang hosannas to their beloved leader, posted signs inveighing against electoral fraud, erected altars, and prayed for divine intervention. In the words of one pro–López Obrador journalist, "Hundreds have made pilgrimages out to the shrine of the Virgin of Guadalupe, some crawling on their knees, to ask the Brown Madonna to work her mojo. 'God doesn't belong to the PAN!' they chant, as they trudge up the great avenue that leads to the basilica. 'AMLO deserves a miracle,' a 70-year-old great-grandmother comments to a reporter as she kneels to pray before the guilded [*sic*] altar."[3] Less pious PRD officials often showed up for meals and media events, only to retire to the comfort of their homes after sundown. Both chiefs and followers appeared for López Obrador's informative assemblies and other activities (shown in Table 26).

The blockage of the downtown tourist and business district dealt a severe blow to local businesses and hotels, whose managers suffered from tens of thousands of cancellations. Meanwhile, motorists fumed at detours required to avoid using a major artery and the Historic Center. In early August 2006, PRD secretary-general Guadalupe Acosta Naranjo, a product of the El Barzón movement, announced that the "For the Good of All" coalition would launch a series of "surprises." Demonstrators, many of them farmers waving the yellow-and-black flags of López Obrador's Democratic Revolutionary Party, blocked the entrance to the Ministry of Agriculture and barred hundreds of employees from getting to work. Other protesters flung open toll barriers across the five major highways linking Mexico City with the cities of Cuernavaca, Toluca, Pachuca, Querétaro, and Puebla, letting tens of thousands of commuters drive through without paying during the morning rush hour. Another surprise involved impeding access to the Stock Exchange building and to the headquarters of major banks.

In the same way that he excoriated authorities in Tabasco for naming Madrazo governor-elect, López Obrador rejected the verdict of the magistrates, who "refused to make the election transparent but acquiesced to a privileged minority that had taken control of institutions and holds them hostage for its own benefit."[4] While he envisioned a "revolution of conscience and outlook," he guaranteed that his struggle to uplift and protect the humble, the dispossessed, and the poor would neither sell out to "political rogues and white-collar criminals" nor kowtow to "the elites, racists and fascists who hypocritically appear to be people of good will."[5]

NATIONAL DEMOCRATIC CONVENTION

López Obrador's gambit of "peaceful civic resistance" cost him popular support to the point that an ever-increasing number of citizens said, according to polls, that, if a second election were held, they would vote for Calderón instead of el Peje. A broad array of individuals and groups began to speak out in support of the fairness of Mexico's electoral authorities: the Roman Catholic Church, leaders of the business community, a majority of the domestic mass media, the international press, notable labor organizations like the CTM, the Revolutionary Confederation of Workers and Campesinos, the SNTE, observers from the European Union, the other losing candidates, and PAN and PRI governors.

Amid this decline in approval levels, and as it became clear that the TEPJF would render a decision favorable to Calderón, López Obrador began to lay plans for a shadow regime reminiscent of the parallel structure that he championed after his loss to Madrazo in 1994. In Tabasco the PRD provided free textbooks to students, connected homes to electricity lines illegally, assisted residents in

TABLE 26. *AMLO's Post–July 2 Activities and Announcements*

DATE	ACTIVITY	MAJOR PRONOUNCEMENT/EVENT
July 3	Press conference	AMLO produced data showing "inconsistencies" in vote tallying and asked for a meticulous recount.
July 5	Press conference	AMLO, with "Por el bien de todos" spokeswoman Claudia Sheinbaum, announced that there were 13,432 voting inconsistencies.
July 8	Informative assembly in the Zócalo involving 500,000 supporters (by AMLO's figures)	AMLO told his supporters that he would prove the election flawed and illegal, and that it violated Article 41 of the Constitution.
July 10	Press conference	Asked the Electoral Court for a vote-by-vote recount and presented evidence of "electoral crimes."
July 13	Press conference	Stated that the IFE was breaking the law and blamed businesses for funding 995 million pesos' worth of PAN attack ads.
July 16	Informative assembly in the Zócalo with more than 1.5 million supporters (by AMLO's figures)	Informed his followers that, if the authorities failed to heed his demands, "Mexico would have neither financial, economic, nor political stability."
July 30	Informative assembly in the Zócalo with more than 3 million supporters (by AMLO's figures)	Told supporters he was certain he would become president. Urged his backers to reject the electoral fraud and participate in peaceful resistance.
August 1	Informative assembly in the Zócalo	Called on the judges of the Federal Electoral Tribunal to make the right decision and said he would not negotiate with the opposition. He also announced that the camps on Reforma and Juárez would keep functioning.
August 5	Informative assembly in the Zócalo	Bashed the decision of the TEPJF not to order a vote-by-vote recount. He reiterated to his supporters that their protesting and efforts were worthwhile.

applying for social programs, helped squatters seize land and construct homes, and provided legal, medical, dental, and veterinary services free of charge. Although the venture is a work in progress, the National Democratic Convention (CND) convened by López Obrador in mid-September had a broader purpose than delivering services.

Some members of his movement compared it to the 1911 Plan of Ayala, which articulated agrarian revolutionary Emiliano Zapata's cry for "Land, Justice, and Law!" This declaration of principles rejected the presidency of Francisco I. Madero, called for free elections once there was political stability, named Pascual Orozco the

TABLE 26 *(cont'd)*. *AMLO's Post–July 2 Activities and Announcements*

DATE	ACTIVITY	MAJOR PRONOUNCEMENT/EVENT
August 6	Informative assembly in the Zócalo	Declared that if the PAN wanted to negotiate, they would first have to respect the will of the people. Quoted Benito Juárez: "The king's power is weak when he opposes the people's will."
August 10	Informative assembly in the Zócalo	Declared that "los mapaches" were succeeding in corrupting the recount.
August 13	Informative assembly in the Zócalo	Announced that he would "save democracy" by not permitting the "imposition of a spurious president." Announced that the National Democratic Convention would be convened on September 16. Also declared that he was willing to fight for years to achieve justice.
August 14–26	Daily rallies in the Zócalo	
August 27	Informative assembly in the Zócalo	Announced the formation of a legitimate national government and the continuation of civil resistance.
August 28–September 5	Daily rallies in the Zócalo	
September 6	Informative assembly in the Zócalo	Announced that 210,000 citizens had registered for the National Democratic Convention.
September 10	Informative assembly in the Zócalo	Announced that more than 500,000 citizens had registered for the National Democratic Convention. Announced that the convention would take place after the *desfile*.
September 11–15	Daily rallies in the Zócalo	
September 16	National Democratic Convention in the Zócalo	More than 1 million delegates attended the convention (by AMLO's numbers). AMLO given title of "Legitimate President of Mexico"—to be inaugurated on November 20. Called for establishment of a parallel government.

SOURCE: Joseph H. Jenkins prepared this table on the basis of information provided on López Obrador's Web site, http://www.lopezobrador.org.mx.

legitimate head of the revolution, demanded land reform, and confirmed the agrarian character of the upheaval. An amendment to the scheme placed Zapata at the head of the revolution and called for the establishment of a government loyal to the short-lived Plan of Ayala.

The legitimacy of the convention, el Peje claimed, derived from Article 39 of the 1917 Constitution, which states: "The national sovereignty resides essentially and originally in the people. All public power originates in the people and is instituted for their benefit. The people at all times have the inalienable right to alter or modify their form of government."

The CND has five objectives: (1) to undertake actions necessary to assist the downtrodden, eradicate poverty, and combat the growing inequality between the rich and the poor; (2) to defend Pemex, the electricity sector, health and social security agencies, and the educational system from privatization, while employing legal means and peaceful civil resistance to safeguard strategic natural resources and national sovereignty; (3) to require that public and private communications media provide access to all political, cultural, and social views even as they disseminate information in a true and objective manner so that people can participate intelligently and freely in decision making; (4) to work to end a patrimonial state in which the government serves a minority and to combat corruption as well as deny impunity to those who use positions of privilege for their own benefit; and (5) to fundamentally renovate political institutions that are now dominated by a small group of power brokers, so as to ensure that economic and fiscal policy no longer benefit the few and that the Supreme Court ceases to protect white-collar criminals.

The Tabascan's campaign coordinator, Jesús Ortega, said that the convention would "oppose the imposition of the president of the Republic," illuminate the "democratic fiction" of the current government, and "prevent the return of antidemocratic life to the country."[6] The organizers claimed that more than 1 million people attended the assembly—with delegates allocated to the thirty-one states and the D.F. based on the number of votes that the "For the Good of All" coalition received on July 2. Thus entities like Mexico City (421,621), México State (370,158), Puebla (31,956), Michoacán (30,720), Chiapas (27,585), and Tabasco (25,643) boasted the lion's share of representatives.[7] The delegates were chosen in an ad hoc manner throughout the country. Meanwhile, López Obrador awarded front-row seats to "special guests" who represented Indian communities, the elderly, and people with disabilities.[8] Groups from peasant, teacher, and university organizations also sent delegations to the CND.

The unwieldy character of the conclave—ridiculed as a "mob" by detractors—militated against the use of ballots for making decisions. Instead, the delegates voted by a show of hands, such as when they unanimously selected the Little Ray of Hope as the "legitimate president" of the nation on September 16, Mexico's Independence Day. Votes were merely symbolic because the Zócalo holds only 110,000 people, a fraction of the number of convention delegates.

López Obrador sought to continue his presidential odyssey by campaigning vigorously for Raúl Ojeda in the October 15, 2006, gubernatorial race in Tabasco. Even though el Peje had carried his home state with 56.3 percent of the votes cast in mid-summer, Ojeda lost decisively to the PRI nominee—a clear sign that the light of the Little Ray of Hope had dimmed in his own bailiwick because of his quixotic antics following Calderón's victory. "López Obrador is like the elephants that return to their homeland to die," said Fernando Moreno Peña, the PAN's secretary of organization.[9] A first-hand observer called Tabasco his Waterloo.[10]

Rather than treat the Tabasco outcome as his Waterloo, political burial, or crucifixion, López Obrador continued his messianic quest. On November 3, he named a parallel cabinet that supposedly emerged from the National Democratic Convention. In making the announcement, he used exceptionally combative language, railing against the "neofascist oligarchy" that neglects the poor while seeking to "govern permanently with repression, intolerance, fear, and political instability." In an obvious allusion to Cuauhtémoc Cárdenas, he condemned those "political leaders who formerly defended the causes of the people but have become tired of thinking and acting as they once did." In castigating the "neofascist right," he stressed that he was embracing the "feelings and problems of the people . . . because the voice of the people is the voice of history."[11]

He then set off on a two-week tour of the Federal District and twenty-four cities in nine states before swearing the oath as legitimate president on November 20, ten days before Calderón's inauguration. He donned a sash whose coat of arms featured the open-winged "republican eagle" favored by Juárez. This was an indication that his would be a government of the people. In so doing, he denigrated the "mocha eagle," literally "the slashed eagle," which became known as "the chauvinistic eagle" under Fox, whom critics deemed arrogant. El Peje also introduced the members of the "Cabinet of the Legitimate Government (Table 27)," noting that the losing PAN presidential candidate in 1988 established a "parallel government" and that Australia, Canada, the United Kingdom, Japan, and Poland also had shadow cabinets. He failed to mention that these cabinet members were elected to their countries' parliaments.

The former mayor paid lip service to using his National Democratic Convention to influence public policy. Successful legislative candidates from the three parties that backed his presidential bid—the PRD, Convergencia, and the Workers' Party—have not only taken their seats in Congress, but have also formed a "Broad Progressive Front." This coalition offers a channel for proposals emerging from the several committees established by the convention. For instance, the front has proposed giving D.F.-type payments to senior citizens nationwide, eliminating pensions for former presidents, and renegotiating NAFTA to curb corn imports from the United States. The problem is that most of the former mayor's platform—energy nationalism, protectionism, subsidies, welfare schemes, and big government—is anathema to the PAN and to progressives in the PRI. Thus his talk about working through the system is at best sterile rhetoric, at worst cant. The PRD's

TABLE 27. *Cabinet Members of the "Legitimate Government"*

POSITION	SECRETARY	PREVIOUS POSTS
Counselors	Elena Poniatowska; Rogelio Ramírez de la O; Federico Arreola; Ignacio Marván; José María Pérez Gay	Advisers in López Obrador's campaign
Coordinator of Social Communions	César Yáñez Centeno	Social Communications Coordinator of his D.F. government and campaign
Secretary of Political Relations	José Agustín Ortiz Pinchetti	Organizer of Citizens Network
Secretary of International Relations	Gustavo Iruegas Evaristo	Retired Undersecretary of Foreign Relations
Secretary of Security and Justice	Bernardo Bátiz Vázquez	Attorney General in D.F. government
Secretary of Honesty and Republican Austerity	Octavio Romero Oropeza	Chief administrative officer of D.F. government
Secretary of Public Finances	Mario Alberto di Constanza Armenta	Former researcher and staff member for the Chamber of Deputies; participated in preparing López Obrador's proyecto alternativo de nación
Secretary of Economic Development and Ecology	Luis Linares Zapata	Worked for SPP, ISSSTE, and other government agencies, served as a private consultant
Secretary of National Assets (Patrimonio Nacional)	Claudia Sheinbaum Pardo	Secretary of the Environment in D.F. government
Controller General	Bertha Elena Luján Uranga	Comptroller-general in D.F. government
Secretary of Social Welfare	Martha Elvia Pérez Bejarano	Secretary of Social Development in the D.F. government
Secretary of Education, Science, and Culture	Raquel Sosa Elízaga	Secretary of Culture in the D.F. government
Secretary of Health	Asa Cristina Laurell	Secretary of Health in the D.F. government
Secretary of Housing and Human Settlements	Laura Itzel Castillo	Secretary of Housing and Urban Development in the D.F. government

SOURCE: López Obrador's Web site, http://www.lopezobrador.org.mx. These secretaries receive monthly salaries of 50,000 pesos (approximately $4,500 per month). Their undersecretaries are paid 40,000 pesos ($3,650), and their advisers, 20,000 pesos ($1,825).

Senate and Chamber of Deputies coordinators failed to appear at a meeting scheduled with two stalwarts of López Obrador's cabinet—Political Relations Secretary Ortiz Pinchetti and Finance Secretary DiCostanzo.[12]

DISENCHANTMENT SETS IN

PRD officeholders realize that Mexico may be a federal republic on paper, but resources flow from the federal government in the capital. Consequently, party bigwigs and their allies have distanced themselves from el Peje's puerile project. Indeed, the governors of Baja California Sur (Narciso Agúndez Montaño), Guerrero (Zeferino Torreblanca), Michoacán (Lázaro Cárdenas), and Zacatecas (Amalia García) have indicated their readiness to work with Calderón.[13] Even Juan Sabines Guerrero, who, with López Obrador's help, barely won the Chiapas statehouse on August 20, 2006, has also cultivated Los Pinos, indicating that his posture did not represent a slight to the Tabascan. "I came to [visit the president-elect] to talk with him about my state [and] the priorities of the *chiapanecos*. This could not offend anyone," he said.[14] They view the convention as a means of promoting López Obrador's personalistic crusade, which is antithetical both to constructing a cohesive political party and to obtaining resources for their jurisdictions. Cuauhtémoc Cárdenas, who lost three presidential races as the leftist candidate, deplored the naming of a parallel president. "It is a grave error that may come at a high cost to the PRD and the democratic movement," he said.[15]

Just as pupil Andrés Manuel López Obrador broke with his maestro, Cárdenas, el Peje's protégé Marcelo Ebrard has started to distance himself from his mentor. The AMLO-Cárdenas split erupted publicly in the Zócalo on the night of July 2, 2000, when López Obrador claimed victory in the mayor's race while Cárdenas's presidential candidacy went down in flames. The AMLO-Ebrard rupture materialized privately between Calderón's swearing in (December 1) and Ebrard's inauguration (December 5).

There was neither fanfare nor public denunciation, but Ebrard eliminated signs and references to "la ciudad de la esperanza." Moreover, the new Jefe de Gobierno named a cabinet that was nearly devoid of *lopezobradristas*. In fact, the only visible positions to go to the Tabascan's followers—and these may be temporary— went to Leticia Ramírez Amaya, who managed Citizen Services under el Peje, Ernesto Prieto Ortega, who was in charge of the city's Civil Registry, and former treasurer, Oscar Rosado Jiménez, who assumed a mid-level post. Two other el Pejelagarto disciples— Martí Batres (secretary of social development) and union leader Alejandra Barrales Magdaleno (secretary of tourism)—landed city jobs, but only by negotiating directly with Ebrard.

Either missing in action or participating in López Obrador's shadow government were such el Peje notables as Encinas Rodríguez, Romero Oropeza, Pérez Mendoza, Ortiz Pinchetti, Pérez-Gay, Sheinbaum, Laurell, Garduño Yánez, Itzel Castillo, Luján, and Sosa Elízaga.

Why has Ebrard gradually turned his back on his patron after decrying Calderón's victory as "manipulated," dispatching lawyers to contest the presidential vote count, and attending the inauguration of the messianic Tabascan as "legitimate president"?

To begin with, the protests and posturing of López Obrador have made him a political liability, as was evident in the Tabasco gubernatorial race. Ebrard, who aspires to Los Pinos, realized that the messianic Tabascan represents a political albatross—to the point that many PRD candidates seeking state and local offices in 2007 have remained at arm's length from the former mayor.

Related to this point is the disorder in the D.F. left by López Obrador that Ebrard must address—for example, the deterioration of the metro, construction flaws in second tiers, and a cascade of lawsuits brought by former employees who were arbitrarily fired. In February 2007, the new mayor won praise by raiding the Tepito market area, the capital's main entrepôt for contraband, cocaine, and marijuana.

In addition, Ebrard was determined to avoid any semblance of co-government in which he would occupy the Antiguo Palacio del Ayuntamiento and López Obrador would dominate grassroots activists. As part of the low-key rupture with his predecessor, the new mayor has taken control of major elements of the city's street vendors, pirate taxi organizations, El Barzón debtors, nightclub proprietors, bar owners, public-sector unions, and other groups that once functioned as AMLO's shock troops.

Like the state executives, Ebrard's administration desperately needs federal resources. While he may have castigated Calderón before taking office, he has gone out of his way as mayor to cooperate with the new chief executive. For his part, Calderón has reciprocated by acceding to Ebrard's request to appoint Rodolfo Félix Cárdenas as the city's attorney general and Joel Ortega Cuevas as the capital's secretary of public security.

Even as he improves relations with the presidency, Ebrard has parted ways with his predecessor over policy toward México State. The mayor and Governor Enrique Peña Nieto, a likely PRI contender for the presidency in 2012, have announced cooperation in areas such as narco-fighting, improving transportation, managing water resources, and protecting the environment.

OAXACA CRISIS: SHIFT TO THE LEFT

The desertion of moderates from his camp means that his most ardent adherents are firebrands who echo the Tabascan's merciless and strident criticism of Calderón, his administration, and his policies. These include elements of El Barzón, the Pancho Villa Popular Front, university rabble-rousers, the SME electrical workers, the social security workers, the STUNAM university workers union, and other militant labor organizations.

In light of the growing distance between him and Ebrard, López Obrador can no longer count on the city's financial backing. As late as summer 2007, however, the PRD provided him with operating funds, and the party's 127 deputies and twenty-six senators contributed 25 percent of their salaries to his cause. This gave el Peje and his cabinet upward of $200,000 per month for their activities. It remains to be seen whether this aid will continue in light of the failure of the "For the Good of All" campaign to report its expenditures to the committee that oversees the PRD's budget.[16]

López Obrador also sought to recruit the Oaxaca-based SNTE Local 22 and the three hundred anarchist, student, and indigenous groups who congregate under the umbrella of the Oaxacan People's Popular Assembly (APPO). In May 2006 SNTE's members went on strike to seek higher pay and staged a sit-in in the central square of Oaxaca City. After negotiations stalled in June, Governor Ulises Ruiz, a PRI hard-liner and confidant of Madrazo, unsuccessfully attempted to dislodge the demonstrators from public places. This inept action further radicalized the teachers and intensified calls for the resignation of Ruiz, who was accused of gaining office through a fraud-ridden election. As the city drifted toward anarchy, the APPO emerged as a repository for malcontents and joined the SNTE local in gradually seizing control of the picturesque colonial city. Armed with truncheons, stones, Molotov cocktails, and firearms, the protesters stormed government offices, turned over cars, and burned buses. "This monster—the never-ending protests, which had been created by these PRI governments—rose up and this colossus said: 'No,'" said sociologist Gloria Zafra.[17] Two days after the death of an American freelance cinematographer on October 27, the Federal Preventive Police moved against the "monster." They employed armored vehicles, water cannons, bulldozers, helicopters, and automatic weapons to regain the city's downtown area. APPO adherents barricaded themselves in local university buildings. Paralyzed by the "Tlatelolco Taboo," Fox refused to allow the police to enter the grounds of the university on the false assumption that they required an invitation from the rector even though students had broken federal laws by using the university radio station to provoke protests, storing weapons, and making Molotov cocktails. Needless to say, they had also shut down classes, harassed opponents, and refused to enter into good-faith negotiations.

Such behavior aside, el Peje—master of Orwellian "newspeak"— extolled the Oaxacan protesters for maintaining their "democratic and peaceful character" despite the repression visited upon them. In an October 31, 2006, rally in the heart of Mexico City, he accused Ruiz of electoral fraud, assassinations, persecution, imprisonment of his opponents, the trampling of human rights, and insatiable corruption and authoritarianism. "The conflict in Oaxaca," he added, "demonstrates that the entire political system is rotten and worn out. The majority of the Mexican people do not want this authoritarian and corrupt system, and sooner than later it will become evident that the right-wing alliance, between the PAN and the PRI cupolas, will be defeated by the popular democratic movement."[18]

He demanded that PAN senators join their PRD counterparts to force Ruiz from office, that the military personnel "disguised as police" leave the state, and that new elections be scheduled so that "the people of Oaxaca . . . can freely and democratically determine their future." Near the end of his speech, he thundered, "To hell with the bosses and their institutions! To hell with repressive and corrupt institutions! Let's move to renovate the country!"[19]

Even before López Obrador declaimed the cause of the "victims" of abuse, some two hundred student zealots in the capital exhibited their solidarity with APPO by occupying academic buildings and blocking roadways in the D.F. A column of protesters a kilometer long formed near the Ministry of Government. This contingent included university students as well as firebrands in the Francisco Villa Popular Front, the Triqui Movement of the Historic Center, and the Popular Revolutionary Front.[20] A pro-APPO contingent even disrupted a sermon by Cardinal Archbishop Rivera in the National Cathedral. In Chiapas, Indians linked to the Zapatistas intermittently closed roads, including one that provides access to Tuxtla Gutiérrez, the state capital, and four that lead into San Cristóbal de las Casas. The stoppages began at 6:00 A.M. on November 1 and lasted until 6 P.M., with two to three hundred people halting traffic every forty-five minutes. Small bands associated with the EZLN's "Other Campaign"—a movement that denounces the political regime and the parties and politicians (including López Obrador) that participate in it—also staged pro-APPO protests in Querétaro, Tabasco, Veracruz, Sinaloa, and Hidalgo.[21] Soon after taking office, Calderón dispatched federal forces to restore order in Oaxaca, thus taking the wind from el Peje's sails.[22]

A NEW SHERIFF IN TOWN

Once in office, Calderón followed up his success in Oaxaca by moving to reconquer large zones of the country infested by incredibly wealthy and obscenely brutal drug bands. For previous chief executives, the war on drugs was a law enforcement matter. By 2007 it had become an issue of sovereignty, as narco-barons held sway over remote areas in states like Michoacán, Guerrero, Sinaloa, Guerrero, and Oaxaca. Meanwhile, they viciously competed for turf, executed enemies in prison, and cowed mayors, police chiefs, and journalists in cities along the U.S.-Mexican border.

Some of these drug lords have become local celebrities, extolled in ballads known as *corridos,* and praised for contributions to charities and churches. Even though in prison, Gulf Cartel boss Osiel Cárdenas Guillén reportedly sponsored a "children's day" in Reynosa featuring ice cream, games, circus attractions, and free toys.[23]

The growing arrogance of the narco-chiefs became evident in 2006, when drug-related murders soared to two thousand, up from 1,304 in 2004 and 1,080 in 2001. This horrific number is complemented by medieval cruelty, as the killings are increasingly accomplished through decapitation. In September 2006, for instance, thugs barged into the Sol y Sombra bar in Uruapan, Michoacán, fired shots into the air, and lobbed five heads onto the dance floor. This appeared to be a warning from one gang to another. A hundred miles away in Zitacuaro, a colonial town once best known as a nesting place for Monarch butterflies, a pair of burned heads were planted in front of an automobile showroom.

Not only have the desperados co-opted and corrupted politicians, but they have turned crime reporting into a dangerous occupation. Since 2004, when its editor was stabbed to death, the *El Mañana* chain, which publishes newspapers in Matamoros, Reynosa, and Nuevo Laredo, has simply stopped running articles about the cartels and their activities. Needless to say, travel warnings issued by U.S. Ambassador Tony Garza in response to the contagion of murders have delivered a body blow to Mexico's tourism industry.

Leaders of the nation's two major opposition forces—the PRI and the PRD—have long scorned the treachery of the drug mobs. However, their internal divisions and, in some instances, links to powerful criminal families has spurred Calderón to cultivate other allies in addition to his own center-right National Action Party. Specifically, he has gone out of his way to propitiate the armed forces, whose leaders profoundly distrusted his predecessor.

Calderón began his courtship on inauguration day. He visited the army's major base in Mexico City before delivering his first speech to the nation. In that address, he emphasized austerity—except for the armed forces, law enforcement agencies, and programs to uplift the poor. His budget contained a robust increase for security, and he has also dined with the top brass, run TV spots emphasizing his pride in the military, visited troops wearing an oversized olive-drab jacket and a military cap adorned with the five stars of the commander in chief, and proposed forming a military Cuerpo de Fuerzas under his command.

In an effort to combat the narco-organizations, Calderón dispatched 6,500 troops to Michoacán, where drug lords have ruled over their own fiefdom in western parts of the state. Thanks to intelligence provided by hundreds of reconnaissance flights, soldiers and marines uprooted and burned thousands of marijuana plants covering more than a thousand acres and made sixty arrests. The second move came in Tijuana, where the army not only pursued the Arellano Félix and Sinaloa cartels but disarmed 2,600 local policemen infamous for their coziness with criminals.

In mid-January he sent fifteen hundred soldiers and federal police to Guerrero, where the Gulf Cartel vies with the Sinaloa Cartel for control of the bountiful marijuana and opium poppy production. Of the nine hundred murders recorded in the state in 2006, 306 were drug related. Attention was also focused on the northeastern states of Tamaulipas and Nuevo León. The president awarded rank-and-file troops a 46 percent salary increase for their success in "protecting the people and the nation."[24]

Some continuity exists between previous strategies and that of Calderón, such as a commitment to extradite vile actors to the United States—a move that, when carried out by the Colombian government, incited even more cartel-authored mayhem. The Cali cartel spread the word that "better a Colombian tomb than an American jail cell." However, Fox set back law enforcement by creating a new Ministry of Public Security. In so doing, he separated intelligence, which remained in the Government Ministry, from the day-to-day pursuit of wrongdoers. For his part, Calderón seems determined to create a single national police force—there are now 1,661 separate federal, state, and municipal agencies—modeled on Canada's Royal Mounted Police and Spain's Cuerpo Nacional de Policía.

What about Calderón's innovations? First, Fox, whose priorities waxed and waned with the phases of the moon, managed to nab some "big fish" among the narco-traffickers, but he never placed the antidrug effort at the top of his agenda. Calderón clearly has.

Second, Calderón has overwhelmingly relied on the army, even as he has explored integrating the thirty thousand members of Federal Agency of Investigations with the Federal Preventive Police—with the possible addition of ten thousand Marines.

Third, rather than deploy a few hundred soldiers in antidrug operations, by mid-2007 Calderón had dispatched more than thirty thousand federal agents and military personnel against his foes in nine states.

Fourth, he has recognized the deep-seated corruption that afflicts local law enforcement bodies. Thus, his forces took the weapons from the Tijuana police as part of their initiative against the locally based cartel headed by the Arellano Félix brothers.

Fifth, in contrast to Fox's Montessori cabinet, Calderón has demanded coordination among the four agencies responsible for the antidrug raids—namely, the Ministries of Defense, Navy, Public Security, and Government, as well as the Attorney General's Office. His attorney general, Eduardo Medina Mora, and public security secretary, Genaro García Luna, have won praise in both Mexico City and Washington, D.C., for their professionalism and skill.

Finally, in the cases of Michoacán and Tijuana, the federal government did not warn their local counterparts of the invasion, lest informers alert the targets of the operation.

How successful will he be in these efforts? What happens when the troops leave theaters of conflict? Can Mexico succeed in the fight against narco-families as long as there is such strong demand north of the Rio Grande? Whatever the outcome, Calderón has shown domestic and foreign observers that he—unlike Fox—is committed to taking back his nation from the drug mobs, even as the military's role increases dramatically.

As a messiah-in-waiting, López Obrador deprecates Calderón's version of the war on drugs, while positioning himself to take advantage of the president's problems and programs. Any move to encourage private investment in the energy arena will spark controversy. In late October 2006, a mélange of malcontents forged the National Front in Defense of Energy Sovereignty (FNDSE), which is made up of the parties that backed el Peje's candidacy, friendly unions, and small antigovernment organizations. Leaders of the front criticized the choice of Agustín Carstens, former deputy managing director at the IMF, as Calderón's finance secretary. They considered this appointment an omen that the new government would cooperate with the IMF and the World Bank to privatize the nation's oil and electricity sectors. According to Martín Esparza Flores, SME's secretary-general, "more than 300 political, popular, social, indigenous, peasant, and labor organizations will defend the national patrimony to avoid having natural resources handed over to foreigners."[25]

A Second Coming?

Even ex-PRI senator Manuel Bartlett showed up at the kick-off of FNDSE. During the early 1990s, a faction of the PAN that became known as the Democratic and Doctrinaire Forum left the party to protest the political deals between *panista* leaders and Salinas. Should the PRI back the president on energy legislation, Bartlett, Fernando de Garay, and fellow strident nationalists could bolt the PRI and support López Obrador's intractable opposition to introducing private capital into the exploration and production of petroleum.

When tortilla prices skyrocketed in January 2007, the erstwhile mayor sought to speak before seventy-five thousand protesters who swarmed into downtown Mexico City. The organizers, which included PRD and PRI peasant and labor activists, refused to allow el Pejelagarto to address the rally.[26] Instead, he held his own meeting after the demonstration had concluded. At his gathering, the self-ordained legitimate president demanded an emergency salary increase for workers, guaranteed prices for farmers, the elimination of corn imports under NAFTA, subsidies for the purchase of tortillas, and passage of legislation on competitive pricing.[27]

Again, Calderón stole the thunder of his nemesis by setting a ceiling on tortilla prices. Meanwhile, the Federal Attorney for Consumer Protection launched an investigation of possible price gouging and noncompetitive practices.

The key to the success of both Calderón and López Obrador lies with the PRI. Although Calderón has impressive legislative experience and knows how to bargain effectively with the opposition, he still labors under the burden of PAN minorities in the Chamber of Deputies (206 seats) and the Senate (52 seats), as depicted in Table 28. The next congressional elections will not take place until

TABLE 28. *Composition of the Mexican Congress, 2006–2009*

PARTY	SEATS IN 500-MEMBER CHAMBER OF DEPUTIES (2006–2009)	SEATS IN 500-MEMBER CHAMBER OF DEPUTIES (2003–2006)	SEATS IN 128-MEMBER SENATE (2006–2009)	SEATS IN 128-MEMBER SENATE (2003–2006)
National Action Party (PAN)	206	148	52	46
Democratic Revolutionary Party (PRD)	127	97	26*	15
Institutional Revolutionary Party (PRI)	106	201	33	60
Greens (PVEM)	17	17	6	5
Convergencia	17	5	5	1
Workers Party (PT)	12	6	5	1
New Alliance (PANAL)	9	0	0	0
Peasant and Social Alternative (PASC)	5	0	0	0
Independents	1	6	1	0
TOTAL	500	500	128	128

* Three PRD lawmakers (Rosario Ibarra, Josefina Cota Cota, and Francisco Javier Obregón Espinosa) switched affiliation to give the PT five members, the minimum required to constitute a "parliamentary group." As a result, the PT faction will receive at least 1,225,000 pesos per month. See Claudia Salazar, "Cede PRD a PT a Rosario Ibarra," *Reforma*, October 18, 2006, http://www.reforma.com.mx/.

mid-2009. In the meantime, the PRI, with 106 deputies and 33 senators, could provide the critical mass of votes on crucial measures.

On February 18, 2007, former Tlaxcala governor Beatriz Paredes Rangel soundly defeated ex-Senate leader Enrique Jackson for the PRI's presidency. Although known for her leftist orientation, Paredes developed an excellent rapport with Calderón when they led their respective parties in Congress during the first part of Fox's regime. After its resounding setback in the mid-2006 race for Los Pinos, Paredes wants to change the party's reputation from one of venality and opportunism to one bristling with creative ideas that demonstrate its capacity to govern responsibly. Such a makeover is essential to prevent the PRI's evolving into a regional entity with a nucleus of governors and law makers dependent on an aging constituency and decaying corporatist groups, but bereft of the ability to regain Los Pinos. While a veteran of her nation's brass-knuckled political infighting, Paredes possesses, in the words of astute analyst Luis Rubio, "a sense of where Mexico should be going."[28] She is intelligent, indefatigable, and articulate. However, she had difficulty building a consensus on a new executive committee for the party, and the PRI faces formidable challenges in upcoming state and local elections, including the 2007 gubernatorial contests in Yucatán (May 20), which the PRI won, Baja California (August 5), and Michoacán (November 11).

While Mexicans will not elect its next chief executive until 2012, several PRI politicians have already begun preparing their candidacies. Natividad González Parás got off to an auspicious start as governor of Nuevo León until an epidemic of narco-killings in 2006 and 2007 cast a dark cloud over his future. Enrique Peña Nieto, Mexico State's dynamic young executive and a vigorous personal and financial supporter of Paredes' bid for the PRI's top post, remains on the short-list of contenders despite acute personal problems. Paredes seems prepared to enter the fray if she can help her party surmount the daunting electoral obstacles that lie in its path.

Yet, in mid-2007, the brightest star in the PRI's firmament was Senate President Manlio Fabio Beltrones Rivera, a savvy, experienced ex-governor of Sonora, who had already begun building his team, forging coalitions, and making international contacts. He even ingratiated himself with Rosario Ibarra de Piedra, a senator from the left-wing Partido del Trabajo and a social activist since the early 1970s when her son, allegedly a member of a guerrilla band, disappeared. Beltrones learned the political ropes from legendary hard-as-nails Government Secretary Fernando Gutiérrez Barrios, worked closely with Salinas, enthusiastically backed Madrazo's candidacy in 2006, helped ensure Paredes' election, has cultivated the Catholic Church and the media, and exhibits a fruitful rapport with his counterpart in the Chamber of Deputies, political heavyweight Emilio Gamboa Patrón. Along the way, he has made relatively few powerful enemies—with the exception of Eduardo Bours Castelo, the rich, ambitious governor of his home state of Sonora. Of course, if his nascent campaign picks up momentum, his detractors will begin ransacking closets for ghosts from his past.

Beltrones has utilized his remarkable political skills to overcome his image of as one of the shrewdest dinosaurs in the PRI's Jurassic Park. He helped Calderón gain overwhelming passage of his first budget; joined Gordillo in spurring passage of legislation to overhaul ISSSTE, the peso-hemorrhaging pension system for public employees; threw his weight behind a measure to enhance the transparency of at all levels of government; and cooperated with Los Pinos on a controversial gambit to fight terrorism.

The 55-year-old Senate leader has embraced a sweeping "reform of the state" as the vehicle for reinventing himself as a responsible, effective statesman. He has enlisted in this endeavor Santiago Creel and Carlos Navarrete, respectively the coordinators of the PAN and PRD factions in the Senate. The three senators often seemed to be completing each other's sentences during an early May 2007 visit to Washington, D.C., where they appeared congenially together at a forum sponsored by the Center for Strategic & International Studies (CSIS) before meeting with high-level U.S. congressional and administration officials.

Beltrones has focused his undertaking on five themes, the first of which relates to the functions of the Executive and Legislature and relations between the two branches. Until the late twentieth century, Mexico's president exercised formal and meta-constitutional powers that made him a Leviathan for six years. Since the political reforms of the mid-1990s and the 1997 congressional and D.F. elections, however, new official power brokers have emerged—among which are IFE, TEPJF, the D.F. Jefe de Gobierno, governors, and Congress—while incentives for cooperation among parties have diminished. For instance, the Chamber of Deputies and the Senate have become formidable actors. But their forte has been to obstruct, not initiate, policies—with the Left resorting to sit-ins, demonstrations, and even violent confrontations to advance its agenda. The parties had until mid-2007 to submit proposals on topics ranging from the reelection of legislators to procedures for selecting presidents to the possibility of independent candidacies for public office.

The July 2006 presidential photo-finish gave rise to the second rubric of study; namely, changes to the conduct of elections. Preliminary talks concentrated on replacing the Federal Electoral Institute with a single electoral body that would register voters and organize contests not only at the federal level, but in the 31 states and the D.F.—each of which has its own institute. Alleging IFE's "favoritism" toward Calderón, the PRD favors broader representation on the institute's political council, as well as prohibiting electoral authorities from engaging in self-serving media campaigns to justify their actions.

The deeply flawed judicial system constitutes the third area of proposed renovation. A study by Mexico's Center of Economic Research and Teaching found that clerks assume much of the responsibility for trials, that there is little open debate between prosecutors and defense attorneys, and that most arguments are presented in written form far from the glare of public scrutiny. Meanwhile, the defendant languishes in jail on the assumption that he is guilty until proven innocent under the Civil Code, an offspring of the Napoleonic Code. He may be able to obtain his release with an "amparo"—a type of injunction—but he must have the cash to hire a lawyer, pay court costs, make bail, and, possibly, grease palms. Often his case will only be heard when he or his family amass sufficient resources to get the attention of court officers. As journalist Kenneth Emmond described the situation: "Pedro, sitting in his cell after his "trial," get[s] a visit from one of the clerks, who tells him, "Bad news, Pedro. You're getting 18 months . . . " Or . . . he [is] summoned to a courtroom to get the news—from a clerk, of course?" He may have no opportunity to see, much less make a statement before the judge who determined his fate, before the verdict is rendered. Such a hermetic, Byzantine, scheme, begs for the authorization of oral testimony, reassessment of the uses of the amparo, public trials, and professionalization of the judiciary.

Beltrones and his colleagues also plan to reevaluate federal-state affairs. Some governors have taken advantage of the weakened presidency to run their states like personal fiefdoms. Mayors have followed suit as evidenced by the travel recorded at public expense—trips equivalent to three times around the world—by representatives of the 125 Mexico State municipalities after they took office in 2006. Still, states and localities derive most of their funds from the federal treasury, all the more so because governors are reluctant to levy taxes on land and water lest they alienate powerful interest groups. A redefinition of the allocation of authority between states and the central government is long overdue, as well as determining whether the Federal District should attain statehood.

Finally, advocates of reform emphasize the importance of "social guarantees" to protect human rights, promote mobility, and close the chasm between the rich and the poor—an issue that nearly catapulted López Obrador into the presidency.

On April 25, 2007, Beltrones formally unveiled the Executive Committee for Negotiation and Construction of Accords of the Congress of the Union. He deftly presided over the two-hour ceremony, which took place in patio of the ornate Palacio de Minería, and brought together the chief justice of the Supreme Court, the secretary of Government, political party leaders, governors, mayors, legislators, and a representative of the president. In the audience were prominent citizens like Muñoz Ledo who headed a commission to achieve a reform of the state during the Fox administration.

The senator from Sonora adroitly emphasized that the projected revisions would provide "an ideal method" to launch a free-wheeling dialogue about critical issues besetting the country—with a view to achieving profound results within a year. "We are paving the way for national reconciliation," he averred. Although calls for root-and-branch reforms filled the air, several participants struck discordant notes. PRD chief Cota harrumphed that he represented "citizens who voted July 2 and were victims of fraud," adding later: "A fraud committed for lack of authority and I am speaking of the authorities of IFE."

Will Beltrones accomplish his goal? If the past is prologue to the future, the best that he can hope for is a "light reform." Since August 2000, the theme of the Senate president's current handiwork has generated 711 talks, 109 round table discussions, 255 initiatives in the Chamber of Deputies, and 34 bills in the Senate, 13 forums, and 44 reform proposals, according to *Reforma*.

Most fundamental changes require substantial funds and, while Calderón and Finance Secretary Agustín Carstens champion an overhaul of the fiscal regimen, they can expect, at the very best, lukewarm support from the PRI's presidential aspirants and outright opposition from the PRD, especially if extending the

IVA to food and medicine appears on the table. A more promising approach would be curb frivolous spending, while closing the loopholes and eliminating the gross inequities that suffuse the current system and inspire rampant evasion.

When asked at the CSIS program about hammering out a strategy that would spur sustained growth, enhance Mexico's competitiveness vis-à-vis China and other Asian powerhouses, and uplift the nation's "have nots," Beltrones, Creel, and Navarrete stressed their tenacious commitment to such a objective. They also voiced readiness to confront the ubiquitous monopolies, oligopolies, and private conglomerates in telecommunications, television, radio, financial services, cement, transportation, processed foods, and other fields. Beltrones advocated inserting in the Constitution a provision that would require "competition." Creel urged providing additional tools to Mexico's existing Federal Competition Commission (CFC), which was created in within the Ministry of Economy in 1993 to implement the Federal Economic Competition Law. As for the labor unions that have colonized public education, Pemex, the electricity sector, and scores of other vital socio-economic areas, Creel and Navarrete underscored the need for greater transparency in their operations and secret ballots in their assemblies. It remains to be seen, though, whether Calderón and fellow reformers will move against kingpins in either monopolies like Telmex and the Petroleum Workers' Union or oligopolies like Televisa and TV Azteca. After all, such behemoths will not forfeit their enormous power just because of tinkering with the Constitution and giving pep talks to the CFC, which already has the mandate (but not the political blessing) to combat anti-competitive practices.

There is also the imperative to allow private investment in Pemex whose reserves are declining rapidly. North Vietnam is the only other country that bans risk contracts in its petroleum sector, but López Obrador, most of the Left, and traditionalists like Bartlett within the PRI equate such a step with selling the national patrimony. Leadership is badly needed to reverse the current counter-productive policy encapsulated in the aphorism: "*El petróleo es nuestro*" ("The petroleum is ours."). Calderón recognizes the problem, but cannot act without a consensus within the PAN and broad support within the PRI. Should Beltrones or Paredes dare to welcome foreign capital, they would become targets of their competitors within the PRI. Moreover, el Peje would lambaste any such opening at the petroleum giant as conclusive proof of his persistent accusation that "PRIAN" pirouettes to the tune piped by Uncle Sam and other devotees of neoliberalism.

In addition, the apparent collegiality between the PAN and PRI protagonists may dissipate over Calderón's naming of delegates from federal agencies to states. The PRI, which long rewarded its faithful with these appointments, has demanded that the process be depoliticized. The PRI also opposes reelection of legislators, which the PAN favors. And the PRI is poised to shrill against "government intervention" when it loses important electoral showdowns. In the aftermath of losing two presidential races, the PRI wants to fortify Congress at the expense of Los Pinos. Actuated by López Obrador's robust showing, the PRD, which undoubtedly will lose seats in the 2009 congressional competition, favors shoring up the presidency.

Beltrones may be able to muster support for revamping IFE and the electoral system in time for the 2009 federal legislative contests. In addition, with or without a comprehensive reform, Calderón will earmark more funds for the poor.

Mexico's establishment has more reason to promote change than at any time in recent memory: López Obrador came within a whisker of defeating Calderón; the public holds politicians in bad odor; pension systems are rolling up enormous debts; proven oil reserves are dwindling; drug barons, which already flaunt their own zones of influence, threaten to compromise the nation's sovereignty; and U.S. law makers—in response to grassroots pressure—have become less enthusiastic about the influx of illegal aliens.

López Obrador has sounded the wake-up call to Mexico's elite, who live extremely well in a country that boasts oil, natural gas, gold, silver, beaches, mountains, museums, historical treasures, and extremely hardworking people. At the outset of Calderón's sexenio, El Peje garnered fewer headlines, attracted smaller crowds, and lost a substantial portion of his funding. Nevertheless, rejuvenated by the birth of another son—appropriately named "Jesús"—he travels sedulously throughout the country, often visiting a half-dozen towns and villages in a day. In an ever-more radical discourse, he savages the Calderón government for the rise in tortilla prices, increases in the cost of gasoline, and the "failure" to provide adequate salary adjustments for workers. In an early May swing through the Cuenca del Papaloapan, el Peje commented that to govern effectively a leader needs more than "servility"; he requires the "three Cs"—*cabeza* (intelligence), *corazón* (heart), and *carácter* (character). He also insisted that crime had skyrocketed under the "usurping government" of Calderón and there was not peace, much less security in Mexico.

Although perceived as an irresponsible gadfly by most middle- and upper-class citizens, the tens of millions of impoverished Mexicans who feel abandoned by the system—the so-called "*jodidos*" or "exploited ones"—resonate to his appeals and regard him as their best hope to escape misery. López Obrador's popularity among the dispossessed has placed the PRD and its leftist allies, which occupy more legislative seats than ever, in a dilemma. Do they continue to maintain ties with the man who generated the votes that swelled their ranks in Congress or do they assist Calderón and Beltrones in resolving major national problems? His National Democratic Convention will enjoy success only if the nation's establishment fails to recognize the wellspring of discontent that the Tabascan has tapped with respect to the abuse of power and the indifference to inequities that beset a nation where 10 percent of the country's households command 39.4 percent of total national income and the bottom 10 percent account for only 1.6 percent.

Self-serving policies permit Mexico's dominant class to live like princes, paying, at best, a widow's mite in taxes. They turn a blind eye toward improving education and healthcare—the primary factors for social development and economic mobility—while protecting the immensely wealthy and powerful moguls who fatten their foreign bank accounts thanks to the economic bottlenecks they have crafted, often with government collusion. Mexico's elite finds it much less expensive and much more convenient to thrust onto U.S. taxpayers responsibility for its malfeasance by using its northern border as an escape valve for its nation's have-nots. If the country's grandees fail to use the country's enormous wealth to address the serious needs of the downtrodden, the Little Ray of Hope—or someone else who proclaims his message of salvation for the humble—may accomplish a "Second Coming" in the 2012 presidential contest.

NOTES

INTRODUCTION

1. A freshwater creature with diamond-shaped scales and long jaws with needlelike teeth that abounds in the rivers and lakes of Tabasco.

2. See Jay Haley, *The Power Tactics of Jesus Christ* (Rockville, Md.: Triangle Press, 1986), 35.

3. Quoted in Hector Guerrero, "Estalla AMLO por tanta corrupción," *Noticieros Televisa,* October 23, 2003, http://www.esmas.com/. All translations from the Spanish are my own unless otherwise noted.

4. Quoted in "Entrevista a Andrés Manuel López Obrador," *La Jornada,* December 4, 2000, http://www.jornada.unam.mx/.

5. Enrique Krauze, "López Obrador, el mesías tropical," *Letras Libres* 8 (June 2006): 20.

6. Ibid., 24.

7. Quoted in Carlos Marín, "Zedillo tuvo más sensibilidad política que Fox," *Milenio Semanal,* May 23, 2004, http://www.milenio.com/semanal/.

8. Ibid.

9. See Haley, *The Power Tactics of Jesus Christ,* 25.

10. Richard Heinberg, "In Search of the Historical Jesus," *New Dawn Magazine* September–October 1998, http://www.newdawnmagazine.com/.

11. Gonzalo Beltrán Calzada, interview by author, June 17, 2005, Villahermosa.

12. Oscar Aguilar Ascencio, interview by author, September 25, 2004, Mexico City.

13. "Les molesta a mis adversarios el que yo actúe de esta manera. Pero yo soy juarista y Juárez decía que la autoridad se adquiere por el recto proceder." Quoted in Marín, "Zedillo tuvo más sensibilidad política que Fox."

14. Quoted in "El oro y el moro," *Reforma,* January 18, 2005, http://www.reforma.com.mx/.

15. Jorge Ramos and Fabiola Cancino, "Marchan miles en favor de AMLO," *El Universal,* August 30, 2004, http://www.eluniversal.com.mx/.

16. Oscar Aguilar Ascencio, interview by author, November 11, 2004, Mexico City.

17. "Las propuestas de AMLO," *El Universal,* August 30, 2004, http://www.eluniversal.com.mx/, appendix 1.

18. Richard A. Horsley, with John S. Hanson, *Bandits, Prophets, and Messiahs: Popular Movements in the Time of Jesus* (San Francisco: Harper & Row, 1988), chapter 1.

19. Heinberg, "In Search of the Historical Jesus," 3.

20. Burton L. Mack, *The Lost Gospel: The Book of Q and Christian Origins* (San Francisco: Harper, 1993), 66.

21. Haley, *The Power Tactics of Jesus Christ,* 23.

CHAPTER 1

1. He was actually born in Macuspana, the municipal center, 2.5 miles from Belén (Bethlehem), where his mother's physician had a clinic.

2. Ernesto Benítez López, interview by author, August 15, 2005, Villahermosa.

3. A close family friend insists that Doña Manuelita was born in Frontera, Tabasco. Hermilo Pérez López, interview by author, June 17, 2005, Tepetitlán, Tabasco.

4. Lic. María de Fátima Castellanos Macossay, interview by author, February 15, 2004, Palenque; Leandro Rovirosa Wade (former governor), interview by author, March 7, 2005, Mexico City. One member of the family told me that Doña Manuelita was actually born in Spain, but to avoid bureaucratic complications, the family registered her as having been born in Frontera, Tabasco. Everyone else with whom I spoke gave Frontera as her birthplace. Some accounts report her birth in 1926.

5. Quoted in Alejandro Almazán, "Retratos desconocidos de Andrés Manuel," *La Revista,* weekly supplement to *El Universal,* March 1–7, 2004, 28.

6. Pedro Arturo López Obrador, interview by Blanca Gómez, March 25, 2004, in Gómez, *¿Y quién es? Historia de un hombre enigmático* (Mexico City: Planeta, 2005), 30.

7. Manuela Obrador González, videotaped interview, 1997, in ibid., 34.

8. Pérez López, interview.

9. Jorge Zepeda Patterson et al., *Los suspirantes: Los precandidatos de carne y hueso* (Mexico City: Planeta, 2005), 10.

10. Pérez López, interview.

11. Quoted in S. Lynne Walker, "Mayor's Popularity Spreading in Mexico," *San Diego Union-Tribune,* April 25, 2005, http://www.signonsandiego.com/.

12. Gómez, *¿Y quién es?* 35.

13. José Ramiro López Obrador (mayor of Macuspana), interview by author, August 10, 2004, Villahermosa.

14. Quoted in Walker, "Mayor's Popularity Spreading."

15. Andrés López Ramón, videotaped interview, 1997, in Gómez, *¿Y quién es?* 46.

16. For information about the films featuring *El Santo,* see http://www.webwasteland.com/santo/santo.htm.

17. Almazán, "Retratos desconocidos de Andrés Manuel," 29.

18. Pedro Arturo López Obrador, interview by Blanca Gómez, March 25, 2004, in Gómez, *¿Y quién es?* 56.

19. Ramiro López Obrador, interview.

20. Benítez López, interview.

21. Fernando Gómez, "AMLO asesino desde niño no 1 sino 2 veces," *Terra Networks,* April 3, 2005, http://www.terra.es/.

22. Walker, "Mayor's Popularity Spreading."

23. Hermilo Pérez López, interview by author, August 19, 2005.

24. Carlos Manuel Rovirosa Ramírez, interview by author, August 15, 2005, Tepetitán, Macuspana.

25. Benítez López, interview.

26. Hermilo Pérez López, interview by author, July 13, 2005.

27. Quoted in Almazán, "Retratos desconocidos de Andrés Manuel," 29.

28. "En la tienda de telas de su padre cayó muerto de un balazo, ayer," *Diario de Tabasco,* July 9, 1960, 1.

29. The most objective account of José Ramón's death appears in Rafael Loret de Mola, *Destapes* (Mexico City: Oceano, 2004), 109. However, Andrés Manuel's brother, José Ramiro, told a different story to a reporter. He said that on July 6, 1969, José Ramón had the gun when Andrés Manuel told him, "Stop playing with that pistol because our father will get mad." José Ramón failed to heed the warning—with fatal consequences; see Walker, "Mayor's Popularity Spreading." Another writer claimed that the shooting occurred on July 9, 1969; see Almazán, "Retratos desconocidos de Andrés Manuel," 29.

30. Zepeda Patterson et al., *Los suspirantes,* 12.

31. Almazán, "Retratos desconocidos de Andrés Manuel," 29.

32. "En 1965, López Obrador asesinó a su hermano," *Rumbo Nuevo,* July 10, 1990, 6.

33. Senator Juan José Rodríguez Prats, interview by author, January 15, 2004, Mexico City.

34. The quotation appeared in an article in *El Universal,* as reported by prize-winning journalist Andres Oppenheimer, *Bordering on Chaos: Guerrillas, Stockbrokers, Politicians, and Mexico's Road to Prosperity* (Boston: Little, Brown, 1996), 201–2.

35. Benítez López, interview.

36. Ibid.

37. Almazán, "Retratos desconocidos de Andrés Manuel," 27.

38. A. Martínez et al., "Se enreda el Nicogate con más parientes incómodos," *El Universal,* January 25, 2004, http://www.eluniversal.com.mx/.

39. Ramiro López Obrador, interview.

40. Castellanos Macossay, interview.

41. Quoted in Rafael Soberanez León, "López Obrador está desgastado políticamente reconocen sus padres," *Tabasco a Día,* April 20, 1995, 3.

42. Pérez López, interview, June 17, 2005.

43. Arturo Núñez, interview by author, January 16, 2004, Mexico City.

44. A quotation by Octavio Romero Oropeza, reported by Rafael López Cruz, interview by author, June 16, 2005, Villahermosa.

45. Andrés Manuel López Obrador, news conference, December 11, 2004, Mexico City.

46. Rodolfo Lara Lagunas, *Juárez: De la choza al Palacio Nacional; historias y testimonios* (Villahermosa, 2004).

47. For this insight I am indebted to Dr. Carlos Ruiz Abreu (archivist of Mexico City), interview by author, July 5, 2005, Mexico City.

48. Lara Lagunas, interview by author, June 13, 2005, Villahermosa.

49. Ibid.

50. Quoted in Andrés Manuel López Obrador, *Entre la historia y la esperanza: Corrupción y lucha democrática en Tabasco* (Mexico City: Editorial Grijalbo, 1995), 73.

51. Ibid., 62–64.

52. Krauze, "López Obrador," 19.

53. Ibid., 64.

54. Quoted in López Obrador, *Entre la historia y la esperanza,* 66.

55. Ibid., 68–70.

56. Ibid., 74.

57. Citlallín de Díos Calles, interview by author, February 16, 2004, Villahermosa.

58. Quoted in López Obrador, *Entre la historia y la esperanza,* 77.

59. "Panorama nacional," *Política* 9 (November 1967): 5, cited in Kathleen Bruhn, *Taking on Goliath: The Emergence of a New Left Party and the Struggle for Democracy in Mexico* (University Park: Pennsylvania State University Press, 1997), 49n32.

60. After leaving the PRI presidency, he delivered many of his key speeches to students and other young people. See L. Darío Vasconcelos, *Madrazo: Voz postrera de la revolución, discursos y comentarios* (Mexico City: B. Costa-Amic, 1971).

61. See José Agustín Ortiz Pinchetti, "Carlos Alberto Madrazo," *La Jornada,* June 6, 1999, http://www.jornada.unam.mx/. When it appeared that his wife was too ill to fly, Madrazo asked future Tabasco governor Manuel Gurría Ordoñez to accompany him. His friend agreed to make the trip, only to step aside when Madrazo's wife recovered. Manuel Gurría Ordoñez, interview by author, December 6, 2005, Mexico City.

62. Bartolo Jiménez Méndez, interview by author, August 9, 2004, Villahermosa.

63. His major rivals for the presidency, Roberto Madrazo and Santiago Creel, compiled 9.2 and 7.5 grade point averages, respectively (Creel subsequently lost the PAN nomination to Calderón); see "Mucha política, bajo promedio," *El Norte,* May 15, 2005, http://www.elnorte.com/.

64. Jiménez Méndez, interview.

65. Quoted in *Testimonio: Los Chontales de Tabasco* (Mexico, 1982), provided to the author by Ernesto Benítez López.

66. Armando Padilla Herrera, interview by author, June 17, 2005, Villahermosa.

67. Gómez, *¿Y quién es?* 61.

68. Dr. Raquel Sosa Elízaga, interview by author, March 28, 2004, Mexico City. Dr. Sosa, who subsequently served as secretary of social development in López Obrador's cabinet, was a fellow student and friend of the future mayor when they were at UNAM.

69. Jiménez Méndez, interview.

70. The thesis was published by the Universidad Juárez Autónoma de Tabasco in 1986.

71. Jiménez Méndez, interview.

72. Quoted in Almazán, "Retratos desconocidos de Andrés Manuel," 30.

CHAPTER 2

1. This section is based largely on Julieta Campos, *Tabasco: Un jaguar despertado* (Mexico City: Aguilar Nuevo Siglo, 1996), 47.

2. Francisco Iracheta, quoted in George W. Grayson, "PEMEX: Threat to Mexico's Environment," *Washington Post,* June 25, 1979, A19.

3. Adrián Lajous Vargas, interview by author, December 5, 2005, Mexico City.

4. Andrés Manuel López Obrador, *Tabasco, víctima del fraude electoral* (Mexico City: Editorial Nuestro Tiempo, 2000), 19.

5. Porfirio Muñoz Ledo, interview by author, January 12, 2005, Mexico City.

6. Krauze, "López Obrador," 21.

7. Leandro Rovirosa Wade, interview by author, August 18, 2005, Mexico City.

8. Rovirosa Wade, interview, March 7, 2005.

9. Ángel Buendía Tirado, interview by author, July 6, 2005, Mexico City. The governor's future private secretary was certain that López Obrador spoke at a rally for Rovirosa Wade in Macuspana.

10. The name of the organization in Tabasco was the Centro Coordinador Indigenista Chontal.

11. Rovirosa Wade, interview, March 7, 2005.

12. Ignacio Ovalle Fernández, interview by author, January 10, 2005, Mexico City.

13. Ibid.; Ovalle Fernández, interview by author, August 18, 2005, Mexico City.

14. Ovalle Fernández, interview, January 10, 2005.

15. Benítez López, interview. Rosario Torres refused to grant me an interview to discuss his relationship with López Obrador.

16. *Revista ABC,* January 16, 1985, cited in Manuel Cedeño del Olmo, *Sistema político en Tabasco: Gobierno, poder regional y federalismo* (Mexico City: Centro de Estudios de Política Comparada, 1999).

17. Omar Castro Castillo (López Obrador's successor as INI director in Tabasco), interview by author, July 5, 2005, Mexico City.

18. Ibid.

19. Ibid.

20. Ovalle Fernández, interviews, January 10 and August 18, 2005. In fact, López Obrador's house, while Spartan, may not have been quite as primitive as Ovalle remembered. Of course, the INI director could have improved the dwelling during his period in Nacajuca.

21. Jiménez Méndez, interview.

22. Luz Rosales Esteva, interview by author, December 9, 2004, Mexico City.

23. Candelaria Lázaro Lázaro, interview by author, January 16, 2005, Nacajuca.

24. Rosa Rojas, "Gestionan reapertura de radio indígena 7 municipios de Tabasco," *La Jornada,* March 19, 2005, http://www.jornada.unam.mx/.

25. Lucas Bernardo Román, interview by author, August 14, 2005, Nacajuca.

26. Pedro Reséndez Medina, interview by author, June 14, 2005, Villahermosa.

27. Buendía Tirado, interview.

28. Ovalle Fernández, interview, January 10, 2005.

29. Graco Ramírez Garrido Abreu, interview by author, July 1, 2004, Mexico City.

30. Campos, *Tabasco,* 88–90.

31. Jiménez Méndez, interview.

32. Mother María del Carmen Muriel de la Torre, interview by author, August 14, 2005, Nacajuca.

33. Almazán, "Retratos desconocidos de Andrés Manuel," 30.

34. Mother Muriel de la Torre, interview.

35. Rovirosa Wade, interview, March 7, 2005.

36. Ovalle Fernández, interview, January 10, 2005.

37. Luis Beltán (Rocío's half-brother), interview by author, June 13, 2005, Villahermosa.

38. Quoted in Guadalupe Loaeza, "Andrés Manuel," *Reforma*, November 18, 1999, http://www.reforma.com.mx/.

39. Beltrán Calzada, interview.

40. Reséndez Medina, interview.

41. Elena Medina del Beltrán (Rocío's mother), interview by author, August 9, 2004, Villahermosa.

42. Benítez López, interview.

43. Carlos Heredia Zubieta, interview by author, July 5, 2004, Mexico City.

44. Padilla Herrera, interview, June 17, 2005.

45. An example was his selecting César Raúl Ojeda Zubieta, an erstwhile enemy, for a Senate seat over Dorilian Díaz Pérez.

46. Luis Beltán, interview. For a collection of essays about Beltrán Medina, see *Rocío Beltrán Medina: Libro de familia* (Mexico City: Palabra en Vuela, 2003).

47. Darvín González Ballina (state deputy), interview by author, August 6, 2004, Villahermosa.

48. Gonzalo Beltrán, interview.

49. Ruiz Abreu, interview.

50. Ibid.

51. Lázaro Lázaro, interview.

52. Quoted in *Rocío Beltrán Medina: Libro de familia*, 3.

53. Rafael López Cruz, interview by author, August 9, 2004, Villahermosa. The former medical student and friend of Rocío is the wife of Rafael López Cruz.

54. Isidra Correa López (wife of former state PRD president Rafael López Cruz), interview by author, June 16, 2005, Villahermosa.

55. Dr. Enrique González Pedrero, interview by author, July 6, 2004, Mexico City.

56. Ibid.

57. Buendía Tirado, interview.

58. González Ballina, interview.

59. Dr. Julieta Campos, interview by author, July 5, 2004, Mexico City.

60. González Pedrero, interview.

61. Ibid.

62. Benítez López, interview.

63. López Obrador, *Tabasco, víctima del fraude electoral*, 19.

64. This section draws on Manuel Cedeño del Olmo, *Sistema político en Tabasco*, 118–31.

65. Campos, interview.

66. López Obrador, *Tabasco, víctima del fraude electoral*, 19.

67. Ibid., 20.

68. Ibid.

69. Rovirosa Wade, interview, August 18, 2005.

70. Luis Priego Ortiz, interview by author, August 16, 2005, Mexico City.

71. For this story, I am indebted to Rafael López Cruz, interview, June 16, 2005.

72. Francisco Peralta Burelo, interview by author, January 17, 2005, Villahermosa.

73. Elena Poniatowska, "La Belisario Domínguez a Carlos Fuentes," *La Jornada*, October 7, 1999, http://www.jornada.unam.mx/.

74. Benítez López, interview.

75. González Pedrero, correspondence to author, August 18, 2005.

76. Reséndez Medina, interview.

77. Ibid.

78. Ramón Bolivar Zapata, interview by author, July 4, 2005, Mexico City.

79. Reséndez Medina, interview.

80. Ibid.

81. González Pedrero, interview.

82. "Renuncia López Obrador a la oficialia mayor," *Rumbo Nuevo,* August 17, 1983, 1.

83. Graco Ramírez Garrido Abreu, interview by author, July 5, 2005.

84. Enrique González Pedrero, interview by author, August 18, 2005.

85. Peralta Burelo, interviews, August 10, 2004, and January 17, 2005, Villahermosa.

86. The state took over Prodecot, changing the organization's name to the Commission for the Development of Petroleum Zones (Comisión de Desarrollo de Zonas Petroleros—Codezpat).

87. Quoted in Juan René Colorado Sosa, "El partido sera vanguardia de la labor revolucionario," *Presente,* August 23, 1983, 1, 12.

88. González Pedrero, interview, August 18, 2005.

CHAPTER 3

1. Pedro Reséndez Medina, interview by author, June 14, 2005, Villahermosa.

2. Ibid. Reséndez scoffed at the idea of charging a family member interest.

3. Andrés Manuel López Obrador, "Revolución y justicia," *Revista de la Universidad* 9 (September 1985): 41–61; and López Obrador, "Sociedad y política," *Revista de la Universidad* 13–14 (September–December 1986): 58–62.

4. Quoted in Guadalupe Loaeza, "Andrés Manuel," *Reforma,* November 18, 1999, http://www.reforma.com.mx/.

5. Ovalle Fernández, interview, January 10, 2005.

6. Clara Jusidman de Bialostozky, interview by author, July 6, 2005, Mexico City.

7. Jusidman de Bialostozky, interview by author, October 8, 2004, Mexico City.

8. Jusidman de Bialostozky, interview, July 6, 2005.

9. INCO had good relations with the business community, whose products the institute evaluated. In addition, average citizens with consumer-related problems were used to contacting INCO, which broadcast its telephone number—5688722—as a jingle on the radio.

10. Jusidman de Bialostozky, interview, July 6, 2005.

11. Jusidman de Bialostozky, e-mail to author, August 11, 2005.

12. Alejandro Páez, "No hay ingenuidad, López conocía a Ponce: Cárdenas," *Crónica,* March 3, 2004, http://www.cronica.com.mx/.

13. Lourdes Galaz, interview by author, August 16, 2005.

14. Arturo Nuñez, interview by author, December 8, 2004, Mexico City.

15. Ruiz Abreu, interview.

16. Ibid.

17. López Obrador, *Tabasco, víctima del fraude electoral,* 22

18. Ovalle Fernández, interview, January 10, 2005.

19. Castro Castillo, interview, July 5, 2005.

20. Castro Castillo calls López Obrador's session with González Pedrero a "taboo" subject that no one will discuss; interview by author, October 22, 2005, Mexico City.

21. This aphorism is attributed to the late teacher-turned-politician-turned billionaire Carlos Hank González (1927–2001), who held public office continuously from 1955 to 1994. He was the only man to serve both as mayor of Mexico City and as governor of México State, and as head of three ministries.

22. This material draws upon Miguel Angel Centeno, *Democracy Within Reason: Technocratic Revolution in Mexico* (University Park: Pennsylvania State University

Press, 1994), 6–7; *La carpeta púrpura*, April 30, 1996, 5; and George W. Grayson, *Mexico: From Corporatism to Pluralism?* (Fort Worth: Harcourt Brace, 1988), 64–65.

23. López Obrador, *Tabasco, víctima del fraude electoral*, 23.

24. The signatories were Cárdenas, Martínez Hernández, Muñoz Ledo, César Buenrostro Hernández, Leonel Durán Solís, Vicente Fuentes Díaz, Armando Labra Manjarrez, Severo López Mestre, Janitzio Múgica Rodríguez, and Carlos Tello Macías.

25. Juan Gabriel Valencia Benavides, interview by author, December 3, 2005, Mexico City.

26. Partido Popular Socialista, "Es necesario y urgente poner otra vez en marcha a la Revolución Mexicana," *84the Pleno del Comité Central* (Mexico City: PPS, 1987), 15, 20; cited in Bruhn, *Taking on Goliath*, 109.

27. The Socialist Workers Party (PST), the Social Democratic Party (PSD), the Green Ecological Party of Mexico (PVEM), the Revolutionary Socialist Party (PSR), the Democratic Union of Progressive Forces (UDFP), the National Worker Peasant Council (CNOC), and the Ecologists Alliance (AE).

28. Bruhn, *Taking on Goliath*, 136; and Adriana Leticia Borjas Benavente, *Partido de la revolución democrática: Estructura, organización interna y desempeño público, 1989–2003* (Mexico City: Gernika, 2003), 188–97.

CHAPTER 4

1. Cuauhtémoc Cárdenas Solórzano, interview by author, October 11, 2004, Mexico City.

2. Bruhn, *Taking on Goliath*, 136.

3. Cárdenas Solórzano, interview.

4. Ibid.

5. Quoted in Cuauhtémoc Cárdenas Solórzano, *Nuestra lucha apenas comienza* (Mexico City: Editorial Nuestro Tiempo, 1988): 154, cited in Bruhn, *Taking on Goliath*, 156–57.

6. Rafael López Cruz, interview by author, August 10, 2004, Villahermosa. Among its activists in the state were Rafael López Julián, Maria Luisa Frias Almeda, and Lisandro Osorio Jiménez.

7. Peralta Burelo, interview, January 17, 2005.

8. Alberto Aguirre M., "La pugna secreta que cimbra al PRD," *Milenio Semanal*, August 2, 2000, 22. Another version has Tabascan painter Daniel Ponce Montuy and Rafael Aguilar Talamantes acting as intermediaries between Cárdenas and López Obrador.

9. Ramírez Garrido Abreu, interview, July 1, 2004.

10. Almazán, "Retratos desconocidos de Andrés Manuel," 31.

11. His major opponents were José Eduardo Beltrán Hernández, who was close to González Pedrero, and José Gamas Torruco, who had close links to President de la Madrid. Other aspirants were Víctor Manuel Barceló and Luis Priego Ortiz.

12. Rovirosa Wade, interview, August 18, 2005.

13. Benítez López, interview.

14. Rovirosa Wade, interview, August 18, 2005.

15. Rovirosa Wade, interview, March 7, 2005.

16. Ibid.

17. Ovalle Fernández, interview, August 18, 2005.

18. Benítez López, interview. Those assembled included Jesús Falcón Becerra, Francisco Rentería, Nicolás Herredia Damián, Manuel Ponce de Huit, Alberto Pérez Mendoza, Lorena del Carmen Hernández, Ramón Bolivar, Ernesto Benítez López, Andrés Madrígal Hernández, Miguel Luna Cabrera, and José Luis Solís Lope. Except for the last three men, all of the participants agreed to assist López Obrador.

19. Ibid.

20. The CNC's state organization was the League of Campesino Unions and Agrarian Communities of Tabasco (Liga de Comunidades Agrarias y Sindicatos Campesinos de Tabasco, LCASCT).

21. Quoted in López Obrador, *Tabasco, víctima del fraude electoral*, 28–29.

22. Héctor Hugo Oliveres, quoted in ibid., 30.

23. Alberto Jiménez Flores (legal adviser to Deputy González Ballina), interview by author, June 16, 2005, Villahermosa.

24. Ovalle Fernández, interviews, January 10 and August 18, 2005

25. Manuel Camacho Solís, interview by author, July 9, 2004, Mexico City

26. Juan S. Millán Lizárraga, interview by author, July 8, 2004, Mexico City. Hernández Galicia personally voted for Salinas. In fact, before depositing his ballot, he showed it to Senator Juan S. Millán Lizárraga, who was the PRI's delegate to the state. As he cast his vote, la Quina said, "I am voting for Salinas even though he doesn't deserve it."

27. Manuel Camacho Solís, *Yo Manuel: Memorias apócrifas? de un comisionado* (Mexico City: Rayuela, 1995), 25.

28. "El secretario del CEN del PRI se reunirá con dirigentes," *Presente*, August 7, 1988; and Miguel Pérez Morale, "Constitúido el movimiento democrática de la unidad revolucionara en Tabasco," *Presente*, August 8, 1988, 1, 13.

29. Quoted in López Obrador, *Tabasco, víctima del fraude electoral*, 30.

30. González Pedrero had become head of the Institute for Economic, Political, and Social Studies (Instituto para Estudios Políticos, Económicos y Sociales, IEPES); in addition, Salinas may have wanted the professor-turned-politician to attract intellectuals and leftists to the PRI campaign.

31. Camacho Solís, *Yo Manuel*, 25.

32. Rovirosa Wade, interview, August 18, 2005.

33. Camacho Solís, interview.

34. "Hoy se inicia la campaña de Andrés Manuel López Obrador," *Presente*, August 7, 1988, 1, 13.

35. Almazán, "Retratos desconocidos de Andrés Manuel," 31.

36. Jesús "Chuy" Falcón, quoted in ibid., 31.

37. Ibid.

38. López Obrador, *Tabasco, víctima del fraude electoral*, 35–45.

39. Muñoz Ledo, interview.

40. López Obrador, *Tabasco, víctima del fraude electoral*, passim.

41. Alvaro Delgado and Armando Guzmán, "Tabasco se une a Chiapas como laboratorio del autoritarismo," *Proceso*, January 2, 1995, http://www.proceso.com.mx/.

42. Jorge V. Alcocer, "Tabasco: Nadie sabe nada," ibid., November 21, 1988, especially 32, 34.

43. López Obrador, *Tabasco, víctima del fraude electoral*, 137–39.

44. Camacho Solís, interview.

45. López Obrador, *Tabasco, víctima del fraude electoral*, 149–50.

46. "Anulación en Tabasco, pide el FDN; impugnaciones a las de Nuevo León," *Proceso*, November 21, 1988, 29.

47. López Obrador, *Tabasco, víctima del fraude electoral*, 151.

48. Guillermo Andrade (former PFCRN member), interview by author, July 1, 2004, Mexico City.

49. Armando Padilla Herrera, interview by author, January 14, 2005, Villahermosa.

50. González Ballina, interview.

51. López Obrador, *Entre la historia y la esperanza*, 114.

52. José Ramiro López Obrador (mayor of Macupana), interview.

53. Samuel Dillon and Julia Preston, *Opening Mexico: The Making of a Democracy* (New York: Farrar, Straus and Giroux, 2004), 265.

54. López Obrador, *Entre la historia y la esperanza*, 112–13.

55. Ibid., 113–14.

56. Francisco Rojas Gutiérrez, interview by author, March 29, 2004, Mexico City.

57. Ibid.

58. Ibid.

59. Lajous Vargas, interview.

60. López Cruz, interview, June 15 and 16, 2005.

61. Almazán, "Retratos desconocidos de Andrés Manuel," 32.

62. Arturo Núñez, interview by author, January 16, 2004; Fernando Valenzuela Pernas, interview by author, February 16, 2004, Villahermosa. Fernando Valenzuela, the twenty-eight-year-old PRI candidate in 1991 and now a highly regarded university professor and legal adviser to the state legislature, is absolutely certain that he won the contest. After the initial results were annulled, he claims that a mixed government council (*consejo de gobierno*) was established to hold new elections within one hundred days; at the end of those hundred days, another council was created, with the result that no new balloting took place.

63. Georgina Trujillo Zentella (senator), interview by author, January 9, 2004, Mexico City.

64. López Cruz, interview, August 10, 2004.

65. Camacho Solís, interview.

66. Ibid.

67. López Cruz, interview, August 9, 2004.

68. Quoted in López Obrador, *Entre la historia y la esperanza*, 100.

69. Ibid., 101.

70. Benítez López, interview.

71. Alejandro Caballero et al., "El banquero, Hank y Bartlett, parte de los activos del gobernador de Tabasco," *Proceso*, September 4, 1995, http://www.proceso.com.mx/.

72. Izundegui Rullán, interview by author, August 11, 2004, Villahermosa. Jesús Madrazo Martínez de Escobar was Neme's choice; Carlos Pratts Pérez headed the opposition.

73. Mario Ibarra Lizárraga, "PRD 'lo peor del PRI,'" *Tabasco Hoy*, March 22, 2005, http://www.tabascohoy.com.mx/.

74. José de Carmen Chablé Ruiz, interview by author, June 14, 2005, Villahermosa.

75. López Obrador, *Entre la historia y la esperanza*, 104.

76. López Cruz, interview, August 10, 2004.

77. Quoted in López Obrador, *Entre la historia y la esperanza*, 129.

CHAPTER 5

1. Carlos Salomón Cámara, interview by author, August 18, 2005, Mexico City.

2. López Obrador, *Entre la historia y la esperanza*, 154.

3. Esteban Moctezuma Barragán, interview by author, July 8, 2004, Mexico City.

4. Roberto Madrazo, "Discurso de toma de protesta como candidato a diputado federal por el 1er. distrito electoral," news release, Villahermosa, Tabasco, May 11, 1991.

5. Priego Ortiz, interview.

6. López Obrador, *Entre la historia y la esperanza*, 159.

7. Ibid., 157–58. The organizations were the Comité de Derechos Humanos de Tabasco and the Academia Mexicana de Derechos Humanos, and the newspapers were *Presente, Tabasco Hoy, Novedades, El Sureste*, and *La Verdad del Sureste*.

8. Ibid., 160–61.

9. Juan Gabriel Valencia Benavides, interview by author, July 2, 2005, Mexico City.

10. Ibid.

11. Juan Gabriel Valencia Benavides, interview by author, May 10, 2005, Mexico City. Valencia said that the Government Ministry had enough background information on Tabasco's politicians to prosecute them if electoral fraud occurred.

12. Jiménez León, interview by author, March 10, 2005.

13. Valencia remembers hiding; Ovalle does not.

14. Valencia Benavides, interview, May 10, 2005.

15. Ibid.

16. Quoted in López Obrador, *Entre la historia y la esperanza,* 174–75.

17. Delgado and Guzmán, "Tabasco se une a Chiapas."

18. Alvaro Delgado and Armando Guzmán, "Sin Zedillo, fueron soldados y poilcías invitados de honor en la toma de posesión de Madrazo," *Proceso,* January 2, 1995, 34.

19. Quoted in ibid.

20. Valencia Benavides, interview, May 10, 2005.

21. Alvaro Delgado and Armando Guzmán, "Los tres poderes de Tabasco ambulantes: No han podido entrar en sus edificios," *Proceso,* September 1, 1995, http://www.proceso.com.mx/.

22. Quoted in ibid.

23. Ibid.

24. Alvaro Delgado and Armando Guzmán, "En Tabasco, el 12 de febrero termina la tregua," *Proceso,* February 6, 1995, http://www.proceso.com.mx/. The businessman was Fernando Alvarez Larios, head of the Businessmen's Coordinating Council.

25. Ibid. Deputies Félix Eladio Sarracino, Raúl Lezama Moo, and Carlos Manuel Rovirosa were named.

26. Quoted in Delgado and Guzmán, "Tabasco se une a Chiapas."

27. Liébano Sáenz Ortiz, interview by author, May 12, 2005, Mexico City. Sáenz pointed out that foreign correspondents were eager for news that would allow them to cover the relatively peaceful situation in Mexico rather than the dangerous war in the Balkans.

28. Ibid.

29. During his term, Salinas had attended the inaugurations of governors of all parties.

30. Sáenz Ortiz, interview.

31. Gurría Ordoñez, interview.

32. Valencia Benavides, interview, July 2, 2005.

33. Valencia Benavides, interview, May 10, 2005.

34. Ibid.

35. Valencia Benavides, interview, July 2, 2005.

36. Moctezuma Barragán, interview.

37. Buendía Tirado, interview.

38. He claimed to hold a Ph.D. from Harvard when he had not earned even an undergraduate degree.

39. Moctezuma Barragán, interview.

40. Sáenz Ortiz, interview.

41. Buendía Tirado, interview.

42. Moctezuma Barragán, interview.

43. "Mexican Financial Crisis Persists," *Facts on File,* January 19, 1995, 28.

44. Jiménez León, interview.

45. Ricardo Martínez Estrada, a union member, said that he required the consent of CTM secretary-general Fidel Velázquez; the two others—Pedro Jiménez Reséndiz and Heberto Taracena Ruiz—feared that they could lose their jobs as notaries if they ran afoul of the national government.

46. Jiménez León, interview.

47. Ibid.

48. Ibid.

49. "En el 95 Madrazo negoció la gubernatura," *Mesa 42,* January 30, 2004, 1, 8–10; Reséndez Medina, interview; and Pedro Jiménez León, interview by author, May 9, 2005, Mexico City.

50. Jiménez León, interview, March 10, 2005.

51. Ibid.

52. Alvaro Delgado and Armando Guzmán, "Vaivenes del gobierno federal: Por las presiones del PRD Madrazo iba a salir; por la rebeldía de priístas, se quedó," *Proceso,* January 23, 1995, 22–23; and Daniel Reyes Dionisio, "Paro generalizado de taxistas," *Presente,* January 19, 1995, 2A.

53. Priego Ortiz, interview.

54. Buendía Tirado, interview.

55. Ramiro López, "Empresarios toman medios electrónicos," *Presente,* January 19, 1995, 2A.

56. J. Joaquín Pérez Morales, "Sondeo político," ibid.

57. Jiménez León, interview, March 10, 2005.

58. Ibid.

59. María de los Angeles Moreno, interview by author, October 12, 2004, Mexico City. For her part, party president María de los Angeles emphasized that she consistently fought the initiative to remove her party's governor. Upon hearing Muñoz Ledo's braggadocio on January 17, she immediately contacted Hank González, who in turn urged Madrazo to hold his ground against Zedillo and Moctezuma.

60. Jiménez León, interview, March 10, 2005.

61. Ibid.

62. Samuel Dillon and Julia Preston, "Open Vote Policy Puts Mexico Leader in Quandary," *New York Times,* April 2, 1999, http://www.nytimes.com/.

63. Jiménez León, interview, May 9, 2005.

64. Jiménez León, interview, March 10, 2005.

65. Gurría Ordoñez, interview.

66. Jiménez León, interview, March 10, 2005. This was a reference to the January 15, 1995, meeting that Muñoz Ledo had arranged between Government Secretary Moctezuma Barragán and Subcomandante Marcos, head of the Zapatista Army of National Liberation.

67. Quoted in Jorge Carrasco Araizaga, "Roberto Madrazo: Las familias y el poder," in Zepeda Patterson et al., *Los suspirantes,* 68–69.

68. Valencia Benavides, interview, May 10, 2005; and Reséndez Medina, interview.

69. Valencia Benavides, interview, May 10, 2005.

70. Ibid.

71. Jiménez León, interview, March 10, 2005.

72. Quoted in "Apoyo político a Madrazo," *Presente,* January 19, 1995, 1A.

73. Jiménez León, interview, March 10, 2005.

74. Delgado and Guzmán, "Vaivenes del gobierno federal," 25.

75. Quoted in Juan Ochoa Vidal and Melesia del Carmen Rodríguez, "Que el pueblo decida," *Presente,* January 24, 1995, 1A.

76. Ovalle Fernández, interview, August 18, 2005.

77. Juan S. Millán Lizárraga, interview, July 8, 2004.

78. Sáenz Ortiz, interview. A key Zedillo official argues that the get-together of top state officials in Campeche turned into a fiasco when none of the governors from U.S. Gulf Coast states showed up. Thus Zedillo wanted to salvage something from his presence in the southeast. Salomón Cámara, interview.

79. Quoted in Ricardo Alemán, "A qué va Zedillo a Tabasco," *La Jornada,* June 1996, http://www.jornada.unam.mx/.

80. Quoted in ibid.

81. Jiménez León, interview, March 10, 2005.

82. Leslie Crawfort and Daniel Dombey, "Isolated Zedillo Trades Policy for Friends," *Financial Times,* July 11, 1996, http://news.ft.com/home/us.

83. The peso-dollar exchange rate for 1995 (6.419) is that published by the U.S. International Trade Administration, http://www.ita.doc.gov. In 1994 Mexico devalued its currency, so that one new peso equals one thousand old pesos.

84. Caballero et al., "El banquero, Hank y Bartlett."

85. As a deputy, Prats had backed a controversial reform proposed by Zedillo, who was education secretary at the time.

86. Sáenz Ortiz, interview.

87. Ibid.

88. Leonardo Curzio Gutiérrez, *Gobernabilidad, democracia y videopolítica en Tabasco, 1994–1999* (Mexico City: Plaza y Valdés Editores, 2000), 148–49.

89. Quoted in López Obrador, *Entre la historia y la esperanza,* 207.

90. Ibid., 207–8.

91. López Cruz, interview, August 9, 2004.

92. Curzio Gutiérrez, *Gobernabilidad, democracia y videopolítica,* 175.

93. López Obrador, *Entre la historia y la esperanza,* 231.

94. Oppenheimer, *Bordering on Chaos,* 83–84.

95. Ibid., 87.

96. Emilio Azcárraga quoted in Salvador Corro, "De los gobiernos priístas, Emilio Azcárraga ha recibido todos los favores y, como priísta confeso, sabe ser agradecido," *Proceso,* July 4, 1994, 6.

97. "El edén tabasqueño," *Voz y voto,* July 1, 1995.

98. López Obrador, *Fobaproa: Expediente abierto* (Mexico City: Grijalbo, 1999), 13. For a list of prominent people whose names appeared in these files, see Ciro Pérez Silva and René Alberto López, "Doce miembros del gobierno de Madrazo, en la lista de dispendio," *La Jornada,* June 22, 1995.

99. Jorge Carrasco Araizaga, "Madrazo: Herencia de poderosos," *Reforma,* November 5, 1999, http://www.reforma.com/. The other was Oscar Sáenz Jurado, the party's former finance secretary, who later became the state's director-general of administration.

100. López Cruz, interview, June 16, 2005.

101. López Cruz, interview, June 15, 2005.

102. Ibid.

103. López Cruz, interview, August 9, 2004.

104. Ibid.

105. Quoted in Carlos Marí, "Revelan origin de pruebas contra Roberto Madrazo," *Reforma,* November 19, 1995, http://www.reforma.com.mx/.

106. López Cruz, interview, June 15, 2005.

107. Luis Rubio, comments to Inter-American Dialogue, November 9, 2005, Washington, D.C.

108. Antonio Lozano Gracia, interview by author, March 25, 2004, Mexico City.

109. "Tabasco Governor's Lawsuit Against Federal Government Becomes Latest Controversy for Governing Party," *SourceMex–Economic News and Analysis on Mexico,* August 30, 1995.

110. Lozano Gracia, interview.

111. Quoted in López Obrador, *Entre la historia y la esperanza,* 226–27.

112. "Tabasco Governor's Lawsuit."

113. Juan Veledíaz, "Denuncio Madrazo secuestro," *Reforma,* August 19, 1995, http://www.reforma.com/. Madrazo insisted that he did not use guards and that his chauffeur had a medical appointment.

114. Lozano Gracia, interview.

115. Ibid.

116. Quoted in López Obrador, *Fobaproa,* 22.

117. Lozano Gracia, interview.

CHAPTER 6

1. Bruhn, *Taking on Goliath,* 13.

2. Cárdenas Solórzano, interview.

3. Quoted in Óscar Hinojosa, "Está muy sólido: Cuahtémoc se debilita; Heberto; seguirá Muñoz Ledo," *Proceso,* February 27, 1989, 22.

4. The twelve groups that constituted the PRD were the Corriente Democrática, Asamblea de Barrios, Asociación Cívica Nacional Revolucionaria, Consejo Nacional Cardenista, Convergencia Democrática, Consejo Nacional Obrero y Campesino de México, Grupo Poliforum, Movimiento al Socialismo, Organización Revolucionaria Punto Crítico, OIR-Línea de Masas, Partido Verde, and Partido Liberal.

5. Borjas Benavente, *Partido de la revolución democrática,* 199; Cárdenas Solórzano, interview. Of the 216,000 participants in the September 6, 1987, poll, 55 percent backed Castillo. Although he was invited to take part in the primary, Cárdenas demurred.

6. Borjas Benavente, *Partido de la revolución democrática*, 296.

7. Guillermo Flores Velasco, interview by author, March 26, 2004, Mexico City.

8. Former PMS member now active in the PRD who asked to remain anonymous, interview by author, March 30, 2004, Mexico City.

9. These men broke with the PRT when its leader, Eduardo Sánchez, refused to back Cárdenas in 1988.

10. Quoted in Daniela Pastrana, "Cuauhtémoc Cárdenas: El ancla y el buen cierre," *La Jornada: Masiosare*, July 2, 2000, cited in Kathleen Bruhn, "The Making of the Mexican President, 2000: Parties, Candidates, and Campaign Strategy," in *Mexico's Pivotal Democratic Election*, ed. Jorge I. Domínguez and Chappell Lawson (Stanford: Stanford University Press, 2004), 156n38.

11. Alvaro Delgado and Maria Scherer, "La disputa entre Cárdenas y Muñoz Ledo llego al límite," *Proceso*, April 18, 1999, http://www.proceso.com.mx/. The Cárdenas-Salinas meeting was revealed in Jorge G. Castañeda, *La herencia* (Mexico City: Aguilar, Altea, Taurus, Alfaguara, 1999), 274.

12. Muñoz Ledo coined this term.

13. José Antonio Crespo, "The Party System and Democratic Governance in Mexico," *Policy Papers on the Americas* 15 (March 2004): 7.

14. Ramón Aguirre Velázquez, interview by author, June 17, 1996, Mexico City. So certain was the PRI nominee, former Mexico City mayor Ramón Aguirre Velázquez, that he had won, that he offered to have a "public count of the votes in the main square of León."

15. Quoted in Elías Chávez, "En San Luis destapan a Camacho y Colosio como aspirantes a la grande ya en combate," *Proceso*, August 13, 1990, 14–16.

16. Flores Velasco, interview.

17. This name derived from their current within the PCM, known as the Movimiento de Acción Popular (MAP).

18. Cuauhtémoc Sandoval Ramírez, e-mail to author, July 31, 2005. Among the *mapaches* who remained in the PRD were political historian Arnaldo Córdova, physicist and union leader Antonio Gershenson, and César Chávez Castillo, a public accountant who won election to the Chamber of Deputies in 2003.

19. Guillermo Flores Velasco, interview by author, January 9, 2004.

20. Quoted in Zepeda Patterson et al., *Los suspirantes*, 138.

21. When Cárdenas ran unopposed for the PRD presidency in 1989, tradition dictated that he should not vote for himself. However, he cast his vote not for long-time CD ally Muñoz Ledo but for his young protégé, López Obrador.

22. This coalition was composed of former members of the CD, the Mexican Communist Party (Partido Comunista Mexicano, PCM), the Unified Socialist Party of Mexico (Partido Socialista Unificado de México, PSUM), the Socialist Workers' Party (Partido Socialista de los Trabajadores, PST), and Punto Crítico.

23. Quoted in Pascal Beltrán del Rio, "Asegura Muñoz Ledo que el PAN busca impeder su liderazgo a la postulatión de Cuauhtémoc," *Proceso*, March 13, 1993, 30–31.

24. Quoted in Borjas Benavente, *Partido de la revolución democrática*, 548.

25. Ibid., 539. This constitutional provision stipulated that a party had to win only 42 percent of the directly elected seats to obtain a majority in the Chamber of Deputies.

26. Quoted in Dillon and Preston, *Opening Mexico*, 274.

27. His followers called themselves the Democratic Change Current (Corriente Cambio Democrática, CCD).

28. Aguirre M., "La pugna secreta," 22.

29. Miguel Angel Granados Chapa, "Plaza Pública/Tres por el PRD," *Reforma*, July 14, 1996, http://www.reforma.com/.

30. Quoted in Sergio Sarmiento, "Jaque Mate/López Obrador," ibid., July 16, 1996.

31. José Luis Sánchez, "Confirman triunfo de López Obrador," ibid., July 20, 1996; and Gerardo Mejía, "Define López Obrador composición del CEN," ibid., July 25, 1996.

32. The figures appeared in José Antonio Crespo, "PRD: ¿El retorno de los duros?" ibid., July 22, 1996.

33. Guadalupe Báez, "En paquete, los perredistas aceptarón la propuesta de López Obrador para el CEN," *Crónica*, August 3, 1996, http://www.cronica.com.mx/.

34. The quotations in this paragraph appeared in Patricia Sotelo and Miguel Pérez, "'Intenta el PRD nueva relación con gobierno," *Reforma*, August 24, 1996, http://www.reforma.com/.

35. Emilio Chuayffet Chémor, interview by author, March 30, 2004, Mexico City.

36. Ibid.

37. This is a rough guess, for the PRD insisted that many people who died of accidents or natural causes between 1988 and 1994 were casualties of Salinas's ruthlessness.

38. Quoted in María de la Luz González, "'Busca PRD perfeccionar procedimientos internos," *Reforma*, September 8, 1996, http://www.reforma.com/.

39. López Cruz, interview, June 15, 2005.

40. PRD Deputy Horacio Duarte Olivares, interview by author, March 8, 2005, Mexico City.

41. Quoted in "El PRD, 34 alcaldías mexiquenses, 10 hidalguenses y una en Coahuila," *La Jornada*, November 11, 1996, http://www.jornada.unam.mx/.

42. Leonel Cota Montaño, interview by author, March 7, 2005, Mexico City.

43. Octavio Romero Oropeza, quoted in René Alberto López, "En general, balance 'favorable' en la Cámara de Diputados, considera López Obrador," *La Jornada*, December 18, 1997, http://www.jornada.unam.mx/.

44. Armando Padilla Herrera, interview by author, January 15, 2005; López Cruz, interview, June 16, 2005.

45. "Comicios QR," *Servicio Universal de Noticias*, Feburary 23, 1999, http://www.sunagencia.com.mx/.

46. Hugo Pacheco León, "El CEN del PRD impugna hoy los resultados electorales en Guerrero," *La Jornada*, February 16, 1999, http://www.jornada.unam.mx/.

47. I am indebted to political consultant Vanessa Ramírez Inches for her valuable input on this section.

48. Jack Willoughby and Lucy Conger, "Under the Volcano," *Institutional Investor* 32 (June 1998): 62–76, http://www.institutionalinvestor.com/default.asp/.

49. Quoted in ibid.

50. "'Casablanca' Shocks Mexico," *News* (Mexico City), May 24, 1998, http://www.thenewsmexico.com/.

51. The source of this anecdote would only agree to an interview off the record.

52. Francisco Gil Villegas M., "El 'tiovivo' de López Obrador," *El Economista*, September 2, 1998, http://www.economista.com.mx/.

53. López Obrador, *Fobaproa*, 32.

54. Ibid., 59.

55. Dillon and Preston, *Opening Mexico*, 367.

56. The PAN did try to have Guillermo Ortiz Martínez removed as head of the central bank, but the best it could do was bar him from sitting on the board of the new banking oversight agency.

57. Alejandra Bordon, "Sugiere AMLO hablar con Fox de economía," *Reforma*, September 7, 2004, http://www.reforma.com/.

58. For this point, I am indebted to Rogelio Ramírez de la O, interview by author, May 8, 2005, Mexico City.

59. A succinct rendition of such sentiment appears in Joseph E. Stiglitz, "Globalizing Globalization's Goods and Expectations," speech before the Economic Club of Washington, D.C., March 13, 2003, http://www.economicclub.org/.

60. López Obrador, *Fobaproa*, 54.

61. Georgina Saldierna, "Hoy será puesto a prueba al nuevo reglamento de elecciones del PRD," *La Jornada*, March 14, 1999, http://www.jornada.unam.mx/. The other candidates were former student leader Raúl Alvarez Garín, actor Carlos Bracho González, and political unknowns Irineo Pablo Reyes, José de Jesús Reyes Angeles, and Felipe Flores Zamora.

62. Quoted in Georgina Saldierna, "Si hay elementos, se anulará la elección nacional en el PRD," ibid., March 24, 1999.

63. Quoted in Aguirre M., "La pugna secreta," 23.

CHAPTER 7

1. Before the Cofipe political reform, Mexico's administrative officer was a "regent," appointed by the president in whose cabinet he served.

2. Diane E. Davis, *Urban Leviathan: Mexico City in the Twentieth Century* (Philadelphia: Temple University Press, 1994), 186–87.

3. Michael C. Meyer and William H. Beezley, *The Oxford History of Mexico* (New York: Oxford University Press, 2000), 601–3.

4. The government infiltrated and eliminated the league in 1973.

5. *Sexto Informe de Gobierno*, September 1, 1982, http://lanic.utexas.edu/larrp/pm/sample2/mexican/portillo/history/820211.

6. Davis, *Urban Leviathan*, 278–81.

7. Soledad Loeza, "Las clases medias mexicanas y la coyuntura económica actual," in *México ante la crisis: El impacto social y cultural de las alternativas*, ed. Pablo González Casanova (Mexico City: Siglo Veintiuno Editores, 1986), 233–34.

8. CBS newsman George Natason, quoted in Patrick May, "'Mighty Blow from Hell' Shatters Mexico," *Toronto Star*, September 20, 1985, http://www.thestar.com/.

9. Quoted in "Housing Minister Finally Resigns," *Latin America Weekly Report* (February 28, 1986), http://www.latinnews.com/.

10. Jonathan Kandel, *La Capital: The Biography of Mexico City* (New York: Random House, 1988), 571.

11. Ibid., 570.

12. Manuel Aguilera Gómez, "Un comentario," e-mail to author, June 30, 2004.

13. Grayson, *Mexico: From Corporatism to Pluralism?* 64–65.

14. David Gardner, "Mexico Minister Sacked over Earthquake," *Financial Times*, February 21, 1986, http://www.ft.com/.

15. Kandel, *La Capital*, 569.

16. Gardner, "Minister Sacked over Earthquake"; J. Ross, "Mexico Barbaro #280," September 29, 2001, http://www.eco.utexas.edu/~archive/chiapas95/2001.09/msa00561/.

17. Lionel Barber, "World Ready to Help If Mexico Makes Request," *Washington Post*, September 21, 1985, http://www.washingtonpost.com/; Mexican Ambassador Jorge Espinosa de los Reyes, who met with Secretary of State George P. Shultz, confined his request for a demolition team, experts to search for persons under collapsed structures, and other technical assistance.

18. Camacho Solís, interview, July 9, 2004.

19. George Wright, *Mexico City, Heart of the Eagle: Democracy or Inequality* (Ottawa: RCW Publishing, 2004), 167–68.

20. Manuel Camacho Solís, interview by author, October 19, 2005, Mexico City.

21. Camacho Solís, interview, July 9, 2004.

22. William Stockton, "Long Wait Ending for Mexico Quake Victims," *New York Times*, August 3, 1986, http://www.nytimes.com/.

23. Camacho Solís, interview, July 9, 2004.

24. Guillermo Flores Velasco, interview by author, July 9, 2004, Mexico City.

25. Quoted in Bertha Teresa Ramírez, "René y Dolores nos olvidaron: Vecinos de la unidad Nueva Tenochtitlán," *La Jornada*, April 28, 2004, http://www.jornada.unam.mx/.

26. Wright, *Mexico City*, 168.

27. Manuel Aguilera Gómez, interview by author, March 24, 2004, Mexico City.

28. Ibid.

29. Camacho Solís, interview, October 19, 2005.

30. Camacho Solís, *Yo Manuel*, 48.

31. Carlos Salinas de Gortari, *Producción y participación: Política en el campo* (Mexico City: Fondo de Cultura Económica, 1987).

32. Jaime Marques-Pereira, "PRONASOL: Mexico's Bid to Fight Poverty," *UNESCO Courier,* March 1995, 25.

33. Bruhn, *Taking on Goliath,* 266.

34. Camacho recalls that José Francisco Ruiz Massieu, former Guerrero governor and Salinas's extremely powerful brother-in-law, approached him, indicating that he would support him over Colosio if Camacho would agree not to prosecute Raúl Salinas and promised to reform the Constitution to permit re-election. Camacho refused both requests. Manuel Camacho Solís, interview by author, July 12, 2004.

35. Ibid.

36. Bruhn, *Taking on Goliath,* 281.

37. Jorge Octavio Ochoa, "Manuel Camacho, hombre de alianzas 'estratégicas,'" *El Universal,* July 23, 2006, http://www.eluniversal.com.mx/.

38. Ibid. The immensely wealthy Martínez Rocillo also had close ties to the Cuban government.

39. Tim Golden, "Rejected Mexican Makes a Comeback," *New York Times,* February 6, 1994, http://www.nytimes.com/.

40. Roberto Campa Cifrián, interview by author, March 29, 2004, Mexico City.

41. Camacho Solís, interview, October 19, 2005; the friend was Enrique Cabot.

42. Campa Cifrián, interview.

43. Ibid.

44. Flores Velasco, interview, March 26, 2004. When Zedillo was secretary of education in the early 1990s, he proposed an education reform, which *inter alia* would have increased slightly the absurdly low tuition at public universities. Cárdenas railed against this legislation. Reportedly, he was angry when then-deputy Bejarano voted for the bill in the education committee of the Chamber of Deputies.

45. Quoted in Zepeda Patterson et al., *Los suspirantes,* 139.

46. Quoted in ibid., 140.

47. Quoted in Niko Price, "Mexico City's First Opposition Mayor Wastes No Time in Overhaul," Associated Press, December 6, 1997, http://ww.ap.org/.

48. Dillon and Preston, *Opening Mexico,* 371–74.

49. Peter M. Ward and Elizabeth Durden, "Government and Democracy in Mexico's Federal District, 1997–2001: Cárdenas, the PRD, and the Curate's Egg," *Bulletin of Latin American Research* 21, no. 1 (2002): 1–39.

50. Quoted in Al Giordano, "The Narco-Media: Drug Corruption in the Press from Mexico to the U.S.," *Media Channel,* May 17, 2000, http://www.mediachannel.org/.

CHAPTER 8

1. Aguirre M., "La pugna secreta," 23–24.

2. Carlos Ramírez, "Indicador Político," *El Universal,* April 24, 2000, http://www.eluniversal.com.mx/.

3. González Ballina, interview.

4. Quoted in Roberto Morales, "Se perfila López Obrador como candidato a Jefe de Gobierno," *El Economista,* July 22, 1999, http://www.economista.com.mx/.

5. Tribunal Electoral del Poder Judicial de la Federación, "Constitución Política de los Estados Unidos Mexicanos," http://www.trife.gob.mx/. A city-born candidate has a three-year residency requirement.

6. "López Obrador Wins in Landslide, but Still Candidacy Is Questioned," *Mexican Weekly Report,* November 22, 1999.

7. Quoted in Sam Dillon, "López Obrador May Be Shaken Out of Mayoral Race," *New York Times,* April 21, 2000, http://www.nytimes.com/.

8. Quoted in Arturo Paramo, "Anucia estrategia López Obrador," *Reforma,* December 17, 1999, http://www.reforma.com.mx/.

9. Gabriela Romer Sánchez, "Descarta AMLO una operación cicatriz," *La Jornada,* November 15, 1999, http://www.jornada.unam.mx/.

10. "Apathy Rules," *Latin America Regional Reports: Mexico and* NAFTA *Report*, March 21, 2000, http://www.latinnews.com/.

11. This alliance included the PRD, the PCD, the Workers Party (Partido del Trabajo, PT), the Nationalist Society Party (Partido de la Sociedad Nacionalista, PSN), the Social Alliance Party (Partido Alianza Social, PAS), and the Convergence for Democracy (Convergencia por la Democracia, CD).

12. Results reported in Dillon, "López Obrador May Be Shaken Out of Race."

13. López Obrador denounced the document as a forgery.

14. Jesús Silva Herzog, interview by author, November 15, 2003, Washington, D.C.

15. Juan Gabriel Valdés, interview by author, December 3, 2005, Mexico City.

16. Ricardo Alemán, "Itinerario político," *El Universal*, April 11, 2000, http://www.eluniversal.com.mx/. On March 28, 2000, López Obrador submitted a notarized document in which three neighbors swore that he had lived for fourteen years at Copilco No. 300, building 16, apartment 1, and that during the last five years his residency had been uninterrupted.

17. Quoted in Dillon, "López Obrador May Be Shaken Out of Race."

18. Alvaro Delgado, "'La mafia me quiere descontar, pero no me doblegará': López Obrador," *Proceso*, April 16, 2000, http://www.proceso.com.mx/.

19. Raúl Llanos Samaniego, "López Obrador se da por satisfecho con los resultados de la consulta ciudadana," *La Jornada*, May 16, 2000, http://www.jornada.unam.mx/. These figures are based on the results from 85 percent of the 5,894 voting places.

20. Alejandra Bordón, "Van 400 mil a consulta perredista," *Reforma*, May 15, 2000, http://www.reforma.com.mx/.

21. "PRI Reacts to Ruling," *News* (Mexico City), May 23, 2000, 2.

22. Silva Herzog, interview.

23. Aguilera Gómez, interview.

24. Juan Manuel Venegas, "Impugnación a López Obrador aviva la polémica entre panistas," *La Jornada*, May 17, 2000, http://www.jornada.unam.mx/.

25. Jesús Reyes Heroles, interview by author, February 27, 2004, Washington, D.C.

26. Commentator Jorge Fernández Menéndez indicated that Zedillo preferred Gurría. This seems improbable because the president needed Gurría, his third finance secretary, to help prepare the country for the transition to the next chief executive. Gurría's leaving his post would have sent negative signals to the international financial community that Zedillo had worked so hard to cultivate (for this point, I am indebted to Jesús Reyes Heroles, interview).

27. Aguilera Gómez, interview.

28. Rojas Gutiérrez, interview.

29. Valencia Benavides, interview, December 3, 2005.

30. Quoted in "Economist Rosario Robles Berlanga Becomes First Woman to Govern Mexico City," *SourceMex–Economic News and Analysis on Mexico*, October 6, 1999.

31. Campa Cifrián, interview, March 29, 2004.

32. George W. Grayson, "A Guide to the 2000 Mexican Presidential Election," *Western Hemisphere Election Study Series* 18 (June 2000): 87.

33. Quoted in Ricardo Olayo and Gabriela Romero Sánchez, "Gana Silva la contienda interna," *La Jornada*, November 8, 1999, http://www.jornada.unam.mx/.

34. Rojas Gutiérrez, interview. As director of credit in the Finance Ministry under President López Portillo, the acerbic Levín Coppel frequently clashed with his boss, Undersecretary Silva Herzog; he often circumvented Silva Herzog to take matters directly to Finance Secretary David Ibarra Muñoz.

35. Aída Ramírez and Sergio Castañeda, "Precisan Silva Herzog y López Obrador sus plataformas en la Ibero," *El Economista*, April 7, 2000, http://www.eleconomist.com.mx/

36. Julia Preston, "Mexico City Journal: Tough, Cheerful Mayor Wins Hearts," *New York Times*, February 28, 2000, A4.

37. Alducín y Asociados conducted interviews that were stratified by delegación; see "Ganó López Obrador el debate, según encuesta," *El Universal,* June 1, 2000, 4.

38. "Santiago Creel, candidato del PAN a la jefatura de gobierno del D.F.," *La Jornada,* November 28, 1999, http://www.jornada.unam.mx/.

39. Quoted in Alejandra Bordón et al., "Fox, crucial para Creel," *Reforma,* May 29, 2000, 6B.

40. Reuters, "Female Politician Faces New Charges," *San Diego Union-Tribune,* June 16, 2001, A11.

41. Ramírez and Castañeda, "Precisan Silva Herzog y López Obrador."

42. Liliana Alcántara, "Construiré 20 mil viviendas en el primer año: AMLO," *El Universal,* April 10, 2000, B10.

43. Alejandra Bordón, "Estudia gabinete Andrés Manuel," *Reforma,* May 26, 2000, 5B. The Robles cabinet members who, el Peje hinted, would keep their jobs in his administration were city attorney general Samuel del Villar, and public works secretary César Buenrostro Hernández.

44. Quoted in Aguirre M., "La pugna secreta," 21.

45. Ibid.

46. Ibid., 21–22.

CHAPTER 9

1. Quoted in Fernando del Collado, "La 'mañanera' de Andrés Manuel," *Reforma,* February 29, 2004, http://www.reforma.com.mx/.

2. Ibid.; and Manuel Durán, "Érase una vez la 'mañanera,'" ibid., April 10, 2005. Including the sessions presided over by Alejandro Encinas, who served as mayor when López Obrador stepped down, the number of mañaneras totals 1,693. See Javier Rodríguez, "Con pendientes se despide la mañanera," *Excelsior,* December 4, 2006, 2.

3. I attended this press conference, which took place on August 17, 2003.

4. I attended this press conference, which took place on January 17, 2004.

5. Kevin Sullivan, "The Man Who Might Lead Mexico; All Eyes on Populist Mayor for 2006 Presidential Election," *Washington Post,* June 25, 2003, http://www.washingtonpost.com/.

6. "Vislumbra AMLO un desastre educativo," *Reforma,* September 12, 2003, http://www.reforma.com.mx/.

7. Durán, "Érase una vez la 'mañanera.'"

8. Del Collado, "La 'mañanera' de Andrés Manuel."

9. Quoted in Manuel Durán, "Retoma Mandatario críticas a la prensa," *Reforma,* January 26, 2004, http://www.reforma.com.mx/.

10. Manuel Durán, "Cambia AMLO predios por concreto," ibid., February 18, 2004.

11. Associated Press, "Mexico City Prosecutor Reveals Corruption Probe," March 1, 2004, http://www.ap.org/.

12. César Yáñez Centeno Cabrera, interview by author, March 26, 2004, Mexico City.

13. Quoted in Lisa Adams, "Latest Mexican Scandal: Legislator Shown Receiving Wads of Cash on Videotape," Associated Press, March 3, 2004, http://www.ap.org/.

14. Raúl Llanos and Gabriela Romero, "Pescan en actos de corrupción a Bejarano," *La Jornada,* March 4, 2004, http://www.jornada.unam.mx/.

15. Manuel Bravo de la Vega, e-mail to author, March 30, 2004.

16. Ibid.

17. Quoted in Francisco Robles Nava, "Se deslinda López Obrador de actos de corrupción," *La Opinión,* March 12, 2004, http://laopinion.com/.

18. César Yáñez Centeno Cabrera, interview by author, August 15, 2003, Mexico City.

19. José Alejandro Sánchez (*La Crónica*), interview by author, July 4, 2004, Mexico City.

20. Ibid.

21. Manuel Durán, "Entrega AMLO taxis a viejitos," *Reforma*, August 18, 2003, 4B.

22. Quoted in Notimex, "Entrega López 219 nuevos taxis a adultos mayores," *Crónica*, August 18, 2003, 20.

23. Pedro Aguilar, interview by author, March 29, 2004, Mexico City.

24. Quoted in Durán, "Érase una vez la 'mañanera.'"

25. Manuel Durán Aguirre (*Reforma*), interview by author, July 4, 2004, Mexico City.

26. Del Collado, "La mañanera" de Andrés Manuel."

27. Quoted in Durán, "Érase una vez la 'mañanera.'"

28. Wilkins quoted in del Collado, "La 'mañanera' de Andrés Manuel."

29. Ibid.; Durán Aguirre, interview; Sánchez, interview.

30. Francisco Cárdenas Cruz, "Pulso Político," *El Universal*, June 9, 2004, http://www.eluniversal.com.mx/.

31. Manuel Moreno Domínguez, interview by author, July 4, 2004, Mexico City.

32. This provision of article 6 of Decree 4 is quoted in del Collado, "La 'mañanera' de Andrés Manuel."

33. Ibid.

34. Alejandra Bordón, "Arranca Luege 'mañaneras,'" *Reforma*, January 7, 2003, B1.

35. Yáñez Centeno Cabrera, interview, August 15, 2003.

36. José Luis Luege Tamargo, interview by author, August 14, 2003, Mexico City.

37. Ibid. The reference to Juárez springs from a reported incident during his youth when he escaped injury from a strong wind by plastering himself to the bottom of a canoe.

38. Jesus Alberto Hernández, "Disputan por la 'mañanera,'" *Reforma*, May 1, 2004, http://www.reforma.com.mx/.

39. Quoted in "Critica Aguilar labor de medios," ibid., September 7, 2005.

40. Quoted in Mark Stevenson, "Mexico's First Fruits of Democracy: Debate on Daylight-Savings Time," Associated Press, January 25, 2001, http://www.ap.org/.

41. Quoted in ibid.

42. He was actually born on November 1, 1953.

43. Bertha Teresa Ramírez, "Llevan las mañanitas a López Obrador," *La Jornada*, November 14, 2003, http://www.jornada.unam.mx/.

44. Manuel Durán, "Festejan a López Obrador por su santo," *Reforma*, May 26, 2005, http://www.reforma.com.mx/.

45. See Rick Yount, "Jesus, the Master Teacher," http://www.ministryserver.com/bible/lectures.

CHAPTER 10

1. Quoted in Raúl Llanos and Gabriela Romero, "Estado de bienestar en el DF, a partir del 2001: López Obrador," *La Jornada*, December 6, 2000, http://www.jornada.unam.mx/2000/12/06/003n1cap.html.

2. Julie Watson, "Mexico City's Mayor Takes Office," Associated Press, December 5, 2000, http://ww.ap.org/.

3. The 2005 figures in this chapter were taken from the Dirección General de Comunicación Social, "Quinto informe del Gobierno de Alejandro Encinas Rodríguez, en la Asamblea Legislativa del Distrito Federal," http://www.comsoc.df.gob.mx/documentos/v_informeencinas.html/.

4. Dirección General de Comunicación Social, "Entrega AMLO 12 mil 560 tarjetas a adultos mayores de 70 años en el Distrito Federal," Bulletin 1140, November 9, 2003, http://www.comsoc.df.gob.mx/

5. Quoted in Alejandra Bordon, "Llama AMLO a defender derechos sociales," *Reforma*, September 4, 2004, http://www.reforma.com.mx/.

6. The material in this section is taken from Gobierno del Distrito Federal, "Apoyo para madres solteras," http://www.df.gob.mx/secretarias/social/programas/madres/html.

7. Quoted in Reed Lindsay, "Mayor Promises Liconsa Refund," *News* (Mexico City), June 13, 2001, http://www.thenewsmexico.com/.

8. Gobierno del Distrito Federal, "Programa de becas para personas con discapacidad," http://www.df.gob.mx/secretarias/social/programas/discapacidad.html/.

9. Quoted in Jason Lange, "New City University Opens," *News* (Mexico City), September 4, 2001, http://www.thenewsmexico.com/.

10. Of the twenty centers, five were in Iztapalapa, three each in Coyoacán and Miguel Hidalgo, two each in Azcapotzalco and Benito Juárez, and one each in Venustiano Carranza, Iztalco, Tlalpan, Alvaro Obregón. (These figures, from the GDF, account for only nineteen centers).

11. Kenya Ramírez and Mirtha Hernández, "Preparan operativa para dar los 'útiles,'" *Reforma*, August 17, 2004, http://www.reforma.com.mx/.

12. Quoted in Alejandra Bordón, "Niega AMLO tregua," ibid., January 13, 2001.

13. "Retirement Home to Open for Mexican Prostitutes," Deutsche Presse-Agentur, June 11, 2005, http://www.dpa.com/.

14. Humberto Padgett, "Acusan politización en plan de vivienda," *Reforma*, May 11, 2004, http://www.reforma.com.mx/.

15. Raymundo Sánchez, "De 313 casas que López Obrador entregó ayer, el 67 por ciento fueron para grupos afines al PRD," *La Crónica*, May 24, 2004, http://www.cronica.com.mx/.

16. Quoted in Humberto Padgett, "Asignan viviendas por apoyar al PRD," *Reforma*, May 14, 2004, http://www.reforma.com.mx/.

17. David Cervantes, "Réplica: Defiende Invi esquema de vivienda," ibid., May 14, 2004.

18. Mario Gutiérrez Vega, "Atrapados por las mafias," *Enfoque*, Sunday magazine supplement to ibid., August 7, 2005.

19. Arturo Páramo, "Absorbe PRD-DF a los ambulantes," ibid., May 22, 2005.

20. In addition to fixed dues, each *taxista* paid three thousand to five thousand pesos for false documents. See Illich Valdez, "Meten taxis piratas 'músculo' a plantón," ibid., August 20, 2006.

21. Manuel Durán, "Justifican el fracaso en combater *piratas*," ibid., August 31, 2005.

22. Illich Valdez, "Crecen al doble los taxis piratas con Garduño, ibid., September 3, 2006.

23. Quoted in Yáscara López, "Dan apoyo a Ebrard," ibid., September 23, 2005.

24. Valdez, "Meten taxis piratas 'músculo.'"

25. Jennifer Dorroh, "Voters Approve Double Decks but Turnout Too Low to Be Binding," *News* (Mexico City), September 24, 2002, http://www.thenewsmexico.com/.

26. Quoted in Jason Lange, "Referendum Highlights Mayor's Unflinching Popularity," ibid., December 10, 2002.

27. Humberto Padgett, "Mide AMLO popularidad desde el GDF," *Reforma*, October 10, 2005, http://www.reforma.com.mx/.

28. Jorge Arturo Hidalgo and Armando Talamantes, "Irrumpen maestros en comparecencia," ibid., December 12, 2000.

29. Marcela Turati, "Intentan maestros disidentes dar 'portazo' en Gobernación," ibid., May 18, 2001; and Fernando Mayolo López, "Despacha Creel desde penthouse," ibid., May 29, 2002.

CHAPTER 11

1. The executive was Carlos Franco Muñiz. See "Momentos para recorder el 2001," *Reforma*, December 9, 2001, http://www.reforma.com/.

2. Manuel Durán et al., "Llevan austeridad al límite," ibid., November 27, 2003.

3. "Anti-Nafta Campaigner Gets Key DF Job," *Latin America Regional Reports: Mexico and NAFTA Report*, December 12, 2000, http://www.latinnews.com/.

4. "Center of Belated Attention," *Economist*, September 14, 2002, http://www.economist.com/.

5. Quoted in Mark Stevenson, "Latin America's Richest Man Lowers Profile," Associated Press, August 1, 2004, http://www.ap.org/.

6. Quoted in Manuel Durán, "Niegan privatizar centro," *Reforma*, August 15, 2003, 3B.

7. Claudia Boyd-Barrett, "Ex-President's Sister Returns Squatted Parkland," *News* (Mexico City), December 13, 2002, http://www.thenewsmexico.com/.

8. La Comisión de Pastoral Social de la Conferencia del Episcopado Mexicano, quoted in Francisco Robles Nava, "López Obrador no quiere la fianza," *La Opinión*, April 22, 2005, http://laopinion.com/.

9. Quoted in Juan Manuel Venegas and Elia Baltazar, "Negociación, práctica obligada para avanzar: Fox a López Obrador," *La Jornada*, May 30, 2003, http://www.jornada.unam.mx/.

10. Martí Batres Guadarrama, interview by author, July 5, 2003, Mexico City.

11. Alejandra Martínez, "Diputados de PRD gastan 1.4m en festivales," *El Universal*, May 12, 2004, http://www.eluniversal.com.mx/.

12. Alejandro Gertz Manero, interview by author, October 22, 2005, Mexico City.

13. "Giuliani Comes Up with 146 Proposals for Mexico City," *Latin America Regional Reports: Mexico and NAFTA Report*, August 19, 2003, http://www.latinnews.com/.

14. Lilia Saúl, "Critica AMLO aumento de la burocracia en gobierno de Fox," *El Universal*, October 9, 2005, http://www.eluniversal.com.mx/.

15. Quoted in Alejandra Bordon, "Llama AMLO a abrir auditorías," *Reforma*, July 28, 2005, http://www.reforma.com/.

16. Tann vom Hove, "Edi Rama, Mayor of Tirana, Elected World Mayor 2004," *City Mayors*, http://www.worldmayor.com/worldmayor_2004/results_2004.html.

CHAPTER 12

1. Martí Batres Guadarrama, interview by author, January 13, 2004, Mexico City.

2. Yáñez Centeno Cabrera, interview, March 26, 2004.

3. This section is indebted to Alejandra Bordón, "Tiene López Obrador círculo tabasqueño," *Reforma*, January 24, 2004, http://www.reforma.com.mx/.

4. His parents named him after Cuban poet José Martí; they named his siblings Vienika (after Vietnam), Lenia (after Vladimir Lenin), and Valentina (after communist labor leader Valentín Campa).

5. Quoted in "Mayor Initiates Federal District Micro-Credit Program," *News* (Mexico City), March 19, 2001, http://www.thenewsmexico.com/.

6. Manuel Durán and Ricardo Zamora, "Cuidan 'Gacelas' a AMLO," *Reforma*, December 5, 2003, http://www.reforma.com.mx/.

7. "Aprueban presencia femenina," ibid., November 22, 2000. Six percent of those interviewed responded that the selection was "neither good nor bad," and 6 percent either did not answer or had no opinion; a clear majority (52 percent to 34 percent) believed that López Obrador named the women because of their competence rather than for the sake of political correctness.

8. Quoted in Angel Bolaños Sánchez, "Entrega López Obrador créditos a productores rurales de 5 delegaciones," *La Jornada*, June 10, 2004, http://www.jornada.unam.mx/.

9. Consulta Mitofsky, "Encuesta de Salida: 2 de Julio, elección presidencial," http://www.consulta.com.mx/interiores/11_elecciones/elec_ENCUSAL_presi.

10. Sosa Elízaga, interview, March 28, 2004.

11. María Cristina de la Cruz, "Obrador: Viudo 'cotizado,'" *Tabasco Hoy* ("El Pais" supplement), June 18, 2005, 8–9.

12. Born in 1937, Ortiz Pinchetti was a prosperous lawyer who had participated in Carlos Madrazo's efforts to democratize the PRI. In 2003 he won a seat in the Chamber of Deputies. He reportedly did not enjoy rising at the crack of dawn to attend cabinet meetings and was delighted to move into the legislative branch, which adhered to a more orthodox schedule.

13. Batres Guadarrama, interview, July 5, 2003.

14. Quoted in Manuel Durán, "Desafía AMLO a difundir más videos," *Reforma*, March 4, 2004, http://www.reforma.com.mx/.

CHAPTER 13

1. See Haley, *The Power Tactics of Jesus Christ*, 43–44.

2. Quoted in Francisco Cárdenas Cruz, "Pulso político," *El Universal*, March 4, 2004, http://www.eluniversal.com.mx/.

3. Quoted in "The Man Who Would Be President," *Economist*, November 15, 2003, http://www.economist.com/.

4. Quoted in John Ross, "Hometown Terror in the Americas," *Peace, Earth, and Justice News*, February 6, 2005, http://www.pej.org/.

5. Cited in Denise Dresser, "¿AMLO autodestructible?" *Reforma*, November 10, 2003, http://www.reforma.com/.

6. Quoted in Ricardo Alemán, "Itinerario político," *El Universal*, May 19, 2004, http://www.eluniversal.com.mx/.

7. Deputy Miguel Angel Toscano Velasco, electronic mail to author, July 13, 2004; Those perredista deputies aligned with López Obrador were Leticia Robles Colin, Dione Anguiano Flores, Adolfo López Villanueva, Alejandro Sánchez Camacho, Susana Guillermina Manzanares Córdoba, and Ricardo Chávez Contreras. Raúl Armando Quinero Martínez headed another faction composed of Edgar Torres Baltazar, Horacio Martínez Meza, Clara Marina Brugada Molina, Carlos Ortiz Chávez, Bernardino Ramos Iturbide, and Gilberto Ensastiga Santiago. Maria del Carmen Pacheco Gamiño began with Quintero but switched to López Obrador. There were also two deputies who acted independently: Ruth Zavaleta Salgado and Iris Edith Santacruz Fabila. Unknown were the positions of Emilio Serrano Jiménez, Marcos Morales Torres, and Ricardo Chávez Contreras.

8. José Luis Luege Tamargo, interview by author, January 15, 2004, Mexico City.

9. Deputy Miguel Angel Toscano Velasco, interview by author, July 7, 2004, Mexico City.

10. César Federico Döring, interview by author, January 15, 2004.

11. Quoted in *Business Mexico*, published by the American Chamber of Commerce in Mexico, April 2001 and May 2002, http://www.amcham.com.mx/ingles/publicaciones/business/.

12. Carolina Pavón and Alberto Acosta, "Rechaza DF aplicar sanciones por SUVA," *Reforma*, December 11, 2002, http://www.reforma.com.mx/.

13. César Federico Döring, interview by author, March 30, 2004.

14. Luege Tamargo, interview, January 15, 2004.

15. Quoted in Caroline Pavón, "Agasaja Asamblea a López Obrador," *Reforma*, January 5, 2004, http://www.reforma.com/.

16. Quoted in "Satisface ALDF a López Obrador," ibid., December 17, 2003.

17. Manuel Durán, "Cancelan el consejo anticorrupción," ibid., March 30, 2004.

18. Carolina Pavón, "Obligan al metro a dar datos," ibid., July 8, 2004, 3B.

19. *La Jornada*, "Contienda inerna causa desbandada de perredistas en el Distrito Federal," January 27, 2003, http://www.jornada.unam.mx/.

20. Carolina Pavón, "Preparan el IEDF sanction para PRD," *Reforma*, May 31, 2004, http://www.reforma.com/.

21. Quoted in Francisco Robles Nava, "Perredistas toman sede del Congreso mexicano," *La Opinión*, October 6, 2004, http://laopinion.com/.

22. Quoted in ibid.

CHAPTER 14

1. Quoted in Ivonne Melgar, "Fracasó política económica de Fox—AMLO," *Reforma*, September 17, 2005, http://www.reforma.com/.

2. In the 1960s and 1970s, the major Coca-Cola bottlers in Mexico were Miguel Barragán (Monterrey), Fernando, José, and Luis Ponce (Mérida and the Yucatán Peninsula/Grupo Peninsular), Fernando Madero Bracho (Sinaloa), Robert Dotson Castrejón (Acapulco/Grupo Yoli), Antonio Echevarría Domínguez (Nayarit), Garza de Lagüera (Mexico City), Roberto Ruiz Obregón (Querétaro), and Burton Grossman (Mexico City and Guadalajara).

3. Quoted in Tim Golden, "Miracle in Mexico: A Clean Election," *New York Times*, May 22, 1995, http://www.nytimes.com/.

4. Quoted in John Ross, "Fox, Inc. Takes over Mexico," *Multinational Monitor*, March 2001, http://multinationalmonitor.org/.

5. Quoted in Stevenson Jacob, "PANistas Reject Mexico City Mayor's Offer of Truce," *News* (Mexico City), June 22, 2001, http://www.thenewsmexico.com/.

6. Elliot Blair Smith, "Questions of Time Still Stir Debates in Mexico," *USA Today*, May 4, 2001, http://www.usatoday.com/.

7. "Encuesta/Pierde López Obrador impulso," *Reforma*, May 3, 2001, http://www.reforma.com/.

8. Will Weissert, "Dirty Scandal Leaves Mexico's New Government Washing Up with $400 Towels," Associated Press, June 21, 2001, http://www.ap.org/.

9. Quoted in Ella Grajeda, "Tregua, para amortiguar la crisis, propone AMLO a Fox," *El Universal*, June 21, 2001, http://www.eluniversal.com.mx/.

10. Stevenson Jacobs, "Mayor, Fox United in War on Crime," *News* (Mexico City), August 31, 2001, http://www.thenewsmexico.com/.

11. Quoted in Alejandra Bordon, "Defiende trato con Fox," *Reforma*, June 28, 2003; and Bordon, "Comparten conceptos Fox y AMLO," *Reforma*, May 30, 2003, http://www.reforma.com/.

12. Alejandra Bordon, "Reprueba AMLO a Fox en política económica," ibid., December 4, 2003.

13. "Mayor Will Test Candidacy," *El Universal*, May 21, 2004, http://www.eluniversal.com.mx/miami/.

14. Quoted in Ella Grajeda, "Rechaza AMLO movilizaciones a su favor," *El Universal*, May 20, 2004, http://www.eluniversal.com.mx/.

15. Manuel Roig-Franzia, "Using FDR as Model, Presidential Hopeful Out to Build New Deal for Mexico," *Washington Post*, June 23, 2006, A18.

CHAPTER 15

1. His first version, with twenty items, appeared as *Un proyecto alternativo de nación* (Mexico City: Grijalbo, 2004). The fifty items appeared as "50 compromisos para recuperar el orgullo nacional," http://www.lopezobrador.org.mx/.

2. Notimex, "Ofrece AMLO ayuda 'desde la cuna hasta la tumba,'" *El Universal*, December 9, 2005, http://www.eluniversal.com.mx/.

3. Manuel Suárez Mier, "Comentarios a los 20 postulados básicos del proyecto alternativo de nación de Andrés Manuel López Obrador," paper, March 2005.

4. George W. Grayson, *Mexico: Changing of the Guard* (New York: Foreign Policy Association, 2001), 41–42.

5. López Obrador, *Comunicado de Prensa 73*, October 14, 2005, and *Comunicado de Prensa 74*, October 15, 2005, both at http://www.lopezobrador.org/mx/.

6. Quoted in Salvador Macías, "Sector privado critica propuestas presidenciales del jefe de gobierno del DF," *El Economista*, July 19, 2005, http://www.economista.com.mx/.

7. Dayna Meré, "Lidera el DF trabjas para abrir negocios," *El Universal*, October 21, 2005, A1.

8. Quoted in Claudia Guerrero, "Propone AMLO reducir salarios," *Reforma,* September 24, 2005, http://www.reforma.com/.

9. George W. Grayson, "Libre comercio y sector agrícola," *Milenio Semanal,* June 12, 2005, http://www.milenio.com/semanal/.

10. Carolina Pavón and Alejandra Bordon, "Piden al GDF revisar la crisis del agua," *Reforma,* June 23, 2005, http://www.reforma.com/.

11. López Obrador, *Un proyecto alternativo de nación,* 40.

12. This section draws heavily on Adrián Lajous Vargas, "Los compromisos petroleros de López Obrador," paper, Mexico City, October 2005.

13. Suárez Mier, "Comentarios a los 20 postulados básicos."

CHAPTER 16

1. Manuel Durán, "Capitaliza AMLO su libro y viajes," *Reforma,* February 28, 2005, http://www.reforma.com.mx/.

2. Manuel Durán, "Obtiene $476 mil AMLO por su libro," ibid., June 1, 2005.

3. "Bajo Reserva," *El Universal,* September 2, 2004, http://www.eluniversal.com.mx/.

4. Quoted at http://www.redesciudadanos.org.mx/.

5. Mariel Ibarra, "Tejen en 3 semanas las redes ciudadanos," *Reforma,* March 28, 2005, http://www.reforma.com.mx/.

6. Grupo Consultor Interdisciplinario (Alfonso Zárate, director), "López Obrador: Proyecto, redes, liderazgo," Report No. 364 (March 25, 2005): 19–23.

7. Quoted in Carlos Marí, "Abandera Raúl Ojeda al PRD en Tabasco," *Reforma,* October 31, 2005, http://www.reforma.com.mx/.

8. The PRI allied with the PVEM in ninety-seven of three hundred electoral districts. For an analysis of these contests, see George W. Grayson, "Beyond the Mid-term Elections, Mexico's Political Outlook: 2003–2006," *Western Hemisphere Election Study Series* (October 2003): 1–10.

9. The name derives from the leadership of Jesús Zambrano and Jesús Ortega in this current; "Chucho" is the nickname for Jesús.

10. Quoted in Claudia Guerrero, "Respaldan perredistas redes de López Obrador," *Reforma,* December 6, 2004, http://www.reforma.com.mx/.

11. Claudia Guerrero, "Acuerdan fundir Redes a estructura del partido," ibid., September 29, 2005.

12. Quoted in Alberto Aguirre, "Recibe AMLO aval de Cárdenas Batel," ibid., October 22, 2005.

13. Quoted in Daniel Pensamiento and Andrea Merlos, "Reta AMLO a hacer campañas austeras," ibid., July 31, 2005.

14. Socorro Díaz Palacios, interview by author, August 16, 2005, Mexico City.

15. López Obrador, *Comunicado de Prensa 40,* September 17, 2005, http://www.lopezobrador.org.mx/.

16. Quoted in Alberto Aguirre, "Prevé López Obrador acuerdo con Cárdenas," *Reforma,* August 28, 2005, http://www.reforma.com.mx/.

17. Quoted in Alberto Aguirre, "Evoca López Obrador a Maquío en Culiacán," ibid., August 14, 2005.

18. Ambassador Jeffrey Davidow, informal discussion with author, February 27, 2004, Washington, D.C.

19. Quoted in Ella Grajeda, "La DEA tiene a Ponce," *El Universal,* March 9, 2004, http://www.eluniversal.com.mx/.

20. José María Pérez Gay, interview by author, December 6, 2005, Mexico City.

21. Jorge Octavio Ochoa, "Desairan redes de AMLO la tregua navideña en EU," *El Universal,* December 14, 2005, http://www.eluniversal.com.mx/.

22. John Authers et al., "Mexican Frontrunner Vows Fiscal Caution," *Financial Times,* May 24, 2005, http://news.ft.com/home/us.

23. Quoted in "Francisco Robles Nava," *La Opinión,* February 17, 2005, http://laopinion.com/.

24. Thomas Black, "López Obrador Reaching Out to Business Class," *Herald* (Mexico City), October 22, 2005, 3.

CHAPTER 17

1. James C. McKinley Jr., "Leftist Outsider's Campaign Surges in Mexico," *New York Times*, March 19, 2006, http://www.nytimes.com/.

2. Lettieri and Corona quoted in Will Weissert, "Venezuelan Leader Figures in Increasingly Negative Mexican Presidential Race," Associated Press, March 29, 2006, http://ww.ap.org/.

3. Enrique Quintana, "Coordenadas/López Obrador y el sector empresarial; desde los que lo repelen hasta los que se han sumado a su equipo, pero AMLO ya no es indiferente al sector empresarial," *Reforma*, March 17, 2006, http://www.reforma.com.mx/.

4. Quoted in James C. McKinley Jr., "Feuding President and Mayor Eclipse Mexican Campaign," *New York Times*, April 7, 2006, http://www.nytimes.com/.

5. Quoted in Marla Dickerson, "Fox Not Shy in Touting Record," *Los Angeles Times*, March 21, 2006, http://www.latimes.com/.

6. Quoted in McKinley, "Feuding President and Mayor Eclipse Campaign."

7. Quoted in ibid.

8. "Mexico: Calderón Plays the Chávez Scare Card," *Latin American Weekly Report*, March 14, 2006, http://www.latinews.com/.

9. The first reported use of *chachalaca* came in Puebla on March 10, 2006; López Obrador called Governor Mario Marín Torres a *patán*, or crude person, and Fox a *chachalaca mayora*; see Mayolo López, "Llama 'chachalaca mayora' perredista al Presidente," *Reforma*, March 11, 2006, http://www.reforma.com.mx/.

10. "Chávez Blasts Nation's Political Right," *Herald* (Mexico City), March 22, 2006, http://www.mexiconews.com/mx/.

11. Quoted in "Escritora Poniatowska sala en defensa de López Obrador en México," Deutsche Presse-Agentur, April 8, 2006, http://www.dpa.com/.

12. "López Obrador Apologises," *Latinnews Daily*, May 23, 2006, http://www.latinews.com/.

13. "Encuesta/Esperan que AMLO pierda votos," *El Norte*, April 26, 2006, http://www.elnorte.com/.

14. For elaboration on these errors, see Denise Dresser, "México: Complot," *La Opinión*, April 30, 2006, http://laopinion.com/.

15. "López Obrador Apologises."

16. Quoted in "The Front-Runner Under Pressure," *Economist*, April 22, 2006, http://www.economist.com/.

17. Quoted in John Lyons, "In Mexico Race, 'Wal-Mart' Voters May Hold the Key," Associated Press, June 7, 2006, http://www.ap.org/.

18. Quoted in "Calderón and Zavala Deny Accusations," *Latinnews Daily*, June 9, 2006, http://www.latinews.com/.

19. Quoted in James C. McKinley Jr., "Electoral Crisis in Mexico as Top 2 Declare Victory," *New York Times*, July 3, 2006, http://www.nytimes.com/.

20. Quoted in "Gamamos la Presidencia y exijo respeto al voto: AMLO," *La Jornada*, July 3, 2006, http://www.jornada.unam.mx/.

21. Quoted in John Rice, "Tight Race Puts Mexico's Electoral System to the Test," Associated Press, July 3, 2006, http://www.ap.org/.

22. Quoted in Claudia Herrea Beltrán and Georgina Saldierna, "Felipe Calderón se proclama vencedor," *La Jornada*, July 3, 2006, http://www.jornada.unam.mx/.

23. "Discurso de Andrés Manuel López Obrador, en la tercera asamblea informativa en el Zócalo de la Ciudad de México," http://www.lopezobrador.org/mx/.

24. Richard Boudreaux, "Mexico's Election May Rest on 7 Votes," *Los Angeles Times*, July 15, 2006, http://www.latimes.com/.

25. Quoted in James C. McKinley Jr., "Election Ruling in Mexico Goes to Conservative," *New York Times*, September 6, 2006, http://www.nytimes.com/.

26. For an exit poll of the July 2 election, see "Encuesta/Pintan en dos la República," *Reforma,* July 3, 2006, http://www.busquedas.gruporeforma.com. utilerias/imdservicios3W.DLL?

27. Roberto Campa Cifrián, interview by author, January 20, 2007, Mexico City.

CHAPTER 18

1. "Discurso de Andrés Manuel López Obrador, en la tercera asamblea informativa en el Zócalo de la Ciudad de México," http://www.lopezobrador.org/mx/.

2. Quoted in Boudreaux, "Mexico's Election May Rest on 7 Votes," *Los Angeles Times,* July 15, 2006.

3. John Ross, "Angrily Awaiting a Messiah," *The Nation,* August 25, 2006, http://www.thenation.com/.

4. Quoted in Enrique Méndez and Andrea Becerril, "Los magistrados se sometieron; no tuvieron la voluntad de actuar como hombres libres," *La Jornada,* September 6, 2006, http://www.jornada.unam.mx/.

5. Ibid.

6. Quoted in Francisco Reséndiz, "Anuncian acciones para hacer frente a un 'gobierno espurio,'" *El Universal,* August 17, 2006, http://www.eluniversal.com.mx/.

7. Francisco Reséndiz, "Coalición garantiza comida y viaje a un millón a delegados," ibid., August 31, 2006.

8. "Reitera AMLO llamado a Convención," *Reforma,* September 6, 2006, http://www.reforma.com.mx/.

9. Quoted in Jácobo García, "López Obrador pierde las elecciones en su ciudad natal, Tabasco," *El Mundo,* October 17, 2006, http://www.elmundo.com/.

10. López Cruz, interview, October 30, 2006.

11. Speech of López Obrador, "Se equivoca la derecha neofascista si piensa que detentará el poder hasta el 2030, asegura López Obrador," http://www.lopezobrador.org.mx/.

12. Daniel Pensamiento, "Desairan a equipo de López Obrador," *Reforma,* February 7, 2007, http://www.reforma.com.mx/.

13. Sergio Javier Jiménez and Mireya Blanco, "Dispuestos gobernadores del PRD a trabajar con Calderón," *El Universal,* October 24, 2006, http://www.eluniversal. com.mx/. Although elected with the support of the PRD, wealthy businessman Torreblanca remains an independent.

14. Quoted in Ernesto Núñez, "Pinta raya Sabines con AMLO," *Reforma,* October 31, 2006, http://www.reforma.com.mx/.

15. Quoted in "Desconocer a Calderón es un error—Cárdenas," ibid., September 19, 2006.

16. Daniel Pensamiento, "Pide órgano fiscalizador al PRD cuentas de 2006," ibid., February 13, 2007.

17. Quoted in Manuel Roig-Franzia, "Oaxaca's Embattled Governor Keeps a Tenuous Hold on Power," *Washington Post,* November 1, 2006, A15.

18. Quoted in "Discurso de Andrés Manuel López Obrador en el mítin de apoyo al pueblo de Oaxaca," October 31, 2006, http://www.amlo.org.mx/.

19. Quoted in ibid.

20. Nadia Sanders and Manuel Durán, "Apoyan a la APPO y cierran 3 escuelas," *Reforma,* October 31, 2006, http://www.reforma.com.mx/.

21. "Miles de simpatizantes del EZLN bloquean carreteras en Chiapas," *La Jornada,* November 2, 2006, http://www.jornada.unam.mx/.

22. In a meeting on November 8, 2006, in Washington, D.C., President-elect Calderón emphasized to the author that he would not be paralyzed by the "Tlatelolco Complex," affirming his determination to "enforce the law."

23. E. Eduardo Castillo, "Party Allegedly Funded by Jailed Drug Lord, 6 Arrested," *Herald,* English-language supplement to *El Universal,* May 6, 2006, http://www.eluniversal.com.mx/.

24. Quoted in "Mexico Raises Troop Salaries in Drug Crackdown," *Reuters*, February 19, 2007, http://today.reuters.com/news/.

25. Quoted in "Anuncian campaña contra planes privazadores de Felipe Calderón," *El Periódico de México*, October 30, 2006, http://www.elperiodicodemexico/.

26. CNN, "Tortilla March Organizers Ask Leftist Leader to Stay Away," *World News*, http://www.cnn.com/2007/WORLD/americas/01/31/tortilla.march.ap/.

27. López Obrador, "Un aumento salarial de emergencia, propuso López Obrador," January 31, 2007, http://www.gobiernolegitimo.org.mx/noticias/discursos.html?id=56070.

28. Quoted in "Can the Old Mexico Play Its Part in Forging the New? The Institutional Revolutionary Party," *Economist*, February 17, 2007, http://www.economist.com/.

SELECT BIBLIOGRAPHY

Aguirre M., Alberto. "La pugna secreta que cimbra al PRD." *Milenio Semanal,* August 2, 2000, 22.

Alcocer, Jorge V. "Tabasco: Nadie sabe nada." *Proceso,* November 21, 1988, 32–34.

Almazán, Alejandro. "Retratos desconocidos de Andrés Manuel." *La Revista,* weekly supplement to *El Universal,* March 1–7, 2004, 28.

Angel Centeno, Miguel. *Democracy Within Reason: Technocratic Revolution in Mexico.* University Park: Pennsylvania State University Press, 1994.

Antonio Crespo, José. "The Party System and Democratic Governance in Mexico." *Policy Papers on the Americas* 15 (March 2004). http://www.csis.org/.

"Apathy Rules." *Latin America Regional Reports: Mexico and NAFTA Report,* March 21, 2000. http://www.latinnews.com/.

Beltrán del Rio, Pascal. "Asegura Muñoz Ledo que el PAN busca impeder su liderazgo a la postulación de Cuauhtémoc." *Proceso,* March 13, 1993, 30–31.

Berry, Charles R. "Porfirio Díaz." In *Encyclopedia of Latin America,* ed. Helen Delpar. New York: McGraw-Hill, 1974.

Borjas Benavente, Adriana Leticia. *Partido de la revolución democrática: Estructura, organización interna y desempeño público, 1989–2003.* Mexico City: Gernika, 2003.

Bruhn, Kathleen "The Making of the Mexican President, 2000: Parties, Candidates, and Campaign Strategy." In *Mexico's Pivotal Democratic Election,* ed. Jorge I. Domínguez and Chappell Lawson, 123–56. Stanford: Stanford University Press, 2004.

———. *Taking on Goliath: The Emergence of a New Left Party and the Struggle for Democracy in Mexico.* University Park: Pennsylvania State University Press, 1997.

Burns, Bradford N. *A History of Brazil.* 2d ed. New York: Columbia University Press, 1993.

Caballero, Alejandro, Álvaro Delgado, and Armando Gúzman. "El banquero, Hank y Bartlett, parte de los activos del gobernador de Tabasco." *Proceso,* September 4, 1995, 20, 22–23.

Camacho Solís, Manuel. *Yo Manuel: Memorias apócrifas? de un comisionado.* Mexico City: Rayuela, 1995.

Campos, Julieta. *Tabasco: Un jaguar despertado.* Mexico City: Aguilar Nuevo Siglo, 1996.

Cárdenas, Cuauhtémoc, et al. *Corriente Democrática: Alternativa frente a la crisis.* Mexico City: Editores Costa-Amic, 1987.

Castañeda, Jorge G. *La herencia*. Mexico City: Aguilar, Altea, Taurus, Alfaguara, 1999.

Cedeño del Olmo, Manuel. *Sistema político en Tabasco: Gobierno, poder regional y federalismo*. Mexico City: Centro de Estudios de Política Comparada, 1999.

Chávez, Elías. "En San Luis destapan a Camacho y Colosio como aspirantes a la grande ya en combate." *Proceso*, August 13, 1990, 14–16.

Consuegra, Renato. "Mil 300 desacatos más de AMLO." May 21, 2004. http://www.kiosco.com.mx/Sem/edit/Archivos/ArchRCons/40521RConsDF.html.

Consulta Mitofsky. "Encuesta de Salida: 2 de Julio, elección presidencial." http://www.consulta.com.mx/interiores/11_elecciones/elec_ENCUSAL_presi/.

Corro, Salvador. "De los gobiernos priístas, Emilio Azcárraga ha recibido todos los favores y, como priísta confeso, sabe ser agradecido." *Proceso*, July 4, 1994, 6.

"Creel condena las impugnaciones de su propio partido y del PRI a la candidature de López Obrador." *Proceso*, April 27, 2000. http://www.proceso.com.mx/.

Cristina Caballero, Maria, with Joseph Contreras. "Looking for a Legacy." *Newsweek* (Latin American ed.), September 29, 2003. http://www.msnbc.msn.com/id/3037881/site/newsweek/.

Curzio Gutiérrez, Leonardo. *Gobernabilidad, democracia y videopolítica en Tabasco, 1994–1999*. Mexico City: Plaza y Valdés Editores, 2000.

Davis, Diane E. *Urban Leviathan: Mexico City in the Twentieth Century*. Philadelphia: Temple University Press, 1994.

Delgado, Alvaro. "'La mafia me quiere descontar, pero no me doblegará': López Obrador." *Proceso*, April 16, 2000. http://www.proceso.com.mx/.

———. "El PRD apostó todo a la democracia y perdío por la falta de institucionalidad como partido." *Proceso*, March 21, 1999. http://www.proceso.com.mx/.

Delgado, Alvaro, and Armando Guzmán. "En Tabasco, el 12 de febrero termina la tregua." *Proceso*, February 6, 1995. http://www.proceso.com.mx/.

———. "Madrazo gobierno inmovilizado; forma su gabinete con acusados de corrupción y fraude electoral." *Proceso*, January 9, 1995, 34.

———. "Sin Zedillo, fueron soldados y policías invitados de honor en la toma de posesión de Madrazo." *Proceso*, January 2, 1995, 34.

———. "Tabasco se une a Chiapas como laboratorio del autoritarismo." *Proceso*, January 2, 1995. http://www.proceso.com.mx/.

———. "Los tres poderes de Tabasco ambulantes: No han podido entrar en sus edificios." *Proceso*, September 1, 1995. http://www.proceso.com.mx/.

———. "Vaivenes del gobierno federal: Por las presiones del PRD Madrazo iba a salir; por la rebeldía de priístas, se quedó." *Proceso*, January 23, 1995, 22–23.

Delgado, Alvaro, and Maria Scherer. "La disputa entre Cárdenas y Muñoz Ledo llegó al límite." *Proceso*, April 18, 1999. http://www.proceso.com.mx/.

Dillon, Samuel, and Julia Preston. *Opening Mexico: The Making of a Democracy*. New York: Farrar, Straus and Giroux, 2004.

Dirección General de Comunicación Social. "50 compromisos para recuperar el orgullo nacional." http://www.lopezobrador.org.mx/50compomisos/.

———. "Entrega AMLO 12 mil 560 tarjetas a adultos mayores de 70 años en el Distrito Federal." Bulletin 1140, November 9, 2003.

———. "Quinto informe del gobierno de Alejandro Encinas Rodríguez, en la Asamblea Legislativa del Distrito Federal." September 17, 2005. http://www.comsoc.df.gob.mx/documentos/v_informeencinas.html.

"Economist Rosario Robles Berlanga Becomes First Woman to Govern Mexico City." SourceMex–Economic News and Analysis on Mexico, October 6, 1999. http://ladb.unm.edu/sourcemex/.

Flynn, Peter. Brazil: A Political Analysis. London: Anchor Press, 1978.

Fox, Vicente. A los Pinos: Recuento autobiográfico y político. Mexico City: Editorial Océano, 1999.

"Giuliani Comes Up with 146 Proposals for Mexico City." Latin America Regional Reports: Mexico and NAFTA Report, August 19, 2003. http://www.latinnews.com/.

Gobierno del Distrito Federal. "Apoyo para madres solteras." http://www.df.gob.mx/secretarias/social/programas/madres/html.

———. "Programa de becas para personas con discapacidad." http://www.df.gob.mx/secretarias/social/programas/discapacidad.html.

Gómez, Blanca. ¿Y quién es? Historia de un hombre enigmático. Mexico City: Planeta, 2005.

González Casanova, Pablo. México ante la crisis: El impacto social y cultural de las alternativas. Mexico City: Siglo Veintiuno Editores, 1986.

Grayson, George W. "Beyond the Mid-term Elections, Mexico's Political Outlook: 2003–2006." Western Hemisphere Election Study Series (October 2003): 1–69.

———. "A Guide to the 2000 Mexican Presidential Election." Western Hemisphere Election Study Series 18 (June 2000).

———. "Libre comercio y sector agrícola." Milenio Semanal, June 12, 2005. http://www.milenio.com/semanal/.

———. Mexico: Changing of the Guard. New York: Foreign Policy Association, 2001.

———. Mexico: From Corporatism to Pluralism? Fort Worth: Harcourt Brace, 1988.

———. The Politics of Mexican Oil. Pittsburgh: University of Pittsburgh Press, 1980.

Haley, Jay. The Power Tactics of Jesus Christ. Rockville, Md.: Triangle Press, 1986.

Heinberg, Richard. "In Search of the Historical Jesus." New Dawn Magazine, September–October 1998. http://www.newdawnmagazine.com/.

Hinojosa, Óscar. "Está muy sólido: Cuauhtémoc se debilita; Heberto; seguirá Muñoz Ledo." Proceso, February 27, 1989, 22.

Horsley, Richard A., and John S. Hanson. Bandits, Prophets, and Messiahs: Popular Movements in the Time of Jesus. San Francisco: Harper & Row, 1988.

"Housing Minister Finally Resigns." Latin America Weekly Report, February 28, 1986. http://www.latinnews.com/.

Kandel, Jonathan. La Capital: The Biography of Mexico City. New York: Random House, 1988.

Kraft, Joseph. The Mexican Rescue. New York: Group of Thirty, 1984.

Krauze, Enrique. "López Obrador, el mesiás tropical." *Letras Libres* 8 (June 2006): 15–24.

Lajous Vargas, Adrián. "Los compromisos petroleros de López Obrador." Unpublished paper. Mexico City, October 2005.

Lara Lagunas, Rodolfo. *Juárez: De la choza al Palacio Nacional; historias y testimonios.* Villahermosa, 2004.

Levy, Daniel, and Gabriel Székely. *Mexico: Paradoxes of Stability and Change.* Boulder, Colo.: Westview Press, 1983.

López Obrador, Andrés Manuel. *Comunicado de Prensa 73.* October 14, 2005. http://www.lopezobrador.org/mx/.

———. *Comunicado de Prensa 74.* October 15, 2005. http://www.lopezobrador.org/mx/.

———. *Comunicado de Prensa 40.* September 17, 2005. http://www.lopezobrador.org.mx/.

———. *Entre la historia y la esperanza: Corrupción y lucha democrática en Tabasco.* Mexico City: Editorial Grijalbo, 1995.

———. *Fobaproa: Expediente abierto.* Mexico City: Grijalbo, 1999.

———. *Los primeros pasos: Tabasco, 1810–1867.* Villahermosa: Universidad Juárez Autónoma de Tabasco, 1986.

———. *Un proyecto alternativo de nación.* Mexico City: Grijalbo, 2004.

———. "Revolución y justicia." *Revista de la Universidad* 9 (September 1985): 41–61.

———. "Sociedad y política." *Revista de la Universidad* 13–14 (September–December 1986): 58–62.

———. *Tabasco, víctima del fraude electoral.* Mexico City: Editorial Nuestro Tiempo, 2000.

"López Obrador: Proyecto, redes, liderazgo." *Grupo Consultor Interdisciplinario* 364 (March 25, 2005): 19–23.

Macías, Salvador. "Sector privado critica propuestas presidenciales del jefe de gobierno del D.F." *El Economista,* July 19, 2005. http://www.economista.com.mx/.

Mack, Burton L. *The Lost Gospel: The Book of Q and Christian Origins.* San Francisco: Harper, 1993.

Madrazo, Roberto. "Discurso de toma de protesta como candidato a diputado federal por el 1er. distrito electoral." News release. Villahermosa, Tabasco, May 11, 1991.

"The Man Who Would Be President." *Economist,* November 13, 2003. http://www.economist.com/.

Marín, Carlos. "Zedillo tuvo más sensibilidad política que Fox." *Milenio Semanal,* May 23, 2004. http://www.milenio.com/semanal/.

Marques-Pereira, Jaime. "PRONASOL: Mexico's Bid to Fight Poverty." *UNESCO Courier* (March 1995): 25.

Mestre Ghigliazza, Manuel. *Invasion norteamericana en Tabasco, 1846–1847.* Mexico City: Consejo Editorial del Gobierno del Estado de Tabasco, 1981.

Meyer, Michael C., and William H. Beezley. *The Oxford History of Mexico.* New York: Oxford University Press, 2000.

Monge, Raúl. "Abusos electorales del gobierno del D.F.: Lerdo de Tejada." *Proceso,* May 13, 2000. http://www.proceso.com.mx/.

Oppenheimer, Andres. *Bordering on Chaos: Guerrillas, Stockbrokers, Politicians, and Mexico's Road to Prosperity.* Boston: Little, Brown, 1996.

"Piden amonestar a López Obrador por instalar circo en el Zócalo." *El Economista,* August 6, 2002. http://www.economista.com.mx/.

Ramírez, Aída, and Sergio Castañeda. "Precisan Silva Herzog y López Obrador sus plataformas en la Ibero." *El Economista,* April 7, 2000. http://www.eleconomist.com.mx/.

Rieff, David. "The Populist at the Border." *New York Times Magazine,* June 4, 2006, 36–41.

Rocío Beltrán Medina: Libro de familia. Mexico City: Palabra en Vuela, 2003.

Ross, John. "Fox, Inc. Takes over Mexico." *Multinational Monitor,* March 2001. http://multinationalmonitor.org/.

Salinas de Gortari, Carlos. *Producción y participación: Política en el campo.* Mexico City: Fondo de Cultura Económica, 1987.

Suárez Mier, Manuel. "Comentarios a los 20 postulados básicos del proyecto alternativo nación de Andrés Manuel López Obrador." Unpublished paper, March 2005.

"Tabasco Governor's Lawsuit Against Federal Government Becomes Latest Controversy for Governing Party." *SourceMex–Economic News and Analysis on Mexico,* August 30, 1995. http://ladb.unm. edu/sourcemex/.

"Times of Trouble." *Business Mexico,* April 2001. http://www.amcham. com.mx/publica/busmex/.

Tribunal Electoral del Poder Judicial de la Federación. "Constitución Política de los Estados Unidos Mexicanos." http://www.trife.gob.mx/.

Villegas M., Francisco Gil. "El 'tiovivo' de López Obrador." *El Economista,* September 2, 1998. http://www.economista.com.mx/.

Ward, Peter M., and Elizabeth Durden. "Government and Democracy in Mexico's Federal District, 1997–2001: Cárdenas, the PRD, and the Curate's Egg." *Bulletin of Latin American Research* 21, no. 1 (2002): 1–39.

Willoughby, Jack, and Lucy Conger. "Under the Volcano." *Institutional Investor* 32 (June 1998): 62–76. http://www.institutionalinvestor. com/default.asp/.

Wright, George. *Mexico City, Heart of the Eagle: Democracy or Inequality.* Ottawa: RCW Publishing, 2004.

Yount, Rick. "Jesus, the Master Teacher." http://www.ministryserver. com/bible/lectures/.

Zepeda Patterson, Jorge, Alicia Ortiz Rivera, Jorge Carrasco Araizaga, Salvador Camarena, Alejandro Páez Varela, Rossana Fuentes-Berain, and Rogelio Hernández Rodríguez. *Los suspirantes: Los precandidatos de carne y hueso.* Mexico City: Planeta, 2005.

INTERVIEWS BY AUTHOR

Aguilar Ascencio, Oscar. July 8, September 25, October 11, November 11, December 10, 2004; January 9, March 12, 2005; May 28 (telephone), December 5, 2006. Mexico City.

Aguilar, Pedro. March 29, 2004. Mexico City.

Aguilar Solís, Samuel. January 13 and June 30, 2004. Mexico City.

Aguilar Talamantes, Rafael. 2004. Mexico City.

Aguilera Gómez, Manuel. March 24, 2004. Mexico City.

Aguirre M., Alberto. July 5, 2005. Mexico City.

Aguirre Velázquez, Ramón. June 17, 1996. Mexico City.

Álvarez Palafox, Fred. March 7, 2002; March 24, July 1, December 7, December 9, 2004; March 14, May 12, October 20, 2005; January 10, 2006. Mexico City.

Alzati Araiza, Fausto. April 9, 2000. Aguascalientes.

Andrade, Guillermo. July 1, 2004. Mexico City.

Antonio Rueda, José. July 3, 2004. Mexico City.

Artz, Sigrid. March 13, 2005 (telephone). Mexico City.

Batres Guadarrama, Martí. July 5, 2003; January 13, 2004. Mexico City.

Beauregard de los Santos, Laura. January 15, 2004, Mexico City; June 14 and 15, 2005, Villahermosa.

Beltán, Luis. June 13, 2005. Villahermosa.

Beltrán Calzada, Gonzalo. June 17, 2005. Villahermosa.

Beltrán Hernández, José Eduardo. January 10, 2006. Mexico City.

Benítez López, Ernesto. August 15, 2005. Villahermosa.

Bernardo Román, Lucas. August 14, 2005. Nacajuca.

Berrueto Pruneda, Federico. January 2, 2004; March 8, October 19, 2005; February 24, 2006. Mexico City.

Bolivar Zapata, Ramón. March 9 and July 4, 2005. Mexico City.

Buendía Tirado, Ángel. July 6, 2005. Mexico City.

Calderón, Felipe Hinojosa. Informal discussion. November 8, 2006. Washington, D.C.

Camacho Solís, Manuel. July 9, July 12, 2004; October 19, 2005. Mexico City.

Campa Cifrián, Roberto. March 29, 2004; January 20, 2007. Mexico City.

Campos, Julieta. March 30, July 5, 2004; August 17, 2005. Mexico City.

Cárdenas Solórzano, Cuauhtémoc. October 11, 2004. Mexico City.

Carreño Carlón, José. January 13, 2006 (telephone).

Carrillo Prieto, Ignacio. October 6, 2004. Mexico City.

Castellanos Macossay, Lic. María de Fátima. February 15, 2004. Palenque.

Castro Castillo, Omar. July 5 and October 22, 2005. Mexico City.

Chablé Ruiz, José de Carmen. June 14, 2005. Villahermosa.

Chuayffet Chémor, Emilio. March 30, 2004. Mexico City.

Córdova Wilson, Ariel. June 16, 2005. Villahermosa.

Correa López, Isidra. June 16, 2005. Villahermosa.

Cota Montaño, Leonel. March 7, 2005. Mexico City.

David González, Félix Jorge. August 6, 2004. Villahermosa.

Davidow, Jeffrey. January 9, 2002; February 27, 2004 (informal discussion). Washington, D.C.

De Díos Calles, Citlallín. February 16, 2004. Villahermosa.

De la Torre, María del Carmen Muriel. August 14, 2005. Nacajuca.

De los Angeles Moreno, María. October 12, 2004; January 11, 2005. Mexico City.

Díaz Palacios, Socorro. August 16, 2005. Mexico City.

Döring, César Federico. January 15 and March 30, 2004, Mexico City.

Duarte Olivares, Horacio. March 8, 2005. Mexico City.

Durán Aguirre, Manuel. July 4, 2004. Mexico City.

Encinas Rodríguez, Alejandro. September 22, 2004, Washington, D.C.; January 11, 2005, Mexico City.

Escobar Toledo, Saúl. March 7, 2005. Mexico City.

Farías, María Emilia. July 5, 2004; August 17, 2005. Mexico City.

Flores Velasco, Guillermo. May 30, 2000; January 7, March 7, 2002; January 9, March 26, July 9, 2004; March 13, August 18, December 5, 2005; February 24, 2006; January 19, 2007. Mexico City.

Funoy Rabanal, César. June 14, 2005. Villahermosa.

Galaz, Lourdes. August 16, 2005. Mexico City.

Gallardo Rincón, Gilberto. December 9, 2004. Mexico City.

Garduño Morales, Patricia. July 7, 2004. Mexico City.

Gertz Manero, Alejandro. October 22, 2005. Mexico City.

González Ballina, Darvín. August 6, 2004. Villahermosa.

González Pedrero, Enrique. July 6, 2004; August 18, 2005. Mexico City.

Gurría Ordoñez, Manuel. December 6, 2005. Mexico City.

Gurría Treviño, Angel. April 27, 2006. Houston, Texas.

Heredia Zubieta, Carlos. January 14, 2003; July 5, December 9, 2004, Mexico City; October 18, 2005 (telephone); January 11, 2006 (telephone).

Itzel Castillo, Laura. January 14, 2005. Mexico City.

Izundegui Rullán, Amador. August 11, 2004. Villahermosa.

Jackson Ramírez, Enrique. May 6, 2004. Washington, D.C.

Jiménez Flores, Alberto. June 16, 2005. Villahermosa.

Jiménez León, Pedro. March 10 and May 9, 2005. Mexico City.

Jiménez Méndez, Bartolo. August 9, 2004. Villahermosa.

Jusidman de Bialostozky, Clara. October 8, 2004; July 6, 2005. Mexico City.

Labastida Ochoa, Francisco. January 12, 2006. Mexico City.

Lajous Vargas, Adrián. December 5, 2005. Mexico City.

Lajous Vargas, Roberta. January 10, 2006. Mexico City.

Lara Lagunas, Rodolfo. January 15 and June 13, 2005. Villahermosa.

Lázaro Lázaro, Candelaria. January 16, 2005. Nacajuca.

López Cruz, Rafael. August 9 and 10, 2004; June 15 and 16, 2005, Villahermosa; October 30, 2006 (telephone).

López Obrador, Andrés Manuel. Author attended his early morning news conferences on August 17, 2003; January 17, April 1, July 4, October 9, December 11, 2004; July 4, 2005.

López Obrador, José Ramiro. August 10, 2004. Villahermosa.

Lozana Gracia, Antonio. March 25, 2004. Mexico City.

Luege Tamargo, José Luis. August 14, 2003; January 15, 2004. Mexico City.

Luján Uranga, Bertha. February 23, 2007. Austin, Texas.

Macossay Gonzaléz, José Francisco. February 15, 2004. Villahermosa.

Martínez Álvarez, Jesús. July 1, 2004. Mexico City.

Marván Laborde, Ignacio. December 9, 2004. Mexico City.

Mastache Mondragón, Aarón. January 11, 2005. Mexico City.

Máynez Gil, Guillermo. May 30, 2000. Mexico City.

Medina del Beltrán, Elena. August 9, 2004. Villahermosa.

Medina Medina, Javier. July 7, 2004, Mexico City; January 25, 2006, Washington, D.C.

Mendoza Garza, Jorge. December 10, 2004. Mexico City.

Millán Lizárraga, Juan S. May 9, 2000, Culiacán, Sinaloa; July 2, 2003, Culiacán, Sinaloa; July 8, 2004, Mexico City, and November 13 and 14, 2004, Culiacán, Sinaloa.

Moctezuma Barragán, Esteban. July 8, 2004; July 4, 2005. Mexico City.

Monreal Ávila, Ricardo. April 9, 2000, Zacatecas; January 12, 2005, Mexico City.

Montaño Martínez, Jorge. March 12, 2002. Mexico City.

Moreno Domínguez, Manuel. July 4, 2004. Mexico City.

Mucio, Fausto. December 7, 2004. Mexico City.

Muñoz Ledo, Porfirio. January 12, 2005. Mexico City.

Núñez Jiménez, Arturo. January 16, March 28, December 8, 2004; May 9, 2005. Mexico City.

Ocaranza Fernández, Antonio. July 6, 2004, Mexico City; February 19, 2007 (telephone).

Ojeda Zubieta, César Raúl. August 6, 2005. Villahermosa.

Olmos Tomasini, Carlos. January 11, 2006. Mexico City.

Ortiz Pinchetti, José Agustín. October 9, 2004. Mexico City.

Ovalle Fernández, Ignacio. January 10 and August 18, 2005. Mexico City.

Padilla Herrera, Armando. January 9, August 9, 2004; January 14 and 15, June 17, 2005. Villahermosa.

Paoli Bolio, José Francisco. October 11, 2004. Mexico City.

Pascoe Pierce, Ricardo. January 10, 2004. Mexico City.

Pastor Medrano, Isidro. March 30, 2004. Mexico City.

Peralta Burelo, Francisco. August 10, 2004; January 17 and August 13, 2005. Villahermosa.

Pérez Gay, José María. December 6, 2005. Mexico City.

Pérez López, Hermilo. June 17, Tepetitlán, Tabasco, July 13 (telephone), August 13, August 19, 2005 (telephone).

Priego Ortiz, Luis. August 15, 2005. Mexico City.

Ramírez de la O, Rogelio. December 6, 2004; May 8, 2005. Mexico City.

Ramírez Garrido Abreu, Graco. July 1, 2004; July 5, 2005. Mexico City.

Ramírez Inches, Vanessa. December 6, 2004. Mexico City.

Rangel M., Jesús. January 14, 2004. Mexico City.

Reséndez Medina, Pedro. June 14, 2005. Villahermosa.

Reyes Heroles, Jesús. January 12, 2002 (informal discussion); February 27, 2004. Washington, D.C.

Robles Berlanga, Rosario. January 13, 2006. Mexico City.

Rodríguez Prats, Juan José. January 15, 2004. Mexico City.

Rojas Gutiérrez, Francisco. March 29, 2004. Mexico City.

Romero Oropeza, Octavio. April 5, 2000. Villahermosa.

Rosales Esteva, Luz. December 9, 2004. Mexico City.

Rovirosa Ramírez, Carlos Manuel. August 15, 2005. Tepetitán, Macuspana.

Rovirosa Wade, Leandro. March 7 and August 18, 2005. Mexico City.

Rueda, José Antonio. July 3, 2004. Mexico City.

Ruiz Abreu, Carlos. July 5, 2005. Mexico City.

Ruiz Ferro, Julio César. October 2, 2000. Washington, D.C.

Sáenz Ortiz, Liébano. May 12, 2005. Mexico City.

Salazar, Pedro Alberto. January 12, 2004. Mexico City.

Salomón Cámara, Carlos. August 18, 2005. Mexico City.

Sánchez, José Alejandro. July 4, 2004. Mexico City.

Sandoval Ramírez, Cuauhtémoc. October 8, December 8, 2004; January 13, 2005; January 12, 2006. Mexico City.

Semo Calev, Enrique. January 12, 2005. Mexico City.

Silva Herzog, Jesús. July 5, 1999, Mexico City; November 15, 2003, Washington, D.C.

Sodi de la Tijera, Demetrio. January 15, 2004. Mexico City.

Soria Narváez, Maricarmen. January 13, 2004; March 8, December 6, 2005; January 11, 2006. Mexico City.

Sosa Elízaga, Raquel. March 26 and 28, 2004. Mexico City.

Toscano Velasco, Miguel Angel. July 7, 2004. Mexico City.

Trujillo Zentella, Georgina. April 6, 2000, Villahermosa; January 9, 2004, Mexico City.

Valdés, Juan Gabriel. December 3, 2005. Mexico City.

Valencia Benavides, Juan Gabriel. May 10, July 2, December 3, 2005; February 25, April 29, November 4 (telephone), 2006; January 20, 2007. Mexico City.

Valenzuela Pernas, Fernando. February 16 and August 11, 2004. Villahermosa.

Vargas Aguilar, Simón. June 1, 2006. Mexico City.

Yáñez Centeno Cabrera, César. August 15, 2003; March 26, 2004. Mexico City.

Zuckerman Behar, Leo. March 14, 2005. Mexico City.

INDEX